D1262176

# WE LOOK FOR A KINGDOM

CARL SOMMER

# WE LOOK
# FOR
# A KINGDOM

The Everyday Lives of the Early Christians

IGNATIUS PRESS    SAN FRANCISCO

Cover art: *The Calling of Saints Peter and Andrew*
Early Christian mosaic, sixth century A.D.
S. Apollinare Nuovo, Ravenna, Italy
Scala/Art Resource, New York

Cover design by Riz Boncan Marsella

© 2007 by Ignatius Press, San Francisco
All rights reserved
ISBN 978-1-58617-079-0
ISBN 1-58617-079-1
Library of Congress Control Number 2005938835
Printed in the United States of America ∞

# CONTENTS

# ACKNOWLEDGMENTS

Special thanks are due to Mr. William VanSmoorenburg of Harmony Media for generously allowing extensive quotations from the CD-ROM *The Early Church Fathers*. These quotations improved this book immeasurably. Thanks also to the librarians at Pius XII Library at St. Louis University, whose patient assistance was invaluable. I am grateful to my friend Cenk Eronat of Ramtur for introducing me to the wonders of ancient Pergamum, Sardis, Hierapolis, Aphrodisias, and Ephesus.

Special thanks to all at Ignatius Press, whose patient work has improved this book immeasurably; and to Jeanette Flood, who copy edited this work and also greatly improved it; and to Gail Gavin, the proofreader, and to the others who worked on this project. As the saying goes, the strengths of this book are due to the hard work of the editors, and the weaknesses are solely the author's fault. I am also profoundly grateful to Father Joseph Fessio, S.J., for his willingness to work with an untried author.

Eternal gratitude goes out to my wife, Anne, whose constant patient sacrifices made it possible for me to complete this book. My love and gratitude know no bounds. Finally, but not last in my thoughts, thanks to my parents, Arthur and Louise; my daughters, Judy and Rebecca; my whole family; and all my friends, for their encouragement and support.

# INTRODUCTION

A common perception is that we live in an age indifferent or even hostile to the study of history. This perception is fed by the stereotype of the teenager bored with the endless memorization of dates and facts. But there are plenty of reasons to think that people are not really bored with history after all. A trip to the local bookseller will confirm one inescapable fact. Every bookstore has a large section devoted to history. There are always two or three people milling around in these sections, thumbing through thick tomes on who-knows-what obscure subject. And plenty of these people finally snap their books shut and stride purposefully over to the cash register with their new possession. The simple fact is there are plenty of people who love history and can't stop filling their bookshelves with books on every imaginable historical subject.

Why do we read history? I suppose there are three reasons. First, and most basically, we love a good story. We read history for the same reason our ancestors told stories around the campfire, with the young-sters hanging on every word. The second reason is related to the first; like the Greeks and Romans themselves, we read history for inspiration. The stories of great deeds from the past motivate us to try harder, to strive to do great deeds in our own time. The third reason is more spiritual in nature. It is trite but true to say that we read history to gain insight into our roots. By studying the past we learn who we are and how we came to be where we are, and, hopefully, how to chart out a wise course for the future.

This third reason, once the most widely cited of all reasons for studying history, is currently in question. In our day, one of the great-est debates among philosophers, theologians, historians, and social sci-entists has to do with the question of human nature. To put the matter plainly, the question is, is there such a thing as human nature? Are there any facts about man that are true of all people, in all times? To you and me, the answer to these questions might seem obvious, but, with some notable exceptions, most historians, sociologists, anthropologists, and philosophers today argue that there is no such thing as human nature.

The basic argument runs something like this: a human being is the product of his environment. Our modes of thinking and acting, our ways of looking at reality, all the things that in fact make us human, are produced in us by the social conditions into which we happen to be born. Since these conditions are constantly changing, modes of thinking, acting, and looking at reality also constantly change. When enough time has passed, and enough social conditions have changed, men become different so there is little point of contact between people of different eras. Thus, the differences between people today and those who lived 2,000 years ago would be so great that we really cannot understand the people of the past. The best we can do would be to study them and gain some insights into their thoughts and behavior, similar to the insights Jane Goodall gains from studying chimpanzees. This position is fed by and in turn provides nourishment for cultural and moral relativism.

Against this position is the traditional stance, a position still held by some Christian theologians and philosophers. This position holds that, despite changes in the outward manifestations of culture, the basic truths of human nature remain the same for all times and peoples.[1] These basic truths are derived primarily from the first four chapters of Genesis. They can be summarized as follows: (1) Man was created in the image and likeness of God. (2) The first human beings freely chose to defy God's will. (3) As a result, all of human nature was broken, distorted, and became prone to sin. (4) God promised to intervene personally to restore humans to their original state.

In the traditional Christian position, all men, despite cultural and historical differences, have certain basic experiences in common. Among these common experiences, one would list on the positive side (1) the desire for union with a transcendent being (God), (2) a deep longing for truth, beauty, and goodness, (3) the desire for freedom, and (4) a tendency on the part of some people to expend noble effort to achieve great good. On the other hand, we also experience (1) a strong tendency toward confusion regarding our true good, (2) an inability to act upon the good even when we can discern it, and (3) a tendency on the part of some people to degenerate to the lowest depths of depravity.

The argument between the "postmodernist" and the traditional Christian positions may seem hopelessly obscure, or even silly, but it is still very important. The consequences of accepting the postmodernist position are devastating. For historians, the main consequence is that we can't really know very much about the past, and consequently can't learn very much from things that happened in the past. This tends to reduce the role of the historian to that of a student of curiosities; the things he can learn might (or might not) be interesting but have no relevance for today.

On the other hand, the Christian position on human nature gives immediate relevance and life to the study of history. By studying how things were done in the past, we can learn many valuable lessons on what to avoid and what to strive for today. It is with this hope that I write this book. The Roman world had many facets that are strikingly similar to elements of modern life. There are problems in the world today that can be overcome only by the practice of largely forgotten Christian virtues. Perhaps we can learn from the practices of the early Church. Perhaps we can learn how to transform the culture in which we live with the power of the gospel. But we can do so only if we truly understand the situation of the world at the time of the early Church and if we have an accurate understanding of the cure the first Christians provided for the ills of their time.

### A Note on Methodology

How does one go about studying the everyday lives of ancient people? There are only two real sources of information about the past: documentary evidence and the archaeological record. Both these sources bring their own strengths and weaknesses to the table. Let's take a brief look at them.

By documentary evidence I mean the letters, treatises, tracts, historical works, poems, plays, and other literature of the age in question. Documentary evidence has the advantage of being sure; as long as historians can read the language with confidence and know the meaning of the words, they can reconstruct the meaning and context of the documents and gain a great deal of information from them. But documentary evidence has three main weaknesses:

1. It is difficult to know how accurate the author was. Some authors lie deliberately, for various reasons, and others are simply mistaken on certain points.

2. Documents are usually written by literate elites and provide few windows into the thoughts and beliefs of ordinary people. This is especially true in historical eras in which the ability to read and write was confined to the privileged.

3. Documents generally represent only the point of view of the author. There is no real way of knowing if anyone else believed what he believed.

Archaeological evidence lacks these weaknesses. When an archaeologist discovers a pot or a house or a burial site, chances are that an ordinary person used that pot or house or burial site. Thus, modern archaeology has provided a remarkable window into the lives of ancient people, but it has its own set of difficulties:

1. It is difficult to tell what to make of a particular archaeological find, without documentary or inscriptional evidence to accompany it. For instance, a burial site tells how a particular group buried a corpse, but nothing about what they believed about death. A burial site accompanied by an inscription is more informative, but without theological or philosophical documents independent of individual tombs, it is difficult to make inferences about beliefs.

2. Archaeological evidence is susceptible to the biases of the archaeologist. If the archaeologist starts with assumptions about a particular culture, ambiguous evidence will probably be interpreted to fit those assumptions.

3. Despite advances in carbon dating, artifacts are difficult to date with precision. Since I am confining this work to the three-hundred-year period at the very beginning of Christianity, this is a crucial weakness. Archaeologists argue, for instance, over the dating of objects and inscriptions in the catacombs. If those objects should be dated to the fourth century, they are of no help to this work, but if they can be dated to the second or third century, they are very useful indeed.

In regard to the period of early Christianity, we have a relatively large number of documents. Generally speaking, they fall into three categories:

1. The writings of orthodox Christians, consisting of letters to neighboring Churches and friends, writings (apologies) intended to defend and explain the faith to non-Christians, theological treatises, and histories.

2. Writings that have been deemed heretical or unreliable by orthodox Christians. This category would include the so-called Gnostic gospels, as well as apocryphal acts of the apostles. These writings are theologically suspect in orthodox circles, and their historical accuracy is questionable.

3. The writings of pagan authors who came into contact with Christians. These writings primarily consist of brief mentions in historical works, satires designed to ridicule Christian beliefs, and the letters of prominent pagans wondering what to do about the problem of Christianity.

Each of these types of documents in turn has its own strengths and weaknesses. The orthodox writings tell us what the Church believed, but practices often have to be inferred, except in the "Church order manuals", which give details about certain rites. Inferences about everyday life can be made from these documents in two ways. Direct inferences can be made about specific practices mentioned in the documents, and indirect inferences can be made when certain practices are criticized. An example would be Tertullian's criticism of Christians who served in the Roman army. One could, from this criticism, reasonably infer that there *were* Christians in the Roman army.

The heretical and historically unreliable writings have to be used with great circumspection. I have used them only in those instances where they might provide a window into the practices prevalent in the time when they were written, not the time about which they purport to write. For instance, the *Acts of Barnabas* purports to be about the life of the Barnabas mentioned in the New Testament, but it was most likely written in Egypt in the third century. It is probably completely worthless in reconstructing the life of the real Barnabas but, if used carefully, can shed light on the beliefs and practices of Christians in third-century Egypt.

I regard the writings of the New Testament to be historically accurate, if one takes into consideration the unique purposes of each book. One will gain very little of direct historical information from the Book of Revelation, for instance, but the book can be helpful to historians in understanding the *sitz im leben* of the community that produced that book. On the other hand, I regard all the Epistles traditionally assigned to Paul as being written while Paul was still alive, either at Paul's dictation, or by his close associates and with Paul's full approval. I also think that the two Letters traditionally ascribed to Peter were produced while Peter was alive and accurately reflect his thought. These are positions held by a minority. Most contemporary scholars think that 1 and 2 Peter, 1 and 2 Timothy, Titus, Ephesians, Philippians, and other Epistles of the New Testament were not written by the authors to whom they were traditionally ascribed.

The question is important and deserves more space than I can devote to it here. For now, I will only observe that my reading of the Christian writers immediately after the New Testament period has convinced me that the early Church placed such an emphasis on apostolic authority that if the apostles were not the authorities responsible for these Letters, all forms of orthodox Christianity have nothing on which to base their authority. The early Christians insisted on concrete historicity. They insisted on the historicity of Christ, in an age uninterested in historicity. And they made arguments based on historicity, arguments that were central to their own authority. Furthermore, they were arguments that in some cases could be verified or contradicted by living witnesses.

For instance, in A.D. 96, when Clement of Rome, in his *First Epistle to the Corinthians*, wrote that the apostles had personally appointed bishops and deacons, and that these authorities should be obeyed, he was making an assertion about which many people would know the truth or falsity. Since this assertion was central to the conclusion of his argument, it must have been believed to be true by his readers.

Similarly, when, in A.D. 107, Ignatius of Antioch repeatedly wrote that Christians should be obedient to their bishops, there would have been people still alive who had known the apostles, and they would have known if Ignatius' letters accurately reflected the true intentions of the apostles. For this reason, this present work "privileges" the authentic writings of Clement of Rome, the *Didache*, Ignatius of Antioch, and Irenaeus of Lyons (who knew men who knew the Apostle John;

Irenaeus wrote *Against Heresies* in the immediate aftermath of a hor-
rific persecution in Lyons). The writings of Clement of Alexandria,
Tertullian, Hippolytus, Origen, and Cyprian of Carthage will also receive
prominence because they testified to the shaping of the ongoing tradition, handed on from the apostles to the earliest bishops, despite the
fact that these writers were not in a position personally to know the
truth, and in some cases did not undergo martyrdom.

Returning to the heretical writings, one final point needs to be
made. It must be acknowledged that many authors deemed heretical
were in fact martyred for their beliefs. We should acknowledge this
fact and honor these martyrs. But the simple fact is that they were not
in a position to know the truth. Despite some of the more extravagant claims made regarding the *Gospel of Thomas*, all the so-called Gnostic texts were most likely the product of that unique period of history
from the middle of the second to the middle of the third century.[2] It
is highly unlikely that any of the Gnostic writings go back to the first
century, as most of the New Testament and some of the postapostolic
writings do. Therefore, these writings are given a secondary status in
this work.

In many ways, the pagan documents are the most useful to historians of the early Church, if used carefully. In the satirical writings, the
authors often thought they were making fun of the Christians, but
they were actually providing the highest praise. For instance, Lucian
of Antioch made fun of the Christians by writing a satire about a
group of Christians who provided charity for a charlatan named Peregrinus. The satire was designed to show how naïve the Christians
were, but what we learn is how widespread and systematic the charitable actions of the early Church were.

From pagan historians and official documents we gain a certain
amount of useful information about Christians, but primarily we learn
what the Romans thought about the Christians, particularly their misconceptions about Christianity. We also gain valuable insight into the
motivation behind the various persecutions the Church experienced.

Archaeological data also have to be handled with care. Archaeology
is a relatively young discipline, existing for fewer than three hundred
years. Nevertheless, in that short period of time archaeologists have
unearthed hundreds of ancient cities, uncovering enormous amounts
of information about the ancient world. This information can be used

quite profitably in reconstructing the everyday lives of the people of the Roman Empire, and quite a bit of this information actually can shed light on the lives of the early Christians. However, for the reasons mentioned above, I am hesitant to use the archaeological data without documentary evidence to accompany it.

As a general rule, archaeological evidence will be used with great circumspection. For example, in ancient Herculaneum, a house has been discovered with a cross-shaped indentation in the plaster in one of its rooms. When it was first discovered, this house created ripples of excitement in Christian circles. The part of Herculaneum that contained this particular house had been destroyed in A.D. 79, when Mount Vesuvius erupted. Could there have been Christians in southern Italy in 79, with crosses mounted in the wall of their home? The thought thrills the imagination. The problem is that there could be other reasons for this particular indentation (a wooden frame could have been sunk into the plaster to allow a cabinet to be mounted, for instance). Also, we have no other reason to think the household was Christian (no artwork, no fish symbols, etc.). Furthermore, there are no other examples of people sinking crosses into the wall plaster of their houses. (Why not simply hang the cross on the wall, rather than sink it into the plaster?)

While I still consider it possible that this house had a Christian symbol, I do not include this particular house in my analysis of early Christian life. The objections are serious enough to raise doubts about what really happened in the house in Herculaneum. It may be that in a few years new evidence will be discovered that will make it more likely that this house contained dedicated Christians, but for now I cannot seriously consider this piece of evidence.

For these reasons, this work relies on both archaeological and documentary evidence to reconstruct the lives of the early Christians. I am not averse to using unorthodox sources to illustrate the lives of the early Christians, but only within certain carefully delineated boundaries. Generally speaking, these documents will be used to shed light on the period in which the work was written, not the period about which it purports to write.

Negative evidence will also be considered; if an author condemns a certain practice, I will be willing at least to consider the possibility that some Christians were engaged in that practice. If a pagan author criticizes Christian behavior that would be considered admirable today, that pagan author will be taken at face value.

## The Boundaries of This Study

It is fashionable, in scholarly circles today, to emphasize the diversity of early Christianity. If these scholars are correct, my task is even more difficult. Rather than describing one set of beliefs and practices, I would be forced to describe dozens, or perhaps even hundreds. Fortunately for me, these modern scholars are only partly right. When they are arguing for the diversity of the early Church, they are including in their definition of Christianity certain heretical groups such as Gnostics, Marcionites, Montanists, and a host of other groups that at one point or another were found to be in heresy. In this study, for purposes of convenience and personal inclination, I have chosen to consider only those Christian communities that later became the Roman Catholic and Orthodox Churches. It will be necessary, on occasion, to mention the beliefs and practices of the heretical communities, but my main focus will be on those branches of Christianity that maintained apostolic succession and orthodox teachings about Christ and the Church.

Some readers will be disappointed to find that my primary focus is not on the New Testament Church, but rather on the two hundred years following the death of the last apostle. Naturally, New Testament data will be included in this work, but my primary focus will be on how the Christians from A.D. 100 to 313 understood the teachings of Christ and the apostles. There have been numerous works, by far better scholars than I, exploring the period of the New Testament. I am interested in the two-hundred-year period immediately following the writing of the New Testament, because the Church of this period was closer to the time when Christ and the apostles walked the earth than the Church is today.[3] We should at least consider the possibility that they understood the teachings of the New Testament better than we do today.

I am also interested in this period because one can clearly trace the development of certain Catholic ideas such as apostolic succession, the Real Presence of Christ in the Eucharist, and the sacraments of baptism, holy orders, and matrimony. At this point, I should make clear my personal presumption: my study of the early Church has convinced me that the first Christians were essentially Catholic in their outlook. All branches of orthodox Christianity (and by this I mean all branches of modern Christianity that adhere to the tenets of the Nicene Creed) owe their basic beliefs and even their canon of Scripture to the proto-Catholics of A.D. 100–313. For this reason alone, the beliefs and practices of the early Christians are worth studying.

It is my hope to introduce the treasures of early Christianity to a large number of people. This work is directed to a nonscholarly audience. I have made few assumptions about the level of historical knowledge of my readership. For this reason, I have included several aids throughout the work. At the end of Chapter 1, you will find a historical timeline that might be helpful. Also, at the end of the work, you will find an appendix giving a brief description of the most important figures mentioned in this work.

But I would urge my readers not to focus too heavily on the historical details of the period and concentrate instead on what we can learn from the lives of the early Christians. They were ordinary people, to be sure, but their lives were touched by grace, and many of them achieved a level of spiritual grandeur we can only marvel at today.

# PART I

# LIFE IN THE ROMAN WORLD

## CHAPTER I

# The World They Knew

The world the early Christians found themselves in was a large, complicated, diverse place. It was a world of bustling trade, intellectual and religious ferment, and constant political turmoil. It was a world of great greed and knavery, as well as a world of high ideals. In short, the world was as human then as it is now. In fact, you could make the argument that of all the periods of history, the world of the Romans was the closest to our own.[1]

In large measure, the complexity of the ancient Mediterranean can be attributed to the large numbers of diverse peoples that were brought under Roman rule. By the time of Christ, the Romans ruled an area that stretched from Spain to Mesopotamia, from Egypt to Britain, with as many different cultures as there were provinces.

We are accustomed to thinking of Roman domination as a disaster for the people of the world. After all, as everyone knows, the Romans destroyed cities, enslaved whole peoples, and later threw the Christians to the lions. On the other hand, the people of the empire obtained many benefits from Roman rule. The *Pax Romana* turned the whole Mediterranean into a massive free-trade zone. Not only did the Romans crush cruel local despots, they suppressed piracy on the sea and banditry in the countryside. They also frequently provided better local government than had many of the rulers they replaced.

Thomas Bokenkotter, a prominent Catholic historian, lists three reasons for the spread of Christianity. Of these three reasons, two actually reflect positively on the way the Romans governed their empire.[2] The first reason Bokenkotter lists is "the favorable material conditions afforded by Rome's dominance of the Mediterranean world".[3] The Romans built roads, promoted the spread of a common culture, cleared the seas of pirates, and did many other things to unite the entire known world. This physical infrastructure made it possible for the gospel to spread with relative ease. Bokenkotter's second reason had to do with the fact that the world was largely at peace for the first hundred years of the Christian era. The Romans employed brutal methods to ensure peace, but these were effective, and in a climate of peace religious systems with a popular appeal could flourish. Bokenkotter's third reason has to do with the spiritual unrest of the time. As we shall see, there were serious deficiencies in the Roman world-view, and Christianity did a better job of providing meaning and hope for people who lived hard lives.

Of the three reasons mentioned above, two reflect well on the Roman system, and one reflects poorly. Like all things human, the Roman Empire had some good and some bad qualities. So it would be a mistake to assume that the Roman influence on the world at that time was purely negative. The Romans accomplished many good and lasting things.

### The Accidental Empire

The Romans themselves were not entirely sure how their city came into existence. In the years before Christ, there were two stories about the founding of Rome. One was that Aeneas, a Trojan hero, traveled to the region after the destruction of Troy and founded the city. The other, more famous, story is told of Romulus and Remus, who were raised by wolves and eventually rescued by shepherds. Romulus murdered Remus, the tale goes, and founded Rome. The tales surrounding the founding of Rome are both obscure and revelatory at the same time. The myths reveal the violence inherent in the founding and advancement of Rome. The murder of Remus, so reminiscent of the murder of Abel in Genesis, proved to be prophetic of the future course the Romans would take. Every new city Rome conquered, every province Rome acquired, duplicated the violence present at the founding of the city.

It took Rome a long time to advance from the mud-walled village of Romulus to the sophisticated world center Peter and Paul found. The traditional date for the founding of the city, proposed by the historian Varro, was 753 B.C. However, this date might not be accurate, since archaeologists have found graves in the region from at least the tenth century B.C.[4] In these early years, a more powerful neighbor, Etruria, dominated Rome. Etruscan power was centered in northern Italy. They had a unique culture, and many elements of it became part of Roman culture as well.[5]

In any case, the Romans did not free themselves from domination by the Etruscans until the fifth or sixth century. By 500 B.C., Rome had allied itself with a dozen neighboring cities.[6] A series of brutal wars secured most of the Italian boot south of the Rubicon by 240. It is most important, however, to realize that Rome did not conquer all this territory. Some of the cities under Roman domination were "allies" rather than conquered territories. This would remain a central component of Rome's modus operandi throughout its history: make allies on the basis of self-interest and later assimilate the allies into Roman territory.

One of the most significant events in early Rome was the expulsion of King Tarquinius in 509 B.C. The monarchy was replaced with a system of two consuls, who were elected for one-year terms. Power was diffused so effectively that when Rome began to rule large overseas territories, it was obvious that a stronger central authority was needed. Empires need an emperor.

The Romans began their overseas conquests during the period of the Punic Wars. This series of intermittent conflicts began in 264 B.C. By 202, the Romans had successfully confined Carthage to a very small area around the North African city. With Carthage decimated, the western Mediterranean (the area now encompassing France, Spain, Corsica, Sicily, and North Africa) was open to Roman domination. Over the next 200 years, the Romans conquered all these lands. They finally destroyed Punic Carthage for good in 146 B.C.

The conquest of Gaul by Julius Caesar in 51 B.C. rounded out the western Roman Empire. (Later, Britain was added by a series of campaigns that were finally concluded in A.D. 84.) Having dominated the West, the Romans cast their covetous gaze eastward, where some of the richest countries in the known world existed.

The eastern Mediterranean—the region that included Greece, Egypt, Mesopotamia (modern-day Iraq), Syria, and Asia Minor (modern-day Turkey)—was accustomed to being united in various empires, but by the time the Romans came on the scene, the whole region was a patchwork of small states, some of them well run, some not so well. Nevertheless, there was a degree of cultural unity that makes it easier to think of the East as a discrete unit. This unity came about as a result of the efforts of Alexander the Great, one of the few true military and political geniuses in the history of the world. So it will be necessary to make a brief digression into Greek history, in order to understand the world the Romans found when they moved east.

In 331 B.C., before Alexander began his career of conquest, the eastern Mediterranean could basically be divided into two parts. The immense Persian Empire controlled Egypt, Palestine, Syria, Mesopotamia, and everything to the east all the way to India. The Persians governed their empire well, allowing a certain amount of local autonomy, keeping taxes relatively low, and thus keeping unrest to a minimum. Against the Persians was arrayed a patchwork of Greek states. Athens, Corinth, Sparta, Thebes, Macedonia, and the rest were as likely to be at war with one another as they were to be fighting the Persians. But the great genius of the Greeks was that they had developed political institutions that allowed a great degree of individual freedom. This freedom allowed the Greeks, particularly the Athenians, to advance in areas of philosophy, science, and the arts, including the military arts.

Alexander's father, Philip, succeeded in uniting the Greek world through a combination of diplomacy and military conquest. When Philip died, Alexander immediately began the campaign he had long dreamed of, the campaign to conquer the Persian Empire. Improbably, Alexander succeeded. In a series of lightning campaigns, Alexander conquered the entire Persian Empire in eight years. Alexander's great accomplishment was to combine the Persian and the Greek worlds. He introduced Greek colonists to the areas he conquered, while continuing to use the Persian administrative system.

Alexander's empire did not survive his death in 323 B.C., of "exhaustion, war wounds, disease, and drunkenness".[7] Three of Alexander's generals divided the empire among themselves, then began to fight one another. Over a period of time the threefold division continued to split into smaller and smaller units. For instance, in 161 B.C., under the leadership of Judas Maccabeus, Judah[8] gained its independence from the Hellenistic kingdom of Antiochus Epiphanes. This process continued, and by the time the Romans came on the scene, the political units were fairly small and quite easy to overcome one at a time.

The lasting achievements of Alexander were all in the area of culture. Alexander gave the eastern Mediterranean a common language (Greek)[9] and a common, though very flexible, religious system. Alexander's conquests made it easy for trade and the mutual exchange of ideas to go on. Alexander united the eastern Mediterranean world culturally. It remained for a sufficiently strong military power to come along and unite the region politically. Ironically, Rome's initial involvement in Eastern affairs was primarily prompted by the actions of those in the eastern Mediterranean.

The historian Edward Gibbon is said to have remarked sarcastically, "The Romans conquered the world in self-defense."[10] Gibbon meant that the Romans always clothed their aggressive actions in the robe of legitimacy. An instance can be seen in the Roman actions in Macedonia. When Macedonia began to interfere in the affairs of other Greek states, Rome made an alliance with the aggrieved parties and defeated the aggressors, but in the end annexed Macedonia. However, there are cases where Rome seems to have behaved in a more admirable fashion. For example, when Antiochus III invaded Thrace in 196 B.C., Rome thoroughly crushed his army, made a peace treaty, and then went home.[11]

What accounts for the difference? The truth is, Rome was extremely hesitant to conquer new territories. Each new territory involved another headache, another administrative and military problem that could be solved only with great difficulty. What the Romans really wanted was free trade. They wanted to grow rich trading with the East. When it became obvious that they could not keep the trade routes open without military intervention, they acted with great ruthlessness.

The Romans may have entered into wars and conquered new territories reluctantly, but once engaged in warfare, they fought with great brutality. In the Macedonian campaign mentioned above, the Roman general Paullus systematically pillaged Molossia and enslaved its entire population, simply as a punishment for fighting on the side of the Macedonians.[12] Incidents like this were quite common in the warfare of that period.

Some parts of the empire came under Roman rule by relatively peaceful means. For instance, the province of Asia, which encompassed a great deal of what we now know as Turkey, was bequeathed to Rome in the will of the last king of Pergamum.[13] Of course, the Romans had to fight off several rival claimants, who understandably doubted the legitimacy of the will. Egypt and Cyrenaica essentially came under Roman possession in the same way, though in the case of Egypt, it took Rome a long time to exert the military force needed to collect the inheritance.[14]

These examples illustrate an important point: there were always powerful and influential people in the East who thought their countries would be better off ruled by Rome. Of course, not everyone agreed with this theory, but enough did that in some areas, Rome came to power with minimal effort. Moreover, the Romans were fairly respectful of local customs, traditions, and religions as long as they did not conflict with Roman administrative authority. This fact also helps to explain why there were relatively few rebellions against Roman rule, and why so few rebellions were ever successful.

The Romans were late in moving into Judea and Galilee. In typical fashion, they came in under cover of legitimacy. A struggle between two members of the ruling family allowed the Romans to act as mediators. When his efforts to resolve the dispute peacefully failed, Pompey the Great besieged Jerusalem and took the city in 63 B.C. Pompey committed the shocking impiety of entering the Holy of Holies, the most sacred part of the Temple, but found nothing there but an empty room.[15]

Rome tried to rule Judea through local allies, but the attempt failed, and in the end the Romans had to send procurators to govern Jerusalem. Galilee, however, ended up in a separate administrative unit. Through clever diplomacy, Herod the Great became "king of the Jews", and his descendants ruled in Galilee after him. This points to another important point of Roman rule. They always preferred to rule local territories through local supporters, but when, as in the case of Jerusalem, the local rulers could not provide order, the Romans would step in and do it themselves.

The Romans frequently found that their wars increased the wealth of individuals and the entire city of Rome. All the loot and slaves that did not become the personal property of the generals and their soldiers ended up in Rome. After particularly successful campaigns, slaves became extremely cheap, to the extent that, at one point, approximately 50 percent of the inhabitants of the city of Rome were slaves.[16]

So military conquest could be highly lucrative and might be said to have become a habit by the time of Christ.

When Roman conquests finally encompassed a relatively easily defended geographical region, the Romans slowed their aggressive military campaigns. They tended to build walls to protect their territories. Thus, in northern England you can still see Hadrian's Wall, built to keep the Picts out of Roman Britain. Wherever there was a good deep river to keep enemies out, the Romans used it as a barrier. For 400 years, the Rhine protected Gaul, and the Danube served to hold Rome's northern frontier. In the east and south, deserts and mountain ranges performed a similar function.

### How Rome Ruled the Empire

In the pages of the New Testament, we find many encounters between Christians and various government officials. Trials before various tribunals are recorded,[17] as well as encounters with governors[18] and conversions of various important officials.[19] It's easy to get lost in all the details. Who was responsible for what? Which government officials were local, and which ones had been sent in by Rome?

Because Rome came to rule the various pieces of the empire in different ways, the government of each territory differed slightly. Rome favored the Persian model of imperial administration, which meant that wherever possible friendly local governments would be set up. Even where this arrangement was not possible, local leadership would be allowed to govern in affairs that were considered purely local. This explains why, for instance, the Sanhedrin could assemble and even conduct trials in Jerusalem, though they lacked the authority to execute anyone. Throughout the empire, local assemblies similar to the Sanhedrin would meet to discuss and decide local affairs, with minimal interference from Rome, unless larger issues were at stake.

As I mentioned earlier, in the sixth century B.C. Rome evicted the last of her kings and set up the Republic. This form of government had two executives, called consuls. The consuls were elected by the tribes of Rome on an annual basis. They had to take monthly turns in governing. The top two vote-getters in consular elections might not have the same political philosophy, and might in fact hate one another, as was the case during the consulships of Julius Caesar and his mortal enemy Bibulus. The Roman Republic worked well until Rome expanded into the eastern Mediterranean, thus necessitating a much more complex administrative model.

Two assemblies governed with the consuls, the Senate and the Plebeian Assembly. The Senate was the more prestigious of the two bodies. There were three requirements for being a senator. You had to have an income of at least 1,000,000 sesterces a year, you could not be engaged in trade, and you had to be a member of a patrician (noble) family. These requirements ensured that the Senate would be conservative in its outlook, tending to look after the vested interests of the land-owning class. The Senate did not represent the interests of either the poor or the rising merchant class.[20]

Late in the Republican period, the Plebeian Assembly became more important, gaining the right to make laws in the domestic field, although any one of the ten tribunes of the plebes could veto any law he did not like. Technically, anyone who was not of the senatorial or equestrian class was a plebe. But in actual practice, the plebes primarily consisted of the poorest citizens of Rome.[21] The members of the Plebeian Assembly were elected by all the plebes, as were the ten tribunes of the plebes. The plebes were primarily interested in debt relief and a more equitable distribution of the land. Since both of these interests directly contradicted the desires of the senatorial class, the two groups were constantly engaged in political struggle.

Politics in the late Republican period were chaotic and prone to corruption, and it was virtually impossible to get anything done. Prominent senators found they could keep the plebes from passing any legislation by keeping a tribune of the plebes on their payroll, to veto any legislation deemed harmful to the patrician interests. The plebes, not as sophisticated as the senators, sometimes resorted to violence to induce the tribunes not to veto their legislation.

Along with internal political strife, the stability of the Roman Republic was also hampered by the growing power of successful generals, who used their military successes and ever-increasing wealth to manipulate the workings of the Roman state in their favor.

All these factors ultimately contributed to civil war. Julius Caesar, Pompey, and Crassus formed a triumvirate, a rule of three men, in an attempt to restore order and get urgent business done. When

Crassus died in 53 B.C., Caesar and Pompey fought, and Caesar emerged the victor. Caesar's seeming efforts to revive a monarchy ultimately led to his assassination, commemorated in Shakespeare's play *Julius Caesar*. The assassins, Cassius and Brutus, had to deal with Caesar's ally Marcus Antonius (Mark Anthony). The affair ended with all the main characters dead. Octavius, Caesar's nephew, assumed the title *Augustus* and began imperial rule, with the consent of the Senate and the people.

The empire had quite a different feel from that of the Republic. The plebes had no power whatsoever. Instead, they took the emperor as their champion. (You might be confused as to how Augustus accomplished this. He evidently had a quite charismatic personality, and he always made sure he provided plenty of "bread and circuses" for the populace. Moreover, he was very cautious in his approach, unlike his uncle. His successors ignored this formula at their own peril.) The Senate, meanwhile, was relegated to an "advise-and-consent" function, with no real power.[22] Outside the imperial family, real power in the empire resided in the military. A wise emperor, which Augustus certainly was, would always make sure to keep the army happy—and make sure no general had too much clout.

Here is the historian Tacitus' description of how Augustus, and all successful emperors, ruled:

> He seduced the army with bonuses, and his cheap food policy was successful bait for civilians. Indeed, he attracted everyone's good will by the enjoyable gift of peace. Then he gradually pushed ahead and absorbed the functions of the Senate, the officials, and even the law. Opposition did not exist. War or judicial murder had disposed of all men of spirit. Upper-class survivors found that slavish obedience was the way to succeed, both politically and financially. They had profited from the revolution, and so now they liked the security of the existing arrangement better than the dangerous uncertainties of the old regime.[23]

The only weakness in this system, from the emperors' point of view, was that the generals had the power to put anyone they wanted on the throne. Throughout the history of the empire, sudden, unforeseen changes in rulers disrupted continuity and severely impeded long-term planning.

Provincial government was not uniform. There were two kinds of provinces: imperial provinces and senatorial provinces. On top of that, there was a third group of territories, like Galilee, governed by local allies.[24] The difference between the various kinds of provinces has to do with how they became a part of the empire. Most of the provinces were acquired before there was an emperor. They were conquered either under the authority of the Senate (which usually had control over foreign policy in the Republic) or by a consul. The Senate retained the authority to appoint governors for those provinces conquered under senatorial orders. However, those provinces conquered by a consul or proconsul (an ex-consul with special authority) came under the direct personal authority of the emperor.

For example, Gaul was an imperial province because Julius Caesar personally conquered it during his proconsular year. Similarly, Syria was an imperial province because the proconsul Pompey conquered it. Thus, in these provinces, the emperor had the privilege of appointing personal friends as governor. Other provinces, such as Numidia and Macedonia, had been conquered under the orders of the Senate, and even after Augustus came to power the Senate was nominally in charge of appointing governors for these provinces. In accord with the ancient practice, proconsuls governed senatorial provinces, and legates governed imperial provinces.

Whether appointed by the emperor or by the Senate, governors were inclined to look upon their provinces as a source of personal enrichment. For instance, if Josephus is to be trusted, the procurator of Judea, Florus, drove the Jews to revolt in 66 A.D. solely so he could loot the province.[25] Some governors behaved more wisely than others. They made numerous improvements in their provinces, such as the construction of aqueducts, the improvement of roads, and the suppression of piracy and banditry.

Motivated primarily by self-interest, the leading men of all the provinces applied for and were granted Roman citizenship. These local leaders contributed greatly to the local improvement projects. Eventually, many of these provincial leaders achieved senatorial rank.

The emperor also had the right to appoint procurators as governors for smaller territories like Judea. The procurators came from the equestrian (knightly) class. They were men of proven ability and great personal loyalty to the emperor. Prefects handled certain tasks deemed

vital to the survival of the empire. For instance, there was a prefect of
the corn supply to insure that the city of Rome received an adequate
food supply. The prefect of Egypt ruled the richest province in the
empire. The elite corps of soldiers who guarded the emperor was commanded by the Praetorian prefect. Aediles and praetors handled the
daily administrative tasks of the cities, such as providing for sanitation
and police protection. Aediles also functioned as treasurers and notary
publics in the communities in which they lived.

Provincial capitals were flooded with a throng of administrators,
accountants, army officers, and other minor officials. By far, the tax
collectors were the most resented of all Roman officials in the provinces. Technically, the tax collectors were not attached to the government, but were private entrepreneurs. Each year, the treasury in Rome
would take bids for the taxes for each province. The tax collectors
would carefully estimate how much they could collect and turn in a
bid that would be high enough for them to get the contract, but low
enough that they could make a huge profit.

The amazing fact is that Rome cared not one whit how much the
tax collectors actually collected. Rome cared only how much the tax
collectors turned in to the treasury. So a tax collector could collect,
say, a million denarii from province A, but if his bid was only 500,000
denarii, he could make a quick 100 percent profit on his year's work.
Of course, it was not as simple as that. To collect taxes in the typical
Roman province one would need a small army of collectors, as well as
legal authority to catch potential cheaters.

The tax collectors often sublet regions within a province. In turn, the
sublease holders would either further divide the pie with more independent contractors or hire locals to do the collecting. In the final analysis, tax collecting might be no more scientific than a group of unscrupulous
men seeing how much they could extort from the local populace.

The system of tax collection facilitated corruption, which in turn
caused considerable resentment. The tax collector might be the only
contact some local populations had with Rome, so the greediest representatives of Roman authority formed people's opinions about Roman
government. Periodically, emperors attempted to reform the system,
but since they made only superficial changes, the basic system remained
in place. Resentment against tax collectors was high and is reflected in
the New Testament.[26]

### The Fate of the Empire

So far, we have traced the history of Rome up to Augustus, described how the empire came to be, and given a thumbnail sketch of Roman rule. This book is intended to cover the entire period from the birth of the Church to A.D. 313 (when Constantine legalized Christianity in the empire). Thus, it will be necessary to trace the outlines of Roman history up to that time, with special attention given to developments of significance to Christians.

The emperors immediately following Augustus were not good rulers. Tiberius, Caligula, Claudius, and Nero were all, in their own ways, unjust and cruel. Nero was probably the worst, although Caligula might have surpassed him had he lived longer. All four died violent deaths in the midst of widespread public revulsion.

Nero gained infamy for setting fire to Rome in A.D. 64 because he wanted to remake it in a manner more to his liking. When the deed was done, and Nero beheld the popular outrage, he proceeded to blame the whole thing on the Christians. Nero's actions launched the first major Roman persecution of Christians and set a legal precedent that lasted for 250 years.

Nero committed suicide in A.D. 68, and chaos followed, as various candidates vied for the empire. The year 68–69 was known as "the Year of the Four Emperors". Army commanders Galba, Otho, and Vitellius all wore the purple for brief periods, but finally the little-known and much-lampooned Vespasian assumed the throne. Vespasian had been sent to Judea in 66 to put down the Jewish revolt. (The historian Suetonius records that Vespasian was sent to Judea because he had the audacity to fall asleep during one of Nero's concerts.)[27] By 68, he had the situation in Judea well in hand and began plotting to become emperor. His troops proclaimed him emperor, and in 69, Vespasian left the siege of Jerusalem in the hands of his son Titus and returned to Rome to secure his new position.

From the Christians' point of view, two significant events of the first century were the persecution of the Christians of Rome, which led to the execution of Peter and Paul, and the destruction of Jerusalem in A.D. 70, which forced the Christians to rethink their relationship with Judaism.

The Roman Empire was at its peak at around A.D. 100. After the death of Vespasian's son Domitian (81–96), a series of relatively effective emperors ruled. Known as the "Five Good Emperors", their wise and far-reaching policies ensured a period of peace and prosperity from 96 to 180. Particularly noteworthy was their policy of choosing their imperial successor based on ability and not blood. By the middle of the second century, however, a new period of tribulations began. A series of plagues swept the empire, and pressure on the frontier with Germania increased dramatically. Emperors like Marcus Aurelius (161–180) were obliged to spend almost all their time on the frontier battling barbarians.

It was thanks to Marcus Aurelius' almost constant warfare that the empire survived this crisis. By A.D. 200, the empire was on firmer footing, but the respite was short-lived. By 250, more pressure, this time from Germanic tribes in the north and Persians on the eastern frontier, led to another period of crisis. Diocletian (284–305) attempted sweeping reforms. He reorganized the empire by dividing it into four parts (to be ruled by two Augusti and two Caesars). He instituted economic reforms. Thinking Christianity weakened the resolve of the empire, he initiated the most brutal of all the Roman persecutions against Christians.

His successor, Constantine, followed Diocletian's lead in all areas except his religious policy. Constantine legalized Christianity in A.D. 313 and subsequently passed a series of laws designed to facilitate the Christianization of the empire. And thus ends the era with which this book is concerned.

# A CHRONOLOGY OF ROMAN HISTORY

*Before Christ*

| | |
|---|---|
| 753 | Traditional date for the founding of Rome |
| 509 | The expulsion of the last king |
| 331–323 | Alexander the Great conquers the Persian Empire |
| 264–146 | Punic Wars |
| 63 | Pompey conquers Jerusalem |
| 58–51 | Julius Caesar conquers Gaul |
| 27 | Augustus becomes first emperor |

*After Christ*

| | |
|---|---|
| 64–67 | Great Fire of Rome, first general persecution of Christians |
| 66–70 | Jewish revolt, destruction of Jerusalem |
| 79 | The Colosseum is built, Mount Vesuvius destroys Pompeii |
| 88–96 | Persecution of Christians under Domitian |
| 97–138 | Persecution under Trajan and Hadrian |
| 160–170 | Plague sweeps the empire for the first time |
| 161–180 | Persecution under Marcus Aurelius |
| 193–211 | Persecution under Septimius Severus |
| 249–251 | Persecution under Decius |
| 296–313 | Last great persecution of Christians |
| 313 | Edict of Milan legalizes Christianity |

## CHAPTER 2

# Religion in the Roman World

In a moment of despair, the Roman historian Tacitus wrote, "Rome is the city where horrible and shameful things from all over the world flow together and are praised." [1] Tacitus would have listed Christianity as chief among the "horrible and shameful things" that had their origins in the shabby corners of the empire and made their way to Rome. But the fact that Tacitus was poorly informed about the nature of Christianity should not deter us from acknowledging the truth of what he wrote.

From the very beginning, Roman religion was a hodgepodge of outside religious influences. First the Romans borrowed heavily from the Etruscans, then from the Greeks of southern Italy, and later from the mystery religions of the East. However, by far the most pernicious of foreign religious ideas was the idea of the divine emperor, an idea that had its ancient roots in the Mesopotamian and Egyptian ideal of the king as the son of a god. Most of the emperors allowed themselves to be worshipped as gods, though some of them knew the idea was absurd. Some of the emperors insisted on such worship as a loyalty test, and this became a major reason for the persecution of Christians.

Human religious systems evolve, and the Roman religious system was no exception. With due attention to the evolution of Roman religion, here is a brief overview of the systems that had an influence on the religious life of the empire.

### The Gods of Hearth and Home

We are accustomed to thinking of Jupiter, Mars, Venus, and friends as the gods and goddesses of Rome. Certainly, there were temples to all these gods and goddesses throughout the empire. But the original gods of the city of Rome were much more complicated, at once intimate and family-centered, yet at the same time mysterious and powerful.

Like most primitive religions, the earliest pagan religions were born out of a desire to control the forces of nature. The Romans believed that all the processes of the world were controlled by spiritual forces. People today might find that thesis acceptable, but the Romans differed from us in that they believed each process had its own spirit that controlled it.[2] Thus, there not only was an agricultural god, but a spirit in charge of plowing, a separate spirit devoted to planting, and a third spirit devoted to the harvest. Each spirit had to be placated in the way it preferred, at the proper time of the year, with the proper ceremony. Failure to perform each rite properly could lead to disaster, not only for individuals but for the entire community.

To a large extent, the state religion, or the official cult of Rome, was nothing more than a larger scale version of the private religion of a small farmer. There were, however, some notable differences. (For this reason, this section will deal exclusively with the private religious life of the Roman family, and the next section will deal with the state religion of Rome, which became the religion of the whole empire.)

At the center of the private religious life of the average Roman were the gods of the household, the *lares* and the *penates*. Each household had its own *lararium*, or cupboard containing the *lares* of the household.[3] Each morning, the family, led by the *paterfamilias*, said prayers and made a small offering of wine or incense to the *lares* of the household. There were also special evening rites to the *lares*, as well as small prayers one would recite upon crossing the threshold (always right foot first).[4]

The *lares* were the deified spirits of dead ancestors.[5] In traditional Roman households they were represented by *imagines*, the masks of the ancestors, which were kept in the *lararium*. The *lares* were believed to take a continuous interest in the fortunes of the family, but they had to be treated with respect. Families who did not show proper respect to the *lares* were likely to find that their affairs did not prosper.[6] Fortunately, the *lares* did not require much. An offering of wine or incense, a gift of garlands, the saying of the morning and evening prayer were all it took to keep the family *lares* on one's good side.

The other household deities that had to be appeased were the *penates*. They take their name from the *penus*, or storeroom. Thus, the *penates* were the "dwellers of the storeroom".[7] More specifically, they were the beings who could make sure the storeroom was full, if they were taken care of. Vesta, the goddess of the hearth, was one of the *penates*. Vesta in particular played a large role in the daily piety of the Romans. Roman families would offer prayers to Vesta before the main meal of the day, and in the middle of a meal particularly devout families would throw a small piece of cake on the fire. It was considered an especially good omen if the cake crackled as it burned.[8]

In addition to the daily rites to the *lares* and the *penates*, every process of life—agriculture, birth, death, travel, returning home— had its own specific gods with specific rites that must be performed in a specific manner in order for events to go smoothly. Just as an example, consider the mysteries of conception and birth. On a wedding night, Virginensis loosened the bride's girdle, Sugibus handed her over to her husband, Prema supervised the marital embrace, Fluonia and Alemona saw to the nourishing of the embryo. Nona (or Decima) brought the child successfully to term, and Postverta and Prosa prevented breech birth. Egeria drew the baby out of the womb, but Parca presided over the birth. Vitunmus imparted life, Sentinus gave sensibility to the child, and Lucina gave the child light (*lux*).[9] Each of these tiny deities had his own rite that had to be performed properly in order for the process to be brought to completion. Ovid records a part of a prayer to Lucina: "I beg thee, good Lucina, spare pregnant women, and when the fruit of their womb comes to maturity, deliver them gently."[10]

For the average Roman every aspect of life was governed by thousands of minor deities. Death, puberty, travel, moving into a new home, and all other matters were each covered by their own rites. The average person at least behaved as if these deities really did exist and had to be courted. We might be tempted to call these people superstitious, but perhaps we should not be too harsh. Lacking any divine revelation or scientific knowledge in these matters, they did the best they could. It was only natural that people who had been touched by hunger, fire, earthquakes, miscarriages, war, illness, and sudden death would wish to come into contact with beings they thought could provide help.

As we shall see, the early Christians in general did not revile the common folks for their religious practices, but instead tried to show how the Christian understanding of God and his relationship to the world was superior. Tertullian even went so far as to assert that angels performed the functions the pagans had ascribed to a thousand minor deities.[11]

The private religion of the Romans, with its simple faith and simple aspirations, was not as dangerous as the public religion of the Romans, with its violent entertainment, its "imperial theology", and its insistence on the deification of the emperors.


## The State Religion

Roman public religion had many of the same features and rites as private religion. The main difference was that in private religion the *paterfamilias* would be the presider, whereas the public religion had priests to perform its rites. With only a few exceptions, the priests were not full-time professional clergy, but rather the leading men of the city who were honored with the ability to perform religious functions deemed necessary to the city.

The chief characteristic of Roman public religion was utilitarianism.[12] The Romans were interested in what worked, and what worked was defined as that which produced military victories, public safety, and economic advantages. Since Rome was usually successful in its endeavors, the people and the leaders thought that their religious practices were responsible and thus should be punctiliously observed. From our vantage point, Rome's success had very little to do with the gods they worshipped, but from the point of view of the Romans, their gods were largely credited for Rome's dominance in worldly affairs, and continued success demanded that the ancient traditions be faithfully observed.

This public sentiment explains how some extremely ancient practices were preserved until the ascendancy of Christianity. There was also, however, another dynamic at work that made it very easy for the Romans to incorporate foreign religious beliefs into their worship, even the public worship of the state. It was considered advantageous for Rome to "capture" the gods of other people and, by assiduous worship, co-opt these gods and make them work for Rome rather than their native people. In this way Minerva became a Roman goddess; her statue was captured from the Falernians in 241 B.C. and installed in her own temple in Rome; she was thought no less loyal to Rome for having been captured in war.[13]

Roman utilitarianism in religious matters was responsible for numerous additions to the ancient religion. One of the most interesting additions was the incorporation of the sibylline prophecies into Roman religious life.[14] The sibylline oracles were a collection of prophecies from Delphi in Greece. In times of national crisis, the ancient scrolls would be pulled out to shed light on the difficulties. In turn, the sibyls often recommended the incorporation of new deities. For instance, in 205 B.C., when Hannibal was ravaging Italy, the sibyls were consulted, and they recommended the addition of a Phrygian goddess named Cybele into Roman worship.[15] Cybele had truly bizarre rites that had to be modified before they could be acceptable in Rome, but this story illustrates that new gods were by no means unwelcome in Rome, and sometimes the addition of one new bit of piety led to others.

New religions were welcome, but they were strictly regulated. A body of men called the *sacris faciendis* was responsible for regulating foreign cults.[16] (They also had the duty of consulting the sibylline oracles when requested by the Senate.) They had a licensing system and were charged with making sure the more ecstatic Eastern cults stayed within the bounds of Roman propriety.

All in all, Roman religion was an extremely well-organized affair. Originally, all sacred matters were organized by the *rex sacrorum*, or "king of sacrifices". This office went all the way back to 509 B.C., when the last king was driven out.[17] Unlike most Roman priests, the *rex* was a priest and nothing else. He held no important political office. His primary duties involved performing certain sacrifices, particularly the sacrifice to Janus on New Year's Day.

Originally, the *rex* was in charge of all religious affairs, but over time the *pontifex maximus* supplanted him. This office was also very ancient. Far back into the dim mists of the past there had been a College of Pontiffs, whose responsibilities originally involved throwing human figures off the *Pons Sublicius* into the Tiber to placate the god of the river.[18] As the name implies, at some point the pontiffs became involved in the building of bridges across the Tiber (in Latin, *pons* is "bridge", and a *pontifex* would be a "bridge builder"). By the imperial times, the most common explanation of the role of the pontiffs was that they served as bridge builders between this world and the world of the gods.[19]

In any case, by the time of Augustus the *pontifex maximus* was the most important religious figure in Rome, which might be why Augustus took this office for himself. The role of the *pontifex maximus* in the time of Augustus was to serve as custodian of sacred laws and rituals, control the calendar, and regulate all acts of public and private worship. The *pontifex maximus* was responsible for choosing the *rex sacrorum* and all the other major priests, as well as the vestal virgins.

Another ancient order of priests was the order of *flamines*. There were fifteen *flamines*, the most famous of which was the *flamen dialis*, the sacred priest of Jupiter Optimus Maximus. The *flamines* were governed by many ancient regulations. The *flamen dialis*, for instance, could not touch iron under any circumstances.

The *flamines* had little real authority by the time of Augustus. Their role was primarily ritual. They were responsible for public and private sacrifices to the various gods they represented. For instance, on a feast day for Jupiter Optimus Maximus, the *flamen dialis* would preside. In the private realm, anyone who wanted to appeal to Jupiter, for whatever reason, would consult with the *flamen dialis*, and he would advise regarding the most efficacious way to approach the god, and preside over the sacrifice if circumstances warranted.

The vestal virgins also played an important role in the public religious life of Rome. Their primary duty was to tend the hearth of Vesta and make sure the sacred fire never went out. It was thought that if the fire went out and was not reignited, Rome would be destroyed. Human nature being what it is, the fire sometimes went out. When this tragedy occurred, the vestal responsible would be beaten, then the fire had to be rekindled in a highly prescribed way.

As their name implied, the vestal virgins were expected to remain chaste. If they broke their vow of celibacy they would be buried alive and left to the gods of the underworld.[20] The vestals took their vows for thirty years, and at the end of their service they were free to marry. Since they usually began their service between the ages of six and ten, they had a significant portion of their life after their service to the state, and many did in fact marry.

Augurs (in its origin, the word means "increaser") also played a role in the civic religion of Rome. In times of national crisis, when the best course of action was not clear, the Senate would consult with an augur, who would typically make arrangements to "take the auspices".[21] He would divide the sky into quarters, then choose one of the four quarters to take his observations from. Any flight of birds in the chosen quarter would be assigned a meaning. Left-handed omens were generally lucky, but interpretation was highly subjective. An augur could even ignore an unfavorable sign simply by calling out, "*Non consulto.*"[22] Obviously, the augurs' duties were politically charged, and wise politicians quickly found ways to manipulate the system.

There was another way anxious people could see into the future, though it was not officially a part of the state religion. *Haruspices* would, for an appropriate fee, slaughter an animal (usually a sheep) and take a look at the liver or other internal organs to make predictions about the future. There were very complicated instruction manuals to help the *haruspex* to make his determinations. In a society where everyone wanted to know about the future, it was easy to make a great living in this highly technical profession.

There were lesser officials who had some role in the public religious life of Rome. The *sacris faciendis* has been mentioned above. The ten *epulones* were responsible for the sacred feasts of the Senate after public sacrifices.

It will be worth taking a look at the practice of public sacrifice, because it will shed light on Jesus' critique of pagan prayer. The Romans were of the opinion that sacrifices had to follow the required steps rigidly, and if anything went wrong, the whole sacrifice would have to be redone from the start.[23] In sacrifice everything mattered. The animal had to be of the right kind, color, size, and sex. An official called a *probatio* made sure that it was not blind, infirm, or otherwise deformed. Once the animal was deemed acceptable, many things could still go wrong. The animal had to be killed with the right instrument: an ox was killed with an axe, a calf with a sledgehammer, a smaller animal with a knife. If the animal resisted in any way or made any noise, or if any other animal wandered through the place of sacrifice, the whole endeavor would be for nought.

During the ritual prayers, if the presider stumbled over any of the words, left out any words, or mispronounced anything, the sacrifice would be invalid.

All these regulations would naturally create a great deal of anxiety in the mind of the sacrificer. Elaborate precautions were taken to avoid an error. The victim would usually be drugged to make it pliant. You could even "take out an insurance policy"; the day before your sacrifice you could make another special sacrifice to atone for any mishap on the day of the festival.[24] In the unhappy event that things did not go well, you could redo the sacrifice until you got it right. There were always extra victims handy, for a price, of course.

Jesus may have had all these elaborate regulations in mind when he solemnly warned his followers, "And in praying do not heap up empty phrases as the Gentiles do." [25]

The average Roman would have little contact with the public cult of the state. He might attend certain ceremonies if there was a chance to get some of the sacrificial meat, but for the most part he left such matters to the professionals. But ordinary Roman citizens had an immense fondness for the *feriae*, the religious festivals of the city. There were an immense number of days reserved for one religious rite or another. (For a list of the fixed *feriae* of the Roman year, see Appendix A.)

Such a large number of holy days might have been disastrous, if everyone was expected to get the whole day off from work or engage in a whole day of prayer and sacrifice. But most of these days did not involve everyone. A particular guild might be expected to take five minutes to perform a small rite, then return to their work. Or, for example, only one gender might be involved in the rituals of the day, as on the feast of *Bona Dea*, when men were forbidden to participate.

Important festivals in which the whole city participated were the *Lupercalia* in February, the *Ludi Romani* in September, and the *Saturnalia* in December. During these times, all but the most essential work would shut down, and everyone would participate in games, eating and drinking immoderately. The Romans (and the Greeks also) believed that what we would call sporting events were especially pleasing to the gods. Religious activities and entertainment became so thoroughly mixed that it was difficult to tell the difference between the two. (For a more detailed discussion of entertainment in the empire, see Chapter 6.)

## The Greek and Roman Pantheon

Everyone knows about the Greek and Roman pantheon. Everyone also knows about the equivalence between Jupiter and Zeus, Mars and Ares, Juno and Hera, etc. As mentioned earlier, these gods and goddesses were not the original deities of the Roman people. The *lares* and *penates*, the spirits of woodland and farm—these were the original gods of Rome. The Olympian pantheon was introduced by Greek immigrants in southern Italy and spread northward to Rome. Linguistically, Greek and Latin are related, and certain odd correlations show up in the names of the gods. For instance, Zeus and Jupiter sound nothing alike, but linguists believe that the name Jupiter is a combination of *Ju*, which is a variation of "Zeus", and *piter*, which is an early version of *pater*, which is "father" in both Greek and Latin. Thus, Jupiter means "father Zeus".[26]

By the time of Augustus, nearly every city in the empire had temples to all the major Greco-Roman gods. This circumstance came about because of a curious melange of factors:

1.  The Greeks had begun the process of correlating local gods long before the Romans came onto the scene. Thus, Ammon of Egypt, Baal of Syria, and a host of other local gods were correlated with Zeus. Greeks governed the eastern Mediterranean from the time of Alexander until the Romans came to power, and they used their authority to promote Greek religion and culture.

2.  The Romans deliberately continued the policies of the Hellenistic rulers. Every city in the empire either had Roman temples built, or temples of local gods rededicated to Roman gods.

3.  The spirit of the age favored religious syncretism. The Greek and Roman religious policy succeeded because the local people, with one notable exception, were receptive to the idea of religious universalism and did not care if their local god was called Baal or Zeus or Jupiter, as long the deity was worshipped properly.

Most cities had a patron god or goddess. For Athens it was Athena. For Ephesus it was Artemis.[27] Rome itself had three patron gods:

Jupiter, Mars, and Quirinus. The people would be open to almost any god or goddess one might care to worship, as long as one was careful to give due homage to the local favorite. When Christians and Jews ran into problems in a local community, it was usually not for the sake of the God they worshipped, but because they would not also worship the local gods.

### The Mystery Religions

There were many strands of thought and practice in Eastern religions. Greece, Egypt, Persia, and Phrygia in particular produced ecstatic, highly mystical religious cults. These highly popular cults spread throughout the empire. The intense practicality of Roman religion caused some people to experiment with other cults out of boredom or in an attempt to achieve a closer union with the divine. Early on, the cult of Dionysius was popular in Rome, but by the time of Augustus the most popular cults were the cult of Cybele, the cult of Osiris, Mithraism, and the Orphic mysteries. There were others, almost too numerous to count, but these four were the most popular.

*The Cult of Cybele.* The cult of Cybele originated in Phrygia, in modern-day Turkey. In 205 B.C., when the outcome of the interminable war with Carthage was still in doubt and there were strange portents in the sky, the sibylline oracles were consulted. A prophecy was found that seemed relevant, and it indicated that victory would be forthcoming if the Romans began to worship the great mother goddess.[28] Accordingly, fifty former magistrates, led by a *vir optimus*, "best man", went to find the great mother goddess and bring her to Rome.

Just how they decided that Cybele was the one they wanted is unclear, but her worship was brought to Rome, and the war with Carthage ended well. But in fact the actual worship of Cybele disgusted and horrified the Romans and had to be modified before it was acceptable.[29]

The Phrygians believed that Cybele had a husband, a minor deity named Attis. In the course of their life together Attis had castrated himself and subsequently bled to death. Consequently, the priests of Cybele, called *galli*, were obliged to castrate themselves. In a state of ecstasy, while dancing through the streets of town, the prospective *galli* would castrate themselves, then attempt to throw their severed part through someone's doorway. If they succeeded in getting it inside someone's house, the people inside were obliged to help the prospective priest. If they failed, no one could help, and the poor man would most likely bleed to death. If a candidate succeeded in castrating himself and did not subsequently bleed to death, he would be a priest to Cybele forever, and dress in women's clothing.

This religion put Rome in quite a bind. On the one hand, the city had been commanded to worship Cybele by the sibyls themselves. On the other hand, the Romans had strict laws that forbade men from mutilating themselves. The Romans solved their problem in typical fashion. They kept the worship of Cybele, as the sibyls required, but modified it so that no Roman citizen was castrated. The priests were imported from Phrygia, where there were enough candidates to fill the needs of both cities. The *quindecemvirs sacris faciendis* was given the task of policing this odd religion, to make sure no trueborn Roman boy mutilated himself in a moment of religious ecstasy.

The cult of Cybele was the first major intrusion of an Eastern cult into Rome. The whole experience helped the Romans to understand that not all religions were as rational as their own and made them aware of the need to regulate Eastern cults carefully. It was a lesson the authorities did not forget. When young Roman men were sent overseas for military or civil service, they often tried out the local cults, out of boredom or simple curiosity. Some of these religions had elements that Roman religion lacked: excitement, mystery, and intimacy with powerful spiritual forces. When the young men returned to Rome from their foreign service, they brought the local cults back to Rome with them, and, again, the *sacris faciendis* would be there to make sure the cult required nothing against Roman custom.

*The Cult of Osiris.* This cult originated in Egypt. It celebrated the death and resurrection of Osiris, who was persecuted by the wicked god Seth, but through the love of his wife Isis, was restored to life.[30]

The simple, beautiful story of Isis and Osiris would seem to be above reproach, but the devotees of Isis were in constant difficulty with the authorities. For one thing, during the annual commemoration of the death of Osiris there would be a procession, during which the priests sometimes got carried away in their great grief and slashed their arms and legs. In the minds of the authorities, this cult was the same as the cult of Cybele.[31] It had to be regulated. It was unseemly and dangerous for solid Roman citizens to be crying in public or mutilating themselves for no good reason. The cult was sometimes outlawed, sometimes allowed with severe restrictions, and sometimes, for brief periods, it was celebrated in its full exuberant force.

The cult of Isis introduced something that Cybele had not required. Periodic celibacy was required of female devotees. During the reign of Tiberius this led to another religious scandal. A certain Decius Mundus desired a lovely young lady named Paulina. He despaired, but when he found out that Paulina was a worshipper of Isis, he hatched a plot. It seems that women would on occasion spend nights in the temple, where they would be visited by Osiris. Decius Mundus bribed a priest to find out when Paulina would be keeping vigil in the temple, and on that night he visited her disguised as the god. A night of lovemaking ensued. Paulina, under the mistaken impression that Osiris himself had favored her, bragged. Decius, under no such impression, also bragged. A scandal ensued, with some of the leading families in the city involved. Tiberius, who was notorious for his temper, had the priest crucified, the temple of Isis razed, and the idol thrown into the river.[32]

The cult recovered from this fiasco and was later reinstated in Rome. It was always very popular, because of the spectacular rites associated with it. A large number of other dying and rising gods, such as Dionysius of Thrace, came to be associated with Osiris. Myths about resurrection were actually quite common in this period. These myths caused Christian apologists to make some very careful distinctions when they began to make the argument that the story of Christ was true, while the other stories were false.

*Mithraism.* This cult originated in Persia. Like the cults of Attis and Osiris, this cult had just enough in common with Christianity to cause trouble. Mithras was a god who saved mankind by slaying a bull. Since Mithras was believed to have slain the bull in a cave, some of the rituals of this religion were performed in caves, or in dark underground rooms called *mithraea.*

There were many superficial similarities between Mithraism and Christianity. The date of Mithras' birth was set at December 25.[33]

One of the rites of initiation for the cult was a kind of baptism, in which a neophyte would stand under a bull while the animal was slain, and the blood was allowed to flow over him. A central feature of Mithraism was a shared meal among worshippers. We know little about the details of this meal, but Justin Martyr records that it included bread and water, and certain ritual prayers.[34]

Mithraism differed from some other religions of the period in that it was concerned with the ethical dimensions of human life. Mithras loved the truth and hated lies. His followers were expected to live a moral life, and their reward would be eternal life. Mithraism was attractive to soldiers in particular, for a number of reasons. Mithraism had a rigid hierarchy of offices and emphasized fellowship, and these are two things soldiers are likely to find attractive.[35]

The similarities between Mithraism and Christianity are striking, but there were also many differences, and, as we shall see, Justin Martyr made much of those distinctions in his attempt to affirm the truth of Christianity and the falsehood of Mithraism.

*The Orphic Mysteries.* The Romans always had an inferiority complex when it came to Greek culture. They were aware that most of their own philosophy, literature, art, and mythology were borrowed from the Greeks. When Romans found themselves in Greece, they always made sure to sample the best that Greek culture had to offer. Invariably, they made their way to Eleusis, a small town near Athens.

In Eleusis, the mystery rite of all mystery rites was performed, that of Orpheus. It is very difficult to gain any clear knowledge about the rites of Eleusis, because it was forbidden for an initiate to speak about what happened, but much can be inferred. Like the cult of Attis and Osiris, the Eleusinian mysteries featured the idea of death and rebirth. In Greek mythology, Orpheus descended into Hades to rescue his love Eurydice, who had died. Orpheus failed in his mission because at the last minute, as he was ascending from the underworld, he looked back (which had been forbidden), and his last sight of Eurydice was her receding in the mist, as she called out, "Farewell." Distraught, Orpheus wandered the earth, playing his flute, until he was torn apart by the maenads.

Out of this romantic tale the priests of Eleusis constructed a rite that was actually quite common at that time. It involved a mystical descent into Hades and rebirth as a new creature. The details are hazy, but the rite must have also included some reference to the agricultural cycle and the "rebirth" of the grain after a long "death" in the winter earth.[36] The imagery of the rite was used to foster the impression that we can all rise to our highest and truest self, which contains the spark of divinity.

The mystery religions, as the name implies, were designed to reveal a mystery to the initiates of the cult. Through *gnosis*, or the knowledge the cult imparted, people were supposed to be able to achieve what was commonly known as *soteria*, or salvation. Scholars have identified three stages in a person's participation in a mystery religion: (1) preparation and probation, (2) initiation and communion, and (3) salvation and blessedness.[37] The idea was that a person would first enter into a period of study, which would culminate in the initiation into the cult, and the knowledge attained by this initiation would empower one to achieve salvation, whatever that might entail.

Numerous scholars have commented on the similarities between the mystery religions and Christianity. These similarities have caused many of these scholars to assume that there was no real difference between Christianity and Orphism, for example. The idea that Christianity is a composite of various pagan cults is nothing new. The first philosophical opponents of Christianity were of that opinion, as are many of Christianity's cultured despisers today. But there is another interpretation of the undeniable facts, an interpretation first put forward by a Christian apologist named Justin Martyr. We will examine Justin's theory in greater detail in a future chapter, but for now it is enough to observe that, unexpectedly, the mystery religions served as a way of preparing the people to receive Christianity. The irony of this observation is obvious. Nevertheless, all the stories of dying and rising gods that circulated around the Roman world accustomed people to the idea that resurrection was possible, if only in a metaphorical sense.

On the other hand, these stories also paved the way for the belief in the divinity of the emperor.

### The Imperial Cult

To the modern mind, emperor worship seems incomprehensible. Conditioned by two thousand years of Christianity, the enlightenment, and the modern scientific revolution, we have a hard time understanding how anyone could worship another human being as divine. But we would do well to remember that in the twentieth century, there was a modern, industrialized nation, Japan, that worshipped its leader as a god. A leading scholar of the religious world of the first century has concluded that even the modern, secular West might be susceptible to emperor worship under certain conditions.[38]

We would never consider worshipping our leader and cannot imagine why ancient people did such a thing. But there was a time when most Romans thought the same. There was no Roman tradition of worshipping a human being as divine. The Romans had to be prepared by hundreds of years of contact with people who *did* worship their rulers as deities before the practice could become acceptable to them, and even then they placed conditions on the practice.[39]

How did the practice of emperor worship come about in the Roman Empire? There were two streams of religious practice that flowed together to form the unique institution that was emperor worship in the Roman Empire. The first stream flowed from Rome itself, in the long tradition of ancestor worship (which is what the *lares* were all about) and in the idea that each person possessed a *genius*, a divine or semidivine spirit that guided the person's actions. The second stream flowed from the Eastern part of the empire. In Egypt, Asia, and Mesopotamia, the people had regularly worshipped their rulers as gods. It was considered natural and even necessary.[40]

In Roman theology, the line between gods and men was never as clear as it was in Judaism or Christianity. The Romans had always worshipped the *lares*, and these beings were always known to be ancestors. So the Romans were not opposed to the idea that those who died in some way became divine. They also believed that each person had a *genius*, or a kind of a guardian spirit that watched over and helped him. This genius was generally held to survive an individual's death. The genius of a particularly powerful, successful person would continue to be of benefit to the nation even after death.[41]

These strands of thought coalesced in the person of Augustus. The Senate declared him a god after his death on the basis of the great good he had done for the state. Before his death, his genius was invoked in sacrifice.[42] After Augustus, most of the emperors followed this formula. Most emperors were deified by the Senate after their death, but while they were alive, the official cult was to their genius.

The Eastern part of the empire saw no need for such fine distinctions. The priests of Egypt, for instance, had cooperated with Alexander the Great in his quest to be declared a god. The reason the Easterners were so acquiescent in these matters was that their own rulers had always been considered divine. The pharaohs of Egypt were always styled the "son of Ammon", and the rulers of Sumeria, Akkad, and Babylon had always been referred to as the son of one god or another. The people of Asia, who had rarely been afforded the luxury of self-governance, came to look on emperor worship as a way of expressing loyalty to Rome.[43] In certain parts of the empire, particularly in Asia, there was a great deal of gratitude to Rome for providing peace and security, and that gratitude received tangible expression in the worship of the emperor.

The emperor cult expressed itself on several levels. In 30 B.C., the Senate decreed that libations should be offered to Augustus' genius at private banquets. Given all that Augustus had done, people thought it would be churlish at best, and disloyal at worst, to refuse this simple request. Public sacrifices to the emperor's genius were made on his birthday and on the anniversary of his accession to the throne.[44]

The imperial cult was administered by the leading citizens of all the major cities of the empire. These citizens would typically arrange a festival on the emperor's birthday or his day of accession. The feast would include the usual features: games, food, drink, and various other entertainments. There would also be a public sacrifice to the genius of the emperor.[45]

The persecution of Christians was associated with the imperial cult. At one time or another during the year each citizen was expected to make his way to the local imperial temple and make his own sacrifice to the emperor's genius. It need not be an elaborate sacrifice. A little wine or some incense would be perfectly acceptable. Nevertheless, anyone who wanted to be considered a good citizen had to make some kind of offering. Some scholars suggest that upon making the sacrifice one would be given a receipt. Lacking this receipt, one would not be able to engage in commerce. Some have suggested that this is the meaning of Revelation 13:11–17, where it is recorded that no one who refuses to worship the beast will be allowed to buy and sell.[46]

This thesis may or may not be correct, but what we do know is that in every city of the empire there was a temple to the emperor, and in that temple serious worship went on. We also know that such worship was reprehensible to Christians and Jews. Jews were given an exemption from worshipping the emperor, but Christians were never given any such exemption, and we know of several martyrs who were executed specifically for their failure to sacrifice to the emperor's genius.

Before concluding this section, a few observations seem necessary. First, not all emperors had the same attitude toward the imperial cult. Domitian, for instance, wanted to be worshipped as a god while still alive.[47] On the other hand, his father, Vespasian, openly joked about his supposed divinity. Some emperors changed their opinion over time as insanity set in. Caligula, for instance, forbade anyone to worship him in the early years of his reign, but later he insisted on divine honors.

Another important fact to bear in mind is that in almost every case the imperial cult had its origins in the desires of the people. The leaders of the local communities organized, financed, and enforced the local cult. There were, of course, many reasons why this was the case, not least of which was the desire on the part of social climbers to ingratiate themselves with the emperor, but the fact remains that, with the exception of Jews and Christians, most people participated in the cult willingly, if not enthusiastically.

A shift in emphasis away from the imperial cult came into being at the time of the emperor Aurelian (270–275). The sun god had given Aurelian a great victory. In gratitude, Aurelian established a great temple to *Sol Invictus* ("the unconquerable sun"). December 25, the festival of *Natalis Solis* from time immemorial, became the festival of *Sol Invictus*. Every emperor after Aurelian, particularly Diocletian, placed great emphasis on the sun god.[48] When Constantine came to power, he also favored *Sol Invictus*, but he had a tendency to relate the sun god to Christ himself.[49] In this way, in the end even the imperial cult led the way to Christ.

### Magic and Divination

The desire to know, and in some measure control, the future was so strong in the imperial age that the practices of augury and the inspection of entrails were not considered enough. In addition to these "tried and true" methods of divination, the people of the empire were devoted to astrology, which came from Babylon through Persian and Greek culture. The emperor Tiberius was addicted to astrology and never made a move without having a chart made.[50] Intellectuals argued against astrology and other forms of divination, but among the common people and the wealthy, recourse to these practices was common.

Magic, charms, and amulets were seen as a valid way of attempting to control events.[51] Romans generally did not participate in such practices as sorcery and witchcraft, but other people in the empire did. Thessalonians, Armenians, and Egyptians were most well known for practices we would associate with witchcraft, particularly the use of human body parts for magic. In general, Romans frowned on these practices, but there were specific cases where Romans became involved in some of these unsavory practices.[52]

### Philosophy

There were several philosophical systems common in the empire that had many of the characteristics of a religion. Prominent among them were Stoicism, Epicureanism, and Neoplatonism. Here are brief overviews of these philosophical systems, with their religious implications.

*Stoicism.* Stoicism was predicated on the idea that "there is nothing good save virtue, nothing bad save vice."[53] The idea was that people should concentrate on behaving in the proper fashion, without giving vent to feelings. The Stoics considered the tragedies and joys of life to be irrelevant. Stoicism was similar to Christianity in that it considered moral traits like justice and piety to be of more worth than extravagant sacrifice. The Stoics thought that sacrifice was worthless, in any case, since they believed that everything that happened was preordained in minute detail. Some notable Stoics were Cato the Younger, Seneca, and the emperor Marcus Aurelius.

*Epicureanism.* The Epicureans were not atheists in the modern sense. They accepted the existence of the gods, but believed that they existed in a realm far removed from us. The gods had not created the world, and they did not bother themselves with its affairs.[54] The Epicureans were committed to the enjoyment of the good things of this world, but, as is frequently pointed out, their philosophy did not necessarily degenerate into hedonism, since personal pleasure is not necessarily increased by gluttony. However, Epicureanism provided no intellectual or spiritual check to the tendency toward the gross physicality to which most Romans were prone. The poet Lucretius was the most notable Epicurean of this period.

*Neoplatonism.* As the name indicates, this philosophical system was loosely based on the philosophy of Plato. Its founder was Plotinus. He believed that a single divine being, called the One, was the ultimate cause of the universe. The One produced the Divine Mind, the Divine Mind produced the Soul, and everything else flowed from the Soul. Individual souls sought to achieve union with the One. Through successive reincarnations, each individual soul could draw closer to the One, if it learned to renounce the things of this world through asceticism.

In some ways, Neoplatonism was very close to Christianity, though in other ways the two systems were far apart. Most Neoplatonists were opponents of Christianity, but some notable early Christian theologians, such as Origen, Augustine, and Pseudo-Dionysius, owed a great deal of their thought to Neoplatonism.

## Judaism in the Empire

The historian Josephus lists four main divisions within Judaism at the time of Christ: the Sadducees, the Pharisees, the Essenes, and the Zealots.[55] Most students of the New Testament are very familiar with these categories, but a brief overview might be helpful.

The Sadducees were largely made up of the priestly families who ran things in Jerusalem. They accepted only the first five books of the Old Testament as Scripture. They did not believe in life after death and did not look forward to the coming of the Messiah as other Jews of that period did. They thought the way to please God was by punctilious observance of the law, as laid down in the Torah. They had a financial interest in Temple worship and always made sure they defended the interests of the Temple in any religious dispute.

The Pharisees believed that a rigorous interpretation of the law was essential, but they differed from the Sadducees in that they accepted the idea of an afterlife. The Pharisees were great religious innovators. They attempted to interpret the Torah in the light of everyday life under the Romans. They created an oral law, which took its place alongside the written law of the Torah. The Pharisees were influential among the common people, and their way of interpreting the law was quite popular at the time of Christ.

The Essenes believed in the immortality of the soul and did not dispute the need for correct observance of the law. They differed from the Pharisees in that they believed that the priesthood of Jerusalem at that time was illegitimate, and that consequently the rites were tainted. They removed themselves from Jerusalem and set themselves up at Qumran. They had their own priesthood, their own rites, and even their own calendar.[56]

The Zealots agreed with the Pharisees on doctrinal matters, but they had a strong desire for liberty and a firm conviction that only God should be their leader. They were the main instigators of the revolt against Rome in A.D. 66.

For their part, the Romans had a very complicated attitude toward Judaism. On the one hand, exclusive monotheism was offensive to the Romans, who were inclined to have a very casual attitude toward the gods of other nations. They might not personally worship all the gods and goddesses of the world, but they were perfectly willing to let other people worship those gods. What was obnoxious to the Romans was any claim of exclusivity. The Jews not only worshipped one God, but they insisted that their God alone was God, and that belief was truly offensive to Romans.

On the other hand, the Jews, with their high moral standards, made excellent citizens when they were motivated to be loyal. They were hardworking and had a better-than-average educational system. They helped the economy, paid taxes, and rarely engaged in criminal activities. They were generally prosperous and respectable citizens. Without indulging in medieval stereotypes, it must be said that some emperors found themselves in debt to Jewish bankers. In return for favorable interest rates, the emperors came up with a policy that exempted Jews from the annual sacrifice to the emperor's genius. The Jews were the only religious group that received this exemption. Judaism was a long-established religious tradition by the time that the Romans incorporated Palestine into their empire. Respect for tradition was a deep-rooted characteristic of the Romans, and so this also influenced their toleration of Judaism.

The Romans learned to be careful in their dealings with the Jews. Early on they made many mistakes and frequently inflamed Jewish religious sensibilities. In A.D. 40, Caligula, intending to establish emperor worship in Jerusalem, sent a statue of himself to the Temple in Jerusalem. The Jews naturally protested this act of desecration. Agrippa, the grandson of Herod the Great, attempted to keep the population calm while working behind the scenes to support a plot against Caligula. The plot was successful. Caligula was assassinated, and Claudius became emperor. The crisis passed. The statue of Caligula was taken away, and, out of gratitude for Agrippa's help, Claudius granted many political privileges to the Jewish communities scattered throughout the empire.

Claudius' favorable policy did not last. The people of Judea, scourged by exorbitant taxes, were constantly on the verge of revolt, and the emperors found it necessary to take Judea under personal control. They sent a series of bad procurators (Pontius Pilate was not the worst man they sent to Judea).[57] The final straw came with a governor named Florus, who drove the Jews to revolt so he could have an excuse to loot the Temple. The Jews obliged by revolting, but Florus was unable to benefit from this fortuitous occurrence. He was driven from Jerusalem, and, as mentioned in Chapter 1, Nero had to send Vespasian to reconquer Judea.

The Roman policy toward the Jews was uneven, but it was essential that the Romans get it right because of the large number of Jews in the empire and because of their economic influence. In an empire of sixty million inhabitants, there were approximately six million Jews.[58] This population was scattered throughout the empire, from Mesopotamia to Spain. In some areas, the Jewish population was denser than in others. In prosperous Asia, for instance, approximately one person in six was Jewish.[59] In Judea and Galilee, the Jewish percentage of the population must have been even higher. There was also a sizable and influential Jewish community in Rome, a community that maintained contacts with most of the emperors.

The Romans always saw their Jewish residents as a source of income. They had long eyed the Temple tax, the tax devout Jews from around the world sent to the Temple in Jerusalem. After the Temple was destroyed (in A.D. 70), the Romans decided that it was only fair that the Temple tax continue to be collected ... and sent to the treasury in Rome!

So on the one hand the Jews were subjected to double taxation, but on the other hand they were the only ethnic group in the empire that was exempt from the imperial cult. This was a tradeoff that most Jews were willing to make for the sake of peace and prosperity. The truth is that most Jews did not participate in the rebellion of A.D. 66, and they were not in sympathy with the rebels.[60]

Judaism underwent a dramatic transformation with the destruction of the Temple. The Romans made certain the Temple was not rebuilt, believing that it was a source of anti-Roman sentiment. Without the Temple, the Sadducees had no source of power, and their influence over Jewish religious life came to an end. The Zealots were destroyed in the war, since they were the most fanatical fighters. It was Zealots who defended Masada to the bitter end, then committed suicide when it was clear they could not win. The Essenes survived until the rebellion of Bar Kochba in 135. At that time, the Romans put an end to their movement also.

Pharisaical Judaism became the foundation of a reconstructed Judaism that organized itself around synagogues in local communities, rather than a Temple in Jerusalem. The local communities handled local matters, but if any serious decisions had to be made, the matter would be referred to councils of scholars. The decisions of the scholars were eventually written down and became the basis for the Talmud.

The synagogue system was already in place before the destruction of the Temple. That is why, whenever Paul visited a new community, the first thing he would do is go to the synagogue, where he would usually be invited to speak. But the synagogue system flourished after the destruction of the Temple and became the foundation of the Judaism of today.

### Conclusion

This brief overview of the religions of the empire is by no means comprehensive, but it is sufficient to illustrate that the Roman Empire was an astonishingly diverse place, where almost any religious system the human mind could imagine was capable of attracting devotees. From the castration rites of Cybele to the austere intellectualism of the Stoics, the Romans had it all.

## CHAPTER 3

# Social Life in the Roman World

The social life of the empire was extremely complicated, bound by thousands of laws and unwritten taboos. At the center of the whole system was the family, but for the Romans "family" meant something slightly different than what it means today, with slaves and other dependents also falling under the authority of the *paterfamilias*. The Romans had no public social welfare system. A person without a family was a person without anyone to help him, and if he got in trouble he would most likely end up a beggar, unless he sold himself into slavery. These aspects of society affected how the early Christians went about their mission of proclaiming the gospel and conditioned the effectiveness of that message.

### Class Distinctions in the Roman World

Roman society was extremely class conscious, and this class consciousness made its way into the legal code. Roman law distinguished between classes based on wealth. At the top of society were, of course, the emperor and his family.

Next came the senatorial class, which required a minimum annual income of 1,000,000 sesterces (and the senators could not earn their income in trade). Next came the equestrian class, with an income of 400,000 sesterces, then the decurions, with 100,000 sesterces a year. Beneath the decurions were the plebes, then freedmen (slaves who had been set free), then the slaves.[1] All these different classifications had their own specific rights and responsibilities in society.

Senators, for instance, could be appointed as legate (army commander) or as proconsul to important provinces, or they could hold an important priesthood in the city.[2] On the other hand, senators were expected to provide *leitourgia*, or public works for the city.[3] These "liturgies" entailed either a public building project or hosting a holiday for the entire city, complete with food, drink, and games.

Equestrians were eligible for a command of auxiliary troops, various posts in the imperial cabinet, and prefectures, or they could be appointed procurators of smaller provinces.[4] It was from this class that Pontius Pilate came.

If you were from the plebeian class and were cursed with ambition, your most viable option was to join the army. If you applied yourself, you could be promoted to centurion and settle down to a nice piece of land in the provinces when you retired.

The client-patron relationship was the grease that allowed the Roman economic machine to run. If you were involved in the economic life of the empire at all, you were either a client or a patron, or, most likely, both. Here is how the system worked: a member of a lower class would visit someone in a higher class with a request for a favor, such as a job recommendation or some sort of advancement. The potential patron would size up the would-be client, and if he agreed, it would be with the unspoken understanding that someday the client would have to do something for the patron. For example, a budding young author might visit a senator, hoping the senator might recommend his book to a publisher. If the senator obliged, it would almost certainly be understood that someday the author would write a flattering biography of his new patron.

Of course, the system could be quite complicated. To continue to use our example, the senator would probably contact a publisher who was already in his debt. In turn, the publisher might ask *his* clients to publicize the young author's work, to make the author more popular. In the end, theoretically, everyone would benefit. One unintended consequence would be, however, that genuine talent might go unrecognized, with skilled social climbers rising to the top of society.

### Family Life in the Empire

Another pertinent aspect of Roman society is the legal status of the family.[5] Under Roman law, all members of a household—wife, children, other legal dependents, and slaves—were all under the rule of the *paterfamilias*. This is why, in the "household codes" (Eph 5:22— 6:9, Col 3:18—4:1), Paul outlines relationships within families and always includes prescriptions for the relationship between slave and master. Paul, in effect, assumes the Roman legal arrangement is the norm and simply makes prescriptions that will make the system as fruitful as possible. The *paterfamilias* was personally responsible for the discipline of anyone in his household. He could also be held legally responsible for their behavior. If a slave misbehaved or ran away, the master was largely at his own discretion in choosing an appropriate punishment. There are cases where a father executed his son for serious misbehavior, and certainly it was not uncommon for masters to crucify slaves for running away.

The absolute power of the *paterfamilias* extended to the power of life and death over his children even after the child was born. Roman law allowed a father eight days to decide whether or not to raise a child. If at any point during those eight days the father decided not to, for whatever reason, he could have his child exposed, presumably to die.[6] Upon the birth of a child, the father would undertake a detailed inspection of the child. Girl children were more likely to be exposed, since boys were more valuable, but children with physical deformities, or those that were weak and sickly, were rejected as well. The Romans considered the benefits of infant exposure to be twofold: the practice kept the population at a manageable level and prevented the "wasting" of valuable resources on children who were too weak to live anyway.

Abortion was also quite common in the Roman world. The Greek physician Hippocrates was opposed to abortion, and there is, or was until quite recently, a line in the Hippocratic Oath pledging not to perform an abortion.[7] But there were plenty of doctors and others who were perfectly willing to help a woman have an abortion. The main reasons for abortion put forward by ancient writers were (1) to conceal the consequences of adultery, (2) to maintain feminine beauty, (3) to avoid danger to the mother, (4) to prevent overpopulation, and (5) to avoid the necessity of dividing an inheritance among too many children.[8]

Odd methods were sometimes attempted to obtain an abortion, including tightly binding the stomach to force the child out before its time.[9] The Greeks and Romans knew that a sharp object inserted into the womb could destroy the developing child, but this method was considered too dangerous. A slight misstep could result in a perforation of the uterus and subsequent death by bleeding or infection. The favored method involved drugs that, if taken before conception, acted as contraceptives, and after conception, as abortifacients. The drugs were derived from common plants well known to the physicians of the ancient world. Without moral or legal impediment, the women of the Greco-Roman world resorted to abortion regularly. Jews and Christians, as we shall see, did not engage in these practices, though not all Jews considered all abortions to be the moral equivalent of murder.

Even children who were not thrown away by their parents had several dangers to undergo before they survived their first week of life. Postnatal mortality was high, given the unhygienic conditions of the ancient world and the state of medical knowledge. But if a child survived his first week, his *dies lustricus*, or "day of purification", would be celebrated. On this day, the child would be named and receive a ceremonial washing, and sacrifices would be made on his behalf. From that day onward, he would be considered a member of the family.[10]

The easy availability of abortion and contraception, coupled with the legality of infanticide before the eighth day after birth, created a demographic crisis in the Roman Empire. Jews, who viewed children as a gift from God and large families as a sign of God's blessing, experienced healthy population growth in the early imperial age. But the Romans were concerned because upper-class families, the families the emperors counted on to help them govern the empire, were dying out. To counter this negative trend, Augustus promulgated a series of laws designed to encourage larger families among the upper class. In A.D. 9, laws were passed penalizing unmarried citizens, giving special privileges to married people, and rewarding those with large families.[11] In the senatorial class, it was well known that there were far more men than women (a circumstance that can be attributed only to the practice of exposing girl children), so laws were passed allowing upper-class men to marry women from lower classes and still have their offspring be counted as legitimate.

These measures appear to have had some success. The Roman upper class stifled its growing aversion to responsibility and had children in order to qualify for the benefits of the new laws. But there is no evidence that the majority desired children or took the time to create loving homes and families.

In wealthy families, children were nursed not by their mothers but by wet nurses, usually slaves. Children were generally weaned at around eighteen months. It was at this time that the harsh discipline that marked childhood in the ancient world would begin, since at this point the child was "old enough to understand blows and threats".[12] The Romans, who had manuals for everything, had their manuals on how to run a household properly. In these manuals, we find that strict discipline was held to be the essential element in the raising of children.

In middle-class and wealthy families, male children would be placed in the care of a *paedagogus*, who was responsible for the care and discipline of the boy. He would take the child to school and see to his daily needs. The child would outgrow the need for a *paedagogus* sometime in the early teen years. At that time, a young man would undergo several rites to mark his coming of age. His first beard would be shaved, and the hair would be kept in the household shrine. Sometime between the ages of fourteen and sixteen, on March 17 (the *Liberalia*), young men were enrolled as citizens and were given their first *toga pura*, the all-white toga that Roman men wore on ceremonial occasions.

For girls, the coming of age was likely to involve a wedding ceremony. The minimum age for the betrothal of a girl was ten, and for marriage the minimum age was twelve for girls and fourteen for boys. However, from inscriptional evidence, we have good reason for believing that most girls were married sometime between the ages of fifteen and eighteen.[13]

The experiences of Jewish children were similar, though with a few major differences. For instance, Jews considered it murder to expose unwanted children.[14] But in other ways, they raised children similarly to their Gentile neighbors. On the eighth day, there was the circumcision rite for male children. Discipline was supposed to be firm, to avoid spoiling the children.[15] There were special rituals for the coming of age of both boys and girls, and girl children were married sometime in their late teens.

What was marriage like in the Greco-Roman world? The first thing that must be observed is that most marriages were not love matches. In Greek, Roman, and Jewish societies, parents arranged their children's marriages. Men married in their twenties, and girls in their teens. For these reasons, divorce, infidelity, and concubinage were rampant.[16] Men could visit prostitutes or keep a concubine without violating the law, but a woman who had intercourse with anyone other than her husband was an adulteress, and the punishment could be severe.

Divorce laws varied by social groups. Among the Jews, it was easy for a man to divorce his wife, but virtually impossible for a wife to initiate divorce proceedings. In Roman law, both husbands and wives could initiate a divorce, and divorce was quite common. Roman divorcees could own property and manage their own financial affairs, but a Greek or Jewish divorcee had few options: she could return to her father's house, or she could rely on a grown son to take care of her. There were few other options available. Seen in this light, it is no wonder Jesus considered divorce to be a symptom of the hardheartedness of men.[17]

We know of happy marriages in the ancient world. But what was considered a "happy" or successful marriage ensued when both parties fulfilled their respective roles faithfully. Men were supposed to represent their families in the public realm, and women were supposed to care for the household. Consider the following inscription, found on a sarcophagus that contained a husband and his wife in the ancient city of Aphrodisias:

> The city council and the people honor the deceased—Pereitas Kallimedes ... who carried out public duties, public offices, and embassies, and his office of temple overseer gloriously, properly, and illustriously, and who did everything in a manner befitting the dignity of his family for which the city council and the people call for the deceased to be honored.... The city council and the people honor Tatia ... a woman who was modest, who loved her husband and children and throughout her life was endowed with dignity and virtue, who was the wife of Pereitas Kallimedes.[18]

Pereitas Kallimedes was an important man in Aphrodisias. He held public offices, he was in charge of embassies, and he was overseer of a temple. But there is no mention among his honors that he fathered children or that he loved his wife. However, when we read the inscription devoted to Tatia, his wife, we find out that she loved her husband and children and was modest and virtuous. Pereitas Kallimedes did what was expected of men, and Tatia did what was expected of women, and for this they were greatly honored. But there is no glimpse of their inner life. The world was not interested if Pereitas wanted to spend more time with his children rather than attend to his duties. Did he ask Tatia for advice, late at night, when they were alone? Did he confide his cares to her, or did he confide only in male friends? What about Tatia? Was she content, or did she long for a more equal relationship? We do not know the answers to these questions. We can only see the surface, the results of their partnership.

But human beings are complex creatures whose essence can rarely be reduced to their function. Perhaps Pereitas and Tatia achieved what many long for, a loving and mutually respectful marriage. But love and respect within marriage were delicate flowers that rarely withstood the heat and dryness of Greco-Roman culture. The concept of the family as a school of love, which the early Christians introduced, was seriously lacking, and desperately needed.

*Women in the Greco-Roman World*

The adult lives of most women got off to a rocky start. They were married at an early age to a man they usually met for the first time on their wedding day, forbidden any choice in their spouse whatsoever. Their husbands would probably be about ten years older and not inclined to view their new wife as anything but a means to create heirs as quickly as possible. And after the heirs were created, there was absolutely nothing to prevent the husband from unceremoniously divorcing his unfortunate wife.

Not all women were so unfortunate, of course. Some were married to decent men they came to love over time. But even under these favorable circumstances, women's lives were narrow and circumscribed by law and custom. The primary role of women was the management of the household. In all the various ethnic groups that populated the empire, women were forbidden from meddling in politics or public affairs.[19] Among certain ethnic groups, women were allowed to own property and live independent economic lives, but if a woman had a husband, he would be expected to perform all public functions on behalf of his family.

The Romans allowed different ethnic groups to govern themselves in local matters, so it is difficult to generalize about women's lives.

Jewish women benefitted from the high moral standards of their religion, but Jewish women who found themselves widowed or divorced faced great difficulties. They were forbidden by custom from inheriting property or engaging in work that would provide an income.[20] Their only recourse was to return to their own father's household, or rely on grown sons, if they had any, to take care of them. A problematic aspect of Jewish religious law regarding widows was that a widow without a son was expected to marry her deceased husband's brother, unless he publicly refused her.[21]

There were provisions in Jewish religious law for the care of widows. Widows wore special clothing,[22] so everyone would know at a glance their special status. The special clothing was significant because Judaism taught that the Lord would hear the cries of oppressed widows and punish their oppressors.[23] Widows were expected to be supported by the public at least a part of the time. For instance, in Deuteronomy 14:28–29, we read that every third year, a full tithe was to be collected in each town for the support of the Levites, the widows, the orphans, and the poor. So it was expected that widows would be cared for by the community. But the unfortunate fact is that if a woman was divorced by her husband, she would have almost no recourse, unless her father or a grown son would take care of her.

In Greek society, the status of women underwent a tremendous evolution in the three hundred years before and after Christ. In traditional Greek society, particularly in those regions dominated by Athens, women rarely left the home, and when they did so, they had to be heavily veiled. But by the time of Christ, we occasionally find women earning their own living, attending public gatherings, and acting as athletes, singers, and doctors.[24]

But for Greek women, as for Jewish women, divorce and widowhood were disasters. A Greek widow would be put under control of a *kyrios*, usually the male head of her husband's extended family. It was the *kyrios'* job to find a new husband for the widow if possible. If it was not possible, he would control the widow's finances and arrange for her livelihood for the rest of her life. Naturally, some were more faithful in their attendance to this duty than others, so the net result was that the widow was in the unpleasant circumstance of having to depend on the kindness of a person she could not necessarily trust.

Greek women whose husbands divorced them were basically in the same situation as Jewish divorcees. They could return to their father's house or depend on a grown son to support them. As mentioned earlier, some women found a way to support themselves. Usually, however, this involved getting a man to act as a "front", since women could not enter into contracts, nor could they own and manage property.

Of all women in the empire, Roman women were the freest. They could give testimony at trials, inherit upon the death of the spouse, enter into legal contracts without a man, and own property without a man to act on their behalf.[25] Roman women were as free as men to initiate divorce proceedings without losing their dowry. In many ways, however, Roman widows suffered worse than either Greek or Jewish widows, since there were no institutional arrangements to care for them. There were laws that required widows between the ages of twenty and fifty to remarry within twelve months of their husband's death.[26] Widows who did not or could not remarry could lose their inheritance from their first marriage.

Greek and Roman women were able to receive an education, though very few were given a good education because women were not expected to enter into the political or legal professions. But women could certainly learn to read and write, and many knew enough math to keep the books of their family businesses.

In general, in speaking about the fate of women in the Roman world, it is important to note that wealth freed women quite a bit. We know of wealthy women in the Roman world who did pretty much what they wanted. In Ephesus, it was a woman, Scholastica, who endowed the public baths. You can see her statue and a plaque dedicated to her, to this day, among the archaeological treasures of that city. It would take a tremendous amount of money to finance and maintain a Roman bath, but Scholastica had the independent means to do so. We have no information as to how she gained her wealth, but she was hardly alone. One thinks of Lydia, the dealer in purple cloth from Thyatira, whom Paul converted to Christianity.[27]

But most women in the ancient world were not wealthy. For a poor woman, being thrust on her own was a great disaster. If her husband died or abandoned her, she could return to her family, but she would simply be another mouth to feed. If she had no family willing to help her, she could try to remarry or turn to prostitution if she was young and attractive, or she could sell herself into slavery. As we shall see, Christianity, with its communitarian ethic, provided a whole new series of options for women.

### Slavery in Roman Law

Slavery was one of the most widespread institutions of the Roman Empire. Estimates vary greatly as to how many slaves there were in the empire, from as high as 30 percent of the total population to as low as 10 percent.[28] Slavery was an urban phenomenon. The percentage of slaves in Rome was much higher, with possibly 50 percent of the population of that city being in some kind of bondage. In Asian cities like Ephesus and Pergamum, the ratio may have been around 30 percent. The physician Galen recorded that Pergamum had a total population of 120,000, and that 40,000 were slaves.[29]

This is a large number of people, and the whole system required careful management and ruthless enforcement of the law to survive. Slaves could not be treated too badly, or they would revolt out of despair, as Spartacus and his followers did in 73 B.C. Conversely, once there was a slave revolt, it was imperative that it be put down as ruthlessly as possible. When Spartacus' revolt was put down, Marcus Crassus lined the Appian Way from Capua to Rome with slaves on crucifixes, for the edification of anyone who might be considering following Spartacus' example.[30]

There were several ways a person might become a slave in the ancient world. (1) Some people were enslaved in the many wars of Rome. (2) Some people were kidnapped by slave hunters. (3) Some people were enslaved for debts they could not pay, or sold themselves into slavery to feed their family. (4) The abandonment of children was common in the ancient world. Each city had a designated area for abandoned children to be left. The slavers would scoop up the unwanted children, raise them, teach them a trade, and sell them when the children were old enough. (5) Most slaves were born into slavery.[31]

Slaves were covered under Roman household law. This meant that the *paterfamilias* could pretty much do what he wanted with them. Therefore, how a slave was treated had everything to do with the personal inclinations of the master. As you might expect, some masters were kind, but an equal number were quite brutal, some in ways that we find difficult to comprehend today. A slave's occupation also affected how his master treated him. Slaves who did hard manual labor, such as in mines, mills, and in large agricultural establishments, could expect routine brutality as a part of their daily existence. Criminals could be enslaved and put to work rowing galleys for the navy. On the other hand, household slaves were usually treated well, depending on the inclination of the master.[32] There were also some extremely valuable slaves who got highly favorable treatment. Intelligent slaves were trained as teachers, doctors, accountants, etc. Others who showed aptitude might be trained in lucrative crafts such as carpentry or stoneworking. These slaves were naturally treated very well.

While there were few legal restrictions on what a master could do to his slaves, by the New Testament era there was considerable pressure from social elites to treat one's slaves well. Owners who mistreated their slaves were viewed with disdain at best. We have in our possession today a letter from Pliny the Younger (A.D. 61–112) to a friend advising that he treat erring slaves with forbearance: "I counsel you in the future to show yourself tolerant of the mistakes of your slaves, even if there be no one to intervene on their behalf." [33]

There is also a truly edifying story about the emperor Augustus. The story, as recorded by the historian Dio Cassius, is that one evening Augustus was dining at the house of Vedius Pollio when a slave accidentally broke a crystal goblet. Vedius, perhaps thinking it would amuse Augustus, ordered the slave to be seized and thrown into a pond full of man-eating lampreys. The slave slipped away from his captors and appealed directly to Augustus. Augustus responded by ordering that the slave be pardoned, that all the crystal goblets in the house be broken, and that the pond be filled in.[34]

This story is illustrative of several points. Dio Cassius is not considered to be a terribly accurate historian by modern standards. His goal was to idealize the reign of Augustus, so he tended to be selective in his use of evidence. However, if his intention was to show Augustus in a good light, surely this story at least demonstrates that among the opinion makers of the Roman Empire cruelty to slaves was considered bad form. On the other hand, the story also illustrates that a truly wicked master could do whatever he wanted with his slaves.

Vedius Pollio almost certainly would have had his way if the emperor had not happened to be among his guests on the night in question. Who knows how many other evenings saw his poor household domestics subjected to a cruel death, with no one to intervene on their behalf?

The Romans considered slavery to be one of the foundations of their economic system and were determined to use all legal means to prevent their slaves from taking too many liberties. It was considered a master's duty to track down and punish runaway slaves. When a slave owner had a runaway, he was expected to take out a warrant on the slave. The warrant would then be posted wherever the runaway might be, with as complete a description of the slave as could be gathered. There were bounty hunters throughout the empire who made their living off the rewards of returning runaway slaves.[35]

Once a slave had been captured, he would be returned to his master. He might simply be returned to his duties, as happened in the case of a slave named Stachys, who was captured by a man named Menes, taken to the house of his master Amyntas, and returned to the slave quarters, with no mention of further punishment.[36] More likely, he would be punished in some way. He might be sold to a harsher master, scourged, branded, mutilated, fitted with a collar, or even crucified, thrown to wild animals, or killed in some other manner.[37]

In order to escape these fates, a fugitive slave would have few options. He could try for asylum at a shrine or temple and hope the priests would help him gain his freedom. He could try to lose himself in a big city (Rome itself might be the best option), or he could head for the country and hire himself out as a field hand. As a last resort, he might join a band of robbers.[38] Any person who became aware of a fugitive slave was expected to turn him in. If he failed to do so, or actively harbored the slave, he could be punished for *furtum*, or "theft of property".[39]

One of the most degrading aspects of ancient slavery was the propensity masters had for sexually abusing their slaves. It was taken for granted that male masters would have slaves, male or female, whom they would use for sexual pleasure.[40] Stories of sexual relations between slave and master are a commonplace in ancient literature. Of course, from the master's point of view such relationships were harmless and fun, but from the slave's point of view they were painful and humiliating. Such relationships were hardly mutual. The slave had no right to refuse, and there were no laws protecting slaves from rape or from punishment for refusing to submit.

There were a few laws intended to mitigate that harshness of the system. If a slave got in trouble with his master, he was permitted to go to the house of a friend of his master's in order to plead with that person to try to persuade the master to be lenient. Some temples offered "sanctuary" to runaway slaves, but the sanctuary lasted only as long as the slave stayed on the temple property, so this was not really a viable option for most slaves.

The most humane feature of Greco-Roman slavery was the readiness with which slave owners freed their slaves. Certainly, not all slaves were freed, but a good number of household slaves were given their freedom.[41]

Even the freeing of a slave did not end the relationship between former slave and master. A *libertus* (freedman) was naturally grateful to his former master and had a moral obligation to come to his former master's aid whenever it was requested. If you were freed under Roman law, you were obligated to present yourself every morning at your ex-master's house. You would be fed breakfast, and if your ex-master had a need of your services on that particular day, he would let you know.[42]

Beyond the daily ritual of the salutation, the freedman had numerous obligations to his former master. The master would typically set the freedman up in a small business, and a percentage of the profits would go to the master in perpetuity. A freedman was forbidden from bringing legal charges against his former master. These numerous ties to their former master insured that the majority of freedmen continued in the same jobs they had before being freed.[43]

It might seem that there were no benefits to being freed, but the status was greatly sought by slaves. For one thing, slaves could not marry, but freedmen and freedwomen could. We even know of some cases where freedmen achieved citizenship, though it was more likely that children or grandchildren could achieve that status.[44]

### Slavery in Greek Thought

Seventy percent of all slave names we have learned from inscriptional evidence are Greek.[45] This does not necessarily mean that 70 percent of all slaves were Greek, or even that 70 percent of all masters were

Greek. What it does indicate is the pervasiveness of Greek cultural influence, especially in the Eastern part of the empire. It also indicates that the majority of the slaves in the empire came from the East. Indeed, Asia was especially known as a good source of slaves.[46]

These facts point to something important for us to consider. We are accustomed to thinking of the Romans as the great slavers of the ancient world, but slavery had always been a part of Mediterranean culture. The Greeks were certainly not the first people to hold slaves, but they were enthusiastic participants in the custom. The Athenians in particular made large numbers of slaves in the course of their numerous conquests.

Aristotle not only defended the custom of slavery, he argued that some people were natural slaves and that others were natural masters. He defined the slave as "an ensouled piece of property".[47]

The Greeks saw few reasons why one person should not own another. It was considered natural and normal. In *The Trojan Women*, the poet Euripides wrote movingly about the fate of noncombatants in times of war. One of the fates that might befall them would be slavery, but slavery was considered preferable to death.[48] In the ancient world, there was no clamor for the emancipation of slaves. It was considered a good thing to reward individual faithful servants with freedom, but the mass freeing of slaves was not only unthinkable, it was considered an extremely dangerous idea.

### Slavery in Hebrew Scripture

Unlike the Greek intellectuals or the Roman lawmakers, the Jews did not approach the question of slavery from the point of view of the master. For, as everyone knows, as a people, the Jews experienced several periods of slavery and other lengthy periods of generalized repression. These national experiences shaped Jewish thought on the subject of slavery and other questions of justice.[49]

Slavery as a social and economic institution was recognized in ancient Israel. Just exactly why it never occurred to the chosen people that it was wrong for one person to own another is a question open to debate. Yet it is the simple truth. Not only is there no passage in the Old

Testament condemning slavery, but one of the classic justifications for slavery can be found in Genesis 9:25–27.[50]

There is a possible answer to this question that is quite consonant with Catholic thought on the nature of scriptural revelation. When we consider the state of thought on slavery before the period in which the Old Testament was written, we see that there were few legal and moral checks on how slaves could be treated. Thus, when we encounter in Scripture such passages as Exodus 21:20, which decrees punishment for a master who fatally strikes a slave, or Exodus 21:26–27, which insists on the emancipation of a slave whose eye or tooth is knocked out by his master, we should realize that these laws represent a step forward in the understanding of the human dignity and rights of the slave.

As a general principle of scriptural interpretation, one can make the most sense of the scattered data of the Old Testament by understanding the principle of the progressive nature of revelation. In this understanding, each new stage of revelation represents a leap forward in ethical awareness. Thus, the Old Testament could be seen as an intermediate stage of revelation, with the fullness of revelation coming in the person of Jesus Christ.[51]

Seen in this light, the Old Testament has numerous limitations on the rights of slave owners and, if followed, would have severely curtailed the institution of slavery in Israelite society. We have already examined Exodus 21:20 and 26–27. Beyond those prescriptions, Exodus 21:2 requires that a Hebrew slave could be owned only for six years and on the seventh year must be set free. A jubilee year, which was supposed to occur every fifty years, was to be a year of general amnesty.[52]

Sirach 33:30–31 was also especially pertinent: "If you have a servant, treat him as a brother, for as your own soul you will need him." Also of some relevance would be Deuteronomy 23:16–17, which said, "You shall not give up to his master a slave who has escaped from his master to you; he shall dwell with you, in your midst, in the place which you shall choose within one of your towns, where it pleases him best; you shall not oppress him." This passage was understood to refer only to Jewish slaves who escaped from Jewish masters.[53]

By the time of Christ, there were two Jewish sects, the Therapeutae and the Essenes, who did not own slaves, on the grounds that "slavery leads to injustice."[54] Any connection between Jesus, Paul, and the Essenes is highly speculative, but on many points the ethical teachings of Jesus are quite similar to the Essenes', and it is possible that Paul also was influenced by the precepts of Qumran, the Essene community.

## Citizenship

Roman citizenship was much prized by the various peoples of the empire, because of the significant rights citizenship entailed. The Romans were, by the same token, extremely reluctant to hand citizenship out, and did so only if it would result in substantial benefits to the state. There were always some influential thinkers in the Roman establishment who argued that everyone in the empire should be granted citizenship to make them more loyal. However, these wise men were always voted down by those who feared that if everyone were a citizen their own privileged status would come to an end. In the end, the emperor Caracalla granted citizenship to all free men in A.D. 212 in order to increase taxation.[55]

Before this happy event, Roman citizenship was available to the leading citizens of a community. If you were wealthy, or a public official (usually the two went together), or you made some extraordinary contribution to the public welfare, you were usually eligible for citizenship.

There were, broadly speaking, four ways you could become a citizen. First, if your parents were citizens, you were automatically a citizen as well. Second, if your community was fortunate enough to get on the good side of an emperor, he might grant citizenship to the whole city.[56] Third, one could apply for citizenship on an individual basis. Of course, this might require a considerable bribe, depending on the personal integrity of the magistrate to whom you applied. The fourth, and, for most people, the surest, route to citizenship was to join the army.[57]

Why was citizenship so highly prized? In principle, the basic distinction between men in the empire was that they were either slave or free.[58] Being free was so much better than being a slave that the distinction between citizen and noncitizen was almost trivial. Nevertheless, there were some important benefits to being a citizen that caused it to be widely sought after. First, the basic distinction: if you were a noncitizen you were subject to the law, but if you were a citizen, the law was designed to protect you.[59] That is a distinction that made an immense difference.

The following were some of the values of citizenship: (1) property became subject to Roman property law, which made it easier to pass it on to heirs;[60] (2) a citizen was exempt from the common practice of torture to extract information; (3) citizens could not be punished without a trial; (4) citizens could appeal to the emperor;[61] and (5) citizens could not be subjected to a humiliating or painful death (crucifixion, wild animals, etc.) if convicted of a crime.[62]

These are not small benefits, but the most important benefits of citizenship had nothing to do with legalities. Citizenship conferred instant prestige and made life easier. Consider the account in Acts 22. Saint Paul was about to be beaten. The centurion was not inclined even to listen to him, until he heard that Paul was a citizen. He was further impressed upon hearing that Paul was born a citizen. No additional legal protection accrued from being born a citizen, but the status it conferred was immense.

After 212, when everyone became a citizen, legal distinctions had to be developed to accommodate the class consciousness of the period. The senatorial and equestrian classes were classified as *honestiores*, and everyone else was classified as *humiliores*.[63] The main difference between the two was that *honestiores* were spared from cruel and degrading punishment, while the *humiliores* could be crucified, thrown to wild animals, or sent to the mines as punishment. In other words, the granting of citizenship to everyone meant very little in actual practice, though it might have raised some people's morale for a time.

## Conclusion

The social system of the Roman Empire was marked by class distinctions based on annual income. The institution of slavery further divided men between slave and free, though the slave of a rich man probably had an easier life than the poorest of freeborn citizens. A large number of freed slaves lived in the empire, and they usually continued to have an economic relationship with their former master. Even men who had never been slaves were likely to find themselves forced to enter into a client-patron relationship with some wealthy man if they wanted to get ahead. Families were governed by a *paterfamilias* who had absolute authority over everyone under his roof. Women who for some reason were not protected by a *paterfamilias* made their way in society with great difficulty, except for certain wealthy Roman women. It was a system in which people had to know, and keep, their own place.

CHAPTER 4

# Life in the Roman Army

The Romans were likely to attribute their success in the world to the favor of the gods, but it was the Roman military system that was in fact responsible for Roman dominance. The superiority of Roman arms and armor, the new military tactics the Romans developed, and the development and improvement of mechanical weapons such as the *ballista* all contributed to Roman military dominance. However, it was the character and makeup of the troops themselves that made the Roman army great. Let us see how all these various elements fit together to make the Roman army the most dominant fighting machine of the ancient world.

### Recruitment and Makeup of the Army

In the period we are dealing with, the Roman army was almost always composed entirely of volunteers. During the civil wars, conscription had been common, but the practice was highly unpopular and was discontinued except for emergencies.[1] This meant that the army was likely to be highly motivated, since only those who freely chose the life served, but it also meant that recruiters had to make enlistment worth it to the potential recruits. Roman citizenship was the most potent inducement recruiters could dangle, and, for reasons listed in Chapter 3, this inducement alone served to keep the ranks full. Recruits also received a signing bonus of seventy-five denarii, called, strikingly, *viaticum*.[2] Young men with poor prospects would join up for adventure, to see the world, and for the steady pay and security, but mostly it was on the understanding that they would receive citizenship at one point or another. Legionaries, soldiers in the regular army, received citizenship upon enlistment. Auxiliaries, soldiers recruited from the provinces, received citizenship upon retirement.

Throughout the life of the empire, the soldiers that defended it came from every province. Generally speaking, however, auxiliaries would be sent to a far-distant province for their service, under the theory that they would be less dangerous away from their own people. Sources of recruitment were abundant. Asia was heavily recruited and produced many good soldiers. Recruiters also worked the colonies of retired soldiers, and many soldiers' sons chose to follow in their fathers' footsteps.

### Daily Life: Camp Life and Combat

It is a truism hardly worth repeating that a soldier's life is hard. However, the life of the Roman soldier was harder than most, for three reasons unique to the Roman system. First of all, the enlistment period was twenty years for legionaries and twenty-six years for auxiliaries. It has always been hard for young men to commit to anything for that length of time, but the Romans knew it took a long time to make a good soldier, and they did not want to lose a man just when he was good for something. But lengthy enlistments were unpopular and made recruitment difficult. Second, Roman soldiers were not allowed to marry. Many settled in with concubines anyway, but that meant their children were not legitimate, and that entailed additional legal burdens. Third, the Roman army was a frontier army, which meant that soldiers would usually be serving far from the centers of population and would have to do without many of the amenities of city life. Even when a legion was stationed in a populous and civilized part of the Empire, long-settled policy was to station the troops outside of urban centers to avoid inflaming the populace.[3] As we shall see, a thriving local economy usually sprang up around the camps, but life was still fairly Spartan compared to the constant excitement of Rome.

From movies and popular books, we are accustomed to thinking that the Romans must have been in a constant state of warfare. Certainly there was much warfare, but there were also long periods of relative peace. Consequently, most soldiers spent most of their time in garrison duty, fighting boredom more often than seven-foot-tall barbarians.

Garrison duty was not without its share of fighting, mostly against small bands of marauders who crossed the frontier looking for plunder. The frontier was guarded almost along its entire length by either *limes* (a boundary, such as a wall) or a river large enough to make crossing difficult. Along the wall or the bank of the river would be a series of watchtowers.[4] Small groups of soldiers would man these watchtowers, ready to send a warning if enemies crossed the border. Approximately two miles behind the front lines would be a series of forts, called *castrum* (hence "castle"; towns in England that end with "caster", "chester", or "cester" had their origins as Roman forts). These forts included barracks, the garrison commander's house, a headquarters where administrative work was done, stables, workshops, and granaries. Some forts also had hospitals.

Since most of the garrison troops lived in forts of this type, we will concentrate on the lives of the soldiers of the *castra*. Officers' quarters were spacious, with hearths, washing facilities, and latrines with a drainage channel to the outside. It is not clear whether each officer had his own space or whether small groups of officers bunked together.[5]

For the enlisted men, each barracks was large enough to house a century (eighty to one hundred men). The barracks was broken down into smaller compartments, large enough for a *contubernium* (eight men). These eight men lived together in close quarters, so it was essential that they find a way to get along with one another. There was an outer room where everyone in the *contubernium* stored his gear, and an inner room for sleeping. The inner room contained a hearth, which would be used for cooking and for warmth. The *contubernium* ate together. Usually, the men took turns cooking, or possibly the best cooks took care of this duty, but there was no mess hall to which the men went for their meals.[6] They drew their rations, prepared the food, and ate in their quarters. Analysis of rubbish heaps indicates that the soldiers ate wheat, barley, figs, dill, coriander, local nuts and fruits, celery, and, when available, meat and cheese. The soldiers' diet was not entirely vegetarian, as some have supposed.[7]

From records discovered in Egypt, it seems that a soldier could draw three pounds of bread, two pounds of meat, two pints of wine, and an eighth of a pint of oil a day.[8] This might seem like an extremely large amount of food, but the legionaries worked hard for their rations. When there was no war going on, they worked on repairing and improving their fortifications, took route marches, and engaged in hand-to-hand combat to keep in practice. If there was nothing of a military nature to do, they built roads, bridges, and other structures to improve the military and economic capacity of the local community.

Towns grew up around the *castra*. When soldiers retired, they would be given land outside the camp. They would most likely take advantage of their new status, get married, and raise a family. Their military service would have given them practical experience in many trades, so a source of income would be readily available. Indigenous people would also settle outside the forts, to open inns, taverns, and shops where the soldiers could spend their pay. So the *castrum*, unless it was in a constant state of siege, would quickly become a thriving town in its own right.

When war broke out, a soldier might be expected to march thirty miles in a single day, with his armor, all his weapons, and his field pack. Care was taken not to force the soldiers to fight without sufficient rest after an exhausting march, but sometimes it was unavoidable. So the legionaries had to keep themselves in fighting shape at all times. Every night on a march the legion would build a camp, consisting of a ditch and an earthen rampart topped with sharpened wooden stakes.

The fighting itself was brutal. Soldiers would stand shoulder to shoulder, four to sixteen ranks deep, and slug it out with their opponents. Casualty rates were extremely high in some of the battles we know about. It was essential, in a pitched battle of this type, that the ranks remain close, so you could protect the person to your left with your shield, and you could, in turn, be protected by the person to your right. If the line were broken, the enemy would get a significant advantage and could possibly force the entire army to flee, which would result in a slaughter. One did not want to be on the losing side of a battle in the ancient world. The best thing that could happen under those circumstances would be that you would be enslaved. Most likely, you would simply be killed, but some of the people the Romans fought had the habit of torturing prisoners to death.

Under these circumstances, two things were necessary to have a reasonable chance to stay alive: trust and discipline. You had to trust that your mates would do their duty and stay in line, and you had to make sure you did the same. When orders were given they had to be obeyed instantly, without question.

This is why discipline in the Roman army was harsh. Individual soldiers who deserted or engaged in other serious malfeasance might be executed, though in picking an appropriate punishment various factors such as age, length of service, and the circumstances surrounding the desertion would be taken into consideration.[9] Punishments like flogging, reduction in rank, and loss of pay were much more common.

The Romans also had a unique military practice that is largely responsible for their reputation for brutal discipline. In cases where a whole military unit, usually a cohort, ran away on a battlefield, or refused to obey an order, or mutinied, they might be subjected to decimation. The whole unit would be lined up, and every tenth man would be pulled out of line and executed. In actual practice there were very few decimations in the Roman army in the age of the empire.[10] For one thing, the soldiers had to obey that order. When it became obvious that the army could simply kill the emperor and set up a new one in his place, unpleasant orders were either not given or were simply disobeyed when they were given.[11] So decimations were extremely rare, except in times of national crisis.

The religious life of the legionaries was considered essential to the success of the legion. Not that the soldiers were expected to be particularly pious, but they were expected to punctiliously perform the rites of Rome. Other gods were allowed, unless those gods made universal claims on a person's loyalty, such as the God of Christianity and Judaism did. It was difficult to be a devout Christian in the Roman army and escape martyrdom, because the legionaries were expected to participate in the rites of the Roman religion, including emperor worship. Every year, on the anniversary of his accession, a sacrifice had to be made to the genius of the emperor.[12]

The hardship and danger of a soldier's life encouraged the development of private religious cults. Mithraism was popular among the officers, and among the private soldiers the cult of Jupiter Dolichenus was quite popular.[13]

### Weapons and Armor

The Roman soldier of the period we are concerned with was extremely well equipped and well trained. Recruits were expected to pay for their own arms and armor, so they were sure to take good care of their equipment. Of course, barring disaster, a good set of equipment could be expected to last a soldier his entire career.[14]

Soldiers were equipped with the *gladius*, a short sword about two feet long, with a sharp point and two sharp edges, good for a straight-on thrust or a forehand or backhand swing. The weapon was kept extremely sharp, and it was light enough to be used for many hours of fighting. The other weapon most legionaries carried was the *pilum*. This weapon would best be described as a javelin, with a wooden shaft about four feet long and a metal head with a razor-sharp point. The *pilum* was designed so that after it was thrown and lodged in the enemy's shield, the head would break off when the enemy tried to dislodge it. This unique design had two advantages: it meant that the enemy could not turn around and use Roman *pila* against the Romans, and it prevented the enemy from using their own shields, since it is hard to manipulate a shield with a foot of iron stuck in it.[15] Each legionary would be issued two *pila*. They would be thrown in battle just before the two armies closed ranks with one another. If the battle were won, the wooden shafts and the iron heads would be gathered up, repaired, and reissued.

Other soldiers, usually the auxiliaries, would be issued slings and stones, bows and arrows, or other weapons, depending on the military tradition of the province they were recruited from. For instance, the Balearic slingers were famous for their ability to sling stones up to a pound in weight, and the Romans always allowed them to fight in this manner. Officers and cavalrymen often carried a spearlike weapon, called a *lancea*, which was lighter and easier to handle than the *pilum*. (It was probably a *lancea* that the centurian thrust into Jesus' side.)

Defensive armor was probably more important than weapons to the average legionary. All the elements fit together to keep the soldier alive to fight another day. First, and perhaps most important, was the helmet. The helmet had ear covers that would allow the soldier to hear but keep the ears from being sliced off by an overhead sword swipe.[16] We are accustomed to visualizing Roman helmets with the stiff red crests, but the common soldiers did not get these crests. Crests were for officers, and the higher the rank, the more impressive the crest. In any case, such gaudy plumage was of no benefit in combat.

The Romans covered the chest and stomach with plate armor designed in such a way that a straight-on thrust would slide off harmlessly. The thighs and groin were covered with a series of flexible plates that allowed movement but still afforded protection. During the period we are discussing, the Romans favored the large, straight-sided, slightly curved shield with the straight top and bottom. Shields were extremely important for fending off sword thrusts, but were primarily for defending against missiles. When a flight of arrows was coming in, the whole cohort would raise their shields over their heads, with no space between them, and they would be relatively safe against the arrows. The shape of the shield also allowed the Romans to employ the *testudo* (turtle) formation, in which a century could arrange their shields in such a way that they were invulnerable to a missile attack, no matter which quarter it came from. The straight-sided shield had many virtues, but it was heavy and awkward in man-to-man combat. In the fourth century it was abandoned in favor of a smaller oval shield.

It seems obvious that all these weapons must have weighed a great deal. It is estimated that the armor and weapons a solider was expected to carry weighed about sixty pounds. When one also considers that they were expected to carry rations for seventeen days when on the march, it is obvious just how fit the Roman soldier must have been.

## The Organization of the Army

In the days of Julius Caesar, there were sixty legions in the Roman army. Augustus reduced that number to twenty-eight after he was victorious in the civil wars.[17] By the time of Trajan, there were thirty legions. Septimius Severus found it necessary to increase this number to thirty-three.[18] Since there were approximately 5,400 men in a legion, it took only between 150,000 and 178,000 men to protect the immense empire.[19]

Tacitus informs us that in A.D. 23 eight legions guarded the Rhine. There were three in Spain, two in Africa, two in Egypt, four in Syria, four along the Danube, and two in Illyria, with easy access to Rome.[20] The numerical placement of the legions fluctuated according to need. In the time of Trajan, there were only four legions along the Rhine, but twelve or thirteen along the Danube.[21] It was not customary to station troops in Italy, much less in Rome itself. The emperor's protection was seen to by the Praetorian Guard, and they also saw to whatever military needs Italy might experience. But as a general rule, if the frontiers were guarded, there was no need to station troops in Italy.

The smallest unit of the Roman army consisted of squads of eight men, the *contubernium*. Ten of these units made up a century, which was commanded by a centurion. Each centurion had an *optio*, or aide, to help him in his difficult work. Ten centuries made up a cohort, and there were six cohorts in a legion. It was at the cohort level that command structure became complicated. Nominally, each legion had six tribunes, one for each cohort, but these tribunes were mostly young men of good families, who were anxious to have some military service so they could begin their political careers. These young men were rarely asked to fight, and in fact most of their actual duties were taken up by the centurions.

The *primus pilus*, or most senior centurion, often became the de facto commander of the whole legion. Technically, the commander of the legion was called the *legatus*. The legates could be divided into two camps, those who were simply doing the job for the sake of having a command to put on their resumés, and those who were legates because they had chosen soldiering as a career.

Because the tribunes and legates would not necessarily be professional fighting men, a special office was created. Above the centurions was the *praefectus castrorum*, or prefect of the camp. The *praefectus castrorum* would be a military man with many years of experience as a *primus pilus*. His job was to command the legion in the absence of the legate and senior tribune, but even when they were present they were likely to defer to the man because of his experience.

Under normal circumstances, legates were under the command of the governor of the province where they were stationed. In times of war, a specific field commander would be appointed and given a number of legions under his command. A perfect example of this arrangement was the appointment of Vespasian to command the legions needed to crush the Jewish Revolt of A.D. 66, over the head of the governor of Syria, who would ordinarily have been in charge. Sometimes, in times of particular national crisis, or just because he thought he was the best man for the job, an emperor might take personal command of a field army. Marcus Aurelius, for example, spent much of his time as emperor personally directing the fighting of various wars.

Each legion had a clerical staff commanded by a *cornicularius*. These clerks kept track of pay, supplies, personnel records, and transfers. A legion would also have 120 cavalrymen, under the command of the *optio equitum.* These horsemen were useful for scouting and raiding, but they did not do much fighting in serious battles.

Legions always had special needs. Roads and bridges had to be built, and special operations had to be conducted behind enemy lines. Soldiers who had special skills in engineering or knew how to write or were fluent in local languages formed a special corps within the legion, and they were known as *immunes,* because they were immune from regular military service.

It is easy to see that in the Roman system everything depended on the centurions. They were responsible for more than the eighty men under their direct command. At times, a senior centurion might find himself in command of the whole legion, so the judgment and skill of the centurions were priceless. Consequently, it took a special man to reach that rank. The youngest man ever known to reach the rank of *primus pilus* was forty-nine years old.[22] The *primus pilus* was paid 60,000 sesterces a year. Ordinary centurions were paid 15,000 sesterces annually, and the *miles* (ordinary soldiers) were paid 900 sesterces a year during the reign of Augustus, though that amount was raised to 2,700 by the time of Caracalla.[23] Upon retirement, a soldier would be given the princely sum of 12,000 sesterces and a piece of land to settle on. The retired *miles* would settle along the frontier in colonies with his former mates, and these colonies greatly enhanced the security of the regions they inhabited, since the retired soldiers could be called up in time of need.[24]

## Conclusion

Encounters with the Roman army were the lot of every inhabitant of the empire. As the encounters described in the New Testament indicate, some of the soldiers were men of good character, and others were not. Paul's comparison of a soldier's armor with the spiritual armor a Christian should put on[25] also indicates that there are some similarities between a soldier's life and the life of a Christian. But it must have been very difficult for a soldier to be a practicing Christian, because of the oaths and sacrifices a soldier was required to make, not to mention the bloodiness of a soldier's duties. So the early Christians had a very complicated attitude toward the profession of arms, and we will explore that attitude later in this work.

## CHAPTER 5

# The Basics of Life: Food, Clothing, Housing, Travel, and Education

Food, drink, travel, clothing, and housing are the constant backdrop to the life of the early Christians. Casual references to such matters in the pages of the New Testament can sometimes provoke questions. What difficulties did one encounter in traveling around the empire? What foods were people accustomed to eating? Did everyone drink wine? What kind of clothing did people wear?

## Food

It is fashionable, these days, to speak of the great benefits of the "Mediterranean diet". It is fascinating to note, then, that the people of the Roman Empire subsisted entirely on that diet.

Roman legends spoke of the great benefits conferred on mankind by the goddess Ceres, who gave human beings agriculture. Before that time, the legends ran, people had to survive on such unsatisfying fare as acorns and berries.[1] When Ceres taught man to plow, she opened up a whole new world of possibilities. Whole grains like wheat and barley became the staples of the diet of the time.

Unfortunately, sufficient grain could not be grown in Italy to feed the population, so grain was imported from Egypt, Sicily, and Tripolitania (a region of North Africa). Consequently, crop failure in these regions meant hunger and hardship in large parts of the empire. Drought, disease, and insect infestation occurred often enough that empire-wide famines were not uncommon events.

All around the Mediterranean, people relied heavily on seafood for protein. Fish, shellfish, octopus, and squid were eaten extensively. As a general rule, people did not eat beef. The Romans considered beef to be tough and tasteless and raised cattle primarily for leather. They liked pork quite a bit and would also eat lamb, though sheep were primarily reserved for their all-important wool.

Vegetables, mushrooms, herbs, and fruit rounded out the diet. In northern regions, such as Gaul, Britain, and what is now Germany, cheese and butter were added to this diet. The Romans and Greeks had a great disdain for butter in particular, and preferred olive oil for all their cooking and dipping needs. They also used goat's milk rather than cow's milk for cheese.

Wine was the drink of choice throughout the empire, because the water supply was likely to be tainted. People found that a little bit of wine mixed with their water would prevent intestinal disorders, so they mixed their wine with water, sometimes as much as ten parts to one. Drinking unwatered wine was reserved for parties where the purpose was to get drunk.[2] At fashionable dinner parties, wine would be mixed with honey to make a drink called *mulsum*. This drink was also served hot on cold winter mornings.

Not all Romans ate breakfast, but those who did started their day with a light meal called *jentaculum*. This meal would consist primarily of bread dipped in honey or wine. For most people, the first meal of the day would be *prandium*, the equivalent of lunch, with bread, cold meats, fruit, and a little wine.[3] The main meal of the day was called *cena* and would be eaten in the evening. This meal would typically consist of *puls*, a wheat porridge seasoned with herbs, mushrooms, vegetables, fish, or whatever meat was handy. Before bedtime, a light meal called *vesperna* might be eaten.

In place of *vesperna*, Romans were fond of dinner parties, and all classes would participate in such activities, although the fare would be much richer if you were wealthy. Great delicacies such as dormice roasted in honey, lark's tongue, peacock, and ostrich might grace the tables of the wealthy, more as a way of showing off than satisfying one's guests, but in more normal homes a dinner party would start off with hors d'oeuvres of salad, radishes, mushrooms, boiled eggs, oysters, and sardines. At this point in the meal, *puls* would be served. The main course at these feasts would consist of various kinds of fish and meat.

Dining out was common, particularly in Rome. It was not normally a family activity, however. Workmen would meet in the *tabernae* after work, to have a meal and a libation.[4] The *tabernae* were the ancient equivalent of a snack bar, with a long marble counter with holes in it for the placement of pots of food. Most had fires underneath the food pots to keep things hot. You could order your food and have a seat on a stool to enjoy your meal, or you could take your food with you and eat outdoors. The fare at these inns and taverns was common. Elaborate, expensive meals could be had only in the homes of the wealthy. In the taverns, simple pottages, sausages, and common wines were the order of the day.

*Clothing*

Throughout the empire, clothes were made primarily out of three materials: wool, linen (which is produced from flax), and cotton, which at that time was produced almost exclusively in Egypt. Silk was used little, both because of its great expense (in the second century A.D., it cost three pounds of gold for a pound of silk dyed purple) and because the sterner critics among the Romans considered it effeminate.[5] Women and extremely wealthy Easterners, unburdened by Roman prejudice, wore silk when they could, but since it had to travel all the way from China, silk was scarce in the best of times.

For both men and women, the main undergarment was a simple shift or chemise, which could also be used as a nightshirt. Throughout most of the empire, a simple tunic would be the main garment for men. There were a wide variety of dyes available,[6] but the Romans considered it unnecessarily flamboyant to wear colored clothes, so the Roman tunic was usually plain white. Men of the senatorial class were allowed to wear purple bands on their tunic, running from the shoulder to the bottom of the tunic on each side. Consuls could wear a wider purple band, and emperors could dress entirely in purple if they chose. Equestrians could wear red bands on their tunics. Other than that, the Roman male wore a white tunic with other colors possibly used as a fringe, or very subtly incorporated. Movies that show Roman men wearing very short tunics are inaccurate; the typical tunic would come down below a man's knees.[7] In the East, it was customary for a man to wear a more voluminous robe that covered his arms and legs. Also, in the East, color was more common in men's clothing, with stripes and elaborate designs incorporated into the fabric.

The toga was a badge of Roman citizenship. It was basically a white sheet draped elaborately in such a way that it would stay on by itself, and allow limited use of the arms. Unfortunately, no matter how skillfully one draped the toga, it was an awkward piece of equipment and was worn only for ceremonial or festive occasions.[8]

Women were allowed more color in their clothing than men. Their main garment was the *stola*, which reached close to the ground. The female equivalent of the toga was the *palla*. Like the toga, it was an inconvenient garment, reserved for special occasions. In the days of the Republic, respectable Roman women were not supposed to go out without her head covered, but this social constraint seems to have died out over time. In the East, although customs varied in different times and places, respectable women were supposed to wear a veil in public; however, it might leave the face uncovered. The prevailing attitude was that if a woman was married, only the husband need see her beauty, and if she was unmarried, it was best if no one but the father and brothers knew what she looked like. But again, in the rich and cosmopolitan empire, ancient customs loosened, and many respectable women went about in public without headgear at all.

Public opinion played a powerful role in people's behavior then as it does now. A man who wore a tunic that was too long might be accused of being effeminate or of having bad legs, while a woman who wore her *stola* too short might be accused of public lewdness.

## Housing

"The subject of private houses is complicated, for there was a great variety of arrangement, and generalization is deceptive."[9] So begins a chapter on household architecture in one of the standard works on the architecture of the Greco-Roman world. Obviously, the primary differences between houses would have to do with the wealth of the homeowner. But there are some generalizations that can be made. In the mild Mediterranean climate of most of the empire, porches and open courtyards (in Latin, *atria*) were common, even in the poorest of houses. The atriums functioned as open inner courtyards to be enjoyed in pleasant weather. Most atriums featured a pool or cistern to catch rainwater.

In Rome itself and in some other large cities, most people lived in *insulae*, multistoried apartment buildings. The ground floor of most *insulae* was devoted to shops, with rooms for rent on the higher floors. The *insulae* were, generally speaking, neither safe nor pleasant places to live. Staircases were rickety. The buildings themselves were often poorly constructed out of wood and susceptible to collapse or fire. Water had to be carried up the stairs, and waste had to be either thrown out the window or lugged back down the stairs.[10] (Most people evidently opted for the automatic disposal system. If you were walking past an *insula*, you would be well advised to stay in the middle of the street!)

The *insulae* lacked central heating or even fireplaces or ovens for each apartment.[11] Heating and cooking were done primarily over portable braziers. You could cook your dinner in the kitchen, then at bedtime move the brazier to the bedroom to make sleep more comfortable on cold winter nights. The braziers, of course, were responsible for most of the fires that periodically swept through the *insulae*.

Concerned about the safety of the *insulae*, Augustus passed legislation limiting their height to twenty meters, tall enough for about four stories.[12] However, Rome's population continued to grow, and since the city could not expand horizontally because of the water distribution system, it had to grow vertically. Consequently, Augustus' wise legislation was ignored later. During the reign of Septimius Severus (193–211), the giant Insula of Felicula was constructed next to the Pantheon. This building towered over the other buildings of Rome "like a skyscraper".[13]

Life on the upper floors of the *insulae* must have been very interesting. As explained above, food, water, and fuel had to be carried up the staircase, and waste had to be either carried down or thrown out the window. The roof did not necessarily keep out the rain. Those on the upper floors were in the most danger of dying in a fire. The satirist Juvenal summarized the situation nicely: "Smoke is pouring out of your third floor attic, but you know nothing of it; if the alarm begins on the ground floor, the last man to burn will be he who has nothing to shelter him from the rain but the tiles, where the gentle doves lay their eggs."[14]

Life on the ground floor was preferable. Some *insulae* even had running water and central heating on the ground level. Consequently, the apartments on this level were much more expensive, and the upper floors were less expensive. The upper-floor apartments could be afforded by the poorest of the poor.

The private dwelling of a shopkeeper might either be fronted by his shop or built over it. You would enter the house through the *vestibulum*, or porch. Upon entering, you would probably encounter bedrooms on both sides, with the atrium directly in front. Behind the atrium would be the *tablinium*, which functioned as an office for the *paterfamilias*; the *triclinium*, or dining room; and the kitchen. Some houses had two stories; if so, there would be a large upper room called the *cenaculum*, where larger groups could meet. Meals would be served in the atrium if the weather was nice, in the *triclinium* otherwise. For larger groups, the *cenaculum*, if the owner had one, could be used.

Wealthier families lived in villas. The basic plan was the same, but everything would be larger and more elegant. There would be, of course, no shop in front of the house, since the wealthy did not work at trades. The house would typically be surrounded by a garden, for privacy and refreshment. Sometimes the atrium would contain a swimming pool. The atrium, *triclinium*, and *tablinium* would be much larger, since the wealthy *paterfamilias* was expected to entertain on a grander scale. There had to be large areas for the wealthy man's many clients and freedmen to make their daily visits in the morning, and there had to be sufficient space for large dinner parties. Most villas included a set of private baths.

From the second century onward, decorations increasingly became an important feature of the wealthy man's house. Wall paintings, marble facades, and mosaics became more and more common in the larger villas. Some homeowners went so far as to have artificial columns painted on the walls, to create the illusion of space and depth. The palaces of the truly wealthy and powerful had no need of such tricks, of course. The spacious halls required majestic columns for support. These columns made it possible for the wealthy to have a *portico*, or porch, off the back of the house. The portico would serve as a dining room during good weather, or simply a good place to enjoy one's leisure time.

The gap between the poor, who had to endure life in their rundown *insulae*, and the wealthy, who enjoyed their private pools, cool porticoes, spacious gardens, and elegant wall paintings, must have been immense. But the gap between the lives of the poor and those of the rich was no greater then than it is now.

### Education

One of the leading scholars of the Roman world thinks the Roman education system was in a state of "decomposition" during the first century A.D., and that the educational system never really recovered from this decline.[15] The study of philosophy, mathematics, science, history, and even literature was eschewed in favor of a system that would culminate in the study of rhetoric. But rhetoric is really useful only in two areas, politics and law.

The best minds of the empire went into the legal profession, arguing civil suits in the forums and agoras of the empire. Of course, there were serious philosophers, mathematicians, physicians, poets, and even scientists in the imperial age, but for the most part their work was dependent on that of Greek thinkers of the previous age.

The Roman system of education was divided into three parts. Most children began the first phase at age seven. These schools were private, but the fees were small enough that most people could afford them. At these schools, teachers would impart the basics of reading, writing, and enough mathematics to get the average person through life.[16]

Primary school started at dawn and ran without a break until noon. The setting of the school was usually the porch of some shop or private dwelling. The goal of the primary schools was to teach the pupils to read, write, and count.

The second phase, which began early in the teenage years, was designed to teach the Greek and Latin classics and prepare the students for their higher education. These schools were taught by a *grammaticus* (grammarian) and were designed to impart the rules of grammar and proper speech.[17]

Some scholars think the methods of the grammar schools, which seem to have consisted primarily of copying out literature on wax tablets, emptied eloquence of all real content.[18] Authentic eloquence requires understanding, emotional and intellectual depth, and above all, the ability to think. In the grammar schools, the study of some of the greatest literature the world has ever produced was reduced to the memorization of grammatical rules and a handful of rhetorical devices. Certainly, exceptionally bright and insightful students could gain knowledge in history, literature, philosophy, and science by osmosis from the study of grammar, but there was no systematic treatment of these subjects.

The third phase was considered essential for anyone who wished to enter public life. The schools of rhetoric were designed to teach people how to persuade. This was considered the essential art for public success. Whether a man wished to enter the profession of law, public service, or politics, to succeed he had to understand the rules of rhetoric.

In the schools of rhetoric, students primarily learned the *chriae*, the formulas for imparting the maxims of wise men. The teachers of rhetoric seemed to be of the opinion that anyone could be turned into an accomplished speaker simply by learning these rules.

You can find traces of these rhetorical rules in the writings of the early Christians. Saint Paul, for instance, used them in his Epistles. Tertullian and Justin Martyr used them in their writings. Other Christian writers, like Irenaeus, deliberately eschewed the techniques of the rhetoricians.[19] However, outside Christian circles, it would have harmed one's career to be ignorant of the rules of rhetoric, so the "finishing schools" of the ancient world were designed solely to teach the effective use of these rules.[20]

### The Working Day

It is not the purpose of this section to provide a catalogue of occupations in the ancient world. With a certain amount of reflection, one can guess the trades at which men (very few women worked outside the home) were employed. The truth is, however, that very few men were what we would call "employees". Most men were slaves, small shopkeepers, or businessmen, and few men went to work for other people for a salary.

The consequence is that most men worked out of their homes or quite near to their homes. Shopkeepers had their small shops either attached to or on the ground floor of their home. Slaves, of course, usually worked out of the home of their master. Artisans like blacksmiths, potters, and metalworkers kept their shops near their homes, and the ringing of the blacksmith's anvil and the metalworker's hammer disturbed the rest of late sleepers in the residential districts of Rome.[21] Warehousemen, porters, and carters worked near the harbors, if the city was a seaport, or in warehouse districts near the city gates.

The workday had its own rhythms, dictated by nature and cultural habits. Most people were, of necessity, early risers. Unless there was a party, people would go to bed when it got dark, and wake up with the sun. Morning ablutions were few, and, as we have seen, most people ate no more than a bit of bread dipped in wine for breakfast.

After breakfast, most people would either go straight to work, or to the house of their patron, if they were in need of employment. Patrons, for their part, were expected to keep office hours in their home first thing in the morning. If a patron needed a client's services, he would arrange for that at this time, when the client presented himself for employment. Conversely, if a client needed help, the patron would be available to offer assistance at this time. Clients owed their patrons *obsequium*, and in turn, if they needed it, they would receive *sportula*, or a free basket of food. As we shall see, as a system of social welfare, this system did not work very well, because it encouraged arrogance in the patron and humiliation for the client, who had to go to his patron hat in hand.

Perhaps the most surprising aspect of the ancient workday for a modern person would be the shortness of the actual working day. After everyone got through the client-patron rituals, actual work would start at around 8:00 in the morning.[22] By what we would call 3:00 P.M., most workers were done for the day. But this simple fact tells very little, because the "hours" of an ancient day were not of uniform length. Days were divided evenly into twelve "hours", starting at sunrise and ending at sunset. This means that in Rome, for instance, an "hour" at the winter solstice would be about forty-five modern minutes, and at the summer solstice an hour would be about seventy-five modern minutes. So in the wintertime, the workday would be fewer than six of our modern hours, and in the summertime it would be slightly more than eight of our hours.

What did people do with the rest of their time? People would visit the baths, which were inexpensive enough for even the poorest person to afford. Or they would go to the forum or agora to watch the trials, political debates, and philosophical arguments that were constantly going on at those places.

You are already, perhaps, detecting a great irony. We are accustomed to thinking that life in the ancient world must have been harder without the modern conveniences, and that people must have worked harder, with longer hours. It is true that most people, particularly slaves, worked harder, but it does not follow that people worked longer hours. The pace of life was slower, and even poor people had time on their hands. The result, as we shall see in the next chapter, was that there was a pressing need for entertainment, to keep people out of trouble.

### Travel

Throughout this work, we have emphasized the great lengths to which Rome went in order to create a universal Mediterranean culture. In large part, they were successful. As a result, a person could travel from the frontiers of northern Britain to the ruins of Babylon in relative safety. Two languages, Greek and Latin, could take you virtually anywhere in the empire.[23]

Of course, safety is always relative. There were real dangers attending travel at that time. In most provinces, deserts and mountainous or wooded regions were infested with bandits. They caused serious problems by robbing travelers, taking important people hostage, and leaving their victims to die on the roadside. On the sea, storms were always troublesome, but in midwinter the Mediterranean was virtually impassable, and few vessels even ventured out.[24] However, during the good sailing season, from May to October, the Mediterranean was a wonderful highway that made travel relatively easy and quick.

The Romans had cleared the Mediterranean of pirates in the days of Julius Caesar and Pompey. Consequently, sea trade flourished. Grain barges would travel from Egypt to Rome. Luxury goods from the East made their way to the far West, and in this way the wealth of Rome spread to every province.

We are familiar with the fact that the Romans were great road builders. Their well-graded and paved roads stretched from one end of the empire to the other, ensuring that any journey that could not be made by sea could be accomplished overland. The Romans built these roads to facilitate the movement of troops, but everyone benefitted from them. Tourists, soldiers, merchants, mail carriers, administrators, tax collectors, and Christian missionaries like Peter and Paul all used the magnificent road system, which was better than anything the world had seen until the twentieth century.[25]

The Romans engaged in a form of travel that few cultures outside our own have engaged in: tourism. The Greeks had begun the habit of traveling for enlightenment and entertainment, but the Romans had the wealth to embrace the practice wholeheartedly. Wealthy Romans would travel to Greece, Egypt, and Mesopotamia to see the famous religious and cultural sights, sample the local culture and cuisine, and experience the local religious rites. Guidebooks were written to help other travelers get the most out of their experience.[26]

Despite all the travel that went on, mail was a constant problem. The government had a postal system, called the *cursus publicus*, but it was reserved for military or administrative use. Of course, most couriers could be bribed to carry private packages (most officials in the Roman world were amenable to financial inducements), but such couriers were considered unreliable. Certainly, nothing dangerous, subversive, or illegal could be sent by government post, since the postmasters routinely opened private mail. This fact primarily is responsible for the fact that the Epistles of the New Testament were sent by private, highly trusted couriers. Most wealthy people retained slaves that they could trust with their mail.[27] Other options were to employ soldiers returning to their distant posts, or fellow travelers who happened to be headed in the right direction. It was a highly inefficient and, in many ways, unsatisfactory system.

With all the travel, it was inevitable that a system of inns and restaurants would arise. Of course, if one were on government service he could rely on public housing, but private travelers were on their own. Or, if a traveler was wealthy, he could simply rent or purchase houses in advantageous locales. Even if he lacked these advantages, he might have friends he could stay with along the way. Jews seem to have had a system involving letters of recommendation that allowed the bearers to stay with other Jews along the way. But other travelers had to rely on inns, which were actually quite common in the towns along the major highways.[28] Most of the inns were simple affairs, involving a chance for a meal, a bed, and a stable for the traveler's animals. Some inns had private rooms; some did not. Homeowners would sometimes rent out spare rooms in their houses. Resort towns like Alexandria, in Egypt, had luxury hotels, but this type of accommodation was definitely rare. The wise traveler made sure he stopped off for the night in a larger town, where he could take his pick.[29]

Inns did not include washing facilities. As we shall see in the next chapter, every good-sized town in the empire had public baths, and a traveler could easily clean up in the Roman manner at one of these baths.

Restaurants were also common. A person could get his meals at the inn, but if for some reason this was unacceptable, he could easily go to a *taberna* for a bite to eat and a libation. However, one had to be careful and use his own nose and common sense to avoid food poisoning.

### Medicine

In the summer of 145, Aelius Aristides, who had been feeling ill for some time, had a dream. In the dream, the god Asclepios visited him and told him to visit the famous *Asclepion* in Pergamum. We are fortunate: Aristides Aelius was an educated man, trained in rhetoric, and he left an informative record of his two-year stay at the *Asclepion*.[30]

What was Aristides' illness? The physician Galen, who began his career at the *Asclepion*, diagnosed him as consumptive. Galen wrote of Aristides: "I have seen many people whose body was naturally strong and whose soul was weak, inert and useless. Thus, their sicknesses have arisen from a sort of insomnia and apoplexy and inervation [*sic*] and sicknesses of the sort of epilepsy. And as to them whose souls are naturally strong and whose bodies are weak, I have only seen a few of them. One of them was Aristides."[31] In short, Galen had no idea what was really wrong with Aristides, except that perhaps his body was not strong. And Galen was the best physician of the age, so good that he ended up as court physician for the emperor Marcus Aurelius.

Aelius Aristides' story ended up fairly well. His health evidently never got much better, but after two years he left the *Asclepion* and returned to his civilian employments, living to the (then) ripe old age of sixty-three.

This brief story fills the mind with curiosity about many things. The *Asclepion* was a temple devoted to healing. What was the experience of visiting one like? Were there physicians who were not associated with temples? How did one become a physician? How were illnesses cured? What was the general state of health in the empire? Fortunately, we have detailed answers to all these questions, thanks to the prolific writings of physicians like Galen and patients like Aristides.

In the early days, the Romans had no physicians. Pliny the Elder declared that "the Romans got along without doctors for six hundred years." [32] Pliny appears to have had it right: the Romans developed no medical ideas on their own. When they came into extensive contact with the Greeks, Greek physicians became increasingly popular in Rome, particularly among the wealthy class. A good Greek physician could make a living anywhere in the empire. The best Greek doctors, like Galen, could even find employment from emperors.

The Greeks believed that somewhere in the far-distant past Asclepios had been born of a human mother, with Apollo as his father. Apollo left Asclepios in the care of a centaur, and this centaur, half-man, half-horse, taught Asclepios medicine. At one point, Zeus killed Asclepios with a thunderbolt in a fit of rage, but later relented, not only restoring Asclepios to life, but making him a god. So Asclepios was associated with medicine and healing because Apollo was his father, he was trained in healing by the centaur, and he was raised from the dead.

There were three main sanctuaries to Asclepios in the Greek world, at Epidaurus, Cos, and Pergamum. All three cities produced famous physicians in the ancient world. In fact, the priests of Asclepios were the first physicians. Their treatments seem to have been a combination of the known healing herbs of the time, common sense aided by personal observation, and the occult, with a heavy emphasis on dreams.

A great deal is known about the Asclepion in Pergamum. It was rebuilt during the reign of Emperor Hadrian (A.D. 117–138). The street leading to the sanctuary was a *via tecta*, a covered street, with columns supporting a vaulted roof over the roadway. The person desiring admittance would walk down this covered street about 500 feet, alone. At the end of this street, he would find himself in a courtyard surrounded by *stoas* (porches supported by columns) on three sides. He would present himself at a huge gate, a barrier that "separated the profane from the sacred".[33]

Once inside the gate, the complex consisted of three long *stoas*; a library; a theater, at which comedies, poetry recitals, and music were featured; a row of apartments for the patients; the temple of Asclepios itself; and an unusual feature usually called the "treatment center". The treatment center was accessed through a 250-foot-long underground tunnel, which had a channel in which fresh spring water ran. When you reached the other end of the tunnel, you would find yourself in a kind of rotunda, and you would walk in a circle, accompanied by the soothing running water and burning incense.

The basic treatment at all the *asclepions* involved the inducement of dreams and visions by means of drugs. The patient would then do whatever "the god" told him to do in the dream. Aelius Aristides, for instance, received a dream in which Asclepios told him to cover himself in mud and run three times around the complex.[34]

One could also visit a physician in a secular environment. Doctors could and did set up in private practice in all the cities of the empire. The emperors did what they could to encourage doctors: in 46 B.C. Julius Caesar granted citizenship to all practicing physicians.[35] We have no idea what the cure rate of ancient physicians was, but most scholars suspect it could not have been very high. Lacking knowledge of the existence of germs, their theory of disease was inadequate. They had a tendency to attribute disease to the actions of various gods, although over time an appreciation for the scientific method increased.

Some physicians, such as Asclepiades, possessed of more common sense than their peers, abandoned failed methods and stressed "diet, exercise, fresh air, light, massage, baths, and regular and sensible ways of living".[36]

Of what did the education of a physician consist? Surprisingly, there do not appear to have been regular schools for doctors. Asclepiades, for instance, was trained in rhetoric, failed in that profession, and set his shingle out as a doctor. Galen was an exception; he studied at the Asclepion at Pergamum, under the priests of Asclepios, and elsewhere for about twelve years before calling himself a doctor. Upon completing his studies, he spent four or five years as a surgeon for a school of gladiators, a good way to learn about human anatomy. At the end of this period of time, he went to Rome, where he quickly became the most eminent physician of his age.

The physical conditions of life were poor by modern standards, but much better than they had been just a hundred years earlier. The aqueduct systems meant that all cities had plentiful supplies of clean water (though the habit of running the water through lead pipes somewhat diminished this advantage). Unfortunately, only a few of the wealthiest houses had water piped into the house and had private latrines with access to the sewage system.[37] Most cities had public latrines[38] and a sewage system that carried waste away from houses, though the waste was usually just dumped into the nearest river. In Rome, for instance, the *Cloaca Maxima* ran waste straight into the Tiber, which is why everyone who could afford to do so left Rome during the summer.

Most people understood that diet had something to do with health. Cato the Younger, for instance, relied heavily on cabbage to maintain his ruddy good health. The Romans ate more fruits and vegetables than the average American, and far less meat. But the poor lived almost entirely on free grain, and that restricted diet led inevitably to poor health.

Two major plagues swept the empire during the period with which we are concerned. We will discuss these plagues at greater length later. For now, it suffices to say that the medical establishment of the time was helpless against them. Galen, for instance, made excuses and fled to the countryside during the plague of 160. Some scholars think the experiences during the plagues undermined the faith of people in medicine altogether and accounted for the rise in superstition and faith in amulets that characterized the period of the late empire.[39]

The poor received few benefits from doctors and medicine: "Whatever benefits medicine may have offered in ancient Rome, they were very unevenly shared, for the poor had little or no access to the best doctors and, apart from military establishments, there were no hospitals or clinics available to treat them until a few were provided under Christian inspiration at the end of the Empire."[40]

Life expectancy is difficult to calculate. The usual figure given is forty years, but this number is somewhat misleading. From the evidence of tombstones, a great number of people died young. Large numbers of children died before the age of two due to unsanitary conditions. Many others, particularly among the poor, died before the age of forty from tuberculosis, smallpox, typhoid fever, malaria, tetanus, and the like. Some people lived to great old age, but a long life was quite rare, except for a few with good heredity and exceptionally clean ways of living.[41]

Some drugs were known and used. The Greeks and Romans knew about opium and hemlock as painkillers. They also knew that overdoses of beneficial drugs could cause death. Dioscorides (ca. A.D. 40–90), who hailed from what is now southern Turkey, classified over a thousand substances, most derived from plants, that had some effect on the body. Dioscorides went so far as to list known side effects, both positive and negative, as well as how to harvest, prepare, and store these substances.[42]

But the ancients did not know what it was in a specific drug that caused a given effect. So every drug administration had an accompanying ritual, a prayer or offering to a specific god. The ancients were unclear as to whether it was the use of the drug, or the incantation, or a combination of both, that actually brought about the desired effect. So even medical treatment was tied closely to pagan religious beliefs, whether you went to a temple of Asclepios or to a private doctor for treatment.

### Conclusion

If a person today were transported back in time to the Roman Empire, he would be surprised, I think, at how good life was in some aspects and how poor it was in other ways. Things we take for granted—for example, good communications—were nonexistent in the Roman world. There was not even a post office box where you could drop off your letters, with any confidence that they would ever be delivered.

The availability of sufficient quantities of good food would be a positive surprise, unless our imaginary person happened to be transported in a year of famine. The Mediterranean region has always been capable of producing large quantities of good and highly nutritious food. The problem the ancient world faced was that not everyone could afford to buy it, so the poor lived almost entirely on free grain, which lacked essential nutrients.

Our time traveler would be unpleasantly surprised by the level of medical knowledge and the lack of sanitary conditions. It is true that most cities had a sewage system of sorts, but they do not appear to have been very efficient.[43]

Our imaginary friend would find much variety in housing. If he visited the homes of the wealthy, he would be impressed by the spaciousness, beauty, and convenience of the homes. Even middle-class homes were reasonable, livable places, although our time traveler might be unaccustomed to the practice of having living quarters attached to places of business. But the housing of the poor, which surpassed anything we have in America today for sheer squalor, would horrify our friend. The poor lived in cramped, dangerous *insulae* with no running water and no system for the removal of waste. The *insulae* were in constant danger of collapse or fire, and landlords were under no obligation to improve conditions.

In some respects, then, life in the ancient world was not as bad as we might fear. Men are marvelously adaptable, and systems were established to make life reasonable. But the ancients were hampered by their lack of knowledge in certain key areas of life, and our time traveler would almost certainly come back grateful to be living in the twenty-first century.

## CHAPTER 6

# Entertainment

The widespread use of slave labor, coupled with the relative material prosperity enjoyed in most parts of the empire, meant that most free men and women had a certain amount of leisure time on their hands. The government provided low-cost grain for the lower-class citizens, so they were protected against the vicissitudes of extreme poverty. These citizens had a special love for the violent forms of entertainment Rome offered. The combination of unemployment and relative freedom from material want meant that the common people were in great need of diversions. The middle and upper classes as a general rule preferred other, more genteel forms of entertainment, such as music or plays, but there were well-known cases where members of the upper class became obsessed with some aspect of the more violent entertainments.[1]

An important aspect of the Roman games was their surprisingly addictive nature. Saint Augustine records a story of a friend of his who was strongly opposed to the games but was lured to the gladiatorial contest. Augustine wrote that he was fascinated by the "madness of the Circensian games".[2] This addictiveness helps us to understand how the emperors used the games to control the people and why the people were so receptive to them.

## The Origins of Gladiatorial Contests

In 246 B.C. the sons of Junius Brutus Pera found themselves in the position in which many sons find themselves: their father had passed away, and it was their duty to honor the great man who had raised them. In addition to the traditional Roman funeral rites, the sons of Junius Brutus Pera honored their father by setting three pairs of men to fight to the death with swords in the *Forum Boarium*, where the whole community could watch. As far as we know, this is the first time such a thing happened in Rome.[3]

We do not know why the sons of Junius Brutus Pera chose to honor him in such a way. There are, as usual, numerous tantalizing historical clues, and numerous theories to match those clues. For the purposes of this study, it is not necessary to analyze these clues and theories in great detail, but it will be interesting and instructive to spend a minute looking at the origins of gladiatorial combat, because the diversity of those origins helps to explain why the custom of sword fighting in an arena spread so easily throughout the empire.

Roman writers themselves ascribed Etruscan origins to the gladiatorial contests, which the Romans called the *munerae*.[4] There is quite a bit of evidence to support this theory. The Etruscans borrowed from the ancient Greeks the practice of "funeral games", honoring great men when they died. But there may not have been a direct cultural exchange between the Etruscans and the Romans. The custom may first have traveled to the Campanian city of Capua, where it eventually was taken up in Rome itself.[5] But the custom may have been much more widespread than we might think. Anyone who has read the *Iliad* knows that after the death of Patroclus, Achilles killed many Trojans in Patroclus' honor. Of course, the Greeks had renounced these customs back in the mists of antiquity. But the custom lingered on in the hinterlands of the Greek world. Herodotus, who wrote in the fourth century B.C., claimed that the Scythians (a Germanic people that lived in the regions of Thrace, modern-day Bulgaria) sacrificed captives to honor dead warriors. From numerous sources it is clear that the Celtic peoples of Gaul and Britain did the same thing. The Carthaginians of North Africa engaged in human sacrifice on a large scale, though primarily for religious purposes.

These practices point to something we must face up to if we wish to understand the Roman use of gladiators. What we consider extreme brutality was built into the fabric of both Rome itself and the surrounding nations the Romans eventually conquered. *Not* to kill prisoners of war, *not* to put on elaborate spectacles that included the death of slaves and prisoners to honor great men, would have marked the Romans off as an odd and weak people in the eyes of many. It is a mark of Roman genius (the word does not connote moral greatness, after all) that they found a way to accommodate their need to execute criminals and prisoners of war, assert their own cultural superiority, and at the same time provide a rousing good show that would be enjoyable to almost everyone who viewed it.[6]

As usual with most Roman practices that became central to imperial policy, the gladiatorial combat became a cultural institution largely by accident. When the sons of Junius Brutus Pera honored their father, they also, incidentally, raised their own status by their extravagance, because of the great store the Romans paid to family connections. The sons of a man who merited the deaths of three men must be great indeed.

The competitive nature of politics in the Republican era insured that the practice would escalate. Other *munerae* (the word *munera* means simply "gift", or "sacrifice") that we know about illustrate this escalation. In 216 B.C., at the funeral of Marcus Aemilius Lepidus, twenty-two pairs of gladiators fought. In 174 B.C., Titus Flamininus hosted funeral games for his father that featured thirty-seven pairs of gladiators. In a mere seventy-two years, the once private practice of holding funeral games for loved ones had escalated into something that could be called a public spectacle.[7]

The common people of Rome loved the *munerae* and were inclined to admire, and more importantly, vote for, men who provided such spectacles for them. This accounts for the rapid development of the games, and it also helps explain a tragic fact of late Republican politics, when public life became the playground of extremely wealthy men. In 65 B.C., when Julius Caesar was an aedile, he planned and advertised games featuring 320 pairs of gladiators, but the Senate, loaded with Caesar's envious enemies, hastily passed legislation forbidding such extravagance.[8] This legislation did not prevent Caesar, Pompey, and other political aspirants from using the games to increase their popularity. Triumphal games came to have greater significance. Great generals like Gaius Marius, Sulla, Pompey, and the aforementioned Julius Caesar all held massive gladiatorial contests to celebrate their military triumphs. For these games, prisoners of war provided a readily available source of trained fighting men.

In 105 B.C. began the practice of having the consuls host the games that were held during their year in office.[9] From this time onward, the funeral aspect of the games declined, and the games became associated with two Roman festivals, the *Saturnalia* (December 17–23) and the *Quinquatrus* (March 19–23).[10] But it was Emperor Augustus who made the games the great imperial celebration the early Christians knew.

## The Games and the Emperors

Augustus recorded that during his long reign (from 27 B.C. to A.D. 14), he personally hosted twenty-seven gladiatorial combats with over 10,000 fighters, and twenty-six wild animal shows in which 3,500 animals were killed.[11] This simple fact reveals a truth of immense importance. Augustus was one of the shrewdest rulers who ever lived, and he understood, with perfect clarity, that the people of Rome needed their *panem et circenses* ("bread and circuses"). Augustus knew that if he wished to rule without continual uproar in Rome, he personally would have to see to the entertainment of his unruly subjects.

Augustus was forced to take on this heavy financial burden by the relentless logic of Roman tradition. The Romans had been enjoying gladiatorial combat and wild animal hunts (*venationes*) for over 200 years, though not on the massive scale provided by some of the later emperors. In Republican times, government officials were required to sponsor public entertainments. Wealthy citizens saw hosting elaborate games as an opportunity to gain popularity and advance their political careers. Powerful men like Julius Caesar and Pompey competed with one another to produce the most elaborate spectacles. Augustus realized that if he was going to rule as an emperor he could not allow anyone to be more popular than he was. Thus, if the route to popularity lay through providing games for the people, Augustus would make sure he was the one to give the people what they wanted.

Augustus' immediate successor, Tiberius (A.D. 14–37), attempted to curtail the mad spending on superfluous entertainment, but he was regarded as excessively penurious. Caligula succeeded Tiberius but ruled for only four years. His successor, Claudius (41–54), loved bloody gladiatorial combat with a passion, and the games reached new heights (or depths) during his reign. After Claudius, the emperors merely vied with one another to provide more spectacular games than their predecessors. To illustrate the progression, consider that Trajan (98–117) put 5,000 pairs of gladiators in the ring to celebrate a military triumph.

(This matched in one festival the total number of gladiators Augustus produced in his entire forty-one-year reign.) Marcus Aurelius (161–180) had a personal distaste for the games, but even he made sure the people had their entertainment. Ironically, his son Commodus (180–192) loved the games perhaps more than any other emperor, even going so far as to appear in the ring himself.[12] However, Commodus' fate revealed that in the minds of the people there could be limits to an emperor's devotion to the games. Commodus neglected his duties and was a cruel ruler in many ways, and eventually he was assassinated.

## *The* Venatio

At the height of the pagan empire, there were three different kinds of wild animal spectacles (called *venationes*): (1) criminals were executed by being torn apart by animals, (2) specially trained men called *venatores* would hunt especially dangerous wild animals, and (3) sometimes animals were made to fight other animals they would not normally meet in the wild.[13] It was, of course, the first type that provided the opportunity for martyrdom for many early Christians, but the people enjoyed the second and third type the best, provided the animals were properly prepared and gave a good fight.

As with the *munera*, no one knows how the *venatio* first came to Rome. Some have supposed that the custom was borrowed from the Carthaginians, who had a ready supply of dangerous wild animals and were known to favor human sacrifice.[14] However, there is no dispute as to when the Romans first began to use wild animals to fight against people. Lucius Caecelius Metellus brought 142 elephants to Rome in 252 B.C. The elephants were made to fight in the circus and were killed with javelins.[15] The first known instance of *damnatio ad bestias* (condemning criminals to wild animals) was in 167 B.C., when Aemilius Paullus had deserters crushed by elephants.[16]

As the Romans conquered new territories, it became the custom to offer animals from those territories in the triumphal games. Thus, one would find bears and aurochs from northern Europe; lions, elephants, rhinoceroses, hippos, and even crocodiles from Africa; and tigers from central Asia, all depending on the resources of the *editore* (the man who saw to the details of a particular set of games). As with the *munerae*, the *venationes* increased in size and violence as the years went by, and the people's appetite for blood increased. At Trajan's victory games, which lasted for 120 days, 11,000 animals of all kinds were slaughtered.[17] Certainly, bloodshed at this level was not the norm, but Trajan's spectacle indicates that no emperor could afford to provide inferior games and expect to satisfy the Roman crowd.

Like the *munerae*, the *venationes* were monstrously expensive and complicated undertakings. There were companies around the fringes of the empire that specialized in capturing the animals needed in the major cities. The trick, of course, was to capture the animals unharmed. From archaeological records, we know that various pits, traps, and nets were used to accomplish this end. The men engaged in this activity took great risks but made large profits from their activities. The local communities encouraged these men in their work, since shepherds, farmers, and other country dwellers benefitted from the reduction in the population of dangerous animals.

After the animals were captured, other companies specialized in transporting them to every city in the empire that had an amphitheater. This involved transport by ship, if the animals were moving from Africa or Asia to Rome, or by cart, if the animals were coming from northern Europe. This work was not as dangerous as that of the catchers, but it entailed great financial risk, since a storm at sea or any other kind of mishap could result in the death of valuable property. As with any risky business in which demand is high, the shippers made immense profits on successful journeys, and this made the business worthwhile to them.

Every city with an amphitheater had a menagerie, where the animals, once transported, could be kept until festival time. Private contractors sometimes ran these menageries, but various cities throughout the empire took this responsibility upon themselves. Whether they were private contractors or city employees, the operators of the menageries had to be knowledgeable about the proper food for the various animals, had to have a rudimentary knowledge of the illnesses that could befall their charges, and had to know how to get the animals into the proper mood for fighting. (Typically, this involved withholding food for several days, but there were other tricks as well.) The keepers were also responsible for transporting the animals to the amphitheater early on the morning of the appointed day, and for keeping them safe in the holding area until it was time to fight.[18]

What about the men who had to face the animals? They fell into two categories. There were the trained professionals who faced the animals for a living and could earn great fame and wealth through their skill and bravery. There were special schools, similar to the gladiatorial schools, where the *venatores* could learn their trade. The careers of these men were necessarily short: even if one escaped death or crippling in the arena, one's career would be over by age forty, due to the inevitable slowing of reflexes. Therefore, the *venatores* were handsomely rewarded for their dangerous and much-appreciated work.

Criminals, prisoners of war, and erring slaves were sometimes executed by being thrown to wild animals. Crimes that could get this sentence were (1) murder, (2) treason, (3) arson, and (4) certain religious crimes (such as robbing a temple or being a Christian).[19] Citizens were not supposed to be executed in this manner. Slaves could be sold to the *editore* of a particular game, but not on a mere whim. The slave had to appear before court to ensure that he had committed some offense that required such as a punishment.[20]

Prisoners of war frequently found themselves condemned *ad bestias*, because when a Roman general won a major victory, he was allowed by the Senate to celebrate a triumph, which involved throwing massive games for the entire populace. In his triumphal procession, the prisoners and animals from the nation conquered were paraded through the city. Later in the triumph, they would fight one another for the entertainment and edification of the populace.[21]

The practice *of damnatio ad bestias* is of special interest to students of early Christianity, since many Christians were martyred in the arena. The Roman practice seems to have been to arm at least some of the condemned, so they could fight for their lives. Since Christians rarely took advantage of this custom, they were not the most popular victims for the Roman audience, which craved a good fight. More popular were the prisoners of war, trained military men who were capable of putting up a good fight. For that was what the Roman public really wanted.

### A Day at the Colosseum

Vespasian (A.D. 69–79), who was in many ways the most parsimonious of the emperors, undertook the massive expense of building the

Colosseum. The massive structure, still a major tourist attraction in Rome today, took about ten years to build.[22] The building is still impressive today but must have been truly magnificent in its day. It was faced entirely in travertine marble (since stripped away) and hung with brightly colored banners. Gilded statues of gods and heroes stood in the archways. Scarlet, blue, and yellow awnings hung over the interior of the Colosseum, to protect the spectators from the vicissitudes of weather.

The Colosseum seated somewhere between 45,000 and 70,000 people.[23] Stone benches were arranged around the amphitheater in three tiers. As one might expect in class-conscious Rome, the plebes were relegated to the upper tier, the middle class got the central tier, and the senatorial and equestrian classes got the best seats. The imperial box was located on the lowest level, and social status could be determined by one's closeness to the imperial box. Special favorites could expect to be invited to view the spectacles with the emperor himself.

A day at the Colosseum would begin before dawn, with animal carts rumbling through town and prisoners marched to the Colosseum in chains. The plebes would arrive early, to fight for a place in line for the limited seats. Once inside, the spectators would be presented with a dazzling scene. Brightly colored awnings would be draped over poles, to provide a temporary roof for the whole building. During the *Saturnalia* (December 17–23), when the days were short and gloomy, there would be lanterns and torches hung everywhere. The scene must have been like a wonderland for the average Roman, who lived out his life in dingy tenements.

The games would start with a flourish.[24] A trumpet fanfare would bring a hush over the crowd. Pantomimes, trick riders, and the like would warm the crowd up. Next would come the *venatio*, with skilled hunters tracking down and killing wild animals.[25] At the noon hour, prisoners would be executed, whether by wild animals, beheading, or whatever other ingenious method the *editore* could devise. If there were no executions, the lunch break would be filled with "farcical interludes ... parodies".[26] Most of the audience would leave at this time to get their lunch.

In midafternoon, the serious fighting would begin, with gladiators fighting to the death. The gladiatorial contests were not haphazard affairs. The men would pair off and fight as advertised, and with strict attention paid to the rules of gladiatorial combat.[27] There were five basic types of gladiators. There was the *Samnite*, who carried a short sword and an oblong shield, wore a plumed helmet with a visor, and had a "greave" or metal piece that covered his left leg (this was the leg that would be out in front as he fought). A second category of gladiator, the *secutor*, evolved from the Samnite and was armed similarly. Another type of gladiator, the *Thracian*, would carry a curved scimitar and a small round or square shield. Thracians got a greave for each leg, as well as leather bands to protect their thighs. A fourth type of gladiator is very familiar to us today, the *retiarius*, or "net man", who carried a trident in one hand and a net in the other. The *retiarius* would normally fight a *myrmillo*, whose scaled armor and helmet were designed to resemble a fish that the *retiarius* would net or spear.[28]

The strengths and weaknesses of the various types of gladiators were well known to the crowd and heightened the crowd's enjoyment, as they assessed the skill with which the fighters used their equipment. A gladiator's life could be saved even if he lost, if he gave the crowd a good fight and somehow earned their sympathy. A fallen fighter could ask for mercy by extending one finger of his left hand. The host of the games (in Rome, invariably the emperor) alone could decide to spare a beaten man, but of course a prudent host would honor the wishes of the audience. The host would signal his decision by the traditional "thumbs up" or "thumbs down", or by waving a handkerchief.[29]

If a fighter was slain in the arena, a macabre ritual was performed to recall the religious origin of the *munera*. A man dressed as Charon, the ferryman of the underworld in Greek mythology, would make sure the man was dead by administering a blow to the head with a wooden hammer. Then another man dressed in the exotic costume of Hermes Psychopomp (Mercury) would remove the body. The body would pass out of the arena through the Porta Libitensis, named after Libitina, the Roman goddess of burials. While all this was going on, slaves would come out and rake fresh sand over the blood of the fallen.[30]

Meanwhile, the crowd would be going insane, shouting at the gladiators to fight harder, excoriating those perceived to be hanging back, and finally, roaring and howling with lust when a stroke went home, and they could watch a man's life-blood drain into the sand.

Arousing a mass of people to such a bloodlust was, of course, dangerous. Riots were frequent and had to be quelled with further violence. And no one will ever know how many murders were committed by men who had imbibed violence and death all day long. But we know of at least one famous case. Suetonius reports that Nero killed his pregnant wife Poppaea by kicking her in the stomach when she reproached him for coming home late from the games.[31]

### The Spread of the Games throughout the Empire

If you travel through western Europe, Asia Minor, and North Africa, even today you will encounter what one author has called "A Scatter of Circles".[32] These circles are, of course, Roman amphitheaters. You can see a magnificent example of this type of building, as well preserved as the Roman Colosseum, in the French city of Nîmes.[33] There are a handful of spectacular examples still standing, but many more that have collapsed with the long passing of years. Some we know about because archaeologists have excavated them, some we know of only from literary references, and others once existed but are not known of at all today. In all, throughout the Roman world, we know of 186 certain and 86 probable amphitheaters.[34]

In order to understand the significance of this prevalence, it is necessary to understand that the only known purposes of a Roman amphitheater were to hold the *munera* and *venatio*. Thus, along with the amphitheaters, archaeologists invariably find the gladiatorial schools and animal housing necessary for Roman-style games. So we know that the Roman games were held in every major population center of the empire.[35]

How did these barbarous Roman customs spread to the provinces, many of which were filled with resentment of Roman rule? Numerous factors have to be taken into consideration to explain the phenomenon, among them the following: most peoples in the empire had their own barbarous practices that needed to be modified only slightly to fit the Roman model. The Gauls (in present-day France) and their cousins the Celts (in present-day Britain) had a practice of executing criminals in public. Sometimes they allowed the criminals to fight one another.[36] In imperial times, the *munerae* were extremely popular in Gaul. In Carthage (in North Africa), the custom was to throw criminals to wild animals, which, of course, were in plentiful supply in the

North African hinterland. In the imperial age, the *venationes* were especially popular in North Africa. So regional practices tended to lend themselves to Roman subversion.

A second reason the games spread so quickly and thoroughly throughout the empire was that the elites in the provinces, eager to endear themselves to the Romans, built amphitheaters at their own expense. The emperors, from Augustus on, encouraged the local elites to do this, believing (rightly) that the amphitheaters would make the populace more loyal to Rome.

Thirdly, Roman games spread throughout the provinces because the Romans planted colonies of Roman natives wherever they could. These Roman colonists naturally wanted the same kinds of entertainments they could find in Rome and more or less insisted that amphitheaters be provided for them.

The fourth reason the games spread into major cities like Ephesus, Corinth, and Antioch was that these cities were flooded with Roman administrators, businessmen, and soldiers. Like the colonists, these Romans required Roman ways in the cities in which they lived. In cities like Colonia Agrippina (now Cologne, Germany), the Roman soldiers (and retired soldiers who settled in the communities) were often the primary builders of the local amphitheaters. During the long years of peace, the legions were employed in building projects to keep them busy and fit. They built amphitheaters willingly, knowing that they would bring a bit of Rome to the lonely life on the frontier.

However the amphitheaters came into being, they were heavily used. Prisoners flowed from the provinces to Rome, to meet the greater needs in the capital, but sometimes prisoners flowed from Rome to the provinces.[37] For instance, following the destruction of Jerusalem in A.D. 70, Jewish prisoners were sent to every city so the provinces could share in the joy of the great Roman victory. The chief men of the provincial cities, the aediles and *duumviri*, would host the games and pay all the expenses, just as the emperor did in Rome. There were, as mentioned, limits on the amount a provincial official could spend. These limits were designed to protect the provincial officials from excessive expense, but they also prevented local elites from gaining a reputation for greater generosity than the emperor.

In most parts of the empire, the amphitheaters were in place before the Christians came on the scene, even in the vicinity of Judea.[38] In

Asia Province, a stronghold of early Christianity, amphitheaters and Roman games were a fixture. The first *munerae* were held in Asia during the governorship of Lucullus some seventy years before the birth of Christ.[39] There were gladiator schools in Philadelphia, Smyrna, and Pergamum, but only Pergamum had a true Roman-style amphitheater.[40] This does not mean the other cities did not have Roman games. The Greek cities of Asia, such as Ephesus, Smyrna, and Laodicea, had theaters that were suitable for the *munerae*. They simply took their Greek-style theaters and added higher walls to separate the audience from the performers, so no spectator could be harmed.

Roman games were an empirewide phenomenon by Christian times. As we shall see, it was not uncommon for Christians to be sentenced to death in the amphitheater. But even during the periods in which the Church was free from persecution, the early Christians had major problems with the games.

### Chariot Races

Like the *munerae* and the *venationes*, the chariot races of the Circus Maximus had their origins in simple religious ceremonies, far back in antiquity. In the ancient religious calendar, two festivals, the *Equirria* (February 27) and the *Consualia* (August 21), featured horse races that evolved into chariot races.[41] As with most things Roman, there were Etruscan elements in the origins of the chariot races. King Tarquinius, the last Etruscan king of Rome, was said to have laid out the boundaries of the Circus Maximus and built the first grandstand. Of course, the crude stands of the early racetrack did not compare to the magnificent Circus Maximus of the imperial age.[42]

There were four teams in the chariot races, each with its own color, blue, red, green, or white. Everyone in Rome, seemingly, had allegiance to one of these four colors. People would support their particular color with great enthusiasm, so much so that "passions aroused in favor of one or the other of these colors could divide families and wreck friendships."[43] The closest modern analogy would be the soccer riots in Europe and Latin America.

In any event, the people of Rome loved the chariot races almost as much as they loved the *munerae* and the *venationes*. As with the games, people would rise early to get the best possible seats. The lowest rows, made of stone, would be saved for the emperor and his favorites, the senators, and the vestal virgins. The upper seats, consisting of wooden stands, were for everyone else—first come, first served. No man could be admitted without a toga, the badge of citizenship.

A day of racing would begin with religious ceremonies appropriate to the god or goddess being honored, complete with processions of priests and priestesses, and images of the gods. The races themselves generally lasted from dawn to dusk, with a constant flow of races. There was plenty of excitement, and quite a bit of bloodshed to satisfy a Roman crowd. The goal was, of course, to finish first, not to kill the opponents, but in the course of the races, accidents were common. The charioteers would wrap the reins around their waist to help control their powerful horses. If they were spilled out of the chariot, they would attempt to cut themselves free with knives they kept in their belt. Of course, in the confusion, some drivers were dragged to death, and even if the charioteer managed to cut himself free, he could be trampled by the other teams or be run over by an iron-rimmed wheel.[44] So the violence to which Rome was accustomed was present in the circus as well as in the amphitheater.

Almost every province in the empire had a heritage of chariot racing, so it was common for the major cities to have chariot racing facilities that would be used as local custom required. Emperors did not encourage the building of circuses, as they did amphitheaters, because the chariot races were not used as a means of executing criminals. The racers themselves were usually slaves or men of low birth. However, if a driver could survive and win his races, he could become rich.[45]

The Christians do not seem to have had as many objections to the chariot races as they had to the *munera* and the *venatio*, but they did have some difficulties with the chariot races.

### The Theater

The Romans did not love the theater as they did the games and the chariot races, but they did attend plays, mimes, farces, musical performances, and the like when there was nothing better to do. The theater did not have its origins in Roman culture, but in Greek, and it never really took hold in the Roman world, though in the Greek parts of the empire you would be more likely to find a theater for the staging of plays than an amphitheater for the staging of fights.[46]

The Greeks, of course, had the great classical poets, the tragedians Euripides and Sophocles, and the comic poets like Aristophanes. The tradition of staging plays during the great religious festivals was deeply ingrained in Greek culture. The Romans were slow to borrow this custom. The first Latin play was staged in Rome in 240 B.C. Most of the best Latin plays were written in the 150 years following this date. After this period, the Romans seem to have lost serious interest in the development of new plays, and theaters in areas dominated by Latin culture were primarily devoted to "mimes, pantomimes and knock-about farces".[47] Even in the "Greek" parts of the empire, the theater seems to have gone into something of an eclipse, as the Roman *ludi* (games) became more popular.[48]

Be that as it may, the traditional Greek theater still had great popularity in many parts of the empire, particularly in the East. The Greater and Lesser Games, as well as the Minor Games, all included plays by classical as well as contemporary authors.[49] A typical amphitheater could hold 50,000 spectators, while the typical theater was designed for 20,000 spectators. This might lead one to assume that the games were more important than the theater, but one should bear in mind that there were far more theatrical shows than *ludi*. As a general conclusion, one could say that people looked forward to the *ludi* and enjoyed them more, but the theater had a great deal of cultural influence, and many people attended the theater on a regular basis.

### The Baths

One of the greatest cultural institutions of the Greco-Roman world was the public bath. Like most Roman customs, this one started out small and grew into a great institution. In the second century B.C., bathhouses were one-room structures used by men only. The water was not heated, so few people used them in the winter months. By the second century A.D., however, baths were cultural institutions, and every reputable city in the empire had at least one, built by the leading citizens.

A Roman *therma* at its best was a multipurpose building, with several different bathing chambers for different water temperatures, places for wrestling, playing ball games, running, walking, reading, and just plain socializing with one's friends. As with other aspects of Roman culture, the baths became more and more impressive as time went by. The Baths of Caracalla (211–217), for instance, covered 270,000 square feet and could accommodate about 1,500 bathers. An impressive building, but the Baths of Diocletian (284–305) were much larger and could accommodate 3,000 bathers at a time.[50]

So what was the experience of going to the *thermae* like in the era of the early Christians? The charge was one *quadrans*,[51] if anything. Local patrons, eager to develop a reputation for largesse, might agree to cover the expenses of a bath for an entire year. So everyone could afford to go to the baths, and everyone did. The wealthy would bring slaves along to carry their towels, rub in oil, and scrape sweat and dirt off with a *stirgil*, an odd object with a handle and a curved blade. Of course, if for whatever reason you did not have your own slave handy, you could hire a bath attendant to do virtually anything you might need.

Bathing was in the nude, and the general custom throughout the imperial age was for men and women to bathe together. There were fines for public immorality, but the general tone of the baths was somewhat lewd. Jews and Christians found this offensive and did not attend the public baths. Some baths were reserved for single-sex bathing or had times set aside for single-sex bathing, and, as we shall see, there is some evidence that Christians would use these baths on occasion.[52]

Most bathhouses had separate rooms with four different water temperatures. The *frigidarium* had cold water, and the air was not warmed. The *tepidarium* had tepid water and slightly warmed air. The *calidarium* was a room with hotter water and quite warm air. An even hotter room, the *laconicum*, was available, but was used mainly by the sick or invalids.[53] The water and air of the various chambers would be heated by fires stoked by slaves. The hot air would be forced through ingenious ducts in the walls and floors of the building.

For their part the bathers would move from room to room as the mood struck them, first, perhaps, enjoying a good sweat in the *calidarium*, then taking an icy plunge in the *frigidarium*, only to end up relaxing in the *tepidarium*. If you were in the mood, you could get a massage, or have your hair plucked, or have any number of services performed. Before or after your bath, you could wrestle a friend, or join a ball game, or race, or enjoy reading or a conversation in a spacious garden. The baths were not intended to be places of prostitution, and occasionally emperors or other officials would issue decrees forbidding lewdness. But the fact that decrees were issued indicates that there were problems in this regard.

The *therma* was like a health spa, a gym, a library, and a coffeehouse all at once. It is difficult to overestimate their popularity, or their necessity, in a society where most houses were without indoor plumbing, and where slavery gave most people a large amount of free time to fill.

## Conclusion

Roman forms of entertainment tended to be rawer than the entertainments we favor today, but if you think about it, essentially, the Romans liked the same things we like today. The baths were similar to the health clubs of today. The chariot races had all the excitement of NASCAR or Formula One racing. The gladiatorial contests and the wild animal hunts were not much bloodier than the movies of today. The main difference, of course, was that the Roman games were *real*. The blood was real, and real men really died in the sand right before the people's eyes. It's difficult to say what effect all this real bloodshed had on the people's psyche. One thing is clear, however, from the literature of the period. The people of the ancient world were much more accustomed to bloodshed and death than we are today.

## CHAPTER 7

# Evaluating the Roman Empire

Understanding the rise of Christianity in the Roman world is difficult. Roman culture is a large house, with many hidden rooms and
unexpected corridors, some blind and some that lead into spacious
chambers of understanding. The only way to know which corridors
lead nowhere and which will lead us someplace worth going is to
explore all the corridors. This might seem like a tedious way to spend
a couple of hours, so we'll take a few shortcuts. We already have the
basic data necessary to understand the unique strengths and weaknesses of Roman culture; it only remains to apply that data to the
question at hand. And when we have finished this chapter, hopefully
we will be ready to begin to understand how Christianity succeeded
in the Roman world.

One of the most commonly asked questions of history is the question of why the Roman Empire fell. Various answers have been proposed for this question, but to me the most likely answer seems to be
that the Roman Empire fell because nothing in this world lasts forever. There is, however, another possible answer. In a very real sense,
one might say that the Roman Empire never fell, and exists yet to this
day. Of course, Rome exists today mostly in the institutions that lie
beneath the surface of our culture, in our laws, religion, and other
institutions. One must also note that the Roman institutions we have
received were Christianized before we received them. Part of the story
of the second half of this book has to do with how those institutions
were Christianized, but let us not get ahead of ourselves.

We will explore this question further in the last chapter of this book,
but to me a much more interesting question, and one closer to the
heart of this book, has to do with why the Roman Empire came into
existence, not why it finally fell. In answering this question we might

gain insights into why Christianity, against all odds, finally gained cultural ascendancy in the Roman world.

## How the Romans Came to Dominate the Ancient World

Historical events are never inevitable. They only seem to be so after the fact. Thus, it was never inevitable that the Romans would rule a territory from Britain to Iraq. In fact, this outcome would have to be judged to be highly unlikely. Historically, the great empires before Rome centered in Mesopotamia or in the Nile valley. In these empires, the large grain supplies afforded by the river valleys freed a large portion of the population to do other things, like make weapons or join the army.

The Greeks changed this dynamic. A small city on the edge of the world, Athens, defeated the mighty Persian Empire in the battles of Marathon (490 B.C.) and Salamis (480 B.C.). Nor were these victories flukes, because for the thirty years after Salamis the intrepid Athenians humiliated the Persians in a series of naval battles and liberated the Greek cities of Asia Minor that had hitherto been under Persian control. Alexander the Great completed the humiliation of the Persians by conquering their entire empire. His empire fell apart, and the Romans eventually entered the vacuum this collapse left. Due to an accident of geography and history, the Romans were uniquely situated to unite the eastern and western Mediterranean, and since it was to their advantage, they did so.

But what were the decisive factors that allowed the Romans to take advantage of their circumstances? Some of the factors that led to Rome's dominance were accidents of history, like the disunity and disillusionment of the people of the eastern Mediterranean. There were other factors, intrinsic to Roman culture, and these are the ones we are most interested in.

*Technological Advantages.* First, the most obvious advantage the Romans had over other peoples was their technological superiority. We can still see, scattered throughout the territories they once ruled, complete, fully functioning aqueducts, bridges, defensive walls, roads, and public buildings. These works reveal that the Romans had developed building techniques that worked far better than those of any other culture. Many of these works were made possible by the discovery or invention and perfection of a product we take for granted, but which for the Romans was a great innovation.[1] The perfection of concrete allowed the Romans to build strong defensive walls and forts, which in turn allowed them to defend the frontier with fewer soldiers. The other technological advantages, such as the aqueducts, allowed Roman cities to grow larger than had previously been possible.

*Military Advantages.* The Romans developed a better way to make war than their predecessors. The legionary tactics were flexible and allowed the same basic military unit to respond to a wide variety of enemy tactics. The Roman system placed a greater reliance on the fighting skill, intelligence, and initiative of individual soldiers, but, fortunately, they had a large pool of people from which to find suitable recruits. This leads into the next, and most surprising, advantage the Romans possessed.

*Human Advantages.* The average person in the Roman Empire, provided he was not a slave, a woman, or a child, possessed a great deal of autonomy in his daily life. Granted, he did not have freedom of religion, in the sense that he could not publicly practice Christianity, and he was not free in the arena of national politics, but he was surprisingly free in his personal economic decisions. He could start a new business, invent a new product and market it, or discover a new way of doing things, all without too many restrictions. Even slaves were sometimes encouraged to use their personal initiative, and, as we saw in Chapter 3, some slaves could hope to be rewarded by being given their freedom. So people became accustomed to thinking for themselves in many areas of life. This insured that the empire always had a pool of intelligent, competent people to call upon in the military and in civic government.

*Legal Advantages.* The Roman legal system was more just than anything that had preceded it. Granted, there were many instances of corruption, and many unjust laws. But on the whole, the people of the provinces found that they liked Roman rule, and that is why, even though there were some rebellions, most people were content to be ruled by Rome.

### Strengths of the "Roman Way"

We have now reached the point where we can evaluate the relative strengths and weaknesses of the Roman system. In exploring these strengths and weaknesses, we will encounter apparent contradictions. For instance, Roman efficiency meant that a relatively small number of people could administer a huge empire, but on a different level the focus on efficiency left many feeling that their individual lives had no meaning. There is no way to reconcile these contradictions. They are simply a part of the human condition. To summarize, then, here are the strengths of what might be referred to as the "Roman Way":

1. The Romans provided peace and material prosperity to every region they ruled.

2. The Romans encouraged individual initiative in the realm of economic and local political activity.

3. The Roman system of roads, coupled with Roman military efficiency, insured that travel was relatively safe and easy.

4. Local communities were free to decide their own affairs, unless there was a compelling national interest at stake.

5. Roman religion emphasized the mutuality of the relationship between people and the gods.

6. The Romans saw to the welfare of the poor by providing free grain and entertainment.

### Weaknesses of the "Roman Way"

The Roman cultural system also had many weaknesses. Some of them correspond to and somewhat diminish some of the positive achievements of the Romans.

1. Though the Romans brought material prosperity to the provinces they conquered, they did it only through warfare and the forced enslavement of many.

2. Free grain and entertainment masked the contempt that the upper class held for the lower class throughout the empire. Because the poor were treated like animals, they often behaved in that way, and riots were frequent.

3. The system of slavery denied personal freedom to almost half the population of the empire.

4. Peace was maintained only by a constant, endlessly expensive military presence on the frontiers.

5. The religious systems of the empire did not do a good job of providing people with ultimate meaning or moral instruction.

6. Roman forms of entertainment were debasing for both the participants and the spectators.

### Setting the Stage for a Christian Empire

We all know the end of this story. Christianity became the dominant religion of the Roman Empire. The Church of the Roman Empire exists today as the Roman Catholic Church in the West and the Orthodox Churches in the East.[2] The specific tactics the early Christians used, under the guidance of the Holy Spirit, will be the focus of the rest of this book, but there are some generalizations that can be made first, to lay the foundation for our study.

Modern liturgists and some theologians speak of a process they refer to as "inculturation". There is nothing new about inculturation, though the word itself is a neologism. Inculturation simply refers to the process by which the gospel is incarnated, or enfleshed, in a particular culture. The process is tortuous, for it requires the Christian community, in communion with the bishops and Pope, to discern which aspects of a particular culture are negative and must be resisted, which aspects are neutral and can be safely tolerated, and which aspects are in fact positive and can be used to help spread the gospel. The Church enters into this discernment process whenever a new culture is evangelized. The process is messy, full of violent disagreements, misunderstandings, and mistakes. It is especially difficult when the discernment process is undertaken in a culture that is persecuting the Church.

Nevertheless, the early Christians undertook this arduous process, in the midst of great difficulty. They were, as we shall see, quite fair with the Roman government and the need for military defense. They took Roman festivals and Christianized them.[3] They stood fast against practices, like the cult of the emperor and the *munerae*, that could not be tolerated by Christians under any circumstances. And when the dust cleared, emperor worship and the gladiatorial contests were finished. Even practices the Church did not outright condemn, such as slavery, slowly faded away under the relentless logic of Christ's love.

# PART 2

# CHRISTIANS AS SALT AND LIGHT IN THE ROMAN WORLD

For the Christians are distinguished from other men neither by country, nor language, nor the customs which they observe. For they neither inhabit cities of their own, nor employ a peculiar form of speech, nor lead a life which is marked out by any singularity. The course of conduct which they follow has not been devised by any speculation or deliberation of inquisitive men; nor do they, like some, proclaim themselves the advocates of any merely human doctrines. But, inhabiting Greek as well as barbarian cities, according as the lot of each of them has determined, and following the customs of the natives in respect to clothing, food, and the rest of their ordinary conduct, they display to us their wonderful and confessedly striking method of life. They dwell in their own countries, but simply as sojourners. As citizens, they share in all things with others, and yet endure all things as if foreigners. Every foreign land is to them as their native country, and every land of their birth as a land of strangers. They marry, as do all others; they beget children; but they do not destroy their offspring. They have a common table, but not a common bed. They are in the flesh, but they do not live after the flesh. They pass their days on earth, but they are citizens of heaven. They obey the prescribed laws, and at the same time surpass the laws by their lives. They love all men, and are persecuted by all. They are unknown and condemned; they are put to death, and restored to life. They are poor, yet make many rich; they are in lack of all things, and yet abound in all; they are dishonoured, and yet in their very dishonour are glorified. They are evil spoken of, and yet are justified; they are reviled, and bless; they are insulted, and repay the insult with honour; they do good, yet are punished as evil-doers. When punished, they rejoice as if quickened into life; they are assailed by the Jews as foreigners, and are persecuted by the Greeks; yet those who hate them are unable to assign any reason for their hatred.

—Mathetes, *Epistle to Diognetus*, 5.1–6

# Baptism by Water, Spirit, Blood, and Fire: Becoming a Christian in the Early Church

If you lived in any one of the major cities of the Roman Empire, from the period of A.D. 100 to 300, chances are there were Christians in your city, perhaps even in your neighborhood. You might not have even been aware of their presence.[1] If you knew anything, it most likely would be the scurrilous rumors about them: that they engaged in cannibalism and sexual immorality at their secret meetings.[2] But, if you were fortunate (or, in Christian terms, if you were touched by grace), you might get to know a Christian under more favorable circumstances. Under these circumstances, you might explore the possibility of becoming a Christian yourself. Eventually, you might undergo the rigorous Christian Rite of Initiation and become a new person.

Sociologist Rodney Stark has estimated that Christianity grew at a rate of 40 percent per decade until around the year 350.[3] Professor Stark thinks other factors, such as a higher birth rate and better care of the sick and poor, account for a part of Christianity's growth, but it is undeniable that for the first 300 years of Christian history, the primary means of growth was through adult conversion. In this chapter, we will explore the process of conversion the early Church employed, starting with the initial evangelization and conversion and moving through the catechumenate, baptism, and postbaptismal formation.

### Why Did People Become Christian?

Conversion involves a twofold action: on the one hand there must be a pool of people willing to proclaim the message, and on the other hand there must be at least a segment of the population willing to hear and accept the message. So in this section we must consider two questions: (1) What methods did the early Christians use to reach out to convince the people of the empire? (2) Why did some people become Christian in spite of widespread ridicule and the very real potential of physical danger?

Readers of the New Testament will be familiar with the Great Commission, the last words of Jesus before his Ascension: "All authority in heaven and on earth has been given to me. Go therefore and make disciples of all nations, baptizing them in the name of the Father and of the Son and of the Holy Spirit, teaching them to observe all that I have commanded you; and lo, I am with you always, to the close of the age." [4] The missionary tactics of the New Testament Church are also familiar. In the Acts of the Apostles and in the Epistles of Paul we gain a picture of the approach the very first Christians took. Paul, for instance, would visit a city and ask to speak in the synagogues. He would accept whatever converts he could make in the synagogue (though more often than not he would arouse the fury of the synagogue authorities) and then begin preaching to the Gentiles. The ministry of the apostles, as presented in the New Testament, was conducted in public. [5]

However, after A.D. 64, [6] it was no longer possible for Christians to preach the gospel publicly. Therefore, the postapostolic Church had to devise other means of fulfilling Christ's command, and they had to do so in a way that would not recklessly endanger the entire Church. We do not know a great deal about the methods they employed, but there are a few passages in the writings of the early Christians that provide knowledge of some specifics of evangelization and conversion. By perusing the writings of this period, it is possible to identify four broad categories of Christian evangelizers: the apologists, the "street evangelizers", the ordinary Christians, and the martyrs. In their own way, each of these groups played a role in presenting the message of Christ to the people of the empire.

*Apologists.* The apologists were authors and philosophers, many with a good pagan education before they became Christians. Upon conversion, they used their gifts to attempt to bring other philosophers into the fold and to convince the emperors to allow Christians to practice their faith in peace. The apologists were only partially successful in their efforts. For instance, Athenagorus' *Supplication for the Christians,*

The main gates of Hierapolis, a center of early Christianity in Asia.

An altar and fish carved on a stone outside the theater of Hierapolis.

Statue of an upper-class Roman woman from the first century A.D., found in the Archaeological Museum of Ephesus.

The massive columns of the temple of Aphrodite in Sardis. The small building on the left side is a fourth-century Christian church.

Scenes of everyday life under the *paterfamilias* depicted on a sarcophagus.

The gymnasium at Sardis. This gymnasium included a library, swimming pool, and other athletic facilities.

The site of the swimming pool inside the gymnasium of Sardis.

A scene from daily life in Roman times, showing a father interacting with three children.

The *via tecta* leading to the *Asclepion* of Pergamum.

The symbol of Asclepios, carved onto a column found in the *Asclepion* of Pergamum.

The stadium of Aphrodisias.

A carving depicting the armor of gladiators, found outside the theater of Aphrodisias.

Carving of a gladiator in action, found outside the theater of Ephesus, grim testimony to what went on inside.

The imperial box of the theater at Hierapolis.

The corridor behind the *skene* of the theater of Hierapolis.

A small shop along the main street in ancient Sardis. The niche in the right corner was for cooking. Sometime during the fourth century, probably, the owner carved crosses into the stone facing.

The sarcophagus of Pereitas Kallimedes and his wife, Tatia.

The library of Celsus, built early in the second century A.D. The structure to the right is a threefold gate leading into the commercial agora.

The agora of Aphrodisias, complete with a swimming pool running down its center. Behind the pool, you can see the columns that would have supported the *stoa* (porch).

The temple of Hadrian in Ephesus.

The *calidarium* of the baths of Ephesus. Note the half-exposed clay pipes running along the ground.

The public toilets of Ephesus.

A geometric design on the wall of the synagogue of Sardis.

A water basin in the vestibule of the synagogue of Sardis.

The *bema* of the synagogue of Sardis. The *bema* was used as a flat surface on which to lay the scrolls of the Torah for reading during services. Note the circular seating arrangement behind the altar, where the presbyters would sit during services.

The theater of Ephesus, where an angry mob threatened Saint Paul. (See Acts 19:22ff.)

A statue of the popular goddess Artemis of Ephesus, from the archaeological museum of Ephesus. (See Acts 19:22ff.)

which he addressed to Marcus Aurelius and his son Commodus (of *Gladiator* fame), had no effect on the policies of these emperors. Likewise, it would seem that the apologists had little success in converting philosophers, whether Jewish or pagan.[7]

The apologists' successes were relatively few, but when they did succeed, their converts made huge contributions to the Church, because they were generally well-educated, gifted members of society. Irenaeus of Lyons and Tatian, who reconciled the four Gospel accounts in a book called the *Diatessaron*, were both disciples of Justin Martyr. In this way, the apologists had a tremendous influence on the early Church.

Most apologists had other functions in the Church. Some operated Christian schools in the city they lived in. Justin Martyr, for instance, taught out of rooms he rented over a Roman bath. Others, like Melito of Sardis, were bishops. Thus, their apologetic work was often a "sidebar", to which we give undue attention because the writings have been preserved, while their oral teaching and quiet work of one-on-one persuasion goes unnoticed.

*"Street Evangelizers".* For obvious reasons, most Christians did not make their Christianity public knowledge. The pagan writer Caecilius accused the Christians of being "silent in the open", with the implication that this silence alone indicated they were up to something shameful.[8] But from Origen we learn that even in the midst of constant danger there were certain Christians who made it "their business to itinerate not only through cities, but even through villages and country houses, that they might make converts to God".[9] We know very little about the methods of these evangelists. In the passage cited above, Origen states that the evangelists would not accept monetary recompense for their work, above their basic needs.

There is reason to believe that the evangelists did not quote Scripture extensively to potential converts, unless they were conversing with Jews. The average pagan knew nothing of the Hebrew Scriptures and would not have considered them authentic anyway. The writings of the New Testament were known to the various Christian communities, but non-Christians would not have been impressed by them, until they had reason to believe that there was something special about Christ. Tertullian summarized the matter thus: "No one turns to our literature who is not already Christian."[10]

If the early Christians did not use Scripture to explain their teachings to potential converts, what did they do? It would seem that the evangelists went to great pains to simplify their message and to present it in an artless manner. Tatian, whom we met earlier in this chapter, wrote, "I was led to put faith in these by the unpretending cast of the language, the inartificial character of the writers, the foreknowledge displayed of future events, the excellent quality of the precepts, and the declaration of the government of the universe as centered in one Being." [11] So the evangelists focused on a simple, clear explanation of the basics of the Christian faith.

There is some thought that the evangelistic process was based on some early versions of the Creed. We know that all communities had creeds; they varied slightly in detail but covered the same ground. As we shall see, a new convert had to memorize the local version of the Creed before his baptism. It might be that the evangelists of this period proclaimed some version of the Creed in their discussions with pagans. But this is a detail about the early Christians that we do not know very much about. What we do know is enough to intrigue, because we have testimony to the fact that the "street evangelists" were effective in their work.

*Ordinary Christians.* Probably the most effective means of evangelization (though we will probably never know for sure) was the quiet work ordinary Christians did in their daily lives. Ordinary Christians evangelized in two ways: (1) quiet, simple conversations with pagan friends, co-workers, and family members and (2) the truly astonishing level of their charity work. The two methods worked in tandem with one another; kindness to a co-worker or neighbor might lead to discussions about religion.

The Christians made charity a central part of their way of life. Believers were constantly urged to charity by the leaders of the community.[12] Alms were collected at every liturgical assembly, but we also read about something called the "oblation". In Hippolytus' *Apostolic Tradition* we read about gifts of oil, milk, and olives, which would be brought forward by those who had no money at the same time the bread and the wine were brought forward.[13] The priest was instructed to pray over these gifts (though not using the same words he would use for the bread and the wine, of course). These gifts would be used to succor the poor and needy: "They who are well to do, and willing, give what each thinks fit; and what is collected is deposited with the president, who succors the orphans and widows and those who, through sickness or any other cause, are in want, and those who are in bonds and the strangers sojourning among us, and in a word takes care of all who are in need." [14]

Most local Christian communities had institutional arrangements for the care of widows, orphans, the sick, and those who were needy within the community. But the early Christians did not engage in only institutional charity. Individual Christians, on their own initiative, would visit prisons and hospitals to provide whatever emotional or physical comfort was needed. Other Christians would frequent the places where the pagans would expose unwanted children to the elements. They would take these poor children home and raise them as their own. All these actions were a part of the daily lives of the early Christians. We will not dwell on them at greater length here, because each of these aspects of Christian life will receive its own chapter later in this book. For now it is enough to understand that these charitable actions were foreign to the spirit of the age[15] and that they had a tremendous impact on the recipients.

People who had benefitted from Christian charity might ask more about the faith that motivated the charitable act. A Christian had to use considerable circumspection in deciding how much to open up to a nonbeliever, no matter how close the relationship might seem; we know of cases where husbands turned in their wives, slaves turned in their masters, and soldiers turned in their officers. So the moment when a Christian decided to invite a nonbeliever to the house of the catechist was a moment of deep significance.

*Martyrs.* The martyrs played a powerful role in the conversion of many. Saint Basil the Great wrote in hindsight, "the blood of the martyrs, watering the Churches, nourished many more champions of true religion." [16] The martyrs proved that there must be more to Christianity than the average person was hearing about. Justin Martyr, who, as his name implies, was himself a martyr, wrote, "For I myself, too, when I was delighting in the doctrines of Plato, and heard the Christians slandered, and saw them fearless of death, and of all other things which are counted fearful, perceived that it was impossible that they could be living in wickedness and pleasure." [17] The knowledge that the Christians were serious people who were being wickedly oppressed by the government caused many people, who were already having grave doubts about the direction their culture was taking, to explore Christianity further.

But more than that, the patient endurance of the martyrs caused many conversions on the spot, particularly among soldiers who were given the task of carrying out the executions. Soldiers always revere bravery above all other traits, and they know how rare genuine bravery really is. They were quick to respond to the bravery of the martyrs. Consider the case of Saint Victor. In the year 285, during one of Emperor Maximian's visits to Marseilles, a Christian soldier named Victor was brought to his attention for his active support and aid to the Christians of the region. Maximian summoned him to appear. The young man was of good background, of strong and intelligent character, the sort that the Roman world admired. Maximian attempted to persuade him to apostatize, but Victor was defiant. First, he suffered only degradation from his military position and public exposition. But he allowed himself to be reviled by the populace without flinching. Then he was imprisoned and tortured. Victor not only remained true to his faith in Christ but managed to convert his three guards. [18]

In the morning, the new Christians, Longinus, Alexander, and Felician, boldly declared their new faith and were beheaded. Victor was eventually beheaded himself, but his witness (for that is what the Greek word *martyria* means) resulted in three conversions that we know of. How many are we not aware of? And for how many converts were Longinus, Alexander, and Felician responsible?

A prominent modern Church historian lists six factors that made Christianity attractive to people: (1) charity offered without expectation of return or profit, (2) fellowship offered to all social levels, (3) Christian steadfastness in the face of persecution, (4) the high moral standards of the Christians, (5) Christians' assurance of victory over demons (this one was much more important than we might think), and (6) the sacraments, which conveyed the promise of salvation. [19] Professor Hinson's categories are comprehensive, and some are even self-explanatory, but there are aspects of conversions in the early Church that need to be explored on a deeper level. In order to achieve the depth the subject requires, we will take a look at the writings of two early Christians who wrote extensively about their own conversion, Justin Martyr and Cyprian of Carthage.

Justin Martyr gave information about his conversion in two passages in his writings. In the first eight chapters of his *Dialogue with Trypho*, he wrote at great length about his exploration of various philosophical systems, first Stoicism, then Pythagoreanism, then Platonism. A seemingly chance encounter with an old man leads to a lengthy conversation in which the weaknesses of the various philosophical schools are laid bare. The old man ends the discussion by suggesting that the Old Testament prophets were superior to the philosophers and that they had pointed to Christ. Justin's response to all this is astonishing:

> Straightway a flame was kindled in my soul; and a love of the prophets, and of those men who are friends of Christ, possessed me; and whilst revolving his words in my mind, I found this philosophy alone to be safe and profitable. Thus, and for this reason, I am a philosopher. Moreover, I would wish that all, making a resolution similar to my own, do not keep themselves away from the words of the Savior. For they possess a terrible power in themselves, and are sufficient to inspire those who turn aside from the path of rectitude with awe; while the sweetest rest is afforded those who make a diligent practice of them. If, then, you have any concern for yourself, and if you are eagerly looking for salvation, and if you believe in God, you may—since you are not indifferent to the matter—become acquainted with the Christ of God, and after being initiated, live a happy life.[20]

On the surface, Justin's conversion seems to be a straightforward intellectual conversion. But there is more to Justin's conversion than meets the eye. As previously mentioned, Justin wrote, "For I myself, too, when I was delighting in the doctrines of Plato, and heard the Christians slandered, and saw them fearless of death, and of all other things which are counted fearful, perceived that it was impossible that they could be living in wickedness and pleasure. For what sensual or intemperate man, or who that counts it good to feast on human flesh, could welcome death that he might be deprived of his enjoyments ... ?"[21]

Some scholars have seen a contradiction between these two conversion accounts and have suggested that one or the other must be inauthentic. We need not linger long over these objections. It is not uncommon for people to have more than one motivation for their behavior, particularly when the behavior in question is conversion to a banned religion. In fact, it would be surprising if a person had only one reason for doing such a dangerous thing. But, as Oskar Skarsaune has shown, the scholars who see a contradiction between Justin's two conversion accounts have fundamentally misunderstood Justin's quest.[22]

Justin did not examine philosophies simply for the intellectual satisfaction of finding the perfect one. His quest was more personal. He was looking for a philosophy that would lead to a satisfying way of life. He found some of the precepts of Stoicism, Platonism, and Pythagoreanism admirable, but until he saw the Christian martyr die, he had never met a person who could actually live according to the teachings of his philosophy. People turned to philosophy in Justin's day as a corrective to the excesses of Roman society. People felt trapped by compulsions they felt they had no control over. As the historian Livy put it, "We can endure neither our vices nor the remedies needed to cure them."[23] The widespread sexual immorality, the violent forms of entertainment, and other aspects of Roman culture were all highly addictive, to put it in modern terms. People who suffered under these compulsions believed they were afflicted by demons. Christ presented the only sure way to defeat the addictions that plagued people, and that is why Justin's quest, which seems at first glance to be purely intellectual, came to an end when he saw a martyr steadfastly renouncing all the goods of this world.

In the writings of Cyprian of Carthage, we see this theme made more explicit. Cyprian was born into one of the most preeminent families of North Africa. He himself seems to have held important offices and lived an immensely rich lifestyle. Cyprian's letter *To Donatus* makes Cyprian's understanding of his state before conversion crystal clear. Cyprian wrote this letter to a young man who was inquiring after baptism, but was wavering. Instead of preaching to Donatus, Cyprian chose to bare his own soul, and this letter of Cyprian is one of the most moving conversion stories ever written, with the exception of Augustine's *Confessions*. In chapter 3 of the letter, we learn about Cyprian's personal state before his conversion:

> When does he learn thrift who has been used to liberal banquets and sumptuous feasts? And he who has been glittering in gold and purple,

and has been celebrated for his costly attire, when does he reduce himself to ordinary and simple clothing?

One who has felt the charm of the *fasces* and of civic honors shrinks from becoming a mere private and inglorious citizen. The man who is attended by crowds of clients, and dignified by the numerous association of an officious train, regards it as a punishment when he is alone. It is inevitable, as it ever has been, that the love of wine should entice, pride inflate, anger inflame, covetousness disquiet, cruelty stimulate, ambition delight, lust hasten to ruin, with allurements that will not let go their hold.

I was held in bonds by the innumerable errors of my previous life, from which I did not believe that I could by possibility be delivered, so I was disposed to acquiesce in my clinging vices; and because I despaired of better things, I used to indulge my sins as if they were actually parts of me, and indigenous to me.[24]

Cyprian went on to explain that his conversion to Christianity made it possible for him to overcome his unsatisfying former way of life. Eventually, Cyprian sold all his properties and gave the proceeds to the poor.[25] Cyprian viewed his conversion as a means to escape from a prison: "What before had seemed difficult began to suggest a means of accomplishment, what had been thought impossible, to be capable of being achieved."[26]

The early Christians were completely earnest when they converted. They knew what form of death they were courting, and they certainly knew that at the very least they would be subjected to considerable ridicule from their old friends and associates. And yet they continued to present themselves for baptism. Their motives were powerful. When a person made the fateful step of approaching his Christian friend and saying "I want to be like you", he was saying, in effect, "I know my way of life is bankrupt and I cannot continue to live this way anymore. I need Christ, the Church, and the sacraments to become the person I want to be."

## The Way of the Catechumens

After months, perhaps years, of discernment, a potential convert might go to the Christian or Christians he knew and express a desire to know more about Christianity, with an eye toward conversion. At this point, the contact person would face a dilemma. The Romans were known to try to plant agents among the Christians. They had little interest in rank-and-file members of the Church. They wanted to arrest bishops, priests, deacons, and catechists, either to force these influential Christians to recant or to make an example of them. So the ordinary Christians, whether they were "street evangelists" or simply people who had a gift for interesting their friends in Christianity, had to develop sound judgment. They had to ask themselves, "How well do I know this person? Is he sincere? Will he make a good convert? Could he be a government agent?" If the answers to these questions were satisfactory, the contact person would become the candidate's sponsor and would take him to see the catechist.[27]

We have already met some of the catechists. Providentially, when they were not teaching they were writing about the faith, and sometimes they explained the process by which one became a Christian, so we know quite a bit about this process. Justin Martyr was a catechist in Rome around the middle of the second century, and Origen was the head of the catechetical school in Alexandria at the beginning of the third century. Tertullian may have filled this role as well. Most catechists are unknown to us today, but their writings live on. The *Didache* gives us a great deal of priceless information about the baptismal teachings and practices of the Church in Syria at the turn of the first century. Over a hundred years later, the *Didascalia Apostolorum* (Teachings of the Apostles) also gives us a snapshot of Syrian Church practice.

Baptismal practice varied slightly from place to place, and there was also an evolution over time, particularly in the methods of preparation. In the New Testament, for instance, an expression of faith and a willingness to be baptized were enough, in the cases of which we are aware.[28] But again, the beginning of systematic Roman persecution in A.D. 64 changed everything. Evangelists had to be more cautious, and they had to protect the catechists and bishops from Roman agents. So an elaborate system evolved. When the sponsor made an initial determination regarding the sincerity and worthiness of a potential convert, he would take the candidate to see the catechist, probably at the catechist's home.[29]

The catechist would not welcome the candidate with open arms, but would subject the person to a series of questions. Here is how Hippolytus, in the *Apostolic Tradition*, explains the process:

New converts to the faith, who are to be admitted as hearers of the word, shall first be brought to the teachers before the people assemble. And they shall be examined as to their reason for embracing the faith, and they who bring them shall testify that they are competent to hear the word. Inquiry shall then be made as to the nature of their life; whether a man has a wife or is a slave. If he is the slave of a believer and he has his master's permission, then let him be received; but if his master does not give him a good character, let him be rejected. If his master is a heathen, let the slave be taught to please his master, that the word be not blasphemed.[30]

The *Apostolic Tradition* goes on to provide a lengthy list of occupations a candidate would have to leave before he could be formally enrolled in the catechumenate: pimps, prostitutes (male and female), teachers (unless they had no other way to make a living), actors, charioteers, gladiators, *lanistae* (the men who arranged the shows), pagan priests, enchanters, astrologers, interpreters of dreams, and military governors had to change their professions or cease their behavior before they could be admitted. Soldiers could be admitted, if they would agree to refuse to execute anyone or take the military oath. However, if a candidate expressed the desire to become a soldier, he would be rejected, for he had "despised God".[31] Magicians could not even be considered for the catechumenate. Special allowances were made for the problem of concubinage. If a woman had been a slave concubine, but faithful to one man, she could be admitted. If a man who kept a concubine wished to be baptized, first he had legally to marry his concubine or permanently separate from her.

Once a candidate had passed this first test, he was formally enrolled in the catechumenate.[32] In Rome, this period normally lasted three years, with allowances made for strongly motivated candidates.[33] The catechumens were broken into two groups, normally referred to as the "hearers" and the "kneelers".[34] "Hearers" were those in the early stages of the catechumenate. "Kneelers" were those who were closer to baptism and were undergoing an intense period of prayer, fasting, and advanced study.

Catechumens were not allowed to attend eucharistic services in orthodox communities. Tertullian wrote in complaint against the heretical sects: "It is doubtful who is a catechumen, and who a believer, they have all access alike, they hear alike, they pray alike—even heathens, if any such happen to come among them."[35]

What were the catechumens taught? We can reconstruct the emphases of various catechists and bishops from their writings. In the *Didache* we find that the late first-century community of Antioch was heavily interested in the moral precepts of Christianity. The "two ways" (the way of life and the way of death) were emphasized. No specific period of preparation is mentioned, only that candidates should be baptized "having first said all these things" (concerning the "two ways").[36] In mid-second-century Rome, Justin Martyr emphasized practical teaching on the Christian life as well as doctrine. A few years later, in Lyons, Irenaeus was emphasizing doctrinal teachings, to combat Gnosticism, which seems to have been more of a problem in his community than others. In mid-third-century Carthage, Cyprian was concerned with the scriptural foundation of doctrine and morality. At about the same time, in Alexandria, Origen developed a comprehensive biblical catechesis. Origen devised a scheme in which he could work through all the major passages of the Bible in a three-year period.[37]

You can see that there was a certain variation in practices from community to community. There are certain generalizations that can be made, however. According to Alan Kreider, the baptismal catechesis of the early Church fits into four categories: (1) the broad sweep of what we now call "salvation history", (2) certain powerful stories from Scripture, such as the story of the three young men in the fiery furnace (Daniel 3, particularly appropriate for a community enduring persecution), (3) the moral teachings of Jesus Christ, and (4) practical teachings on how to live a good Christian life.[38]

A particularly rich source on catechesis is Cyprian's *Letter to Quirinus*.[39] This letter consists of three parts, one on salvation history (with an emphasis on scriptural references), one on Christology, and one containing 120 precepts, the vast majority of which were moral. This three-part letter was intended to summarize the entirety of Cyprian's catechesis and to make the work of his catechists easier.

When the catechist made the judgment that the candidates were ready to move to the next stage, another examination was made of their lives, to see "whether they have lived soberly".[40] At this time, sponsors and others who knew the candidates could speak on their behalf. Some of the more rigorous writers made it clear that by no means should everyone be baptized: "They whose office it is, know that baptism is not rashly to be administered."[41] So the candidates were rigorously evaluated, and if they passed scrutiny they would become "kneelers". At this point, asceticism was the order of the day. Candidates were encouraged to engage in daily fasting and prayer, with the catechists fasting and praying alongside them.[42] In some communities, the candidates would receive the Rite of Exorcism daily, with the bishop himself administering the last exorcism.[43]

Sometime in the third century, the season of Lent began to be observed in some communities.[44] Since Easter or sometimes Pentecost was the normal time for baptism, it was natural that the period of the "kneelers" came to be associated with Lent. So the fasting, prayer, almsgiving, and confession of the catechumens were united with the practice of the whole Church. Candidates were also encouraged to confess their sins.[45] At this time, confession was public, before the whole community, so this might have been the most difficult thing the catechumens had to do.

A final matter had to be disposed of before baptism. The catechists taught the catechumens the Creed.[46] At some point during the baptismal rite, the catechumens had to be able to recite the Creed. In later times, this came to be known as the *traditio symboli* (handing over of the Creed) and the *reditio* (giving back). Some communities asked the candidates questions based on the Creed, which had to be answered in the affirmative.

After this rigorous preparation, the catechumens must have experienced considerable relief with the approach of baptism. The truth is, the system was set up to induce this feeling, because the primary theological meaning of baptism was the participation in the death and Resurrection of Christ.

### The Rite of Baptism

The actual Rite of Baptism varied slightly from community to community. Liturgists detect a significant difference between the Syrian and the Western rites of this period. The Church of Syria anointed the candidates only once, while the Western practice was to anoint before and after immersion.[47]

Hippolytus' *Apostolic Tradition* provides the best description of the Western rite. The rite described would be the one used in Rome at the beginning of the third century. It is very similar to the rite used in Carthage at the same time, and is thought to be the representative Western rite of this period.

At cockcrow prayer shall be made over the water. The stream shall flow through the baptismal tank or pour into it from above when there is no scarcity of water; but if there is a scarcity, whether constant or sudden, then use whatever water you can find.

They shall remove their clothing. And first, baptize the little ones; if they can speak for themselves, they shall do so; if not, their parents or other relatives shall speak for them. Then baptize the men, and last of all the women; they must first loosen their hair and put aside any gold or silver ornaments that they were wearing: let no one take any alien thing down to the water with them.

At the hour set for the baptism the bishop shall give thanks over the oil and put it into a vessel: this is called the "oil of thanksgiving". And he shall take other oil and exorcise it: this is called the "oil of exorcism". [The anointing is performed by a presbyter.] A deacon shall bring the oil of exorcism, and shall stand at the presbyter's left hand; and another deacon shall take the oil of thanksgiving, and shall stand at the presbyter's right hand. Then the presbyter, taking hold of each of those about to be baptized, shall command him to renounce, saying:

I renounce thee, Satan, and all thy servants and all thy works.

And when he has renounced all these, the presbyter shall anoint him with the oil of exorcism, saying:

Let all spirits depart far from thee.

Then, after these things, let him give him over to the presbyter who baptizes, and let the candidates stand in the water, naked, a deacon going with them likewise. And when he who is being baptized goes down into the water, he who baptizes him, putting his hand on him, shall say thus:

Dost thou believe in God, the Father Almighty?

And he who is being baptized shall say:

I believe.

Then holding his hand placed on his head, he shall baptize him once. And then he shall say:

Dost thou believe in Christ Jesus, the Son of God, who was born of the Holy Ghost of the Virgin Mary, and was crucified under Pontius Pilate, and was dead and buried, and rose again the third day, alive from the dead, and ascended into heaven, and sat at the right hand of the Father, and will come to judge the quick and the dead? And when he says:

I believe,

He is baptized again. And again he shall say:

Dost thou believe in the Holy Ghost, and the holy church, and the resurrection of the flesh?

He who is being baptized shall say accordingly:

I believe.

And so he is baptized a third time.

And afterward, when he has come up out of the water, he is anointed by the presbyter with the oil of thanksgiving, the presbyter saying:

I anoint thee with holy oil in the name of Jesus Christ.

And so each one, after drying himself, is immediately clothed, and then is brought into the church.[48]

Hippolytus' description of the Rite of Baptism speaks for itself, far better than I could describe it. There are, however, a couple of points that require further discussion. First, in every description of baptism we have from this period, the neophytes would join the congregation, exchange the sign of peace, and then participate in their first eucharistic celebration. Since, as we have seen, the catechumens were not allowed to attend the Liturgy of the Eucharist before baptism, this must have been a quite powerful experience. It must have felt like a resurrection from the dead (and this is exactly what was intended).

Secondly, the candidates were baptized completely naked. The early Christians were particularly concerned about seeing members of the opposite sex naked, so much so that it was forbidden to attend co-ed public baths. In *Apostolic Tradition*, there is no indication that any kind of arrangement was made to protect the nudity of any of the candidates, but other communities had very careful arrangements to keep men from seeing naked women. In the *Didascalia Apostolorum* (Teaching of the Apostles), which was written in Syria around 250, we learn that this community had deaconesses to submerge and anoint female candidates.[49]

## A Note on Infant Baptism

It will not have escaped your attention that the *Apostolic Tradition* made provisions for the baptism of children, even children so young that they could not speak for themselves. That is, of course, contrary to what modern Evangelicals have told us. They have said that infant baptism did not begin until after Constantine, when the Church became corrupted by close cooperation with the prevailing culture. There are indications that the Evangelical position is simply wrong. Infant baptism is not ruled out in the New Testament. Several passages speak of the baptism of entire households. Then as now, the concept of an entire household encompassed whatever children there might have been. It is not likely that all four households mentioned in these passages were childless; therefore it seems likely that the New Testament assumes, without specifically mentioning, infant baptism.[50]

We must also bear in mind that the *Apostolic Tradition* purports to represent the traditions of the Church all the way back to apostolic times. The fact that Hippolytus mentions, without bothering to defend, infant baptism, indicates that at least in his mind, the practice went back to the time of the apostles. Tertullian, a contemporary of Hippolytus, opposed infant baptism in terms that indicate the practice was fairly widespread.[51] Both Origen and Cyprian of Carthage favored infant baptism.[52] Origen went so far as to assert: "The Church has received the tradition from the Apostles to give baptism even to little children."[53] Were Hippolytus and Origen wrong? Less than two hundred years after the apostles, in communities that went to great lengths to preserve the authentic apostolic teaching, could these men have been mistaken?

Fortunately, we have additional sources of information on the baptismal practices of the early Church. We have uncovered numerous inscriptions at early cemeteries and in the Roman catacombs that indicate the age of baptism and the date of death. Here is a particularly heartrending one from the third century, from the catacombs of Priscilla, Rome: "Sweet Tyche lived one year, 10 months, 15 days. Received grace on the 8th day before the Kalends ... gave up her soul on the same day."[54] A careful perusal of a good sample of these inscriptions indicates that usually infants were baptized if they were on the point of death. It is not hard to see how this could come about. Infant mortality was quite high in those days. Parents desired to pass on the gift of salvation to their children, and the Church joyfully conferred this gift.

### Forgiveness for Postbaptismal Sins

The early Church did not teach, nor did any early Christians believe, the doctrine of "once saved, always saved". In fact, if anything, the early Christians believed that willful sins after baptism were even worse than those sins committed before baptism. They took seriously the words of Hebrews:

> If we sin deliberately after receiving the knowledge of the truth, there no longer remains a sacrifice for sins, but a fearful prospect of judgment, and a fury of fire which will consume the adversaries. A man who has violated the Law of Moses dies without mercy at the testimony of two or three witnesses. How much worse punishment do you think will be deserved by the man who has spurned the Son of God, and profaned the blood of the covenant by which he was sanctified, and outraged the Spirit of grace? [55]

The early Christians took sin seriously, more seriously than we do today, perhaps. There was a fear that serious sinners could die as a direct result of their sins. [56] Paul recommended casting serious sinners out of the Church. [57]

Of course, nobody can go through life without sinning, even with the grace of baptism and the best of intentions. The early Church found it necessary to make provisions for the repentance of postbaptismal sins and the restoration to fellowship of erring Christians. Jesus, of course, also foresaw this problem, and there are several passages in the New Testament that address the process for the forgiveness of sins.

In James 5:14–16, we find the first passage that speaks directly about the power of confession of one's sins. In this passage, sinfulness and sickness are linked, and the cure is the same: one must go to the presbyters for anointing and prayer. In this passage, the confession of the sin acts in the same way as the telling of one's symptoms to a doctor. First John 1:8–10 urges a similar course of action: "If we say we have no sin, we deceive ourselves, and the truth is not in us. If we confess our sins, he is faithful and just, and will forgive our sins and cleanse us from all unrighteousness. If we say we have not sinned, we make him a liar, and his word is not in us."

To whom would one confess one's sins? John is not specific. James, however, says one should go to the presbyters. As we shall see, this did not necessarily mean that the presbyters were the only ones who would hear someone's confession. Some sins had to be publicly confessed and public penance done. But in James' approach, the presbyters, as the "doctors of the soul", would be the ones who would determine which approach would be used in specific cases.

Jesus was the one who had the authority to forgive sins, and he passed this authority on to his apostles. In Matthew 18:18, Jesus told the apostles: "Truly, I say to you, whatever you bind on earth shall be bound in heaven, and whatever you loose on earth shall be loosed in heaven." The power of binding and loosing was a common figure in rabbinical literature and had to do with the ability to judge difficult cases and determine guilt or innocence. Since this passage is in the context of Jesus giving his authority to the Church, there can be only one meaning here: the apostles were given the authority to forgive sins in Jesus' name.

In John 20:22–23, Jesus says the same thing to the apostles in a different way. He breathes on them (a sign of giving the Holy Spirit), and then he says, "Receive the Holy Spirit. If you forgive the sins of any, they are forgiven; if you retain the sins of any, they are retained."

In our time, various Christian denominations construe these passages in different ways. In this work, we are concerned only with one question: How did the early Christians understand these passages? What were their beliefs and practices? The first clues we receive are in Clement's *First Epistle to the Corinthians* (written ca. 96). This letter was written to address the fact that a faction in the Corinthian Church had deposed their duly appointed presbyters. Clement held that this faction was in the wrong and called for the restoration of the presbyters and the repentance of the rebels. Toward the end of the letter, he wrote: "You therefore, who laid the foundation of this sedition, submit yourselves to the presbyters, and receive correction so as to repent, bending the knees of your hearts. Learn to be subject, laying aside the proud and arrogant self-confidence of your tongue." [58]

Our next clue comes from the *Didache* (written ca. 90–110). At one point we read, "In the Church you shall acknowledge your transgressions, and you shall not come near for your prayer with an evil conscience." [59] Reconciliation was considered a prerequisite for the reception of the Eucharist: "Let no one that is at variance with his fellow come together with you, until [he] be reconciled, that your sacrifice may not be profaned." [60] The first passage speaks of public confession before prayer. The second seems to speak only of the reconciliation between two believers who have fallen out. But the principle is clear: no one with an uneasy conscience should approach the Eucharist. *The Epistle of Barnabas* (written sometime between 70 and 135) emphasizes this point: "Thou shalt confess thy sins. Thou shalt not go to prayer with an evil conscience." [61]

*The Pastor of Hermas* (a series of visions recorded sometime between 140 and 155) marks an interesting period in the understanding of the Church. Hermas had a vision in which an angel spoke to him. The angel spoke at great length regarding the need to live a sinless life after baptism. Daunted, Hermas asked the angel about the chance of repentance after baptism. The angel replied, "If any one is tempted by the devil, and sins after that great and holy calling in which the Lord has called His people to everlasting life, he has opportunity to repent but once. But if he should sin frequently after this, and then repent, to such a man his repentance will be of no avail; for with difficulty will he live." [62]

This passage has two implications. On the one hand, it seems to allow only one opportunity for forgiveness. On the other hand, if you keep reading, you will find that Hermas was exceedingly grateful for this one opportunity. Some scholars have deduced from this passage that the early Church taught that one could receive formal forgiveness for sins only once. It is important to remember, however, that Hermas provides only one data point. Other passages from roughly the same period speak of people being forgiven several times for the same sin. There is a way out of the dilemma, if we patiently cull though the sources.

Irenaeus of Lyons writes about one Cerdo, a heretic, who persisted in teaching heresy in Rome: "Coming frequently into the church, and making public confession, he thus remained, one time teaching in secret, and then again making public confession; but at last, having been denounced for corrupt teaching, he was excommunicated from the assembly of the brethren." [63] We see that Cerdo, upon being confronted, made at least two public confessions, and remained in communion, until at last the exasperated community excommunicated him.

It seems likely that the early Church made a distinction between different kinds of sins. There is scriptural warrant for this kind of distinction. "If any one sees his brother committing what is not a mortal sin, he will ask, and God will give him life for those whose sin is not mortal. There is sin which is mortal; I do not say that one is to pray for that. All wrongdoing is sin, but there is sin which is not mortal." [64]

The distinction between "mortal" or deadly sins and "venial" or lesser sins had already begun in the New Testament. Most scholars who carefully study the early Church's penitential practices believe that there was a distinction between serious sins and less serious sins. Less serious sins could be repeatedly confessed, as James implies. More serious sin could, evidently, be confessed only once, in public, and was followed by a public penance before the sinner could be restored to fellowship. Three questions remain: What sins were serious enough to require public confession and penance? What was the process one had to undergo to receive forgiveness for these sins? And what was the process for lesser sins? All these questions can be answered, thanks to those voluminous writers Tertullian of Carthage and Origen of Alexandria.

From a careful reading of the sources, it seems likely that sins that were serious enough that they could be repented of only once, had to be publicly confessed, and required the penitent to do public penance were limited to adultery, murder, and apostasy. [65]

What was the process for the forgiveness of these sins? Tertullian laid out the whole process in a treatise aptly titled *On Repentance*:

> The narrower, then, the sphere of action of this second and only remaining repentance, the more laborious is its probation; in order that it may not be exhibited in the conscience alone, but may likewise be carried out in some external act. This act, which is more usually expressed and commonly spoken of under a Greek name, is *exomologesis*, whereby we confess our sins to the Lord, not indeed as if He were ignorant of them, but inasmuch as by confession satisfaction is settled, of confession repentance is born; by repentance God is appeased. And thus *exomologesis* is a discipline for man's prostration and humiliation, enjoining a demeanor calculated to move mercy. With regard also to the very dress and food, it commands the penitent to lie in sackcloth and ashes, to cover his body in mourning, to lay his spirit low in sorrows, to exchange for severe treatment the sins which he has committed; moreover, to know no food and drink but such as is plain,—not for the

stomach's sake, to wit, but the soul's; for the most part, however, to feed prayers on fastings, to groan, to weep and make outcries unto the Lord your God; to bow before the feet of the presbyters, and kneel to God's dear ones; to enjoin on all the brethren to be ambassadors to bear his deprecatory supplication before God. All this *exomologesis* does, that it may enhance repentance; may honor God by its fear of the danger; may, by itself pronouncing against the sinner, stand in the stead of God's indignation, and by temporal mortification, expunge external punishments. Therefore, while it abases the man, it raises him; while it covers him with squalor, it renders him more clean; while it accuses, it excuses; while it condemns, it absolves. The less quarter you give yourself, the more will God give you.[66]

What about those sins not considered "mortal"? Origen makes it plain that those sins can always be forgiven through confession. Actually, Origen lists seven channels through which the grace of forgiveness might flow: (1) baptism (only once, through which original sin and all sins committed before conversion are forgiven), (2) martyrdom, (3) almsgiving, (4) willingness to forgive, (5) the conversion of sinners, (6) fervent love, and (7) penitence (by which Origen meant the whole process of confession and the doing of penance).[67]

The first step in all repentance would have to be a private interview with a priest or bishop. At that time, the priest might forgive the sin, imposing a light penance, or decide the sin was too serious and public penance had to be performed.[68]

During the third century, the penitential structure of the early Church underwent some modifications. Hippolytus complained that Pope Callistus forgave adultery without the *exomologesis*.[69] Hippolytus was inclined to exaggerate where Callistus was concerned, but there is reason to believe that Callistus introduced a more lenient system of repentance for certain sins, including adultery. Tertullian may have been referring to Callistus when he wrote, "The Pontifex Maximus—that is, the bishop of bishops—issues an edict: 'I remit, to such as have discharged the requirements of repentance, the sins both of adultery and of fornication.' "[70] Tertullian was seething with rage when he wrote this. The Bishop of Rome had evidently made some change in the rules regarding adultery and fornication, and Tertullian did not like that change. (For a detailed discussion of the role of the Bishop of Rome in the early Church, see Part 2, Chapter 3.)

## Conclusion

The lengthy process of conversion and catechesis that early Christians had to go through before baptism must have discouraged many potential converts. Others were, undoubtedly, rejected by the Church for one reason or another. The seeming harshness of the early Church is jarring to our modern sensibilities, but there were reasons for these actions. Not only were they necessary to protect the Church from government agents, but they ensured that those who were baptized were prepared to live an authentic Christian life and die for the faith if necessary.

## CHAPTER 2

# How the Early Christians Prayed

In 251, Cyprian, Bishop of Carthage, returned from exile to his flock. He found many problems: sacred books and vessels had been destroyed, heresy abounded, the region was in the grip of plague, and, worst of all, there was a dispute over what to do with those Christians who had denied the faith under threat of death and now wanted to return to the Church. Cyprian acted with great energy to attack these immediate problems (though his solution to the problem of the *lapsi* was later overruled by Rome), but he also devoted time to the long-term spiritual health of his community.

Cyprian wrote a series of treatises on the spiritual life during this period after the Decian persecution. Among them are *De Unitate Ecclesiae* (On the Unity of the Church), *De Gratia Dei* (On the Grace of God), and *De Dominica Oratione* (On the Lord's Prayer). The treatise on the Lord's Prayer is a remarkable document: deep, subtle, and of immense spiritual benefit to those who read it.[1] Cyprian, like other leaders of the early Church, cared about the prayer life of everyday Christians and wrote on the subject at great length.

From Cyprian's choice of topics, we can make two initial observations: (1) the prayer life of individual Christians was of immense interest to the leaders of the early Church and (2) the Lord's Prayer was considered the form, or model, of all Christian prayer.

These two points deserve more attention, but for now, there is one important preliminary observation to make. Life for the early Christians was hard, harder than we can even imagine today. Not only did they suffer from the threat of persecution and constant personal insult, but there was the additional difficulty of the extremely high moral standard of the Church and the practice of public penance. The individual Christians feared falling back into sinful ways.

This fear was not, primarily, something that was imposed on the Christians by a prudish and abusive hierarchy, as some have supposed. It was primarily self-imposed. The early Christians were, for the most part, men and women who had been sickened by the excesses of their former way of life. Their firmest desire was never to return to that way of life, but more than that, they desired to transcend the temptations of this world and be transformed into the image of their Savior.

Prayer, an intense communal experience of the presence of God, was their way of allowing this transformation to work in their lives. As we shall see, in addition to the liturgy on the Lord's Day, the early Christians had a strong program of daily prayer. They believed in the communion of the saints (that the saints in Heaven can intercede on our behalf) and that we should pray for our departed loved ones. The overarching theme of the prayer of the early Church is the idea of connectedness: communion with God, with one another, and with the extended community of faith.

### Daily Prayer

The earliest Christians were, for the most part, Jews. In particular, the leaders of the early Church were Jewish. Perhaps we say this too often, but it is true, and it is essential to understand how the Jewish heritage of the Church has influenced the development of Christian prayer. The early Church borrowed prayer forms from Jewish practice, and in turn those prayer forms were used by the monks and nuns of the Middle Ages and survive to this day in the Liturgy of the Hours, the Divine Office, prayed by priests, religious, and an increasing number of laypeople in our time.

In discussing the Jewish origin of Christian daily prayer, one has to be careful. Jewish practices in the first century were quite different from those in the second and third centuries.[2] This point, obscure though it seems, matters because Christians borrowed their prayer forms from Judaism in the first century, and in the second and third century the split between the two communities grew wider and wider.

The essential elements of first-century Jewish daily prayer were the morning and evening prayer. There were two scriptural sources for this custom. The Torah records that the major daily sacrifices of the

day were held in the morning and the evening.³ Also, Scripture calls
for the *Shema* ("Hear, O Israel, the Lord thy God, the Lord is one
...") to be recited twice daily, "when you lie down, and when you
rise."⁴ The Mishnah (an early commentary on the Torah) called for
benedictions to be prayed before and after the recitation.⁵ The practice of morning and evening prayer was established long before the
coming of Christ.

In addition to these prayers, it was also the practice of pious Jews to
pray at the third, sixth, and ninth hours.⁶ Various scriptural passages
were used to justify this practice, but it may have simply been a matter
of convenience. These hours were announced by the watch in some
cities, and they would be convenient times to stop work for a few
minutes to pray.⁷

There are other interesting facts about first-century Jewish prayer,
some of which have a bearing on early Christian prayer: communal
synagogue services were held on Saturday, Monday, and Thursday. At
these services, a quorum of ten people was required.⁸

The New Testament testifies that the very first Christians, in addition to distinctively Christian forms of worship, also engaged in traditional prayers. "They devoted themselves to the apostles' teaching and
fellowship, to the breaking of bread and the prayers."⁹ Acts 10:9 is especially relevant in this context, since it explicitly mentions Peter stop-
ping to pray in the middle of the day.¹⁰ So we have reason to believe
that the very first Christians prayed according to the Jewish pattern.

New Testament prayer had two main characteristics: it was communal and informal. Saint Paul is frequently seen offering prayers of
thanksgiving and petition.¹¹ He also recommends singing "psalms, hymns
and spiritual songs", though we do not know the form or musical
style of these songs.¹²

When we move into the postapostolic Christian literature, we find
that the hours of prayer were the same, but the prayers were somewhat different. The *Didache*, our first nonbiblical source on Christian
prayer, recommends fasting on Wednesday and Friday and praying the
Our Father three times a day:

> But let not your fasts be with the hypocrites; for they fast on the sec-
> ond and fifth day of the week; but do ye fast on the fourth day and the
> Preparation [Friday]. Neither pray as the hypocrites; but as the Lord

commanded in His Gospel, thus pray: Our Father who art in heaven, hallowed be Thy name. Thy kingdom come. Thy will be done, as in heaven, so on earth. Give us to-day our daily [needful] bread, and forgive us our debt as we also forgive our debtors. And bring us not into temptation, but deliver us from the evil one [or, evil]; for Thine is the power and the glory for ever. Thrice in the day thus pray.[13]

Other than the Lord's Prayer, we have little idea of the content of first-century Christian prayer. It seems safe to assume that the Psalms were used extensively, since they were so well known to the early Christians.[14] Perhaps in this period, the more informal practice of singing "psalms, hymns and spiritual songs" was continued. We simply don't have any evidence to go on until early in the third century.

Tertullian, Cyprian, and Origen are our best sources for Christian prayer in the third century. We find that in Carthage, Tertullian speaks of the pattern mentioned above: morning and evening prayer; shorter prayers at the third, sixth, and ninth hours; and rising in the middle of the night to pray. Tertullian also recommended praying before meals, or going to the bath, or whatever one did.[15] Clement of Alexandria and Origen testify to similar practices in Alexandria. The *Apostolic Tradition* describes the same practice in Rome. So we have a remarkable thing. Evidently, in the first three centuries of Christianity, the whole Church observed the whole range of prayer times that in later ages only monks and nuns observed.

Of course, allowances were made for those who had work to do at the prescribed times. The *Apostolic Tradition* has this recommendation: "If at the third hour thou art at home, pray then and give thanks to God; but if thou chance to be abroad at that hour, make thy prayer to God in thy heart."[16] We do not know what the exact content of the daytime prayers might have been. It might be that believers simply prayed the Our Father, as the *Didache* called for. For the prayer in the middle of the night, it was recommended that husband and wife pray together, if both were Christians. Otherwise, the Christian spouse was to go to another room to pray.[17]

The morning and the evening prayers seem to have been communal, while the prayers during the day must have been either individual, or with family, or in small groups that could gather conveniently. Cyprian discouraged private prayer, insisting that all Christian prayer was communal, for "we do not say, 'My Father'." [18] Of course, Cyprian understood that slaves and those who worked for a living could not drop everything to go to communal prayer. His point was that Christians should gather together for prayer whenever possible, but even when they prayed alone they were with the whole community in spirit.

Christians faced to the east in prayer. We learn from Origen that some private houses had special rooms for prayer. From other sources, we learn of houses that had crosses on the east wall. [19] Tertullian noted that there were various opinions regarding kneeling for prayer. His recommendation was that kneeling should be reserved for the Lord's Day, for the Wednesday and Friday fasts, for morning prayer, and for the confession of sins. [20] His point seems to have been that kneeling for other prayers might be too ostentatious, especially in public places.

Some Christians appear to have worn amulets or "seal rings" with gems shaped in the form of a cross, with Christ's initials carved into the stones. These rings served both as a mark of Christian identity and as a reminder and an aid in daily prayer. [21] In an age when public Christian prayer was impossible, these rings must have provided comfort and a much-needed visual reminder of the faith.

As mentioned, Wednesdays and Fridays were days of fasting. On these days, Christians observed what were known as "Stations". [22] This term seems to have had a military origin, and the connotation is that on these days Christians are on watch like a soldier keeping his station, or post. The fasts ended at the ninth hour with a prayer service.

As mentioned, the content of prayer is a matter of some speculation. Tertullian provides some interesting evidence on this subject. In his treatise on prayer, he stated that the Lord's Prayer was the prescribed and regular prayer, but that other petitions could be added to it. In his *Apology*, he added the following information: "We pray, too, for the emperors, for their ministers and for all in authority, for the welfare of the world, for the prevalence of peace, for the delay of the final consummation." [23] The Lord's Prayer was considered the "form" or template of all Christian prayer, because it was given by the Lord himself, and because it was considered to have all the petitions for which we should rightly pray. [24]

The writers of the early Church all understood the clause "give us this day our daily bread" in both the physical and the spiritual sense. More specifically, many of the Fathers interpreted this clause as a reference to the Eucharist. Here is what Cyprian of Carthage wrote in his treatise *On the Lord's Prayer:* "We say, 'Our Father,' because He is the Father of those who understand and believe; so also we call it 'our bread,' because Christ is the bread of those who are in union with His body. And we ask that this bread should be given to us daily, that we who are in Christ, and daily receive the eucharist for the food of salvation, may not ... be separated from Christ's body." [25]

This, of course, brings us to the next aspect of the spiritual life of the early Church: the firm conviction that the Eucharist was the "food of salvation". What did this phrase mean, and how did they celebrate this awesome mystery?

## *The Eucharist*

On August 15, 255, a young man named Tarsicius, either an acolyte or a deacon of the Church of Rome, was walking the Appian Way, carrying a very special burden, the eucharistic Body of Christ. He moved carefully, to avoid dropping the Hosts in his possession, and it may have been the very care with which he moved that attracted attention. A group of nonbelievers confronted Tarsicius and demanded that he hand the Sacrament over to them. Tarsicius, fearing sacrilege, refused. The group then proceeded to attack Tarsicius with sticks and stones, beating him so violently that he died. But when the men searched Tarsicius' body, they found no trace of the Precious Body. After the mob, perhaps shaken by the miracle that had occurred in their midst or by their own casual brutality, dispersed, then the local Christians came and carried Tarsicius to the catacombs of Callistus for a Christian burial.

To this day, if you go into the catacombs of Callistus, you can read about the martyrdom of Tarsicius. Some one hundred years after the actual incident, Pope Damasus set up a memorial to this gruesome event, complete with a poem Damasus had composed himself: "While the holy Tarsicius was carrying the sacraments of Christ, an impious band pressed upon him, anxious to expose them to a profane gaze. He chose rather to give up his life than to betray the heavenly limbs to mad dogs." [26]

So far we have a simple story of tragedy, heroism, and faith. Tarsicius was martyred while carrying the Eucharist from one part of

Rome to another. But there are questions we could ask, given the paucity of information Damasus' inscription provides. Where was Tarsicius coming from, and where was he going with the eucharistic Bread? What did he believe about that Bread, and why did he face death rather than see it ridiculed, destroyed, or consumed by nonbelievers? In answering these questions, we can learn about the early Christians. Tarsicius was not alone in his particular beliefs, and he was not the first person to hold them.

When Jesus blessed and broke the bread with his disciples at the Last Supper,[27] he did not do so in a cultural vacuum. He was a Jew, sharing a meal with fellow Jews. He wished to invest that meal with special significance and do it in such a way that they would understand and remember his words and repeat his actions.[28] The Jews of the first century were used to sharing holy meals together, meals that included a unique type of prayer called the *berakah* (plural *berakoth*). The *berakah* was a prayer that blessed God, giving thanks for all the good that he had done, both in the lives of individuals and for the whole nation of Israel. This kind of prayer would typically begin, "Blessed are you, Adonai, Lord God, King of the Universe, who has given us the fruit of the vine ..."[29]

The *berakah* would typically be prayed at three types of meals, all of which may have had an influence on the development of the liturgy. The first, and the one that comes most readily to mind, is the Seder. This meal was eaten on the Passover and included lamb, unleavened bread, four cups of wine, and bitter herbs. An unblemished lamb would be sacrificed by the head of the household, and the blood of that lamb was smeared over the doorposts of the house. In the New Testament, Jesus was compared to the Passover lamb,[30] and the synoptic accounts of the Last Supper indicate that it was a Passover feast. For instance, in Mark 14:12, the author writes, "On the first day of Unleavened Bread, when they sacrificed the passover lamb, his disciples said to him, 'Where will you have us go and prepare for you to eat the passover?'" Shortly thereafter, the Last Supper is eaten. The implication is clear, that the Last Supper was a Seder.

In John 19:14, the author states just as clearly that Jesus was crucified on "the day of Preparation for the Passover", meaning that, if John is correct and Matthew, Mark, and Luke are mistaken, the Last Supper was not a Passover meal, but some other kind of meal. But what other kind of meal could it have been? There are two possibilities, both with strong and able advocates. There was a custom in Judaism at that time to celebrate a friendship meal, called the *chaburah*, on the night before the Sabbath. A small piece of bread would be broken at the beginning of the meal, with appropriate blessings, and at the end of the meal, again with a *berakah*, a cup of wine would be passed around for everyone to take a sip of.[31]

A third type of meal that might have influenced the proceedings at the Last Supper was the *todah*. This was a thanksgiving meal that a pious Jew might hold at any time, if there was something in particular for which he wanted to give thanks. At this type of meal, the host would gather his friends together and offer a prayer, perhaps Psalm 22 or 116.[32] In addition to the prayer, the host would offer a simple meal of bread and wine. The fascinating aspect of this meal, commented on by numerous scholars, is that the Jews of that time believed that when the Messiah came "all sacrifices [would] cease except the *todah* sacrifice. This will never cease in all eternity."[33]

So what we have are three different meals, and you could make a good case that the Last Supper was based on each one. We need not choose between the meals, however. It is possible that the Last Supper was a mingling of all three meals.[34] In any case, it is enough for our purposes to know that first-century Judaism was full of meals that featured bread and wine, blessings and prayers of thanksgiving, and a gathering of friends. In a meal of this sort, Jesus took bread, gave it the typical blessing, and proclaimed, "This is my body." He did the same with the wine at the end of the meal.

How did the early Christians understand this gesture? Did they think Jesus was speaking symbolically, or did they take him at his word? The evidence is overwhelming. In obedience to Christ's command, the early Church celebrated the Lord's Supper on a weekly basis.[35] Those in the Church clearly believed that the bread and wine of which they partook were truly the Body and Blood of Christ. Theological understandings of this mystery were not far advanced, but already in A.D. 107 we find Saint Ignatius, Bishop of Antioch, writing of the Eucharist as "the flesh of our Savior Jesus Christ".[36] This belief had its practical application. The early Christians took great care with the Eucharist. In Hippolytus' *Apostolic Tradition*, we read, "Let each one take care that no unbeliever taste the eucharist, nor a mouse nor any other animal, and that nothing of it fall or be lost; for the body of Christ is to be eaten by believers and must not be despised." [37]

Given this understanding, it is not to be wondered that Saint Tarsicius would rather die than expose the Eucharist to dishonor. Like us, the early Christians believed that Christ was truly present in the eucharistic Bread and Wine. They based this belief not only on the institution narratives referenced above but also on the sixth chapter of the Gospel of John, particularly verse 51: "I am the living bread which came down from heaven; if any one eats of this bread, he will live forever; and the bread which I shall give for the life of the world is my flesh." The early Christian placed the eucharistic Presence of Christ in the context of the Incarnation and the paschal mystery. By this I mean that when the early Christians celebrated the Eucharist, they understood that what they were remembering was Christ's death and Resurrection, and that by partaking of the Eucharist they were spiritually participating in that death and Resurrection. [38]

Because of this association, the early Christians fully accepted the notion that the Eucharist was a sacrifice that the table the Eucharist was offered on was an altar, and that the minister who presided over the sacrifice was a priest. Here is what Cyprian of Carthage wrote on this topic:

> For if Jesus Christ, our Lord and God, is Himself the chief priest of God the Father, and has first offered Himself a sacrifice to the Father, and has commanded this to be done in commemoration of Himself, certainly that priest truly discharges the office of Christ, who imitates that which Christ did; and he then offers a true and full sacrifice in the Church to God the Father, when he proceeds to offer it according to what he sees Christ Himself to have offered. [39]

How, then, did the early Christians celebrate this mystery? We are fortunate in that we have several sources on this subject. We have Eucharistic Prayers in the *Apostolic Tradition*, part of another Eucharistic Prayer and a Prayer of Thanksgiving after Communion in the *Didache*, and two complete descriptions of the entire liturgy in the *First Apology* of Justin Martyr. [40]

Here is Justin's description of the liturgy. It will sound a lot like what we experience every Sunday, and there is every reason to believe that this is how the liturgy was experienced throughout the Christian world during Justin's lifetime:

On the day called Sunday, all who live in cities or in the country gather together to one place, and the memoirs of the apostles or the writings of the prophets are read, as long as time permits; then, when the reader has ceased, the president verbally instructs, and exhorts to the imitation of these good things. Then we all rise together and pray, and, as we before said, when our prayer is ended, bread and wine and water are brought, and the president in like manner offers prayers and thanksgivings, according to his ability, and the people assent, saying Amen; and there is a distribution to each, and a participation of that over which thanks have been given, and to those who are absent a portion is sent by the deacons. And they who are well to do, and willing, give what each thinks fit; and what is collected is deposited with the president, who succors the orphans and widows and those who, through sickness or any other cause, are in want, and those who are in bonds and the strangers sojourning among us, and in a word takes care of all who are in need. But Sunday is the day on which we hold our common assembly, because it is the first day on which God, having wrought a change in darkness and matter, made the world; and Jesus Christ our Savior on the same day rose from the dead.[41]

How was the liturgy experienced by those who participated in it? We know that the early Christians worshipped in houses. The New Testament frequently refers to this practice. Acts 20:7 reads, "On the first day of the week, when we were gathered together to break bread, Paul talked with them, intending to depart on the morrow; and he prolonged his speech until midnight." As the communities grew larger, it became necessary to move out of private houses and find some other places of worship.[42] The Christians could not build churches, with huge crosses on top, so they developed the practice of modifying houses to meet the public worship needs of the community. Typically, the houses in use would be donated by wealthy members, or they would be purchased with community funds, and walls would be knocked out, an altar would be placed near the east wall, and in some cases, a baptistery would be installed.

We know about these house churches from documents and archaeological sites. In Dura-Europos, a city on the far-eastern edge of the empire, a house has been found that had been modified to provide one large meeting room and a smaller room for baptisms. We know about the purposes of these two rooms from the wall frescoes, which

The House Church of Dura-Europos, A.D. 232–256

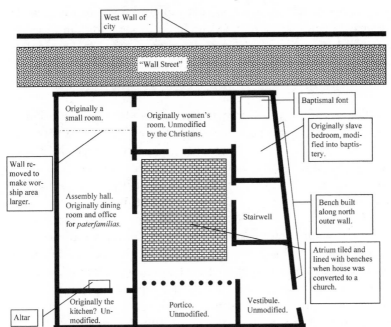

West Wall of city

"Wall Street"

Baptismal font

Originally a small room.

Originally women's room. Unmodified by the Christians.

Originally slave bedroom, modified into baptistery.

Wall removed to make worship area larger.

Assembly hall. Originally dining room and office for *paterfamilias*.

Stairwell

Bench built along north outer wall.

Atrium tiled and lined with benches when house was converted to a church.

Originally the kitchen? Unmodified.

Altar

Portico. Unmodified.

Vestibule. Unmodified.

This house was modified from a residence to a *domus ecclesiae*, or house church, in 232–233. Relatively few modifications were needed: (1) a bedroom wall was knocked out to make the main assembly area larger, (2) an altar was placed at the east end of this room, (3) the slave's bedroom was fitted with a baptismal font, with a canopy over the font, (4) the atrium was tiled over and benches were built along the inner walls, and (5) a bench was built along the entire north outer wall. The purpose of some of the modifications is perfectly clear, but it is not clear what the atrium was used for (possibly for outdoor liturgies and for *agape* meals). It also remains unclear what the bench along the north outer wall was for. Perhaps it was simply a waiting area for people who arrived early for services, or perhaps it was where the catechists instructed the candidates, after they were dismissed from the liturgical assembly. But of course it could be used for these purposes only in times of no persecution. This house church, along with the entire city, was destroyed by the Persians in A.D. 256.

depicted liturgical scenes.[43] This particular building has to be dated before 256, since the Persians destroyed the city in that year.

We also know, from Roman documents, that during the reign of Alexander Severus (222–235), a Roman Christian community contracted with an innkeeper to purchase a building for use as a church. There were approximately 40,000 Christians in Rome at this time, so there must have been many "house churches" in operation, and the scene described here must have been replayed many times.[44] Archaeologists have also reconstructed the process by which an entire floor of an *insula* was converted into a *titulus* (the Roman term denoting a "house church") in third-century Rome.[45]

In the fall of 2005, a Christian church building, that is, a building that was designed and built to be a house of worship, was found in Megiddo, Israel.[46] Archaeologists have tentatively dated this building to the third century, based on the style of pottery found near it, the style of the mosaics on the floor, and the general architectural features of the building. Other experts in the field have cast doubt on the dating of this building, but if it turns out to be a third-century Christian church building, it would be the earliest anyone has found within the Roman Empire. It may be that the church was built during one of the long periods of the third century when the Church was left in relative peace, in a region where a high percentage of the population was Christian.

In Rome, a beautiful custom evolved concerning the eucharistic Bread. Since there were so many house churches in Rome, the papal Mass would be held early in the morning. Fragments of the Eucharist from this Mass, called *fermentum* (the word means, literally, "leaven"), would be taken to all the *tituli*, so everyone could share in the same Eucharist.[47] This fact might provide an answer to the question of what Saint Tarsicius was doing transporting the Eucharist across Rome. It may very well be that he was taking it to the sick, or to prisoners, but he may also have been taking *fermentum* to the other churches of Rome.

Another fascinating source of information about what actually happened in the house churches is the *Constitutions of the Holy Apostles*. In this document, we learn that the preferred shape for a house church would be "long, with its head to the east, with its vestries on both sides at the east end, and so it will be like a ship".[48] The priests and the altar would be in the east end of the building, with the bishop's chair in the center, behind the altar.[49] The deacons were to stand close at hand, ready to help out in whatever way they might be needed. The lectern would be in the center of the room.

The laity would enter from the west and be met by a deacon, who would speak with the people that entered, to make sure they were

Christian. If they were guests from another city or parish, he would make sure they were welcome. This deacon would also arrange the people in their proper groups, with widows, married women, unmarried women, children, and men all seated in different sections. It was expected that some would have to stand, and preference for seats was to be given to the poor, elderly, and widows. The *Didascalia Apostolorum* (written ca. 250) goes so far as to state that if a poor person comes to visit the community, he must be seated, even if it means the bishop himself must give up his seat.[50] During the liturgy, the deacons brought the gifts of bread and wine up and stationed themselves throughout the congregation to make sure there were no improprieties. "Let the deacon also see that no one whispers, or falls asleep, or laughs, or makes signs."[51]

The artwork of the Roman catacombs can also shed light on the eucharistic beliefs and practices of the early Church. Let us take a look at one remarkable example, described by Father Ernest Lussier in vivid detail:

> In the cemetery of Priscilla, there is a fresco called the *Fractio Panis* [breaking of the bread], a name given it by Wilpert, its discoverer. It is found in the *Capella Graecae* [Greek Chapel] and is the oldest known representation of the Eucharist, dating back before the middle of the second century.
>
> Seven persons are gathered in a half circle around a slightly rounded table on which are placed a plate with two fishes and another with five small round loaves of bread. Seven bread baskets are ranged on either side of the table, four to the left and three to the right. The third guest from the right is a veiled woman, her presence indicating probably the universal character of the gathering.
>
> The person on the extreme left has his hands outstretched and somehow his feet are clearly seen above the table. This is probably due to the artist's failure in perspective, in his effort to make the character more conspicuous. In any case, a large cup with two handles is before him, and he is apparently breaking one of the loaves, while the second, fourth, sixth, and seventh banqueters are attentive to his action. The third and fifth, [the women] are looking the other way, possibly for artistic variety.[52]

Father Lussier's vivid description stands on its own merits, but there are a couple of points that should be explored more deeply. First, there is the question of the minister. Is the man Christ himself, or a priest acting in the person of Christ? We do not know. The fact that the feet are above the table indicates the former, but, as Father Lussier indicates, artists of that period did not employ perspective. The question is important, because it touches on the early Church's theology of ministry. Is the artist trying to indicate that the human minister, the priest, represents Christ in this Holy Meal? We do not know the answer to that question.

Another important detail of the painting is the presence of fish on the table alongside the bread and wine. Here we have wandered into a complex and fascinating subject all of its own. We know that in New Testament times the Christians would combine the eucharistic celebration with a full meal, perhaps a potluck meal called the *agape* (love feast). Saint Paul was forced to criticize the Corinthian community for its tendency to abuse this practice.[53] He even went so far as to tell the Corinthians, "If any one is hungry, let him eat at home." [54]

The Christians continued to celebrate *agape* until the fourth century, but at some point it was separated from the eucharistic rite. Dom Gregory Dix thinks the practice became to celebrate the Eucharist, as Justin Martyr described it, on Sunday morning and to gather again on Sunday evening for the *agape*. Both the *Apostolic Tradition* and Tertullian's *Apology* describe the *agape* in great detail.[55] Tertullian contrasted the solemnity and simplicity of the Christian feast with the grasping and excess of the pagan feasts. Hippolytus provides us with a liturgy to accompany the *agape*, with responsorial prayers, psalms, and even a prayer over the bread and wine. But Hippolytus was clear on one point. At the *agape*, "it is 'a blessing', not 'a thanksgiving', as is the body of the Lord." [56]

The leaders of the Church, from Paul to Hippolytus, strove, for pastoral reasons, to distinguish between the Eucharist and the *agape*. Yet they allowed the *agape* to continue, as long as there were no abuses. To ensure this, Hippolytus specified that only bishops should preside.[57]

The *agape* should not be confused with the modern custom of parishes holding potluck dinners. It is true that everyone brought his own contribution to the feast, but the meal was structured with prayers and Scripture readings throughout, much more like the Jewish Seder than the modern potluck dinner in the church basement. It is possible, then, that the meal depicted in this picture is an *agape*, but the evidence does not allow us to say this with any degree of certainty.

But what about the fish on the table with the bread and the wine? My surmise is that the fish are a symbolic aspect of the artwork. We know that for the early Church, fish symbolize Christ.[58] My guess is that the fish in the *Fractio Panis* were meant to symbolize the Presence of Christ in the Eucharist, though I must caution that other explanations are also plausible.

One final question remains in our discussion of the liturgy of the early Church. Did the early Christians celebrate Mass in the catacombs, as popular imagination has it? Most modern scholars believe that they did not. The catacombs consisted of narrow corridors, with small niches for the bodies. There was simply no room for large groups of people to congregate and celebrate the Eucharist.[59] Sometime in the early third century, the popes began the custom of celebrating the Eucharist at the tombs of the martyrs, but they must have gone with small groups of priests and deacons for this purpose. We know that Pope Sixtus II was martyred on August 6, 258, along with four of his deacons, while he was preaching at a Mass in the catacombs.[60] So it seems clear that, although the whole community did not enter the catacombs to celebrate the Eucharist, small groups of Christians did.

There was a ceremonial meal in the catacombs in which the laity participated. Above ground, usually at the entrance to various catacombs, archaeologists have found funeral meal chambers, called *tricliae*. In these chambers, the Christians of Rome celebrated meals called *refrigerium* (refreshment). We know the meals were Christian, because the artwork and graffiti represent Christian themes.[61] One might think that such meals would be dangerous, if not impossible, to participate in. We must remember, however, that the majority of those buried in the catacombs were not Christian. The practice of holding funeral meals above the catacombs was not explicitly Christian; pagans ate these kinds of meals as well. So the Christians could engage in this practice without fear.

All the meal practices described above paled in comparison to the Eucharist, in the minds of the early Christians. For them, the Eucharist was truly "the source and summit of the Christian life".[62] In order to understand why, let us return to Ignatius of Antioch, who called the Eucharist the "medicine of immortality". By this phrase, Ignatius did not mean that the mere consumption of the Eucharist would guarantee salvation. He meant something much more profound. In the very next phrase, Ignatius called the Eucharist "a cleansing remedy driving away evil".[63] The grace the early Christians needed to combat evil and receive the gift of salvation was given to them primarily through the Eucharist. It was the Eucharist that helped them to triumph over persecution, ridicule, and the dangerous temptation of a culture gone insane.

### Veneration of Saints and Martyrs

On January 21, 259, Fructuosus, Bishop of Tarragona, and his deacons, Augurius and Eulogius, were put to the test. The three men bravely admitted to being Christians and were executed in the amphitheater of Tarragona. Emperor Valerian was determined to stamp out Christianity. In fact, he was so determined that he ordered not only the execution of Christians but the destruction of their remains, so those Christians who remained could not set up another martyr's shrine. So Fructuosus, Augurius, and Eulogius were burned to death, with the intention that their ashes would be scattered. Night fell and the job was not completed, so the bodies were left in the amphitheater, with the expectation that the work would be finished the next day.

Fructuosus' faithful flock—shocked, grieving, and scared out of their wits—had a choice. They could have faded into the background and waited for the storm to blow over, and no one would have blamed them. Instead, they chose to do something almost as incomprehensible to the modern mind as it was to the Romans. At great personal risk, a small band of Christians sneaked into the amphitheater and removed the still smoldering ashes of the three martyrs.[64]

What motivated these Christians, so removed in time and culture from our own that we almost cannot understand their behavior? Were they motivated by a fear that Fructuosus and his companions would not be able to participate in a general resurrection of the dead if their bodies were not properly assembled?[65] No. The early Christians did not subscribe to that theory, though the pagans constantly attempted to mock them for their belief in a bodily resurrection. To comfort his friends, Ignatius of Antioch wrote, "When I [my body] shall have disappeared, then I shall be truly a disciple of Christ."[66]

When the Christians spoke of resurrection, the Romans misunderstood them, thinking they meant a purely physical restoration of the body. But the Christians knew that the resurrection they hoped for was more than physical, and that if a man died by beheading be would not have to endure the afterlife without his head. If then, the early Christians did not believe such things, why did they take such great care, as in this case, to collect the remains of the martyrs? A look at the evidence reveals four reasons. These follow, in no particular order.

The early Christians wished to honor the holy lives and ultimate sacrifice of the martyrs. The careful collection of the remains of the martyrs was simply a prelude to an honorable burial. The local churches kept cemeteries, and if it was necessary to move the remains of a particular saint, careful records were kept. At any given time, the leaders of the Christian communities could direct people to the gravesites of the main martyrs of the city. Around 200, the Roman priest Caius could assure his readers, "I can show the trophies of the apostles. For if you will go to the Vatican or to the Ostian Way, you will find the trophies of those who laid the foundations of this Church." [67]

The burial sites of the martyrs were kept not only for private visitors, who would come and pray for the salvation of loved ones, but for liturgical celebrations. On the anniversary of the martyrs, small groups would visit their tombs to celebrate the liturgy.[68] At a very early date, then, accurate lists of the martyrs and their feast days would be kept. This was the origin of the calendar of saints that we know today.[69]

Typically, the tombs of the martyrs would be marked, sometimes only with a small "m" (if the inscription was in Latin). Other tomb inscriptions were more straightforward:

DP III. IDVS SEPTEMBER YACINTHUS MARTYR[70]
[Buried on the third of the Ides of September, Hyacinthus, a martyr]

A tomb marked in this manner was safe. It was generally acknowledged in Roman law that once bodies had been properly interred, visitors should not be bothered.[71] However, those who came to visit, pray, or say Mass at tombs so clearly marked had to be careful.

This manner of honoring the dead was not unknown in the Old Testament. One thinks of the Israelites, who dug up the bones of Joseph and took them back to the Promised Land.[72] Like the ancient Israelites, the early Christians were careful to distinguish between the worship due to God and the veneration proper to the saints. In the

*Martyrdom of Polycarp*, we read, "Christ we adore, because He is the Son of God. To the martyrs, on the other hand, we offer the love which is due to disciples of the Lord, on account of their unsurpassable devotion to their King and Teacher."[73]

The early Christians loved the martyrs and wished to keep physical reminders of them. Let us return to the story of Fructuosus, whose followers risked their lives to retrieve his still-smoking ashes from the amphitheater. The account of Fructuosus' martyrdom records that "he was much beloved of pagans and Christians alike. For he was all that the Holy Spirit, through Paul, the vessel of election and the teacher of the Gentiles, declared that a bishop should be. For this reason his brothers, who knew that he was going on to such great glory, were happy rather than sad."[74] There are numerous records that stress this point. The early Christians felt a deep and personal love for the martyrs. When Ignatius of Antioch was being transported to Rome for his execution he had to write a letter to the Christians of Rome asking them not to intervene on his behalf.[75] Human affection, denied its natural impulse to save the object its affection, will seek other means of expression. So, after their death, the remains of the martyrs would be carefully gathered up and buried with great reverence.

The early Christians believed and taught that the communion of the saints was not broken by death. This doctrine was a great comfort amid the tragedy and death of that time. Cyprian of Carthage wrote to his flock, to comfort them in a time of plague, "A great number of our dear ones wait for us, fathers and brothers and sons are longing for us, who being already assured of their own safety are mindful of ours."[76]

The belief that the saints in Heaven could and would intercede on the behalf of the living was a powerful motivator for the early Christians. Innumerable inscriptions found in the catacombs attest to this belief. Here are just a few, from the catacombs of Callistus:

> "O Atticus, may thy soul be in bliss, and do thou pray for thy parents."
> "Dionysius, an innocent child, rests here among the saints. Remember in thy holy prayers both the sculptor and the writer."[77]

Throughout the catacombs, there are hundreds of similar inscriptions. They attest to the belief of the early Christians that the saints were alive and could give powerful intercession before God. This belief did not arise out of thin air; it is derived from the pages of Scripture. In Revelation 6:9, the author states that the souls of those martyred are "under the altar". The altar here described is the sacrificial altar of the sacrificial Lamb, Christ. The souls of the martyrs are under the altar because their sacrifices have somehow been joined to the sacrifice of Christ.[78]

In a later age, the custom of the Church was to put the relics of the saints under the altar stones of churches, and this passage of Scripture is the origin of this custom. But in the period we are examining, it was not possible to put relics in the houses of worship, so the community would visit the tombs of the martyrs on their feast days, to celebrate Mass and pray.

Miracles were associated with the relics of the martyrs. In the acts of the martyrs, we read of many miracles occurring at the time of death. Here is a sample, from the death of Polycarp:

> When he had pronounced this amen, and so finished his prayer, those who were appointed for the purpose kindled the fire. And as the flame blazed forth in great fury, we, to whom it was given to witness it, beheld a great miracle, and have been preserved that we might report to others what took place. For the fire, shaping itself into the form of an arch, like the sail of a ship when filled with the wind, encompassed as by a circle the body of the martyr. And he appeared within not like flesh which is burnt, but as bread that is baked, or as gold and silver glowing in a furnace. Moreover, we perceived such a sweet odor coming from the pile, as if frankincense or some such precious spices had been smoking there.[79]

The story told here is by no means unique. Almost every account we have of the death of a martyr contains similar wonders. These circumstances caused the early Christians to view the relics of the martyrs as precious objects. But there were also miracles associated with the places where the martyrs were executed, and with the location of the tomb, as this quote from Eusebius of Caesarea indicates:

> The very place where those conducted to death had been decapitated, and which previously was not approached on account of ghosts, was now purified, and those who were under the influence of demons were released from the disease, and many other notable miracles were wrought at the tomb. These are the particulars which should be stated

concerning Martyrius and Marcian. If what I have related appears to be scarcely credible, it is easy to apply for further information to those who are more accurately acquainted with the circumstances; and perhaps far more wonderful things are related concerning them than those which I have detailed.[80]

As Eusebius conceded, these types of miracles are difficult to believe, and perhaps prudence dictates caution in accepting some. But, as Eusebius also indicated, this particular case had witnesses still alive at the time Eusebius wrote, and he had no hesitation whatsoever in sending people to them. In any event, the early Christians believed them, and they had scriptural warrant for their belief. In Acts 19:11–12, we read that "God did extraordinary miracles by the hands of Paul, so that handkerchiefs or aprons were carried away from his body to the sick, he and diseases left them and the evil spirits came out of them." Note that in this case Paul himself did not go to lay hands on the sick, but simply sent an item of his clothing (one might even call it a "relic"), and the sick were healed. So these things are possible, and we modern sceptics doubt their possibility to our own loss. In any event, the early Christians were convinced that miracles were associated with the relics of the martyrs, and they acted accordingly.

### Prayers for Departed Loved Ones

Praying for the dead, particularly for loved ones, is so natural to man that one author called it "an instinct of natural piety".[81] We know that the Jews in the time of Christ prayed for their dead. In 2 Maccabees 12:44–45,[82] the author writes, "If he [Judas Maccabee] were not expecting that those who had fallen would rise again, it would have been superfluous and foolish to pray for the dead. But if he was looking to the splendid reward that is laid up for those who fall asleep in godliness, it was a holy and pious thought. Therefore he made atonement for the dead, that they might be delivered from their sin." Second Macabees was written sometime between 150 and 50 B.C. and can be taken as reliable evidence that Jews at the time of Jesus prayed for the dead.

It is true that Jesus did not give a positive endorsement of the practice of praying for the dead, but neither did he condemn it, even though he did not hesitate to condemn other Jewish practices of which he disapproved. Saint Paul himself evidently prayed for the dead, as we can see in 2 Timothy 1:18: "May the Lord grant him [Onesiphorus] to find mercy from the Lord on that Day." This prayer might be unexceptional, except that in verse 16, Paul wrote, "May the Lord grant mercy to the household of Onesiphorus", suggesting that the man in question had passed away and that his family was in need of comfort.

There is also another odd passage, 1 Corinthians 15:29, in which Paul asked the rhetorical question, "What do people mean by being baptized on behalf of the dead? If the dead are not raised at all, why are people baptized on their behalf?" In context, Paul is arguing for the resurrection and using the very behavior of the Corinthians to reinforce his argument. He does not condemn the practice of being baptized on the behalf of someone who has already died, though the practice seems extremely odd to us today.[83] The point is that the Corinthians thought that they could do something to affect the salvation of someone already dead, and Paul did not challenge their belief. So in the pages of Scripture, the seeds have already been sown for the practice of praying for the dead.

In the 250 years after Saint Paul's death, we have so much literary and archaeological evidence that Christians prayed for the dead that it is impossible to quote more than a fraction of it here. It should be noted, however, that the earliest evidence of this practice comes from the middle of the second century. This need not be taken as proof that the earliest Christians did not pray for the dead. The earliest writings, the *Didache*, and the letters of Ignatius and Clement of Rome were devoted to other topics.[84]

We learn more from later writings that focus on the prayer life of the Church. For instance, the apocryphal *Acts of Paul and Thecla* contains the following prayer, for one Falconilla, deceased daughter of Tryphaena: "God most high, grant to this woman according to wish, that her daughter Falconilla may live forever." [85] This has been understood to be a work of fiction since the days of Jerome, but even fiction can provide insights into the beliefs and practices of the time it was written. Scholarly consensus dates the *Acts of Paul and Thecla* to the middle of the second century. If this date is correct, we can surmise that it was an acceptable and even common practice to pray for the dead at that time.

Some fifty years after the *Acts of Paul and Thecla*, Tertullian wrote with great eloquence and confidence about prayers for the dead. In *On Monogamy*, he wrote about the duty of a wife to her deceased husband: "She prays for his soul, and requests refreshment for him meanwhile, and fellowship with him in the first resurrection; and she offers her sacrifice on the anniversaries of his falling asleep." [86]

One of the most powerful documents in the entire history of Christianity outside the New Testament is the *Acts of Saints Perpetua and Felicity*. Perpetua, Felicity, and their companions were martyred in 203 in Carthage. The work consists of three parts: the first part is a narrative of the events leading to Perpetua's arrest, the middle part is a prison diary written by Perpetua herself, and the third part is an epilogue written by the same person who wrote the first part. [87] In the middle part, Perpetua's diary, we find the following passage:

> While we were all praying, on a sudden, in the middle of our prayer, there came to be a word, and I named Dinocrates; and I was amazed that that name had never come into my mind until then, and I was grieved as I remembered his misfortune. And I felt myself immediately to be worthy, and to be called on to ask on his behalf. And for him I began earnestly to make supplication, and to cry with groaning to the Lord. Without delay, on that very night, this was shown to me in a vision. I saw Dinocrates going out from a gloomy place, where also there were several others, and he was parched and very thirsty, with a filthy countenance and pallid color, and the wound on his face which he had when he died. This Dinocrates had been my brother after the flesh, seven years of age, who died miserably with disease—his face being so eaten out with cancer, that his death caused repugnance to all men. For him I had made my prayer, and between him and me there was a large interval, so that neither of us could approach to the other. And moreover, in the same place where Dinocrates was, there was a pool full of water, having its brink higher than was the stature of the boy; and Dinocrates raised himself up as if to drink. And I was grieved that, although the pool held water, still, on account of the height to its brink, he could not drink. And I was aroused, and knew that my brother was in suffering. But I trusted that my prayer would bring help to his suffering; and I prayed for him every day until we passed over into the prison of the camp, for we were to fight in the camp-show ... and I made my prayer for my brother day and night, groaning and weeping that he might be granted to me. Then, on the day on which we remained

in fetters ... I saw that that place which I had formerly observed to be in gloom was now bright, and Dinocrates, with a clean body well clad, was finding refreshment. And where there had been a wound, I saw a scar; and that pool which I had before seen, I saw now with its margin lowered even to the boy's navel. And one drew water from the pool incessantly, and upon its brink was a goblet filled with water; and Dinocrates drew near and began to drink from it, and the goblet did not fail. And when he was satisfied, he went away from the water to play joyously, after the manner of children, and I awoke. Then I understood that he was translated from the place of punishment.[88]

Let us consider that practical implications of this passage. Perpetua had a dread, which must have been quite disturbing, for she saw her deceased brother suffering. But having seen this vision, she did not despair. Rather, she began to pray, with great intensity. She did not assume that, even though Dinocrates had died years before, his eternal destiny was fixed. She, and those around her, believed that praying for the dead was exactly the right thing to do. So we seem to have forceful evidence that the early Christians prayed for the dead.

But we need not rely solely on the literary evidence. If we descend into the Roman catacombs, we will find numerous inscriptions, carved near the tombs of loved ones. Here is one, dated from 268 or 269:

MARCIANE, VIBAS INTER SANCTIS[89]
[Marcian, live with the saints]

Here is one from the cemetery of Priscilla:

PRIVATA, DULCIS IN REFREGERIO ET IN PACE[90]
[Sweet Privata, may you be in solace (*refrigerio*) and in peace]

Next let us examine one that specifically invokes God:

BOLOSA, DEUS TIBI REFRIGERET QUAE VIXIT[91]
[Bolosa, may God grant you rest]

Finally, let's take a look at one that both asks for rest for the beloved and asks the loved one to pray for those left behind:

ATTICE SPIRITUS TUUS IN BONO ORA PRO PAREN TIBUS TUIS[92]
[Atticus, may thy soul be in bliss and do thou pray for thy parents]

The early Christians prayed for the deceased as a matter of love, piety, and faith. They believed that their prayers could help those who had died, and they believed that the prayers of those in Heaven would help them as well.

## A Brief Note on Mary in the Early Church

Since the saints played such a large, conspicuous role in the early Church, it may come as a surprise and a disappointment to some to find so few references to Mary in the life of the early Church. But the truth is that there are more references than we have been led to believe, and in our lifetime one of the greatest mysteries about Mary is being unraveled, on the outskirts of the ancient city of Ephesus. Before discussing this mystery, though, let's take a look at the literary and artistic references to Mary in the first three centuries.

The New Testament references are familiar. We all know the stories surrounding Jesus' birth, in the beginning of the Gospels of Matthew and Luke. Let us pay specific attention to Luke 1:28, where the angel of the Lord visits Mary and greets her, *"Chaire kecharitomene!"* This alliterative greeting is translated in modern translations as something like, "Greetings, favored one"[93] or "Rejoice, favored one!" Older translations, particularly Catholic ones, read, "Hail, full of grace!" It is not my purpose here to argue between translations. *Chaire* means both "greetings" (or "hail") and "rejoice".[94] *Kecharitomene*, though, is an odd word, which appears only here. Its meaning depends on how you translate the root word, *charis*. *Charis* means "loveliness or charm", "good will or favor", or "the kindness of a master toward his servants" (hence, the kindness of God toward mankind).[95] *Kecharitomene* means "one who is full of charis". So, the translation "Hail Mary, full of grace" is not as preposterous as some modern scholars make it seem.

Jesus' Virgin Birth, which is clearly attested to in the New Testament,[96] was accepted by the early Church. Ignatius of Antioch affirmed that Jesus was "truly born of a virgin".[97] The Fathers of the early Church all understood Isaiah 7:14 to have predicted the virginal birth: "Hear again how Isaiah in express words foretold that He should be born of a virgin; for he spoke this: 'Behold, a virgin shall conceive, and bring forth a son, and they shall say for His name, God with us.'

For things which were incredible and seemed impossible with men, these God predicted by the Spirit of prophecy as about to come to pass."[98]

One of the strangest documents of early Christianity, the *Protoevangelium of James*, tells of the conception and birth of Mary. The circumstances surrounding these events, as depicted in the *Protoevangelium*, seem remarkably similar to the Catholic doctrine of the Immaculate Conception.[99] In the *Protoevangelium*, we read, among other things, the following: "An angel of the Lord came to her and said: 'Anna, Anna, the Lord has heard your prayer. You shall conceive and bear, and your offspring shall be spoken of in the whole world.' "[100] We also read that Mary was examined by a midwife named Salome after giving birth to Jesus, and that Salome attested to her virginity after giving birth.[101]

The *Protoevangelium of James* is not considered a very reliable source for anything of historical or theological interest. It was probably written sometime in the latter half of the second century, clearly not by any of the Jameses associated with the New Testament. But it had a great deal of influence on the beliefs of the ordinary Christians of the time. It was translated into Syriac, Ethiopic, Georgian, and Coptic. So at least some of the Christians of the early Church believed in something very similar to the Immaculate Conception, though you will not find those particular words used to describe their beliefs.[102]

The great mystery to which I alluded earlier is quite fascinating. Outside the walls of the ancient city of Ephesus, on Nightingale Mountain, there is a small house nestled deep in the forest. This house is clearly quite new, but if you look closely at the foundation stones, you will see that those stones are extremely old. The foundation of this house was discovered as a result of the visions of a nineteenth-century German nun, Anne Catherine Emmerich. Sister Emmerich, who never left Germany, had a series of visions in which she seemed to see the house the Virgin Mary lived in when she dwelt in Ephesus.

Against all odds, following clues derived from Sister Emmerich's visions, a group of Jesuit archaeologists actually found the house exactly where she said it would be. This strange story leads to more questions than answers. Is it possible that the Blessed Virgin Mary lived in Ephesus? Could she have lived in this particular house? The answer to these questions appears to be maybe. We know from the Gospel of John that from the Cross, Jesus placed his mother in the care of the Apostle John.[103] We have a great deal of evidence that John, after being driven out of Jerusalem by persecution, eventually settled in Ephesus. So if Mary was still alive when John went to Ephesus, it seems reasonable that he would have taken her with him.

But what about the house in question? Could it have been the house in which Mary lived? The answer appears to be a qualified yes. The bottom courses of stone on this house are quite old, and in fact archaeologists date those stones to the first century. But there is no plaque written in Greek, Latin, and Hebrew saying, "Mary, the Mother of Jesus, lived here".[104]

There are in fact some texts that write about Mary's life in Ephesus. We have no idea how authentic these documents are, but they indicate that Mary lived "in Ephesus with Salome, Joanna, and some of her girlhood companions from the Temple, where they turned the house of John into an evangelical center devoted to the spreading of Jesus' message".[105] The information in this quote was gleaned from the apocryphal *Acts of Bartholomew*, an Egyptian work from some time in the third or fourth century. It cannot be taken as proof that Mary really lived in Ephesus, but it does point to that possibility. Other Egyptian documents from the same period depict Mary spending the last years of her life in Jerusalem.[106]

The same group of Egyptian documents contains stories about the last days of Mary's life. Some scholars think these documents are the source of the Catholic dogma of the bodily Assumption of Mary into Heaven. The problem is, the documents, or more accurately, fragments of documents, do not tell a consistent story about Mary's last days. One manuscript mentions one Evodius as an eyewitness of what can be described only as Mary's Assumption into Heaven. But the document is wildly inaccurate on other important details. The Evodius we know of was the Bishop of Antioch before Ignatius.[107] If Eusebius is to be believed, Evodius was the first bishop of that city, so he must have been appointed by an apostle. He must have known John, Peter and Paul, and even Mary herself if she really lived in Ephesus, since there were always many connections between the Churches in Antioch and Ephesus.

But in the document Robinson has entitled "The Falling Asleep of Mary", Evodius is referred to as the "Archbishop of the great city of

Rome, who was the second after Peter the Apostle".[108] If the author of this obscure Egyptian work really knew what Evodius said about Mary, is it not reasonable to think that he would at least have known where Evodius lived?

So we have no proof of the dogma of the Assumption in the literature of the very early Church. What we do have is a collection of perhaps a dozen fragments of manuscripts attesting that in the third and fourth century many people in Egypt believed that something mysterious and wonderful happened to Mary when she passed from this life.

Mary can be found in some of the artwork of the early Church. In the *Cappella Graecae*, deep in the vaults of the catacombs of Priscilla, there are two wall paintings clearly depicting Mary with the baby Jesus. One shows a woman with a child on her breast, while a man dressed in the garb of a philosopher points at a star shining above her head. The other picture shows the visit of the magi to the Holy Family and is considered the oldest artistic representation of Mary that we now possess, going back to the middle of the second century.[109] Both these paintings show Mary seated, with the Child in her arms.

Another group of objects found in the catacombs deserves mention, although we are not sure what they mean. Some of these praying figures, dated to the third and fourth centuries, are engraved with the Latin name MARIA. Were these figures statues of Mary? Were people asking Mary to pray for them? Or is there some other explanation? We simply do not have enough information to answer these questions. But there are two things we do know. These figures are found in great numbers near the tombs of Christians in the catacombs, and the figures have their arms extended, presumably in the act of prayer.[110]

What are we to make of this disparate collection of clues regarding the role of Mary in the early Church? Well, we have no clear evidence of a cult of Mary, as we clearly do have evidence of a cult of the martyrs. The idea of Mary's sinlessness was alluded to in some documents, as well as the idea that Mary was somehow taken up to Heaven on her deathbed. In the catacombs, we find evidence that might lead one to conclude that Mary was asked to intercede for departed loved ones (although this evidence is open to other interpretations). What we do have, I think, is evidence that many of the beliefs and practices that later became common in the Church were nascent in the beliefs and practices of the early Church.

## Conclusion

The prayer life of the early Christians can be summed up with one word: communion. They believed that through prayer they could achieve communion with God and with the Body of Christ, both on this earth and in Heaven. Daily prayer, Eucharist, and special prayers for the deceased were the components that molded the lives of the Christians and gave them the strength to live their hard and dangerous lives.

## CHAPTER 3

# The Organization of the Early Church

The early Christians lived lives of community, by necessity and by choice. By this I do not mean that they lived in communities, as did the monks of a later age. The first Christians tended to live in family units, or in small groups of friends, as most people do today. But they lived in community in the sense that members believed themselves to be responsible to and for one another. Provisions were made for the systematic care of widows and orphans, and appropriate people were appointed to see to these tasks. Local decisions were usually made publicly, with input from as many members as possible.

On a larger scale, leaders fostered a sense that the local Christian community was a part of something much larger. The house churches, or *tituli*, as they were called in Rome, of a single city were all united under the headship of one bishop. The bishop presided over a council of presbyters, and the bishop, in communion with his presbyters, would govern the church of a city. The bishops of the various cities, in their turn, would write to one another with astonishing regularity, and regional bishops would sometimes meet in synods to decide important matters.

At a very early date, decisions that could not be decided locally were referred to the Bishop of Rome. The Bishop of Rome, for his part, would attempt to resolve these disputes with the advice of his own presbyters. Sometimes the decisions would be made well and wisely, and other times not so well and not so wisely, but local bishops believed that communion with the Bishop of Rome was a goal for which it was worth striving no matter what the difficulty. The constant theme of the early Church, whether at the local or the universal level, was "unity in the truth". The early Christians were not interested in unity without truth; they frequently withdrew fellowship from those they considered heretics. But within the confines of truth, charity and accommodation were the rule.

Today we have a tendency to idealize the early Christians. A careful study of their history will quickly dispel this tendency. They were as human as we are today and just as prone to childishness, pride, careerism, and even treachery. They differed from us in two ways: (1) the average Christian tended to be much more serious about his faith, since it cost so much to be a Christian, and (2) they were closer to the origins of Christianity.

The second point is actually quite important. Human nature being what it is, from the very start distortions of the Christian message began to develop everywhere. Some heretics denied the divinity of Christ, while others denied his humanity. There were those, called Gnostics, who taught that the flesh was evil, that only the spirit was good, and that only those who were in possession of special knowledge could be saved.

These doctrinal difficulties were not merely theoretical; they caused real problems in the Church and had to be dealt with. When you consider these doctrinal difficulties along with the ever-present danger of persecution, it seems clear that the early Church needed strong leadership.[1] It would be a mistake to think the early Church was organized like a modern democracy. It is true that bishops were elected by popular acclamation. It is also true that most important decisions were made by a bishop conferring with his presbyters (if the matter were local) or by local synods (if the question involved more than one *ecclesia*). But once decisions were made, it was expected that everyone would abide by them. As mentioned, if controversies proved intractable, an appeal would be made to Rome, and if an appeal was made to Rome, then Rome's decision had to be followed.[2]

The ways in which the early Church exercised authority varied from the ways it is exercised today in subtle but important ways. This is necessarily the case, since our ways of thinking and organizing society have changed. It is also true that within the period we are discussing, there were already evolutions in understanding and in actual practice. But it is my thesis that the early Church was organized in essentially the same way the Roman Catholic Church is organized today.

*From Synagogue to* Ecclesia

There is a book on the early Church, written in 1990, with the very first chapter titled "The Wonderful Time When There Was Neither Clergy nor Laity".[3] My purpose in mentioning this chapter title is simply to point out a modern assumption that skews our understanding of the early Church. In the modern, egalitarian West, we assume that hierarchies are bad things. Since we also assume that the early Church was a model Christian community, our conclusion, without examining the facts, is that the early Church did not have any form of rank or distinction between members. But it is easy to discover that this was not the case, even in the New Testament Church.

Alexandre Faivre's argument rests on the undeniable fact that the words "clergy" and "laity" are not used in the New Testament. It is true that the words are not used, but the ideas behind the words are clearly present. During the lifetime of Jesus we find "the Twelve" (also referred to as the twelve apostles) and "the Seventy-Two" (disciples). Moreover, he gave these groups of men authority he did not grant to others. It seems clear, then, that Jesus had some kind of hierarchy in mind, and to deny this would be to do violence to the spirit of the New Testament itself.

The Church, if we believe there is such a thing, is an unusual institution in that she has both divine and human origins: divine in that Christ is ultimately always the one who calls people forth to ministry; human in that it is always human persons who are called, and human offices to which they are called. The question of succession to office, which brought the mystery of the humanity of the Church to the fore, came about when the apostles came to the end of their lives, with no sign that Christ was coming back anytime soon. When it became clear that the fast-growing Church was going to exist beyond the death of the Twelve, we find the apostles appointing *episkopoi* (overseers), *presbyteroi* (elders), and *diakonoi* (servants) to fill the administrative and ministerial needs of the Church.

Before talking about the offices the apostles created, it is important to first discuss the nature of apostleship, as it is presented in the New Testament. We are all familiar with the calling of the Twelve, which is recounted in all four Gospels.[4] The significance of the Twelve is fairly obvious. There were twelve patriarchs of Israel and twelve tribes. The twelve apostles signify the continuity of the New Covenant with the Covenant God made with Israel. Jesus seems to have chosen twelve apostles as a symbolic action to make the relationship clear.[5]

The title "apostle" comes from the Greek word *apostolos*, which simply means "one who is sent", or, more specifically, "an ambassador, envoy, delegate or messenger".[6] In Christian usage, the word is associated with the special friends of Jesus, who were called for the specific ministry of proclaiming the gospel to the world. But in the ancient world, many people were called apostles. In fact, important members of the Jewish Sanhedrin were called apostles. They would travel the Mediterranean, visiting synagogues, and they were empowered to act on behalf of the whole Sanhedrin if circumstances required it.[7]

This fact explains what otherwise would be a rather significant problem: the existence of the Apostle Paul. Jesus Christ did not call Paul before his Crucifixion and Resurrection; indeed, it is unlikely that they ever met. Yet in the New Testament, and not just in his own letters, Paul is repeatedly referred to as an apostle.[8] Not only is Paul called an apostle, but he gives the title of apostle to men who clearly were not of the Twelve.[9] So just what was an apostle, and how did one get the title?

The problem is complicated, but can be resolved by understanding one simple fact: in the writings of Paul, there are two kinds of apostles. There are "apostles of Jesus Christ" such as himself, Peter, and the other apostles in Jerusalem, whose authority he does not deny. There are also apostles of the Church. This is the category that includes the "brothers" mentioned in 2 Corinthians 8:23 and Epaphroditus in Philippians 2:25. They were simply "sent" by the local church, or by Paul himself to perform some unspecified task.[10]

Of all the titles Paul gives himself, "Paul, an apostle of Jesus Christ", or some variant, is by far the most common. It is also significant that in his first and second letters, Peter uses the same phrase to describe himself.[11] So being an apostle per se was not special, but to be an apostle of Jesus Christ conferred authority and a special charism. Paul was an apostle on the same level as the Twelve because the risen Christ did indeed appear to him and because the original apostles accepted him as one of them.[12]

This is an important point because Scripture shows Jesus conferring special authority on the Twelve. In Matthew 18:18, Jesus tells them (among other things), "whatever you bind on earth will be bound in heaven, and whatever you loose on earth will be loosed in heaven." Furthermore, in John 20:19–23, Jesus breathes on the apostles and says, "Peace be with you. As the Father has sent me, so I send you. Receive the Holy Spirit. If you forgive the sins of any, they are forgiven them; if you retain the sins of any, they are retained."

It is not necessary here to give a detailed exegesis of these passages, but it is clear that significant authority is given to the apostles. The authority to make judgments in matters of faith and morals is implied in Matthew 18:18. These are the powers that in the Old Testament were given to the levitical priesthood.[13] In addition, in John 20:23, Jesus explicitly gives the apostles the power to forgive sins. Since the twelve apostles, on a symbolic level, were meant to signify the continuity of the New Covenant with the Old, it makes sense that on a practical level the apostles would be given the same authority as the Old Testament priesthood. One important question remains, however. We are discussing apostolic succession: were they given the authority to choose and anoint successors?

## The Beginnings of Apostolic Succession

You will search the New Testament in vain for a passage that depicts Jesus actually telling the apostles to choose successors before they died. But why would Jesus give them this authority and not expect them to pass it on? The levitical authority was designed to continue in history, so why not the apostolic authority? In any event, after Jesus' Ascension, we find numerous passages that show the apostles appointing officers to minister to the Church. The first and most obvious was the choosing of Judas' successor in Acts 1:15–26. Other instances quickly come to mind: in Acts 6, deacons are chosen to provide services the apostles are unable to see to personally.

Now we have reached the point where we can discuss the episcopacy in the New Testament. The Greek word *episkopos* simply means "overseer". So it is fascinating that in Acts 1:20, when the successor of Judas is being chosen, the Psalm quoted to justify their action says, "Let another take his position of overseer [*episkopos*]" (author's translation from the Greek). The apostles saw themselves as overseers and were already appointing new overseers as needed. Paul, since he was an authentic apostle, called by Christ and confirmed by the other apostles, also appointed overseers as the need arose. Let us focus on Acts 20. Paul is on his way back to Jerusalem, a mission so full of danger that his followers rightly fear that they will never see him again. In verse 28, he tells the elders assembled, "Keep watch over yourselves and over all the flock, of which the Holy Spirit has made you overseers [*episkopoi*], to shepherd the Church of God." In Philippians 1:1, Paul addresses this letter to "all the saints in Christ Jesus who are in Philippi, with the bishops and deacons".

How did Paul confer his authority to the bishops he chose to guide the local flocks? In 2 Timothy 1:6, Paul urges Timothy to "rekindle the gift of God that is within you through the laying on of my hands." Similarly, in 1 Timothy 4:14, Paul tells Timothy, "Do not neglect the gift you have, which was given by prophetic utterance when the elders laid their hands upon you." Paul believed that the Holy Spirit was ultimately the one who called people forth to ministry. The human instruments of the divine will were the apostles and elders, who by the imposition of hands conferred authority on those who were chosen. Furthermore, when someone had been called to the episcopacy, he had the authority in turn to anoint others who were chosen. In 1 Timothy 5:22, Paul warns Timothy not to "ordain anyone hastily" (author's translation). In Titus 1:5, Paul reminds Titus that he was to "appoint elders in every town".

So here we see very clearly the origin of the offices of the Church, the *episkopoi*, the *presbyteroi*, and the *diakonoi*. The machinery had been set in place for these offices to continue through time, for as long as they were needed. From the levitical priesthood to the New Testament Church, a line of authority was established, with the apostles as the living bridges between the two covenants. Now let us examine how the various offices established by the apostles actually functioned in the early Church.

*From Apostles to Bishops*

The apostolic age did not end suddenly, but over a period of time. The Apostle James was martyred in about A.D. 51 in Jerusalem. Peter and Paul were martyred sometime between 64 and 67 in Rome. The last of the twelve apostles was John, who died of natural causes sometime between 92 and 98. We know that there were numerous small, local Christian communities scattered throughout the world.[14] We know that many of these communities were founded by apostles. But it is about fifty years before we hear from most of these communities again. When we do hear from them, they have bishops, presbyters, and deacons in positions of ministry. Most scholars think these structures arose gradually in the local communities. But for the following reasons there is no real reason to postulate a gradual evolution of the episcopacy: (1) as we have seen, the process of systematizing the ministry of local communities was already under way in the New Testament period; (2) the documents we have from the generation after the death of the apostles do speak of episcopal governance; (3) from 150 on we have numerous documents attesting to apostolic succession, some of which actually trace the succession from bishop to bishop all the way back to the apostles; and (4) as we shall soon see, the structures of the early Church were borrowed from the Jewish synagogue structure of that time, so there was no need to "invent" new offices, titles, and functions.

Since we have already discussed the New Testament evidence, let us move on to the next-generation documents. There are only three relevant Christian documents from this period: the *Didache* (written ca. 90–100), Clement of Rome's *First Epistle to the Corinthians* (ca. 96), and the letters of Ignatius of Antioch (107–115).

Scholars agree that the *Didache* was most likely written as a manual for new Christian communities, because the instructions contained in it are so basic.[15] It was written quite early in the history of the Church, so much so that apostles and prophets are still mentioned.[16] The apostles referred to are probably apostles of the Church, that is, emissaries from other local communities, rather than the apostles of Jesus Christ. The prophets mentioned were itinerant preachers, who wandered from community to community, celebrating the Eucharist, preaching, and moving on. There were also wandering teachers, who had similar customs. The problem with these itinerant preachers was, of course, that it was hard to tell who was authentic and who was not. The *Didache* lays down a simple rule: if a prophet or apostle stays longer than three days and asks for money when he leaves, he is false and should be shunned. In this context, the *Didache* recommends, "Appoint, therefore, for yourselves, bishops and deacons worthy of the Lord, men meek, and not lovers of money, and truthful and proved; for they also render to you the service of prophets and teachers." [17]

With this data in mind, let us construct a reasonable scenario. The *Didache* was probably written in Antioch, one of the oldest communities in the Church. As a service to the newer communities, someone put together a manual of the things he had learned. The new communities, excited by their newfound faith, were susceptible to charlatans. It was important that they appoint reliable men to lead them, so they could avoid chaos and disillusionment. Some scholars have seen in these passages evidence that the episcopal structure of the Church evolved late, and that the *Didache* represents an early stage of this evolution. But it seems to me more likely that the episcopacy was well established in the community that produced the *Didache*. Furthermore, it seems that that community was anxious for the newer communities to get off to the right start. Therefore, the authors of the *Didache* were careful to recommend the episcopal structure over the looser structure that featured wandering prophets and teachers. [18]

Clement's *First Epistle to the Corinthians* (or *I Clement*) is a long letter written from the Church of Rome to the Church at Corinth, [19] in response to some question posed by the Corinthians. [20] The salutation indicates no particular author, but the letter has always been attributed to Clement for the following reasons: (1) the Church historian Eusebius (ca. 260–340) attributes it to him, [21] (2) if you follow the chronology of the bishops of Rome provided by Hegessippus, Clement must have been Bishop of Rome at the time the letter was written, (3) the letter shows a unity of thought that is incompatible with production by a committee, [22] and (4) a later bishop of Corinth wrote that he had in his possession the letter from Clement and that it was still read in his church.

I have laid out the arguments for Clement being the author of this letter because some modern scholars, Catholic as well as Protestant, have theorized that there was no one Bishop of Rome at this time, and that the Roman Church was governed by a council of presbyters, of which Clement may or may not have been the chief.

To whom the letter was written is another contentious point for this letter. Who were the leaders of the community in Corinth? Clement is clearly writing to the whole Church, but he has some things to say about the leaders: "You lived in accordance with the laws of God, submitting yourselves to your leaders [*hegoumenois*] and giving to the presbyters among you the honor due them." [23] Later in the letter he writes, "Let us respect our leaders [*prohegoumenous*]; let us honor our presbyters." [24] Presbyters are mentioned by their correct title, but there is no mention of a bishop in these passages. For this reason, some scholars have supposed that in fact Corinth did not have a bishop.

If this theory is true, then thirty years after the death of Peter and Paul, the two most important Western churches did not have bishops, and the idea that there was a steady, traceable line of succession from the apostles to the bishops down through the ages would be in question. But is this theory in fact true? I have argued that Clement was the Bishop of Rome and the author of this letter, and now I am going to argue that the Bishop of Corinth is in fact mentioned in the letter as well.

Eusebius provides the clue to unraveling the mystery of why the Bishop of Corinth is not mentioned in *I Clement*. In his writings on *I Clement*, this piece of information is found: "In this epistle he gives many thoughts drawn from the Epistle to the Hebrews, and also quotes verbally some of its expressions, thus showing most plainly that it is not a recent production.... [T]he epistle of Clement and that to the Hebrews have a similar character in regard to style, and ... the thoughts contained in the two works are not very different." [25] This fact is significant because the Epistle to the Hebrews also uses the Greek word *hegoumenoi* to describe the leaders of the Christian community.[26] The Letter to the Hebrews does not use the word *episkopoi* to describe leaders. Since Clement borrowed terminology from Hebrews, it is reasonable to assume that the word *hegoumenoi* is also borrowed from Hebrews. It is not too far a stretch to suppose that *hegoumenos* and *episkopos* are synonyms, and both words refer to the highest authority in the local community, and that highest authority is what today we would call a bishop.

In support of my argument let me go back to the two passages from *I Clement* quoted earlier. The author speaks of leaders *and* presbyters. Who are these "leaders" if they are distinct from the presbyters? If there are higher authorities than the presbyters, are they not, ipso facto, bishops? We need not, in my opinion, be unduly concerned by Clement's use of the plural in writing about leaders. He is not implying that Corinth had more than one bishop at a time. He is simply observing that the Corinthians had a history of following their bishops.

Besides, later in the letter, Clement does mention bishops. "Christ therefore was sent forth by God, and the apostles by Christ. Both these appointments, then, were made in an orderly way, according to the will of God. . . . And thus preaching through countries and cities, they appointed the first-fruits, having first proved them by the Spirit, to be bishops and deacons of those who should afterward believe." [27] Why would Clement write about the appointment of bishops by the apostles if neither Rome nor Corinth had a bishop?

The evidence leads one to the conclusion that both Corinth and Rome were ruled by individual bishops, who worked in close conjunction with a council of presbyters, and that these offices could trace their origins to the apostles themselves.

The third author we need to consider from the first generation after the apostles is Ignatius, Bishop of Antioch. Ignatius was arrested, tried, and convicted for being a Christian sometime around 107.[28] He was transported to Rome for his execution, and on the way he wrote a series of letters to the Churches at Ephesus, Magnesia, Smyrna, Tralles, Philadelphia, and Rome. He also sent a letter to his friend Polycarp, Bishop of Smyrna. The five letters to the Churches of Asia are all basically the same. These letters provide a great deal of information on the status of the episcopacy in the early Church. The letter to the Church at Rome is unique, because it was written to ask the Roman Christians not to try to get him a pardon. This letter will be dealt with in the next section. The letter to Polycarp is fascinating in its own right and will be discussed in the next section.

The letters to the Ephesians, Magnesians, Smyrneans, Trallians, and Philadelphians were written while Ignatius was still in Asia, on his way to Rome. He was able to meet and confer with some of the Asian bishops on an individual basis after his arrest, but he sent the letters to have a more permanent record of his final thoughts. Or were they instructions? Some scholars have plausibly suggested that Ignatius exercised some kind of regional authority over the bishops of Asia.[29] In any event, Ignatius' letters are important because they shed light on the attitude of the Church toward her bishops at a very early time.

Ignatius is especially significant because there is a good chance that he knew the apostles. Eusebius wrote that Ignatius was the second

Bishop of Antioch after Peter left.[30] Assuming that Ignatius was seventy when he was martyred, he would have been a young man in his twenties when Peter and Paul were in Antioch. He could have learned much from these two men, and it seems unlikely that he would have distorted their teachings or ignored their intention for the Church of Antioch. Besides, if he had done so, there would have been plenty of people in Antioch who would have known and protested.

So what did Ignatius wish to impart to the bishops, clergy, and people of Asia? Ignatius seems to have been primarily concerned with the unity of the local communities. The Churches of Asia and Syria were wracked by heresy and division. In each of the five letters, Ignatius warns against false teachers who were moving among the communities, sowing dissension and false doctrine: "Some that are without God, that is, the unbelieving, say, 'He became man in appearance only.'"[31] It is clear, from reading Ignatius, that the problems with the heretics were not purely intellectual. They were destroying love in the communities they inhabited: "But consider those who are of a different opinion with respect to the grace of Christ which has come unto us, how opposed they are to the will of God. They have no regard for love; no care for the widow, or the orphan, or the oppressed; of the bond, or of the free; of the hungry, or of the thirsty."[32]

For Ignatius, the antidote to false teaching was to remain loyal to one's properly appointed bishop. Over and over again, Ignatius writes something like this: "It is fitting that you should act together in accordance with the will of your bishop, as indeed you do. For your justly renowned presbytery, worthy of God, is fitted as exactly to the bishop as the strings are to the harp. Therefore in your concord and harmonious love Jesus Christ is sung. And you, man by man, become a choir, that being harmonious in love, and taking up the song of God in unison, may with one voice sing to the Father."[33] Ignatius was convinced that communion between the bishop, his presbyters, and the whole people of God was an essential sign of the true Church, and that the bishop himself was to be the focus and source of that unity. Thus, he also writes: "As therefore the Lord did nothing without the Father, being united to Him, neither by Himself nor by the apostles, so neither do you anything without the bishop and presbyters."[34] Such was the great emphasis Ignatius put on unity of belief, thought, and action.

Ignatius wrote that a bishop's authority comes from Christ, as Christ comes from God, but he took this thought a step farther. He also believed that bishops were in some way Christ's representatives on earth: "We ought to receive every one whom the Master of the house sends to be over His household, as we would do Him that sent him. It is manifest, therefore, that we should look upon the bishop even as we would upon the Lord Himself." [35]

Ignatius also believed that the bishop should be the sole authority in liturgical matters in his community: "It is not lawful without the bishop either to baptize or to celebrate a love-feast; but whatsoever he shall approve of, that is also pleasing to God, so that everything that is done may be secure and valid." [36]

It is easy to misunderstand Ignatius' writings, particularly when they are presented out of context. Ignatius could seem to be merely seeking more power for the bishops. But the communities to which he wrote were troubled by the ongoing persecution and by schismatics who taught heresy and were lacking in Christian love. In this context, Ignatius' insistence on obedience to and unity with the bishop can be understood more clearly. Ignatius' primary concern was the unity in faith and love of the Christian communities of Asia, and he believed that the bishops were the best guarantors of that unity.

I have focused on these three early authors because I wanted to establish that the episcopacy was an important part of Church organization from the start. Next, we shall look at two later authors who have advanced the Church's understanding of the episcopacy: Irenaeus of Lyons and Cyprian of Carthage. It was Irenaeus who introduced the phrase "apostolic succession" and did so much to help us understand the implications of that teaching. From Cyprian of Carthage we can learn much about the procedures used in the election of bishops and the employment of synods of bishops to solve regional problems. As we shall see later, Cyprian also had numerous, sometimes controversial, dealings with various bishops of Rome.

Heresy, division, and controversy were powerful motivators for Irenaeus of Lyons. Irenaeus was born and raised in Asia. He knew Polycarp, Bishop of Smyrna, as a youth. At some point, he must have traveled to Rome and spent considerable time there. His writings contain ideas and phrases first used by Justin Martyr, and it has been suggested that he may have been a student of Justin. [37] In any event, he was in Rome in 155, when Polycarp paid a visit to Pope Anicetus, and he provided an eyewitness account of a liturgy at which Anicetus graciously allowed Polycarp to preside. It was in Rome that Irenaeus first became aware of the teachings of the Gnostics Valentinus and Marcion.

From Rome, Irenaeus traveled to Lyons, where he became a presbyter. In 177, a brutal persecution came upon the Church of Lyons. Bishop Pothinus and many other members of that community were arrested and tortured horribly. Irenaeus was sent to Rome to inform Pope Eleutherius what was happening, and it may be that this was the reason he was able to escape death himself. When he returned to Lyons, Bishop Pothinus was already martyred, and the Church chose Irenaeus as his successor. Sometime in the mid-180s he wrote a monumental work, *Against Heresies*. In this work, he first gave a highly detailed account of the beliefs of the Gnostics and then presented a series of scriptural, philosophical, and historical arguments against the sect.

What was Irenaeus' problem with the Gnostics? "These men falsify the oracles of God, and prove themselves evil interpreters of the good word of revelation."[38] False interpreters of revelation have to be countered with those who have the right and responsibility to interpret the Word correctly. For Irenaeus, those who have been given the charism to interpret the Word of God are the bishops of the universal Church. But how would one prove that these bishops were authentic? Irenaeus chose to argue that the bishops could be trusted as authentic interpreters: "We have learned from none others the plan of our salvation, than from those through whom the Gospel has come down to us, which they did at one time proclaim in public, and, at a later period, by the will of God, handed down to us in the Scriptures, to be the ground and pillar of our faith."[39] This is an important point to realize. For Irenaeus, it was not the physical succession, from apostle to bishop and on down, but the succession of correct teachings that were passed on from the apostles to the bishops, that really mattered.

Nevertheless, authentic teaching has to be carried on by somebody, and in Irenaeus' mind, there was no doubt that it was the bishops who were given the spiritual gifts to transmit that teaching faithfully. So Irenaeus' argument runs thus: "It is within the power of all, therefore, in every Church, who may wish to see the truth, to contemplate clearly the tradition of the apostles manifested throughout the whole world; and we are in a position to reckon up those who were by the apostles instituted bishops in the Churches, and to demonstrate the succession of these men to our own times; those who neither taught nor knew of anything like what these heretics rave about." [40]

What conclusion did Irenaeus draw from his line of argument? Basically the same conclusion Ignatius drew seventy years earlier: "It is incumbent to obey the presbyters who are in the Church—those who, as I have shown, possess the succession from the apostles; those who, together with the succession of the episcopate, have received the certain gift of truth, according to the good pleasure of the Father. But it is also incumbent to hold in suspicion others who depart from the primitive succession, and assemble themselves together in any place whatsoever." [41] Notice that Irenaeus believed that the presbyters who were in communion with the bishop also possessed "the certain gift of truth". Irenaeus' position can be summed up thus: "Only by listening to those who maintained this original succession could one be sure of hearing the truth taught by the apostles." [42]

So far, we have focused on proving that the episcopal ministry was important in the early Church. This is important because many modern writers have tended to downplay the importance of the episcopacy for the early Church. But other questions concern us. How were bishops chosen? What did their daily ministry look like? Did they cooperate with one another on matters of mutual concern? How did the people really feel about their bishops? Some of these questions can be answered by perusing the writings of Cyprian of Carthage, who presided over the Church of Carthage during one of the most tumultuous periods of its history.

Cyprian has become a favorite today of those who wish to democratize the Catholic Church. This is a debate into which I have no desire to enter, but I will say that it is an undeniable fact that in the early Church, bishops were elected by popular assent. We should be aware, however, that the practice was discontinued in the Middle Ages because the election of bishops had been captured by powerful political forces who wished to control the Church for their own purposes. What happened once could happen again, so those who think that all our problems would be solved if only we could elect bishops should think twice. It might be that the election of bishops worked only when the Church was a persecuted minority. [43]

Having said all this, the procedure the early Church used in choosing bishops has much to commend itself, in terms of transparency and openness of process. Here is how the *Apostolic Tradition* describes the selection and ordination of a bishop:

> Let the bishop be ordained after he has been chosen by all the people. When he has been named and shall please all, let him, with the presbytery and such bishops as may be present, assemble with the people on a Sunday. While all give their consent, the bishops shall lay their hands upon him, and the presbytery shall stand by in silence. All indeed shall keep silent, praying in their heart for the descent of the Spirit. Then one of the bishops who are present shall, at the request of all, lay his hand on him who is ordained bishop.[44]

Bear in mind that the *Apostolic Tradition* was written around A.D. 200. The bare bones of the procedure outlined above can be fleshed out by additional information from one of Cyprian's letters. In January 250, Fabian, Bishop of Rome, was martyred. Due to the ongoing persecution, his successor, Cornelius, was not chosen until March 251. A Roman priest named Novatian challenged the election. A crisis ensued; some of Cyprian's neighbors were inclined to support Novatian over Cornelius.

Cyprian, for his part, supported the validity of Cornelius' election, and sent a letter to his fellow bishop Antonianus, outlining his reasons:

> I come now, dearest brother, to the character of Cornelius our colleague, that with us you may more justly know Cornelius, not from the lies of malignants and detractors, but from the judgment of the Lord God, who made him a bishop, and from the testimony of his fellow bishops, the whole number of whom has agreed with an absolute unanimity throughout the whole world. For ... he was not one who on a sudden attained to the episcopate; but, promoted through all the ecclesiastical offices, and having often deserved well of the Lord in divine administrations, he ascended by all the grades of religious service to the lofty summit of the Priesthood. Then, moreover, he did not either ask for the episcopate itself nor did he wish it; nor, as others do when the swelling of their arrogance and pride inflates them, did he seize upon it ... but he himself suffered compulsion, so as to be forced to receive the episcopal office. And he was made bishop by very many of our colleagues who were then present in the city of Rome, who sent to us letters concerning his ordination, honorable and laudatory,

and remarkable for their testimony in announcement of him. Moreover, Cornelius was made bishop by the judgment of God and of His Christ, by the testimony of almost all the clergy, by the suffrage of the people who were then present, and by the assembly of ancient priests and good men.[45]

From these two sources, we can make the following generalizations about the ordination of bishops in the early Church:

1. It was understood that bishops are chosen by the will of God and that God would use human instruments to affect his will.

2. The clergy were given the right to testify on behalf of candidates.

3. The people were given *suffragio*, which should probably be understood as the right to vote, for the episcopal candidates. In any event, in some way the people were given a forum for expressing their approval or disapproval.

4. It was essential that as many neighboring bishops as possible should be on hand to supervise the selection process and to ordain the newly chosen bishop.

As illuminating as these points are, there are still many unanswered questions: How were candidates nominated? How did the people get to express their opinion? Was there a ballot, a voice vote, or a show of hands, or did the candidate whose supporters could shout the loudest win? What happened if the bishops favored one candidate and the people preferred another? Sooner or later these questions would have come up. The early Christians prized harmony, peace, and unity among the community so greatly that they must have had a system designed to ensure the orderly succession of authority. Regarding episcopal elections, we know for sure only the things I've outlined above. It is, however, possible to construct a plausible scenario, based on the evidence, that answers the questions I have enumerated.

Let us take a look at the way civic elections were held in Roman colonies. In the Republican period, most free men of all Roman cities had a voice in the election of their local leaders. The preferred method of balloting involved the voters writing the name of their candidate on *tabellae*, small pieces of paper or wood.[46] But in the imperial age, the voting rights of ordinary people slowly atrophied. By the middle of the third century, the normal procedure was for appointed magistrates to select suitable candidates. The people were then given the right to give *testimonium* on the qualifications of the candidates, and then they would vote.[47]

Given the state of the evidence, I am prepared to construct a scenario that can fill in the gaps. First, I think it likely that the local presbyters were given the responsibility of selecting a list of qualified candidates, probably only two or three. To prepare this list, it seems likely that they would have had to have a series of meetings, and perhaps votes, to narrow down the field. They also, I think, would have sent the candidates' names to the bishops who would be present on the day of voting. Any candidate unacceptable to the bishops would automatically be removed from the ballot. On the day when the neighboring bishops were in town, the priests would present the candidates to everyone and provide a summary of the candidates' qualifications. The people would then be allowed to voice their own opinions. When everyone who wished to speak had been given an opportunity, the people would vote. I think the *tabellae* would have been used, to preserve confidentiality and prevent the humiliation of the losing candidates. Under the supervision of the bishops, the priests would count the ballots. When a winner was determined, the assembled bishops would take over and ordain the candidate.

This scenario steps outside the bounds of the evidence, but it does not contradict the evidence, and it has the advantage of maximizing order and harmony. Yet, as we saw in the case of Cornelius and Novatian, Church elections were not without controversy. The only process devoid of difficulties had been when Jesus walked near the Sea of Galilee, calling forth this man and that, for reasons he alone knew.

Once ordained, bishops were expected to rule their dioceses with love and humility. We have already discussed the rule in the *Didascalia Apostolorum*, to the effect that if a visitor comes to his church, particularly an old man, the bishop should yield his chair if there are no other seats available. We have numerous documents that quote 1 Timothy 3:2, "Now a bishop must be above reproach ..." Here is how the *Didascalia Apostolorum* puts it:

> But concerning the bishopric, hear ye. The pastor who is appointed bishop and head of the presbytery in the Church in every

congregation, it is required of him that he be blameless, in nothing reproachable, one remote from all evil, a man not less than fifty years of age, who is now removed from all the manners of youth and from the lusts of the Enemy, and from the slander and blasphemy of false brethren, which they bring against many because they understand not that word which is said in the Gospel.[48]

So a bishop, once elected, was not to be a tyrant. Nevertheless, if a bishop somehow were to offend his flock, it is clear that the laity could not take action to remove him from office, except in those cases where the bishop was among the *lapsi*, who renounced Christ under threat of persecution.[49] For their part, the people were expected to obey their bishop in all matters: "The layman loves the bishop and honours and fears him as father and lord, and as God after God almighty, for to the Bishop it was said through the apostles: 'Everyone that heareth you heareth me, and everyone that rejecteth you rejecteth me, and him that sent me.' "[50]

As mentioned earlier, some bishops achieved some measure of regional primacy. The bishops of Antioch supervised all the bishops of Syria, Alexandria ruled all of Egypt, Carthage ruled all of North Africa, and Rome had primacy over all the bishops. But the regional primates generally did not exercise their primacy in a dictatorial manner. Regional problems were usually solved by regional synods.

We have detailed information on three different series of regional synods: (1) from 229 to 231, a series of synods in Alexandria condemned the writings of Origen,[51] (2) from 251 to 256, five synods were held in Carthage to discuss three different controversies, and (3) between 264 and 268, a series of synods was convened to deal with heresy charges against Paul of Samosata, who happened to be the Bishop of Antioch at the time. There must have been cases in the second century as well, but we do not know about them. Of the three cases we do know about, we will discuss the synods of Carthage and the strange case of Paul of Samosata at greater length, but first, a brief word about the idea of universal Church councils.

In the period in question, there was only one universal or ecumenical council in which the apostolic leaders of the entire Church met to solve a problem that affected the whole Church.[52] This council occurred in 49 or 50, and there was not another ecumenical council until 325. Reasons for this gap are not hard to find. In an age when

Roman authorities were on the lookout for bishops of whom to make examples, it was dangerous for bishops to travel so far and convene together all in one place. It was also difficult to arrange the logistics of such a meeting, which would have required a large hall, great quantities of food and drink, plus housing. The Church simply did not have sufficient resources to arrange such meetings. It also might be the case that perhaps there was no pressing need for an ecumenical council during those years.[53]

For whatever reason, there were no ecumenical councils in the period in question, but there were quite a few regional synods. The synods we know the most about are those that occurred in Carthage between the years 251 and 256. We happen to know so much about these synods thanks to the copious correspondence of Cyprian, Bishop of Carthage.

The first of Cyprian's synods was convened in 251, shortly after Cyprian returned from exile. This synod had to deal with the question of what to do with the large number of people who apostatized during the persecution of Decius. Here is what Cyprian has to say about this particular synod:

When the persecution was quieted, and opportunity of meeting was afforded; a large number of bishops, whom their faith and the divine protection had preserved in soundness and safety, we met together; and the divine Scriptures being brought forward on both sides, we balanced the decision with wholesome moderation, so that neither should hope of communion and peace be wholly denied to the lapsed, lest they should fail still more through desperation, and, because the Church was closed to them, should, like the world, live as heathens; nor yet, on the other hand, should the censure of the Gospel be relaxed, so that they might rashly rush to communion, but that repentance should be long protracted, and the paternal clemency be sorrowfully besought, and the cases, and the wishes, and the necessities of individuals be examined into, according to what is contained in a little book, which I trust has come to you, in which the several heads of our decisions are collected. And lest perchance the number of bishops in Africa should seem unsatisfactory, we also wrote to Rome, to Cornelius our colleague, concerning this thing, who himself also holding a council with very many bishops, concurred in the same opinion as we had held, with equal gravity and wholesome moderation.[54]

There are three significant points to be derived from this letter. First, note that the synod was not packed. Arguments were heard, as were Scriptures supporting both sides, and in the end a moderate, balanced decision was achieved. Second, Cyprian stressed twice that a large number of bishops had been present at the synod. A large number of bishops confers legitimacy on the deliberations of a synod, because no one could say that the opinion of a few was being foisted on the whole Church. Third, Cyprian was also careful to stress that the decision of this synod was in agreement with the decision of the Roman synod, under the leadership of Pope Cornelius. For Cyprian, being in harmony with the Roman Church was always a mark of legitimacy in its own right.

The second group of synods dealt with a more specific problem. The synod of 251 had decided that the *lapsi* could be allowed back into the Church, after a period of penance, but what about lapsed clergy? What about cases in which priests, deacons, and even bishops had given in under the threat of torture? Could they resume their ministry? The synod decided that, in accord with previous decisions, the lapsed clergy could be readmitted into the Church, but could not resume their ministry.[55]

In this case, the local synod was in disagreement with the will of Stephen, the Bishop of Rome, though Cyprian understood himself to be in agreement with the decision of Stephen's predecessor, Cornelius. This was also the case in the matter of the third set of synods Cyprian convened, having to do with the rebaptism of those baptized by schismatics, particularly those baptized by the followers of Novatian. But we will leave the discussion of these cases for the next section.

Before we move on, it will be worth our while to take a look at the case of Paul of Samosata. Paul was Bishop of Antioch during the 260s. Problems arose because Paul took the Antiochene Church's historical position on the humanity of Christ to an unacceptable extreme. The Antiochene community had always stressed the humanity of Christ over his divinity. His position was that Jesus did not eternally preexist, but that he came into being in Mary's womb and became God at the descent of the Holy Spirit at his baptism.[56] This position was heretical and deeply offensive to many bishops, particularly Maximus, Bishop of Alexandria.[57] A synod was convened, consisting of a large number of bishops from Asia and Syria. Three synods were held, and at the third, Paul "rejected any idea of essential unity between Christ and the Word".[58] Essentially, Paul denied that Jesus was God from all eternity.

The bishops present at the synod explained in a letter to Pope Dionysius and Bishop Maximus what they did next: "Therefore we have
been compelled to excommunicate him, since he sets himself against
God, and refuses to obey; and to appoint in his place another bishop
for the Catholic Church. By divine direction, as we believe, we have
appointed Domnus."[59]

There is an interesting footnote to this story. Paul, evidently supported by some of the clergy and laity of Antioch, refused to leave his
diocese. The bishops who had voted to depose him appealed to the
emperor Aurelian, who was not entirely opposed to Christianity. Aurelian used the power of the state to depose Paul, some forty years before
Constantine made Christianity legal in the empire.

From the examples we have considered, we can draw some con-
clusions about synods in the early Church. They were used mostly to
decide issues of heresy and church discipline. Synods strove for consensus and harmony, but what happened when decisions could not be
reached at the regional level? What happened when one synod decided
a question one way, but another synod came up with a different answer?
What about cases that could be decided only by an authority accepted
by everyone? To whom did the various local Churches look when all
other authorities failed to come to a universally satisfactory decision?

### The Nature of the Primacy of the Bishop of Rome

The title of this section may be somewhat jarring to some, since I
take it as a given that the Bishop of Rome exercised primacy in some
way. In this work, it is not my purpose to argue ecclesiology but to
show how the early Christians did things, and I believe that an unbi-
ased reading of the documents we have will reveal that all the local
churches *assumed* that the Roman Church was in some way their leader.
In some cases, it would seem that the local Churches wanted Rome to
be more forceful in exercising leadership than Rome was prepared to
be.[60] What is not clear from the documents is how, or under what
circumstances, Rome exercised its universally accepted authority.

One might object that the early Christians must have appealed to
the authority of Scripture, rather than mere men. Clearly, they did
not consider Scripture a final authority, for two reasons. First, the

canon of Scripture was not finalized until the fourth century. Some books, such as the four Gospels, the Epistles of Paul, and the Acts of the Apostles, were pretty much universally accepted as scriptural, but others, most notably the Letter to the Hebrews, the Letter of James, and the Book of Revelation, were not accepted by all the Churches. So, obviously, Church A could not appeal to one of these books in a dispute with Church B if Church B did not accept the book as Scripture. Second, even when a book was accepted as Scripture, it was susceptible to different interpretations. It is obvious, for instance, that Paul of Samosata and Maximus, Bishop of Alexandria, would not have agreed on an interpretation of the prologue of the Gospel of John.[61] Under such circumstances a human authority, instituted by Christ and guided by the Holy Spirit, was necessary.

The basic question before us is, how were decisions affecting the whole Church made? We have already discussed the dearth of ecumenical councils in the early Church and some reasons for that lack. However, it seems likely, given the immediate recourse to ecumenical councils in the fourth century, that if the early Church had been free from persecution there could have been numerous ecumenical councils in the first three centuries.[62]

Actually, the first ecumenical council, the Council of Jerusalem, recorded in chapter 15 of the Acts of the Apostles, can give us some insights as to how the early Church made decisions affecting all the Churches. The dispute that prompted the Council of Jerusalem was started by a group who were telling Gentile converts they had to be circumcised or they could not be saved. Paul and Barnabas debated with the Judaizers, but the matter was not settled. What happened next is instructive: "Paul and Barnabas and some of the others were appointed to go up to Jerusalem to the apostles and elders about this question."[63] The apostles and elders discussed the matter, then Peter stood up and made a decisive intervention:

> Brethren, you know that in the early days God made choice among you, that by my mouth the Gentiles should hear the word of the gospel and believe. And God who knows the heart bore witness to them, giving them the Holy Spirit just as he did to us; and he made no distinction between us and them, but cleansed their hearts by faith. Now therefore why do you make trial of God by putting a yoke upon the neck of the disciples which neither our fathers nor we have been

able to bear? But we believe that we shall be saved through the grace of the Lord Jesus, just as they will.[64]

After Peter's testimony, the assembly listened to Barnabas and Paul tell about their experiences among the Gentiles. Then James delivered the concluding remarks, in which the decision of the Council was stated. This sequence has led some commentators to assume that James was the leader of the New Testament Church, not Peter. This assumption is mistaken. The debate and dissension ended when Peter spoke. In verse 12, immediately after Peter spoke, we read, "The whole assembly kept silence." But before Peter spoke, "there had been much debate."[65]

The basic decision was guided and shaped by Peter, under the influence of the Holy Spirit. James spoke last for two reasons. First, James was the Bishop of Jerusalem,[66] and as such represented the Jewish Christian concerns. Any decision had to have his agreement, or it would not have preserved Church unity. Second, the Council was held in Jerusalem, and protocol probably required that the local bishop would chair the meeting and publicly announce the decision. For these reasons, it is not surprising that James spoke last, acquiescing in Peter's opinion, merely making some minor stipulations regarding diet and sexual morality.

In the four Gospels, it is abundantly clear that Jesus assigned Peter a special role. Here are some of the highlights:

1. In Matthew 16:18–19, Jesus said that Peter was the rock on which the Church would be built, and he gave Peter the keys of the kingdom of heaven, telling Peter: "Whatever you bind on earth shall be bound in heaven, and whatever you loose on earth shall be loosed in heaven."

2. In Luke 22:31–32, Jesus tells Peter that he has prayed that Peter's strength will not fail, then he charges Peter with the ministry of "strengthening the brethren".

3. In John 21:15–17, Jesus asks Peter three times, "Do you love me?" and three times tells Peter to feed his sheep.

4. The lists of the apostles, found in Matthew 10:1–4, Mark 3:16–19, Luke 6:14–16, and Acts 1:13, all list Peter first.

5. Peter is mentioned 191 times in the New Testament, while the rest of the apostles combined are mentioned 130 times.

6. In Acts 1:15, it is Peter who initiates and presides over the process that led to the addition of Matthias to the twelve apostles.

These are only some of the distinctions Peter was given in the New Testament. All these special signs of favor indicate that after Jesus, Peter was the leader of the apostles, and thus, the leader of the whole New Testament Church.[67]

An important question remains, however. Did the special role of Peter in the New Testament translate to some kind of special authority for the bishops of Rome after Peter's martyrdom? But first a more basic question can be raised: How did Peter come to be associated with Rome?

Catholic tradition has it that Peter was Bishop of Rome for twenty-five years.[68] We have good reason to believe that Peter was martyred in Rome sometime between 64 and 67, so if he presided in Rome for twenty-five years, he must have first arrived in that city sometime between A.D. 39 and 42. However, this presents difficulties. The Council of Jerusalem was held in 49 or 50, so Peter was in Jerusalem at least part of that time. Also, in Galatians 2:11, Paul states that Peter was in Antioch at some time in what must have been the late 40s. Other than these scraps of information, we have very little solid information on Peter's movements in the 40s, 50s, and 60s. Various ingenious chronologies have been constructed to show how Peter could have moved from place to place and still have been an effective Bishop of Rome. These theories are interesting, but as one perceptive Catholic scholar of the early twentieth century put it, "The coming of Peter to the capital of the Empire and his laying of the foundations of that Church are historically certain, but neither the date of his arrival nor the length of his stay can be accurately fixed."[69]

It can be regarded as fairly certain that Peter was martyred in Rome during the persecution of Nero.[70] The fact that Peter's sojourn in Rome is not mentioned in the New Testament is only slightly problematic. The author of the Acts of the Apostles, the book one would most expect to mention this fact, is silent on the entire subject. But Luke might have been silent on this point because he did not want to endanger Peter, who was wanted by the authorities in several jurisdictions. After all, Luke was silent about the Apostle John moving to

Ephesus, but if you travel to that ancient city, you can see John's tomb there.[71]

The silence of the New Testament on Peter's presence in Rome is offset by a great deal of evidence in the postapostolic period, some of which has already been mentioned.

1. Clement makes an allusion to Peter's martyrdom in Rome in *I Clement*.[72]

2. Ignatius of Antioch, in his *Epistle to the Romans*, states, "I do not, as Peter and Paul, issue commandments unto you", indicating that Peter and Paul had ruled the Church in Rome at one time.[73]

3. Eusebius quotes a letter from the Bishop of Corinth written about A.D. 150, which states that Peter and Paul had sown the Word in Rome.[74]

These are only a small portion of the testimonials of the early Church that make it clear that Peter was in Rome; that he, along with Paul, organized and governed that Church; and that Peter was martyred in Rome. There can be no real doubt that these things occurred. The question that remains is, what significance did the Christians of the generations after Peter attach to these facts? The fact is that until the second half of the second century, there is little information that will help us. The Church was in hiding. The Bishop of Rome was the prime target of every persecution. Christians would be reticent to discuss the presence of a successor of Peter in Rome.

We do, however, have a few documents that provide tantalizing glimpses of the organization of the early Church. In the second half of the second century, these glimpses become a mosaic, and we are able to get a fuller picture of how the Church was organized.

Our first glimpse comes from an earlier document we have already discussed in a different context: Clement's *First Epistle to the Corinthians*. The letter begins thus:

> The Church of God which sojourns at Rome, to the Church of God sojourning at Corinth, to them that are called and sanctified by the will of God, through our Lord Jesus Christ: Grace unto you, and peace, from Almighty God through Jesus Christ, be multiplied. Owing, dear

brethren, to the sudden and successive calamitous events which have happened to ourselves, we feel that we have been somewhat tardy in turning our attention to the points respecting which you consulted us.[75]

Two points are significant in this introduction. The letter is not from Clement himself, but from the Church of Rome. This has led some commentators erroneously to assume that this indicates that the office of Bishop of Rome either did not exist at this time, or that it had no real authority that would be comparable to what we know as the papacy. We dealt with this objection earlier, but it is worthwhile to remind ourselves of the reasons we think Clement wrote this letter in his capacity as Bishop of Rome. First, at around 150, Dionysius, Bishop of Corinth, wrote a letter to the Church of Rome, stating that his community still had the letter Clement wrote to them. Secondly, the tone of *I Clement* indicates one author, expressing his will and the will of his advisors. Finally, Clement must have been the author, acting in his capacity as Bishop of Rome, because in Hegesippus' list of the bishops of Rome, written around 150, Clement would have been Bishop at the time the letter was written. All these pieces of evidence argue strongly that Clement was the author of this letter.

So if Clement wrote the letter, why did he use the plural voice, speaking of "we", not "I"? There are several reasons for this. First, Clement was urging the Corinthians to show humility before God and their ordained leaders, so he probably felt it would be in good form to exercise humility himself. Late in the letter, he wrote, "These things, beloved, we write to you, not merely to admonish you of your duty, but also to remind ourselves."[76] Second, Clement used this tone because it is the tone recommended by Peter, the first Bishop of Rome: "not as domineering over those in your charge but being examples to the flock."[77] Third, Clement used the plural voice because *he had not made the decision alone*. This is an important point because Protestants and Catholics alike have a tendency to think of papal authority being exercised in solitude. However, in the history of the Church, most often papal decisions have been made in close consultation with a council of trusted advisors. In the modern Church, these people are the cardinals and bishops who work in the Curia. In the early Church, the bishops of Rome consulted with the presbyters of the Roman Church. So Clement used the plural because a group, not just one individual, truly had made the decision. Clement's ministry amounted to effectively and authoritatively communicating the consensus of a group of wise men. However, if necessary, the Bishop of Rome could have exercised authority alone, as we shall see.

Another important point to glean from the introduction of *I Clement* is that the letter was written in response to an inquiry from the Church of Corinth. An envious clique had deposed presbyters who had been performing their duties blamelessly. Evidently the local community was unable to adjudicate the matter properly, so an appeal was made to the Roman Church. But the question that is relevant to our current inquiry is, why Rome? Ephesus, the home of the Apostle John (who may have been still alive when the letter was written), was much closer, and it would have been much easier to send letters back and forth to that city. But the authorities in Corinth chose to send their appeal to Rome, the Church of Peter and Paul. This fact alone leads inevitably to the conclusion that the Roman Church was held to have some special authority, thirty years after the death of Peter and Paul.

The decision promulgated in *I Clement* was twofold: the deposed presbyters should be restored, and those who plotted against them should repent. The justification for this decision was as follows:

> Our apostles also knew, through our Lord Jesus Christ, and there would be strife on account of the office of the episcopate. For this reason, therefore, inasmuch as they had obtained a perfect foreknowledge of this, they appointed those already mentioned, and afterwards gave instructions, that when these should fall asleep, other approved men should succeed them in their ministry. We are of opinion, therefore, that those appointed by them, or afterwards by other eminent men, with the consent of the whole Church, and who have blamelessly served the flock of Christ in a humble, peaceable, and disinterested spirit, and have for a long time possessed the good opinion of all, cannot be justly dismissed from the ministry.[78]

The decision, made by Clement with the assistance of the Roman presbyters, was premised on the idea that the ministry had been handed down from the apostles, for the sake of good order. In appealing to Rome, the Corinthians were tacitly acknowledging that order, and in the decision passed on, the Roman Church considered that it was merely upholding the divinely ordained order of the Church.

After the decision was promulgated and announced, Clement wrote, "Let us then also pray for those who have fallen into any sin, that meekness and humility may be given to them, so that they may submit, not unto us, but to the will of God." [79] We see here true humility in action. Rome's authority is not for its own sake, nor is it an occasion for arrogance. It exists merely as a channel, a conduit, through which the grace of God can be made manifest.

In the conclusion, Clement requested a return letter: "Send back speedily to us in peace and with joy these our messengers to you: Claudius Ephebus and Valerius Bito, with Fortunatus: that they may the sooner announce to us the peace and harmony we so earnestly desire and long for among you, and that we may the more quickly rejoice over the good order re-established among you." [80] This brief passage illuminates a practice of the Roman Church. In a later date there was a constant stream of information passing from Rome to the other Churches, and from those Churches back to Rome. We see this most clearly in the letters of Cyprian of Carthage.

After Clement, there is a gap in the information about the role of the Bishop of Rome in the universal Church. This is not surprising; in the first half of the second century there are very few Christian writings on any topic. There are the letters of Ignatius of Antioch and the writings of Justin Martyr, and neither one says much that is helpful to our current topic. In his letter to the Romans, Ignatius refers to the Roman Church as "worthy of God, worthy of honor, worthy of the highest happiness, worthy of praise, worthy of credit, worthy of being deemed holy, and which presides over love, is named from Christ, and from the Father, and is possessed of the Spirit". [81]

Ignatius does not mention a Bishop of Rome in this greeting, which is odd, since he explicitly mentions by name the bishops of the other communities to which he writes. There are four possible explanations for this lapse: (1) there was at that time no office of Bishop of Rome, (2) there was a Bishop of Rome but he had no real authority, (3) at that time there temporarily was no Bishop of Rome due to persecution or death, or (4) there was a Bishop of Rome, but Ignatius did not wish to call attention to that fact, in case his letter fell into the hands of the authorities.

Of these four options, the third or fourth seems most likely. In order to hold the first or second, you must believe that Peter and Paul

were in Rome, but despite the fact that Paul appointed bishops for
other communities, neither Peter nor he did so in Rome. Further,
you must hold that in approximately 96 there was a Bishop of Rome
named Clement, who had the authority to send a letter to another
community telling them how to resolve a dispute, but after this anomalous bishop the office mysteriously died out once again. (Remember
that Ignatius wrote his letters in about A.D. 107.) This theory becomes
insupportable when your consider that after 150 there is a great deal
of evidence of the importance of the Bishop of Rome to communities
outside of Rome.

In addition to this negative evidence, there is some positive evidence to support the third or fourth option. We know that the Romans
targeted the bishops of Rome for special attention in their persecutions. The emperor Decius, after disposing of one Pope, commented
that he would rather hear about a rival claimant for the throne than
the election of a new Bishop of Rome.[82] There is a Catholic tradition
of long standing that every Bishop of Rome to the time of Constantine was martyred. So it seems likely that when Ignatius fails to mention the Bishop of Rome in his salutation, it is a reflection of the
ongoing persecution the bishops of Rome faced, not the lack of existence of a Bishop of Rome.

Writing at around 150, a man named Hegesippus ended the gap in
our knowledge about the bishops of Rome. He traced the bishops of
Rome all the way back to Peter. In turn, his list of the bishops of
Rome was copied by Irenaeus of Lyons, who wrote in the 180s. Here
is Irenaeus' list of the bishops of Rome:

> The blessed apostles, then, having founded and built up the Church,
> committed into the hands of Linus the office of the episcopate. Of this
> Linus, Paul makes mention in the Epistles to Timothy. To him suc-
> ceeded Anacletus; and after him, in the third place from the apostles,
> Clement was allotted the bishopric. This man, as he had seen the blessed
> apostles, and had been conversant with them, might be said to have the
> preaching of the apostles still echoing in his ears, and their traditions
> before his eyes. Nor was he alone in this, for there were many still
> remaining who had received instructions from the apostles. In the time
> of this Clement, no small dissension having occurred among the breth-
> ren at Corinth, the Church in Rome dispatched a most powerful letter
> to the Corinthians, exhorting them to peace, renewing their faith, and

declaring the tradition which it had lately received from the apostles.... To this Clement there succeeded Evaristus. Alexander followed Evaristus; then, sixth from the apostles, Sixtus was appointed; after him, Telephorus, who was gloriously martyred; then Hyginus; after him, Pius; then after him, Anicetus. Soter having succeeded Anicetus, Eleutherius does now, in the twelfth place from the apostles, hold the inheritance of the episcopate. In this order, and by this succession, the ecclesiastical tradition from the apostles, and the preaching of the truth, have come down to us. And this is most abundant proof that there is one and the same vivifying faith, which has been preserved in the Church from the apostles until now, and handed down in truth.[83]

In addition to producing this list, Irenaeus said the following about the authority of the Church of Rome and her Bishop: "It is a matter of necessity that every Church should agree with this Church [Rome], on account of its preeminent authority, that is, the faithful everywhere, inasmuch as the apostolic tradition has been preserved continuously by those faithful men." [84] It is worth noting that Irenaeus made this stunning comment shortly before making his list of the bishops of Rome, and there can be no doubt that in his mind the source of the authority of the Roman Church had its origins in the faithful passing on of authoritative teaching from one Bishop of Rome to the next.

Nor was Irenaeus alone in his belief. Tertullian, writing from Carthage shortly after Irenaeus, stated:

Come now, you who would indulge a better curiosity, if you would apply it to the business of your salvation, run over the apostolic churches, in which the very thrones of the apostles are still pre-eminent in their places, in which their own authentic writings are read, uttering the voice and representing the face of each of them severally. Achaia is very near you, in which you find Corinth. Since you are not far from Macedonia, you have Philippi; and there too you have the Thessalonians. Since you are able to cross to Asia, you get Ephesus. Since, moreover, you are close upon Italy, you have Rome, from which there comes even into our own hands the very authority of apostles themselves. How happy is its church, on which apostles poured forth all their doctrine along with their blood ... against such a discipline thus maintained she admits no gainsayer.[85]

The bishops of the East also acknowledged that they had some accountability to Rome. Eusebius records that Polycarp, Bishop of

Smyrna, traveled to Rome in the hope of resolving the dispute over the proper date of Easter.[86] Forty years later Polycrates, Bishop of Ephesus, made the same journey, to confer with Pope Victor on the same question. This time, Pope Victor threatened the Eastern Churches with excommunication if they did not change their calendars. This action caused a great deal of consternation and anger in the Eastern communities, but no one on either side of the issue seems to have doubted that Victor had the authority to act as he did. "Thereupon Victor, who presided over the church at Rome, immediately attempted to cut off from the common unity the parishes of all Asia, with the churches that agreed with them, as heterodox; and he wrote letters and declared all the brethren there wholly excommunicate. But this did not please all the bishops, and they besought him to consider the things of peace, and of neighborly unity and love." [87] (This incident had a happy ending. Irenaeus of Lyons acted as an intermediary between Victor and the bishops of the East, effecting a compromise that lasted until the middle of the third century.)

The examples given above are sufficient to show that throughout the Christian world the Roman Church and her Bishop were accorded a special respect, love, and authority. In the third century, this trend became more pronounced. As the Church grew in numbers, spreading into new communities, the desire for unity required a stronger central authority. Rome, with its powerful, vibrant community, its tradition of strong bishops, and its status as the community in possession of the relics of Peter and Paul, was the natural focus of unity. We will leave aside the question of whether Christ willed Roman primacy. The question of this book is what the early Christians actually believed and acted upon. With this sole criterion in mind, there can be little doubt that in the third-century Church, everyone (including some obvious heretics) accepted Roman primacy.[88]

The case of the heretic Marcion is a perfect example of how Roman primacy operated. Marcion (early second century), from Pontus (in modern-day Turkey), was a wealthy merchant who became a Christian. He studied Scripture and developed a dislike for the Old Testament. He settled on the heretical notion that the God of the Old Testament was different from the God of the New Testament, and that in fact the God of the Old Testament was Satan. He further decided that only the Gospel of Luke, the Acts of the Apostles, and some of the Letters of Paul should be accepted as authentic Scripture. He succeeded in attracting numerous followers and came to the attention of the Church authorities. When the bishops of Asia condemned Marcion's ideas, he went to Rome and attempted to present the Roman Church with an immense sum of money. The Roman Church refused Marcion's gift and denied him the right hand of fellowship.[89]

Clearly, Marcion went to Rome to appeal the decision of the Eastern bishops. Just as clearly, Marcion's "gift" to the Roman Church was a poorly concealed bribe, and Rome was right to return it. The implications of the story are clear: "Until Rome has condemned him he is still a Catholic Christian."[90] Just as clearly, Marcion must have reasoned that if Rome accepted him he would also be accepted in his native Pontus.

In the third century, the Montanist controversy was debated in Rome, though Montanus himself never left Asia. Montanus, who taught that the third age, the Age of the Spirit, had begun in his lifetime, caused quite a bit of havoc in the Churches of Asia. The bishops of that region were greatly relieved when the Roman Church condemned Montanus' teachings. When Abercius, Bishop of Hierapolis, made his anti-Montanist inscription, it is to far distant Rome that he directs his praise. "He sent me to Rome, to behold a kingdom and to see a queen with golden robe and golden shoes. There I saw a people bearing the splendid seal."[91] The Eastern bishops saw Rome as the guarantor of orthodoxy, and they were grateful, not resentful, for this ministry.

Of course, reliance on the Bishop of Rome for the adjudication of disputes could be a two-edged sword, as Cyprian of Carthage found out in the middle of the third century. Cyprian was a strong supporter of the *idea* of Roman primacy. Cyprian called Rome "the throne of Peter ... the chief church whence priestly unity takes its source",[92] and "the root and matrix of the Catholic Church".[93] Notice the emphasis Cyprian places on the role Rome had in insuring unity. For Cyprian, this was the essential function of the Bishop of Rome, and the real point of Rome's authority.

Cyprian had extensive dealings with two popes: Cornelius, with whom he had excellent relations, and Stephen, with whom he quarreled over the matter of the rebaptism of heretics. Cyprian worked closely with Cornelius on the problem presented by Novatian, whom we mentioned in the previous section. Novatian, after losing the election to Cornelius, had declared himself Bishop of Rome anyway. Cyprian wrote a letter to his fellow North African bishops advising them that Cornelius was the rightful Bishop of Rome and that Novatian should not be followed.[94]

After the martyrdom of Pope Fabian, but before the election of Cornelius, Cyprian worked closely with the Roman presbyters on the question of the lapsed, that is, those who had failed to confess Christ under threat of martyrdom. He showed the presbyters of Rome the same deference he would have shown the Bishop of Rome: "You counseled that comfort should be given to those who fell ill after their lapse.... I have decided that I too should take my stand alongside your opinion."[95]

After Cornelius was martyred, Stephen was elected Pope. At first, Cyprian had cordial relations with Stephen. Cyprian respected the office of Bishop of Rome so much that he requested that Stephen intervene in the affairs of Marcianus, Bishop of Arles. Marcianus had refused to grant absolution to the lapsed, as the Roman presbyters had decided. In a letter to Stephen, Cyprian wrote: "Let letters be directed by you ... to the people abiding at Arles, by which, Marcian being excommunicated, another may be substituted in his place, and Christ's flock ... may be gathered together."[96] Notice that Cyprian does not send a letter to Marcianus himself. He knew such an action would be futile. The only one who could command the bishops of Gaul to excommunicate Marcianus was Pope Stephen, and that is why he begged Stephen to exert "the full weight of your personal authority".

In the end, though, Cyprian was embroiled in a controversy with Stephen that he took so seriously that he had difficulty deferring to Roman authority. The hitherto unresolved conflict had to do with the rebaptism of those who had been originally baptized into a heretical sect. At the time of Cyprian, many who had been baptized by heretics wished to come into communion with the universal Church. The bishops of North Africa convened a synod, which decided that these people had to be baptized again. Cyprian innocently wrote Stephen a letter, informing him of the synod's decision.[97] He also wrote a letter to a fellow bishop, one Jubaianus, excoriating those who disagreed with this decision as "betrayers of unity"[98] and "partaker[s] with blaspheming heretics".[99]

Perhaps Cyprian was unaware that the established practice of the Roman Church was against rebaptism, if the original baptism had been done in the name of the Trinity. In any case, his letter to Jubaianus made its way back to Pope Stephen, who was not pleased with this opinion. Stephen wrote a letter to Cyprian, which has not been preserved. We can, however, reconstruct what Stephen must have written from a later letter of Cyprian. Stephen must have forbidden the rebaptism of those who had been baptized in the name of the Father and of the Son and of the Holy Spirit and threatened anyone who disobeyed with excommunication.

There must have been passages in Stephen's letter that Cyprian perceived as abusive and arrogant, for in a letter to a fellow bishop, Cyprian referred to "other matters, which were either haughtily assumed or not pertaining to the matter, or contradictory to his own view, which he unskillfully and without foresight wrote".[100]

It is unclear how this controversy was resolved. As a matter of Church practice, Stephen's position prevailed. To this day, the Catholic Church does not rebaptize anyone who was baptized in the name of the Trinity. On a personal level, we do not know what happened next in the relationship between Cyprian and Stephen. Stephen was martyred in 257, shortly after this dispute came to a head, and Cyprian was martyred in 258. It seems likely that Cyprian, though he disagreed with the decision and disliked the promulgator, obeyed Stephen. It must be the case that Stephen never actually excommunicated Cyprian, since Cyprian has always been counted among the saints of the Roman Catholic Church. Had he been excommunicated this would not be the case.

It is clear from these events that the course of Church unity never did run smoothly, and the Bishop of Rome sometimes was a blunt instrument in her service. Nevertheless, for the early Christians, the authority of the Roman Church was almost always accepted and usually welcomed as the only sure way to avoid endless dispute and schism.

### From Presbyters to Priests

There was a religion in the ancient world that had its headquarters in Jerusalem. This religion had local communities scattered throughout the Roman Empire, in major cities like Rome, Ephesus, Antioch, Sardis, Lyons, and Carthage. The headquarters kept in touch with the local communities by means of emissaries called "apostles". The apostles had authority to depose and appoint leaders to the local communities, anointing the new leaders with oil to seal their position in the community. When the apostles were not present, the local communities were governed by a highly revered older man who presided over the prayer services of the community. This leader was advised and aided in his administrative duties by a council of elders. This religion may sound familiar. You may be thinking that I am referring to early Christianity, in the period before the destruction of Jerusalem. If so, you are mistaken. The description I am providing certainly fits early Christianity, but the religion to which I am referring is actually Judaism. All the elements I have described were present in the Judaism of the first century, including the presence of apostles,[101] although their function as emissaries of the Jewish authorities was not exactly the same as the function of the apostles of Jesus in early Christianity.

From the fifth century before Christ, Jewish communities existed in many of the cities of the Mediterranean world.[102] These communities found themselves in a largely hostile world, with the polytheistic religions of Greece and Rome holding sway. To combat the potential influence of paganism, the Jewish communities had to establish strong institutions. However, it was not possible to build a temple in every city with a substantial Jewish population, since the sacrifices of the Temple could be performed only in Jerusalem. Thus, it was during this era that the synagogue became an important institution in Judaism. The earliest reference to a synagogue comes from Egypt, in the third century.[103]

The institutions that made the synagogues strong evolved over time, but by the time of Christ the synagogues of the Diaspora generally were presided over by a single man called the *archisynagogos* (which translates literally as "leader of the synagogue").[104] The *archisynagogos* was primarily a liturgical leader, presiding over Sabbath services and the various rituals of Judaism. Assisting the leader of the synagogue was a council of elders, the *presbyteroi*.[105]

In Diaspora Judaism, the presbyters had no direct liturgical function. Their primary duties were to advise the leader on financial and administrative matters and to represent the synagogue in its dealings with local government and business leaders. During synagogue services, the presbyters would seat themselves on marble benches in a semicircle behind the leader while he led the prayers. They also might involve themselves with the collection and distribution of alms and with the interpretation of the law.[106]

When Paul traveled through the Eastern end of the Roman Empire, establishing Christian communities, it was natural that he should use terms for certain ministries already used in the synagogues. Paul did not consider that he was establishing a new religion, and he always considered himself a good Jew. When he traveled to a new community, he visited the synagogue first and would preach in the synagogue if invited.[107] Often, the Christian "house church" would be set up right next to the synagogue.[108] In fact, in Corinth the *archisynagogos*, a man named Crispus, became a Christian.[109] Against this background, it is perfectly reasonable that Paul would appoint presbyters for his new Christian communities.

Many of the references to presbyters in the New Testament are found in the Acts of the Apostles. In Acts 14:23, we find Paul and Barnabas appointing presbyters for the communities they founded: "And when they had appointed elders for them in every church, with prayer and fasting, they committed them to the Lord in whom they believed." In Acts 15, we find the elders aiding in the deliberations of the Council of Jerusalem. In Acts 20:17, we find Paul summoning the elders of Ephesus for a meeting.

Elsewhere, Paul wrote about the elders. In Titus 1:5, Paul tells Titus, "That is why I left you in Crete, that you might amend what was defective, and appoint elders in every town as I directed you." In 1 Timothy 5:17–19, Paul laid down some rules regarding elders: those who did well, particularly in preaching and teaching, should be supported by the whole community, and accusations against elders had to be supported by two or three witnesses.

Paul was not the only New Testament author to discuss the presbyters. In James 5:14, we find that those who are sick should have the elders pray over them and anoint them with oil. In 1 Peter 5:2 we find that the author calls himself an elder and asks his fellow elders to "tend the flock of God that is in your charge"; he also asks the younger men to accept the authority of the elders. In John's Second and Third Epistles, the author refers to himself simply as "the Elder". In the Book of Revelation we find various images involving elders.[110]

These passages are sufficient, I think, to show that before the end of the apostolic age, councils of elders were in place in most of the early communities. Sure enough, the earliest Christian documents we possess, apart from the New Testament, mention presbyters in a prominent way. In Clement's *First Epistle to the Corinthians*, we find that some of the presbyters of Corinth had been unjustly removed from office. The response in the letter is firm: Clement reiterates that the offices of the Church were ordained by Christ, and he compares the New Testament ministers to the priesthood of the Old Testament. Clement excoriated the Corinthians in the following manner: "Blessed are those presbyters who, having finished their course before now, have obtained a fruitful and perfect departure from this world; for they have no fear lest any one deprive them of the place now appointed them. But we see that you have removed some men of excellent behavior from the ministry, which they fulfilled blamelessly and with honor." [111] In the end, Clement and the presbyters of Rome ruled that the presbyters who had been removed from ministry should be restored, and that those responsible for the problem should do penance.

It is noteworthy that the *Didache* does not mention presbyters at all. This document, which many scholars think was probably written around 90–110 in Syria, directs the communities to appoint bishops and deacons, but the document does not mention presbyters. Some commentators have come to the conclusion that this indicates that the Syrian community did not know about presbyters at this point. This position seems unlikely, given the relatively large number of references to presbyters in the New Testament (and some of the New Testament documents originated in the regions quite close to Syria).

The lack of a single reference to presbyters in the *Didache* can perhaps be explained by the fact that in many early documents the Greek words *presbyteros* and *episkopos* are used interchangeably. Perhaps the *Didache*'s reference to *episkopoi* was understood by its author to refer to the same ministry as that of *presbyteroi*.

There must be some explanation for the lack of reference to presbyters in the *Didache*. As I demonstrated above, we know from Scripture that there were presbyters throughout Asia in the period from 52 to 90. We also know, as we shall see next, that there were presbyters in Syria, the province most scholars think the *Didache* comes from, as well as in Asia, in approximately 107. So in order to say that there were no presbyters in the community of the *Didache*, one must hold that the apostles came through the region and established Christian communities but did not appoint presbyters, despite the fact that they appointed presbyters in the next province (Asia).

We know about presbyters in Syria and Asia in 107 because of the letters of Ignatius, Bishop of Antioch. We have examined Ignatius' writings in other sections, but a brief review is in order. Ignatius was on his way to Rome, where he would be martyred. He was allowed to write letters to some of the neighboring Churches, and in those letters he wrote a great deal about Church organization, with a special emphasis on practices that would promote harmony within the community. Here are some of the things he wrote about the office of presbyter:

> Since therefore I have, in the persons before mentioned, beheld the whole multitude of you in faith and love, I exhort you to study to do all things with a divine harmony, while your bishop presides in the place of God, and your presbyters in the place of the assembly of the apostles.[112]

> Continue in harmony among yourselves, and in prayer with one another; for it becomes every one of you, and especially the presbyters, to refresh the bishop, to the honor of the Father, of Jesus Christ, and of the apostles.[113]

> See that you all follow the bishop, even as Jesus Christ does the Father, and the presbytery as you would the apostles.[114]

These few examples will suffice to show that when Ignatius wrote the Churches of Asia all had presbyters. But what did they do? They seem to have advised and assisted the bishop in governing the community. They are admonished to be obedient to their bishop, and in turn the people are admonished to obey them as they would the apostles.

At this period the presbyters did not generally preside at the liturgy. Ignatius reserved this function for the bishop. "It is not lawful without the bishop either to baptize or to celebrate a love-feast; but whatsoever he shall approve of, that is also pleasing to God, so that everything that is done may be secure and valid." [115] This passage by itself cannot be interpreted to mean that the presbyters never presided over the liturgy. If the bishop gave a presbyter the capacity to preside, he could do so: "Let that be deemed a proper Eucharist, which is administered either by the bishop, or by one to whom he has entrusted it." [116]

The bishop could appoint another man to preside over the liturgy, but the normal practice was that there would be one liturgy in each community, presided over by the bishop, with the presbyters assisting him: "Take heed, then, to have but one Eucharist. For there is one flesh of our Lord Jesus Christ, and one cup to show forth the unity of His blood; one altar; as there is one bishop, along with the presbytery and deacons, my fellow-servants: that so, whatsoever you do, you may do it according to the will of God." [117]

We can reconstruct the situation in the Churches of Asia at this time. The communities must have been fairly small. In Magnesia, we find one bishop, two presbyters, and one deacon. [118] It is hard to imagine that the situation in, say, Tralles would be much different. Under circumstances such as this, there would be no need for anyone but the bishop to preside, unless he was sick or traveling. Of course, if the bishop were martyred, the senior presbyter would preside until a new bishop was ordained.

As the years went by and the Church grew, it became necessary to have more than one house of worship and more than one liturgy in a given community on Sunday morning. Under these circumstances, the bishops would have used their right to appoint as many presiders as were needed. For instance, in a letter from Pope Cornelius to Fabius, Bishop of Antioch, in 251, we read that the Church in Rome had "forty-six presbyters, seven deacons, seven sub-deacons, forty-two acolytes, fifty-two exorcists, readers, and janitors, and over fifteen hundred widows and persons in distress, all of whom the grace and kindness of the Master nourish". [119] We know that in this period Rome had numerous *tituli*, or house churches, at which the Eucharist was celebrated on the Lord's Day. We know that the practice was that a deacon would carry fragments of the Eucharist from the Pope's Mass to all the *tituli*. But there are many things we would like to know. We do not know if the *tituli* had their own presbyter assigned to them on a permanent basis, or if the presbyters rotated among the *tituli*. But we do know that in the third century the presbyters of Rome celebrated their own Masses, with, of course, the faculties granted them by the Bishop of Rome.

With this information in mind, it is possible to understand something of how the presbyterate developed and how the Church came to understand its sacramental, priestly nature. As was demonstrated in Chapter 2, at a very early time, the Eucharist was understood as a sacrifice. There can be no sacrifice without a priest. Therefore, in the early Church, the bishop of a given community was often compared to the high priest of ancient Israel.[120] It was natural, then, as the Church grew and more presiders were needed, that the additional presiders would be taken from the ranks of the presbyters, and that they would come to be known as priests in their own right. But technically, in the early Church as in the Catholic Church today, the priestly authority of the priesthood derives solely from the priestly authority of the bishops.[121]

It needs to be said, however, that in the early Church, even when presbyters functioned as presiders at local liturgies, their primary duty was to help the bishop guide and govern the local Church. Here is a segment of Hippolytus' ordination prayer for presbyters: "God and Father of our Lord Jesus Christ, look upon this thy servant, and grant to him the spirit of grace and counsel of a presbyter, that he may sustain and govern thy people with a pure heart; as thou didst look upon thy chosen people, and didst command Moses that he should choose presbyters, whom thou didst fill with thy spirit, which thou gavest to thy servant."[122] In this prayer notice the emphasis on the care and guidance of the people of God.

Because the presbyters were involved in leadership roles in the community of faith, it was imperative that they be men of excellent character. Here is what Saint Polycarp had to say about the character of a presybter:

> And let the presbyters be compassionate and merciful to all, bringing back those that wander, visiting all the sick, and not neglecting the widow, the orphan, or the poor, but always providing for that which is becoming in the sight of God and man, abstaining from all wrath, respect of persons, and unjust judgment; keeping far off from all covetousness, not quickly crediting an evil report against any one, not severe in judgment, as knowing that we are all under a debt of sin.[123]

Evidently not all presbyters lived up to their high calling. In his *Commentary on Matthew*, Origen criticized presbyters for haughtiness and a lack of concern for the poor. He also criticized the careerism of some presbyters, who thought only of being elevated to bishop. Origen went so far as to criticize some clergymen for simulating virtue they did not possess in order not to be deprived of their power.[124]

Because of the danger of abuse of power, Cyprian of Carthage had to enforce a rule against presbyters executing estates.

> Each one was desirous of increasing his estate; and forgetful of what believers had either done before in the times of the apostles, or always ought to do, they, with the insatiable ardor of covetousness, devoted themselves to the increase of their property. Among the priests there was no devotedness of religion. . . . They sought to possess money in hoards, they seized estates by crafty deceits, they increased their gains by multiplying usuries.[125]

Despite these problems, Cyprian had a high regard for his presbyters. He rarely made a decision without consulting them, as a matter of principle: "From the commencement of my episcopacy, I made up my mind to do nothing on my own private opinion, without your advice."[126]

Cyprian delegated his responsibilities to his presbyters when he was forced into exile during the persecution of Decius: "Relying, therefore, upon your love and your piety, which I have abundantly known, in this letter I both exhort and command you, that those of you whose presence there is least suspicious and least perilous, should in my stead discharge my duty, in respect of doing those things which are required for the religious administration. In the meantime let the poor be taken care of as much and as well as possible."[127]

The normal process by which a presbyter was chosen was designed to insure that the men chosen would be worthy. Tertullian seems to indicate that the presbyters were chosen by the entire people, based on their wisdom and good character. "The tried men of our elders preside over us, obtaining that honor not by purchase, but by established character."[128]

How was good character established? Who decided who was worthy of becoming a presbyter? In Cyprian's North Africa, everyone—bishop, presbyter, and layperson—had a say in the discernment process. "God commands a priest to be appointed in the presence of all the assembly. That is, he instructs and shows that the ordination of priests ought not to be solemnized except with the knowledge of the people standing near."[129]

One should not, however, assume that Cyprian's practice was universal. In the community of the *Didascalia Apostolorum*, for example, the bishop alone chose presbyters. "So now does the bishop also take for himself from the people those whom he accounts and knows to be worthy of him and of his office, and appoints him presbyters as counselors and assessors." [130]

We also know of another way in which a man could become a presbyter: by virtue of standing firm as a confessor. "On a confessor, if he has been in bonds for the name of the Lord, hands shall not be laid for the diaconate or the presbyterate, for he has the honour of the presbyterate by his confession." [131] This passage is not crystal clear. There were a number of men in the early Church who were arrested and tortured, in an attempt to make them renounce the faith. Many of them stood firm, but for various reasons were not executed. While they were in prison, these men were highly revered. The custom was for lay people to visit them, bringing gifts and hoping for a blessing of some sort. Often the Eucharist was celebrated in prison by a priest who was one of these confessors. In similar manner, such priest confessors heard confessions and absolved sins. Hippolytus said that they had the right to do so by virtue of their suffering. [132]

The presbyters began as counselors of the bishop and ended up sharing in the sacramental and teaching ministries of the bishop. Whatever their ministry, its source was in the authority of their bishop, and for the sake of harmony and charity in the body of Christ, they were expected always to remain obedient to their bishop.

### Deacons

Many scholars regard the diaconate as the oldest ministry among the three orders of bishop, presbyter (priest), and deacon. According to this view, it was instituted by the apostles themselves, before the episcopate and the presbyterate. Its necessity in a religion that promoted practical love is obvious.

In Acts 6, we find the apostles living and teaching in Jerusalem, with the numbers of believers continually growing. A dispute arose because the widows of the Hellenists [133] were being neglected in the daily distribution of food. Therefore, seven men, among them Stephen, the first martyr, were chosen to see to the fair distribution of food. Despite the fact that nowhere in this passage are these men referred to as *diakonoi*, the story has often been regarded as the origin of the order of deacons. As we have seen above, in Rome the number of deacons was limited to seven, despite the fact that a Church that large might easily have used more deacons.

The word *diakonos*, as it is used in the New Testament, has three different meanings: a general meaning, a general Christian meaning, and a specific ministerial meaning. In general, in Greek usage, the word simply refers to a household servant—not a slave who does heavy manual labor, but someone who serves meals, cleans, and does general household duties. The Latin word *minister* has the same meaning. The New Testament uses this meaning quite often, but also adapts the term to apply to everyone who is involved in Christian ministry. An example of this meaning would be Colossians 1:25, where Paul writes, "I became a minister [in Greek, *diakonos*] according to the divine office."

There are three other passages in the New Testament where *diakonos* is used as a technical term to refer to a specific order of ministry. First Timothy 3:12 is the clearest case of this usage. Philippians 1:1 is significant because it mentions the deacons along with the bishops. (Romans 16:1 may also be a case where *diakonos* is used in a special, technical sense, but this passage is subject to more than one interpretation. We will deal with Romans 16:1 in another section, since it touches closely on the question of women in ministry.) For now, let us consider Acts 6, 1 Timothy 3:8–12, and Philippians 1:1 to see what these passages can tell us about the development of the special ministry of deacons.

In Acts 6:5, we find that the whole community chose the Seven, and that one of the men chosen was Stephen, an outstanding Christian, "full of faith and the Holy Spirit". In verse 6, we find that they stood before the apostles, who laid hands on them and prayed over them. A little bit later, in verses 8 to 15, we find that Stephen, in the power of the Holy Spirit, did great signs and wonders, and engaged nonbelievers in debate. This debate led to Stephen's martyrdom, recounted in Acts 7. From this whole section, we can see that the diaconate was not an insignificant institution in the early Church. In addition to seeing to the care of widows, orphans, and the poor, deacons engaged in evangelism, apologetics, and other public ministries.

First Timothy 3:8–12 is significant because in this passage Paul[134] lays out the requirements for deacons: they must be serious, honest, not greedy or drunkards, strong in faith and character, married only once, and good husbands and fathers. To appreciate the significance of this passage, we must bear in mind that one of the purposes of this letter was to help Timothy in his task of setting up the ministries of the Church. It must be noted, however, that even though Paul lays out the requirements for these two ministries, he does not define their roles.

It is significant that Paul discusses deacons immediately after his discussion of the requirements of a bishop. It would seem that as the shape of the Church's ministries became clearer in Paul's mind, deacons and bishops were linked together in a special way. We see this linkage clearly in the salutation of Paul's Letter to the Philippians, where Paul greets the Church of Philippi, along with "the *episkopoi* and the *diakonoi*".[135]

Once again, however, Paul specifically mentions the ministry of deacon, but does not define it. The best definition of the role of the *diakonoi* in the New Testament is found in Acts 6 and in those passages that describe Christian ministry in general. Like the other ministries of the Church, the diaconate evolved, and we can get a clearer picture of how this ministry evolved from the postapostolic literature.

We know that deacons were functioning in the Church at the end of the first century. They are mentioned in both the *Didache* and *I Clement*. As in Paul's Letters, we find the deacons and bishops closely linked to one another. This will be a theme throughout the writings of the early Church. We will also find, in *I Clement*, an attempt to link the ministries of the Church to the Old Testament: "And thus preaching through countries and cities, they [the apostles] appointed the first fruits of their labors, having first proved them by the Spirit, to be bishops and deacons of those who should afterward believe. Nor was this any new thing, since indeed many ages before it was written concerning bishops and deacons: For thus says the Scripture in a certain place, 'I will appoint their bishops in righteousness, and their deacons in faith.' "[136]

In the *Didache*, the diaconate is presented as an alternative to the unreliable traveling prophets and teachers. The readers are told: "Appoint, therefore, for yourselves, bishops and deacons worthy of the Lord, men meek, and not lovers of money, and truthful and proved; for they also render to you the service of prophets and teachers." [137] Based on the information that the deacons performed the same functions as prophets and teachers, a modern scholar has presented the essential functions of the deacons of the late first century in the following list: "to preach (1 Cor 12:10), to serve the community (1 Cor 14:4), to teach, encourage, reprove, correct, and console (1 Cor 14:3). By preaching the mystery of Christ (1 Cor 13:2), they brought men to the faith (Rom 16:26)." [138]

Ignatius of Antioch, from whom we gain a clearer picture of the three-part ministry of bishop, priest, and deacon, always referred to his deacons as "fellow servants". [139] Ignatius wrote: "I have had the privilege of seeing you, through Damas your most worthy bishop, and through your worthy presbyters Bassus and Apollonius, and through my fellow-servant the deacon Sotio, whose friendship may I ever enjoy, inasmuch as he is subject to the bishop as to the grace of God, and to the presbytery as to the law of Jesus Christ." [140] He also wrote: "It behooves you also, in every way, to please the deacons, who are ministers of the mysteries of Christ Jesus, not just ministers of meat and drink, but servants of the Church of God." [141]

Ignatius indicates that deacons could preach: "Philo the deacon, of Cilicia, a man of reputation, who still ministers to me in the word of God...." [142] He also frequently used deacons as letter carriers, not an insignificant task, since the letter-bearer also had to give a personal account of events: "Elect a deacon to act as the ambassador [apostolos] of God to the brethren there, that he may rejoice along with them when they are met together, and glorify the name of God." [143] We find Ignatius giving a wide variety of tasks to the deacons, but always we find him calling them his "fellow servants", and even "special friends". [144]

In the Rome of *The Pastor of Hermas* (ca. 150), we find deacons engaged in active and important ministries. The author of this work experienced a series of highly symbolic visions, and in one of them, deacons figured with great prominence: "Hear now with regard to the stones which are in the building. Those square white stones which fitted exactly into each other, are apostles, bishops, teachers, and deacons, who have lived in godly purity, and have acted as bishops and teachers and deacons chastely and reverently to the elect of God." [145]

On the other hand, "the ones with blemishes are deacons who served badly and stole the livelihood of widows and orphans and profited for themselves, from the service which they received to perform." [146] Deacons worked on a personal basis with the poor, widows, and orphans, and there would be many chances for them to gain control of funds that did not belong to them, so it was imperative that they be honest. A dishonest deacon would be a blemish on the entire Church.

From Justin Martyr we find that the deacons had a liturgical function: "When the president has given thanks, and all the people have expressed their assent, those who are called by us deacons give to each of those present to partake of the bread and wine mixed with water." [147] Later, "to those who are absent a portion is sent by the deacons." [148]

From Tertullian we learn that deacons could baptize if given a commission by their bishop: "Of giving it [baptism], the chief priest who is the bishop has the right: in the next place, the presbyters and deacons, yet not without the bishop's authority." [149]

In Hippolytus' Rome, deacons were ordained, but only by the bishop:

> When one ordains a deacon, he is chosen according to what has been said above, with only the bishop laying on his hand in the same manner. In the ordination of a deacon, only the bishop lays on his hand, because the deacon is not ordained to the priesthood, but to the service of the bishop, to do that which he commands. For he is not part of the council of the clergy, but acts as a manager, and reports to the bishop what is necessary. He does not receive the spirit common to the elders, which the elders share, but that which is entrusted to him under the bishop's authority. [150]

In Cyprian's North Africa, it appears that deacons performed the same functions as in other places. Since Cyprian spent some time in exile, he had to rely heavily on his presbyters and deacons. It has been argued by some that the deacons of Carthage actually heard confessions during extreme emergencies. [151] It should be noted, however, that this extraordinary privilege was granted only in cases when a martyr (one who was in prison awaiting execution) gave the penitent a certificate recommending forgiveness. Later Church teaching makes it clear that deacons do not have the authority to grant sacramental absolution.

Cyprian had some troubles with his deacons. Not all were obedient. Some peculated Church funds or ran off with the widows' savings. Cyprian describes one very questionable situation in his own words:

We have read, dearest brother, your letter which you sent by Paconius our brother, asking and desiring us to write again to you, and say what we thought of those virgins who, after having once determined to continue in their condition, and firmly to maintain their continency, have afterwards been found to have remained in the same bed side by side with men; of whom you say that one is a deacon; and yet that the same virgins who have confessed that they have slept with men declare that they are chaste … you have acted advisedly and with vigor, dearest brother, in excommunicating the deacon who has often abode with a virgin; and, moreover, the others who had been used to sleep with virgins.[152]

We should be very clear what was going on here. The virgins were young women who had taken a perpetual vow of celibacy. They were sleeping with men, one of whom was a deacon, and yet they claimed that they were maintaining their chastity. We should note that there is no indication that the young women were lying. Cyprian decided that the virgins should be examined by midwives, and if they were telling the truth they should be readmitted to their status in the Church. The deacon, for his part, was excommunicated because, whether he had in fact had intercourse with the young women or not, he had violated the high standards of his office.

We should not leave this as our last word on the deacons of the early Church. Probably the vast majority fulfilled their duties with heroic love. When Cyprian was martyred, on September 14, 258, his deacons stepped forward to stand beside him. That same year, Pope Sixtus was arrested with four of his deacons while saying Mass in the catacombs. All five men were martyred on August 6. And who could forget the blessed Saint Lawrence, Archdeacon of Rome, who faithfully cared for the poor until he was martyred during the persecution of Valerian. And these are only a small number of deacons who gave their whole life to the service of Christ and his Church.

### Subdeacons, Acolytes, Lectors, and Exorcists

The offices of bishop, presbyter, and deacon were already established by the beginning of the second century. Over the next 150 years other ministries evolved; these fall under the heading of "minor orders".

*Subdeacon.* The office of subdeacon was first mentioned in the *Apostolic Tradition*, so the office must have been in existence from at least around 170 to 180.[153] Of them Hippolytus says only, "Hands shall not be laid upon a subdeacon, but his name shall be mentioned that he may serve the deacon",[154] and "each of the deacons with the subdeacons shall be alert on the bishop's behalf, for the bishop must be informed if any are sick."[155] Cornelius' list of the ministers of Rome, which we noted above, indicates that in his time (around 250), Rome had seven deacons and seven subdeacons. Since we know that Rome was divided into seven districts, with a deacon in charge of the charitable work of each district, it seems reasonable to assume that each deacon was assisted by his own subdeacon.

Subdeacons could have varied duties. We learn from Cyprian of Carthage that he made a man named Optatus a subdeacon and assigned him the duty of teaching the catechumens.[156] Cyprian also used subdeacons as letter-carriers for many of his letters.[157] This would have been an extremely important duty, since Cyprian ruled his diocese from exile during a period of persecution, and he also needed letter-carriers for his important letters to fellow bishops throughout the world.

The office of subdeacon appears to have been made necessary by a belief in the early Church that no community should have more than seven deacons. This belief, which of course was taken from Acts 6, insured that as the communities grew (and also the needs of the community), something like the office of subdeacon would be necessary.

*Acolyte.* The office of acolyte was also derived from that of the deacon, as seven deacons and seven subdeacons were not enough for some communities. We first hear about them from Cornelius and Cyprian. Since we do not hear about them in the *Apostolic Tradition*, the office must have originated sometime between 200 and 250. Cyprian used acolytes as letter-carriers[158] and ministers for those in prison.[159]

*Lector.* Subdeacons and acolytes were associated with and subservient to deacons. Lectors, on the other hand, were associated with the presbyterate. In some cases, it was a "gateway to the ministry of presbyter".[160] Justin Martyr is the first Christian writer to mention the specific office of lector: "The memoirs of the apostles or the writings of the prophets are read, as long as time permits; then, when the reader [lector] has ceased, the president verbally instructs".[161] Hippolytus states, "The reader is appointed by the bishop's giving him the book, for he is not ordained."[162] This would indicate that Hippolytus did not consider lectors (who are in minor, not major, orders) to be members of the clergy. However, some scholars hold that lectors were evidently regarded as members of the clergy in Carthage,[163] although that would have been an anomalous view.

*Exorcist.* One of the most touching aspects of the early Christians concerns the great care they gave to people they considered possessed by demons. Of course, Jesus himself showed great care for demoniacs,[164] so in this regard the Church was simply imitating her Master.

We find exorcists mentioned among the ministers of Rome in Cornelius' letter to Fabius. Cyprian also made reference to exorcists in Carthage.[165] It was evidently possible to be an exorcist and a member of another order at the same time.[166]

What did the exorcists do? The early Church seems to have known two kinds of exorcisms. As you will have remembered, in the early Church, baptisms were preceded by daily exorcisms all during Lent. It is possible that the exorcists were responsible for these exorcisms, except for the last one, which had to be done by the bishop.

There was also another type of exorcism. The ancient world had many people that were classified as possessed by demons. Many, if not most, of these were probably what we today call mentally ill.[167] For these unfortunates, the Church had a special ministry. Reconstructing how that ministry was exercised in the first three centuries is difficult: the office of exorcist is mentioned in the documents mentioned above, but there are no descriptions of an actual exorcism until the fourth and fifth centuries.

In the fourth century, we find that demoniacs (called *energumenoi*) were given a special place in the porch of the basilicas, that there were special prayers for them during the liturgy, and that the bishop would give them special blessings.[168] In the canons falsely attributed to the Fourth Council of Carthage, the exorcists are bidden to visit the *energumenoi* daily, to provide them with food and lay hands on them.[169]

The plight of the mentally ill in the ancient world was truly desperate. No one knew the cause of their problems or knew what to do for them. They were frequently ignored or abandoned by their families, and since they had a hard time finding work, they had to be helped or they would die. The Church at least made sure they had food and a place to stay, and it is possible that in some cases their prayers and kindness actually helped.

Let us conclude this section by contemplating the teaching of Saint John Chrysostom (late fourth and early fifth century):

> For indeed the showing of mercy is a mystery. Shut therefore the doors, that none may see what it is not pious to display. For our mysteries too are above all things, a showing of God's mercy and loving-kindness.... And the first prayer too is full of mercy, when we entreat for the *energumenoi*; and the second again, for others under penance seeking for much mercy; and the third also for ourselves ... but the mystery itself, of how much mercy, of how much love to man it is full, the initiated know.[170]

The Church treated the *energumenoi* with much greater tenderness than did society as a whole, and the exorcists were on the front line of this ministry of mercy.

### Women and Ministry

The question of women in ministry in the early Church is a controversial one today, not so much because of the state of the evidence from the period, but because of the state of the controversy in our times. Today, some people see the ordination of women as a question of justice. Traditionally minded Christians look at Church history and see no precedent for or possibility of the ordination of women within the Catholic or Orthodox tradition. As usual, there are complicating factors that make analysis more difficult. The problem, as I see it, is that at any given time in Church history, there have been more women than men active in Church-related activities. The early Church period was, in my judgment, no different in this regard.

In the introduction of his study on the subject, Father Jean Danielou states the matter well: "On the one hand, there has never been any mention of women filling strictly sacerdotal offices. We never see a woman offering the eucharistic Sacrifice, or ordaining, or preaching in the Church. On the other hand, all Christian history, particularly in the first centuries, shows that women have played a considerable part in missionary work, in worship and in teaching." [171]

Father Danielou has it right, if you consider only those Churches in the communion of the Catholic Church. Among heretical sects, the Marcionites and Gnostics in particular, women engaged in priestly ministry. We know this because Tertullian strongly criticized these sects for their behavior. In *Prescription against the Heretics*, he indicated that a characteristic of heretical sects is that they allow women to teach, dispute, and even to baptize. [172]

Perhaps because they allowed women to participate in these ministries, women tended to be attracted to heretical sects. Irenaeus wrote about a charlatan named Marcus, who tricked women by flattery, seducing them spiritually and physically and allowing them to participate in his liturgies. [173] One might argue that Irenaeus was exaggerating, driven by jealousy, misogyny, or desire to protect his own authority. But we have seen enough examples of spiritual charlatanry in our own time to know that such things are possible, and we also know that women (and men) are sometimes vulnerable to such charlatans. [174]

The question of women in sacramental ministry is vexed by the problem of what evidence is to be considered. The orthodox communities did not allow women to function as priests. Some of the heterodox communities did, but they had a host of other problems. They frequently denied either the humanity or the divinity of Jesus. Many of them found it impossible to escape from a radical dualism that caused them either to forbid sexual relations even in marriage, or, paradoxically, to advocate free love. [175] So the sincere Catholic proponents of women's ordination have to ask themselves if they wish to use the evidence of heretics and charlatans in arguing their case.

In this work, I have made the methodological decision (based, admittedly, on my personal faith commitment) to write about the lives, beliefs, and practices of orthodox Christians. Therefore, I can wholeheartedly endorse the judgment that the orthodox communities never allowed women into the sacramental ministries of the Church, even though there were more women than men in Church-related activities in the early Church.

What were the ecclesial roles in which women were involved? A survey of the writings of the early Church reveals three specific ones:

there are deaconesses, widows, and virgins mentioned in the relevant literature. Here is a review of the history and function of these states.

*Deaconesses.* Early in 112, the emperor Trajan sent a new governor, Pliny, to the province of Bithynia. The province had been badly managed, and Pliny encountered many difficulties. He was obliged to send numerous letters to Trajan for instructions, and the letters have been preserved for us today. These letters provide an invaluable window into the life of one province at one particular period of history. One letter is of special interest to our current inquiry. The local temples had experienced a serious loss of income due to the success of a strange cult of Christians. Entirely unfamiliar with Christianity, Pliny investigated the cult, not hesitating to torture to gain the information he needed: "This made me decide it was all the more necessary to extract the truth by torture from two slave women [*ancillae*], whom they call deaconesses [*ministrae*]." [176]

We note several important facts, not the least of which is that an educated man saw nothing wrong in torturing two women without any evidence of wrongdoing. It is possible that he saw nothing wrong with it based on a false impression. In Roman law, it was legal to torture slaves to gain information in criminal cases. Pliny said the two women were slaves, then that the Christians called them *ministrae*. This Latin word is the root of the English word "minister". It is the word that is routinely used to translate the Greek *diakonos* (female, *diakonia*). As we saw, *diakonos* meant "household slave or servant" before the Christians used the term for a type of ministry. It is quite possible that the two women Pliny tortured were not servants at all, but deaconesses.[177]

Other authors have cast doubt on this interpretation of Pliny. They think the two women were Christian servant girls with no specific ministry in the Church at all. This interpretation is plausible because of the double meaning of *diakonos*, but it is not likely, since Pliny used two different words to describe the two women. "Servants who were called by them deaconesses" seems the most likely translation to me. But if this is true, the implication is that at a fairly early date the Church had an established office of "deaconess". How did this ministry come about? What did the deaconesses do? What were the requirements?

We first read about deaconesses, or think we do, from the pages of the New Testament. There are two relevant passages, Romans 16:1 and I Timothy 3:8–12, and several ancillary passages that will help us deduce the role of deaconesses in the New Testament Church.

The earliest reference would be Romans 16:1. Paul has reached the end of this important letter and is ready to make his farewells. A woman named Phoebe has accompanied the letter. Paul describes her as "our sister Phoebe, a deaconess [*diakonon*] of the Church of Cenchreae . . . a helper of many and of myself as well". Again, some scholars have suggested that this not a reference to a specific ministry, but simply an acknowledgment that Phoebe has served many of her fellow believers in one way or another.

The second alleged mention of deaconesses in the New Testament is even more ambiguous. In I Timothy 3:8–13, we find Paul laying out the requirements of a deacon. This is not surprising. He has just finished explaining what Timothy should look for in bishops. In verses 8 to 10, he writes that deacons should be serious, honest, sober, not greedy, possessing a strong faith, and blameless in their personal lives. Then, in verse 11, he writes, "Women likewise must be serious, no slanderers, but temperate, faithful in all things." In verses 12 to 13 he goes back to talking about male deacons. The interpolation about women in verse 11 is interesting. He might be talking about the wives of deacons, or he might just have a misplaced reference to women in general.

What did the deaconesses do? Paul was clear on this point: "Women should keep silence in the churches. . . . If there is anything they desire to know, let them ask their husbands at home." [178] So the deaconesses probably did not preach or lead prayers during the early liturgy. They may have taught and led prayer services for the women of the community, but this is somewhat speculative. [179]

The primary duty of the deaconesses must have been to take personal care of the sick and poor, the widows and the orphans. Outside of the New Testament, the *Didascalia Apostolorum* makes several mentions of deaconesses. They are to act as ushers for the women's section during the liturgy, see to hospitality to women during the liturgy, act as intermediaries between the bishop and the women of his flock, supervise the widows, distribute material goods to the widows, generally see to the care of all women in the congregation, and assist in the baptism of women. [180]

The last function deserves a closer look, since it is very different from our current practice. Here is what the *Didascala* says: "In the first place, when women go down into the water, those who go down into the water ought to be anointed by a deaconess with the oil of anointing; and when there is no woman at hand, and especially no deaconess, he who baptizes must of necessity anoint her who is being baptized. But where there is a woman, and especially a deaconess, it is not fitting that women should be seen by men."[181] The passage is fairly self-explanatory. Deaconesses were needed because baptisms were performed in the nude, and it was undesirable for the bishops and deacons to behold the nakedness of female catechumens and lay hands on them. After baptism, the deaconesses would see to the further instruction of the neophytes. The *Didascalia* required that a deaconess be "a pure virgin; or, at the least, a widow who has been but once married, faithful, and well esteemed".[182]

From the evidence of Pliny and the *Didascalia*, we find the office of deaconess in the East during the second and third centuries. There is no document from the Western Church that mentions deaconesses. Late in the third century, the office seems to have died out even in the East, its duties taken over by senior widows.[183]

*Widows.* The early Christians inherited their concern for widows and orphans from Judaism. The Old Testament is full of admonitions to take care of the widows and orphans. The great care for widows was justified. In Jewish as well as Greco-Roman society, all women were expected to marry shortly after puberty. In Jewish law, women could not own property, make financial transactions, or inherit without a man to act as an intermediary. To make matters worse, a widow without a son was supposed to wait for her husband's brother to marry her, in fulfillment of levitical prescriptions.[184] For these reasons, widowhood was greatly feared by first-century Jewish women. The Hebrew word for widows is eloquent: *almanah* has as its root the word that means "unable to speak".[185] Because of the legal restrictions that prevented widows from taking care of themselves, the law required that widows be taken care of by the whole community.[186]

In Greek culture, the status of widows was hardly better. They did not have to worry about marrying their husband's brother, but they were still unable to make a living on their own. The root of the Greek word for widow means "forsaken", or "empty". Upon the death of her husband, a widow was subject to a *kyrios*, or "lord" (usually her deceased husband's brother), who was responsible for her. The *kyrios* was supposed to find a new husband for the widow, and if he was unable to do so, he would be responsible for her upkeep. The *kyrios* was supposed to administer the woman's dowry, so she could live on the interest. If the *kyrios*' behavior was in any way objectionable to the widow, her only recourse was to return to her father's household, if that was even possible.

There is some evidence that the lot of Greek women had improved by the time of Christ, particularly in the further reaches of the empire. Athens was at the forefront in the restriction of women's freedom, and the further away from Athens, the better the lot of Greek women, as a general rule.[187]

In Roman law, widows fared somewhat better. Widows could remarry as they willed. They could give testimony in court, own and manage property, and accumulate wealth. These freer customs gradually spread throughout the Roman Empire, and in the New Testament we find women with considerable freedom.[188] But the world was still full of poor widows with few means of support, and the Church took it upon herself to take care of them.

The clearest example of this care is in Acts 6:1, where we find a special ministry set up just to see to the fair distribution of goods to all widows in the community. At some point the Church grew to such numbers that it was not enough to have deacons appointed to take care of the widows.

Evidently the widows were taking up too much of the community's resources, and it became necessary to find out which widows had no other means of support and enroll only those widows. In 1 Timothy 5:3–6 we read, "Honor widows who are real widows. If a widow has children or grandchildren, let them first learn their religious duty to their own family and make some return to their parents; for this is acceptable in the sight of God. She who is a real widow, and is left all alone, has set her hope on God and continues in supplications and prayers night and day; whereas she who is self indulgent is dead even while she lives." A little further on, in verses 9 to 16, Paul expands on his ideas:

Let a widow be enrolled if she is not less than sixty years of age, having been the wife of one husband; and she must be well attested for her good deeds, as one who has brought up children, shown hospitality, washed the feet of the saints, relieved the afflicted, and devoted herself to doing good in every way. But refuse to enroll younger widows; for when they grow wanton against Christ they desire to marry, and so they incur condemnation for having violated their first pledge. Besides that, they learn to be idlers, gadding about from house to house, and not only idlers but gossips and busybodies, saying what they should not. So I would have younger widows marry, bear children, rule their households, and give the enemy no occasion to revile us. For some have already strayed after Satan. If any believing woman has relatives who are widows, let her assist them; let the church not be burdened, so that it may assist those who are real widows.

In this passage, Paul introduces three rules. The first is that widows are to be enrolled. That is, the deacons or some other responsible party would investigate the case of every widow and determine who was genuinely needy. Only these widows would be supported by the community. The others would be supported by their families.

The second rule was that widows would be made responsible for helping other widows. This proposal, which seems harsh on the surface, was actually a stroke of inspired genius. Widows, like all human beings, have a strong need for useful work, after basic needs are met. So we see Paul urging widows to take the initiative in seeking out other widows and providing assistance to them.

Paul's third rule was that younger widows should be encouraged to remarry, presumably out of fear that they would take a vow of celibacy that they would later find themselves unable to keep. This implies, though Paul does not come right out and say it, that widows were expected to take vows of celibacy.

In the postapostolic Church, widows are in great evidence. As already noted, at around 250, there were 1,500 "widows and persons in distress" supported by the Church of Rome alone.[189] Widows were not ordained, but instituted. Hippolytus explains why: "The widow shall be appointed by the word alone. . . . Hands shall not be laid upon her because she does not offer the oblation nor has she a sacred ministry. Ordination is for the clergy on account of their ministry, but the widow is appointed for prayer, and prayer is the duty of all."[190]

As mentioned, in addition to receiving charity, many widows engaged in service themselves. They made clothes for the poor,[191] prayed for the whole Church,[192] cared for other widows, visited the sick and prisoners,[193] and taught other women and orphans the basics of the faith.[194]

Polycarp, Tertullian, and other writers used a curious metaphor to describe the widows. Polycarp wrote, "Teach the widows to be discreet as respects the faith of the Lord, praying continually for all, being far from all slandering, evil-speaking, false-witnessing, love of money, and every kind of evil; knowing that they are the altars of God."[195] What could Polycarp possibly have meant? When one considers the purpose of an altar, his meanings become clearer: (1) an altar is where a community places its offerings, and the widows were the ones who received the offerings of the Church, either to use for themselves or to distribute to others; (2) the altar signifies the prayer of the Church, and widows were asked to serve as "prayer warriors" in the early Church; and (3) widows were themselves asked to make numerous sacrifices in their personal lives, taking vows of chastity, living simple lives, aiding the poor, and avoiding gossip.

The final point is worth considering further. In ministering to widows, the sick, and the poor, the widows were privy to many secrets, which they had to share with their superiors (probably the deacon), but no one else. For this reason, widows were frequently admonished to refrain from gossip.[196] Because the widows were expected to be sober and industrious, and because of the requirement of chastity, some communities set the minimum age for enrollment at sixty years.

The widows were truly on the front line of the Church's practical ministry in the first three centuries. Through their countless acts of loving kindness, they genuinely earned the title Polycarp bestowed on them, "the altars of God".

*Virgins.* In the culture surrounding the early Christians, the overwhelming impetus was for young men and women to marry and have children. In Judaism, children (particularly sons) were considered a blessing, and there was a great deal of social pressure on men and women to marry. Concerned about the dearth of young Roman citizens, Emperor Augustus passed a law requiring members of the upper class to marry. In a society with few social services, it was considered necessary to have children to make sure there would be someone to care for one in old age. Despite these powerful impediments, a large number of Christian young women (and men) chose a life of consecrated virginity. For the most part, Church leaders, who feared scandals, did not encourage young people to take this step. However, when it became obvious that the young people were eager to give their lives to Christ, the Church found a place for them.

Given that the surrounding pagan culture did not favor virginity,[197] why did so many Christians want to live a life of virginity? There appear to be three factors that encouraged Christian virginity. First, ascetic Jewish cults, such as the Essenes of Qumran and the Therapeutae of Egypt, seem to have practiced celibacy along with other ascetic practices.[198] Second, women appear to have been going through a period of dissatisfaction with the institution of arranged marriage. In many of the accounts of female virgin martyrs that we have, a pagan suitor was the villain.[199]

A third factor in the popularity of virginity among Christian women was undoubtedly the virginity of Mary. Scripture affirms that Mary was a virgin.[200] Ignatius of Antioch mentioned the virginity of Mary in three of his letters.[201] In the third century, devotion to the Blessed Virgin seems to have flowered. Numerous apocryphal writings, in particular the *Protoevangelium of James* and the *Gospel of Bartholomew*, attempted to fill in the periods of her life not mentioned in Scripture.[202] These documents seem to have inspired a relatively large number of young women to live a celibate life.[203]

In the third century, celibacy as a way of life may have increased in popularity, but we find female virginity from the beginning. In the Acts of the Apostles, four virginal daughters of Philip are mentioned. These young women had the gift of prophecy, which may have been linked to their virginity.[204] In 1 Corinthians 7:25–38, Paul dealt with the question of marriage and virginity in a deeply subtle way. He affirmed the goodness of both marriage and celibacy, but indicated that his preference was that those not married remain in that state, due to the uncertainty of the times.[205] Paul also affirmed that he himself was celibate.[206]

By no means did the practice of celibacy die out in the postapostolic period. Ignatius of Antioch mentioned virgins in his letters: "Virgins, have Christ alone before your eyes, and His Father in your prayers, being enlightened by the Spirit. May I have pleasure in your purity, as that of Elijah, or as of Joshua the son of Nun, as of Melchizedek, or as of Elisha, as of Jeremiah, or as of John the Baptist, as of the beloved disciple, as of Timothy, as of Titus, as of Evodius, as of Clement, who departed this life in perfect chastity." [207]

Clement of Rome found it necessary to write two letters devoted strictly to the subject of virginity. He reminded some young women, who were not sure exactly what they were undertaking, about the reality of the life to which they were aspiring: "You desire, then, to be a virgin? Do you know what hardship and irksomeness there is in true virginity—that which stands constantly at all seasons before God, and does not withdraw from His service, and is anxious how it may please its Lord with a holy body, and with its spirit?" [208] Clement was not intent on dissuading anyone from taking a vow of perpetual virginity, but he wanted to make sure the candidates knew exactly what they were going to experience.

Justin Martyr attested to the beauty of the celibate life well lived: "Many, both men and women, who have been Christ's disciples from childhood, remain pure at the age of sixty or seventy years; and I boast that I could produce such from every race of men." [209]

What did the virgins do in and for the Church? As the reference to Philip's daughters indicates, many undoubtedly functioned as prophetesses. As we have seen elsewhere, in Scripture, prophecy does not so much entail foretelling the future as much as simply speaking the truth. The virgins appear to have spent much time in charitable work. Some virgins, as we shall see, were independently wealthy. These virgins were asked to share their wealth with those in need. Others, who were not wealthy, were expected to visit the sick and poor. Prayer was also an important part of the lives of the virgins. [210]

Not all was perfect in the world of consecrated virginity, however. The careful rules that were developed at a later time were not yet in place. Adequate supervision of younger celibates was sometimes lacking. A lack of clearly defined roles meant that some celibates tended toward idleness. Some celibates were tempted by the vice of spiritual pride. These problems were addressed by various writers in their customary manner. The only writer of the early Church who actively discouraged celibacy was Clement of Alexandria. The rest acknowledged the existence of celibacy, and even encouraged it, but wanted greater discipline among the ranks of the celibates. Sexual incontinency caused the greatest problems, since it seemed to confirm to the pagans that the Christians were living lives of debauchery.

Third-century writers, primarily Cyprian of Carthage, began to attack these problems. The problems of idleness and unchastity were related to one another. Cyprian urged virgins to use their time and resources to aid the poor:

> You say that you are wealthy and rich, and you think that you should use those things which God has willed you to possess. Use them, certainly, but for the things of salvation; use them, but for good purposes; use them, but for those things which God has commanded, and which the Lord has set forth. Let the poor feel that you are wealthy; let the needy feel that you are rich. Lend your estate to God; give food to Christ. Move Him by the prayers of many to grant you to carry out the glory of virginity, and to succeed in coming to the Lord's rewards.[211]

Cyprian also had to ask the virgins of Carthage to dress modestly: "Your shameful dress and immodest ornament accuse you."[212] He even had to ask some virgins not to attend those public baths where they would see nude men and be seen in the nude themselves.[213] Cyprian laid out a series of rules for dress and behavior designed to protect virgins from the dangers of temptation and public scandal. In the fourth century, when Christians were free to live their faith publicly, the virgins were settled in religious orders, where they could carry out their various charisms with other like-minded women, who would help them live out their vocations. These orders were forerunners of the religious orders that exist to this day.

In the early Church, the vast majority of virgins lived out their vows in faith, hope, and love. As already noted, many were martyred for their faith. They provided examples of continence in a society that was every bit as obsessed with sex as ours is today. In this way, they provided a valuable witness to the power and beauty of the Christian life. Let us conclude this section by returning to the thoughts of Cyprian, that wise servant of God: "This [virginity] is the flower of the ecclesiastical seed, the grace and ornament of spiritual endowment, a joyous disposition, the wholesome and uncorrupted work of praise and honor, God's image answering to the holiness of the Lord, the more illustrious portion of Christ's flock."[214] Cyprian likened virginity to a flower, which is not the whole plant, or even the most important part, but the most visible part and the most beautiful. Contrary to all expectations, the virgins of the early Church were fruitful in a wholly unexpected way, as a sign of faithfulness and a call to repentance.

### The Rich and Varied Role of the Laity

One of the aspects of Christian life of which pagans particularly disapproved was the Christian habit of entrusting their deepest teachings to the poor and uneducated. The pagan philosopher Celsus complained about this habit:

> We see, indeed, in private houses workers in wool and leather, and fullers, and persons of the most uninstructed and rustic character, not venturing to utter a word in the presence of their elders and wiser masters; but when they get hold of the children privately, and certain women as ignorant as themselves, they pour forth wonderful statements, that they alone know how men ought to live, and that, if the children obey them, they will both be happy themselves, and will make their home happy also ... that if they wish to avail themselves of their aid, they must leave their fathers and their instructors, and go with the women and their playfellows to the women's apartments, or to the leather shop, or the fuller's shop, that they may attain to perfection—and by words like these gain them over.[215]

In Celsus' world, only the well educated would presume to teach children. The poor workmen stuck to their own work and did not interfere in deeper matters that were deemed beyond their understanding. The early Christians, however, believed that each person had a unique calling and unique gifts from God, and that each person should use those gifts for the benefit of the entire Church and all mankind. The source of this belief is not hard to find: the Christians had a profound belief in God's personal care for them, exemplified in Jesus' teachings on the worth of human life. They also took seriously the teaching of Saint Paul on the Church as the Body of Christ and believed that each Christian was responsible for fulfilling the function that had been designated for him.[216] Finally, they believed in the doctrine of the priesthood of all the baptized, made explicit in 1 Peter 2:9: "But you are a chosen race, a royal priesthood, a holy nation, God's own people, that you may declare the wonderful deeds of him who called you out of darkness into his marvelous light." [217]

Throughout the first three Christian centuries, there was a steady consolidation of the authority of the clergy. The growth in the sheer number of Christians required an increasing level of organization and discipline. The presence of heresies and periodic persecutions made organization even more imperative. As we shall see, this increased clericalization did not affect the roles of the laity. Throughout the period in question, the same specific ministries and obligations were in effect for the laity. Broadly speaking, these ministries and obligations can be divided into four categories: (1) liturgical functions, (2) constitutional functions, (3) supportive functions, and (4) evangelical and catechetical functions.

We will discuss each of these functions in greater detail, but first it seems necessary to discuss the origin of the terms "laity" and "clergy". Both words have Greek roots. The term "laity" comes from *laos*, which means simply "the people". In early Christian thought, the entire Christian community was the *laos tou theou*, the people of God, holy and chosen. There was nothing derogatory or condescending about the term. The fact that there were apostles, bishops, presbyters, deacons, and countless other specific ministries did not detract from the dignity of the people of God.

The term "clergy", which we find coming into common use at around the beginning of the third century, can refer to an heir, but its primary meaning is "a lot", or "that which is assigned by lot". [218] To understand the significance of this meaning, think of the replacement of the Apostle Judas, recorded in Acts 1:15–26. Two worthy men were identified, and lots were cast. The lot (*kleros*) fell on Matthias, and he was added to the Eleven. The significance of this passage is immense. Either man, Matthias or Barsabbas Justus, would have made a fine apostle. The will of God was revealed in the casting of the lots, and Matthias had no reason for feeling pride, just as Barsabbas Justus had no reason to feel shame. The point is that the belief among the early Christians was that God called whomever he willed, for whatever purpose he willed, and there was neither special merit nor disgrace in God's specific call.

*Liturgical Functions.* We do not know of a single instance where a layman presided over the liturgy in the early Church. The question of exactly who presided over the liturgies of the very earliest communities is simply not answerable. In the few liturgy-like meetings described in the New Testament, apostles presided. Presumably, there could have been a period in these communities in which the apostle would be absent but no bishop and presbyters in place. Exactly how these communities handled the situation is unknown. But for the period we know more about, it is clear that laypeople were not allowed to preside at the Eucharist.

Regarding preaching, the evidence is mixed. We know that Origen got in trouble with Demetrius, Bishop of Alexandria, for preaching as a layman during his first trip to Caesarea. But Eusebius records that the bishops of Caesarea and Jerusalem responded to Demetrius with examples of lay preaching. Here is what Bishop Alexander of Cappadocia has to say about Demetrius' assertion that laymen were never allowed to preach:

> In this assertion he has departed evidently far from the truth by some means. For, wherever there are found persons capable of profiting the brethren, such persons are exhorted by the holy bishops to address the people. Such was the case at Laranda, where Evelpis was thus exhorted by Neon; and at Iconium, Paulinus was thus exhorted by Celsus; and at Synada, Theodorus also by Atticus, our blessed brethren. And it is probable that this is done in other places also, although we know not the fact.[219]

It seems that laymen were allowed to preach in the Eastern communities, but not in the West. We have no record of laymen preaching in Rome, or Corinth, or Carthage, or Lyons. Clearly, it was not allowed in Alexandria. Equally clearly, it *was* allowed in some Eastern communities. But even where it was allowed, the stipulation was that the lay preacher must be "capable of profiting the brethren", i.e., he had to be well trained, as would be the case for an ordained minister, or he had to have some special experience to share.

The primary role of the laity in the early Church liturgy was to add their individual prayers and spiritual sacrifices to those of the whole community. In the context of the liturgical celebration, Clement of Rome wrote, "Let every one of you, brethren, give thanks to God in his own order, living in all good conscience, with becoming gravity, and not going beyond the rule of the ministry prescribed to him." [220]

Another primary responsibility of the laity during the liturgy was to add physical offerings to the spiritual offering of the liturgy. Laymen in the act of making their offering were called *prospherontes*. This offering could take the form of money or other goods. Justin Martyr affirms that the offering was entirely voluntary: "They who are well to do, and willing, give what each thinks fit; and what is collected is deposited with the president." [221] The *Apostolic Tradition* gives detailed instructions regarding the blessing of nonmonetary gifts, such as oil, cheese, and olives. [222] It would seem that the well-to-do would support the Church financially, while the poor would make offerings from their produce. Laymen would also provide the elements of bread and wine that would be transformed into the Eucharistic sacrifice.

*Constitutional Functions.* We have written at great length about the process of choosing bishops, priests, and deacons. The laity were allowed to express their opinions in the choosing of all these ministers. A curious side note is related to this practice. The emperor Alexander Severus, who was well disposed toward Christianity, developed the practice of posting the names of candidates for important offices and soliciting the comments of citizens on the grounds that "he used to say, it was unjust that, when Christians and Jews observed this custom in announcing the names of those who were to be ordained priests, it should not be similarly observed in the case of governors of provinces, to whose keeping were committed the fortunes and lives of men." [223]

*Supportive Functions.* As mentioned above, the laity made offerings to the Church, and those offerings were used to support the ordained ministers of the Church, as well as the needy members of the community. Tertullian expounds on this point: "Though we have our treasure-chest, it is not made up of purchase money, as of a religion that has its price. On the monthly day, if he likes, each puts in a small donation; but only if it be his pleasure, and only if he be able: for there is no compulsion; all is voluntary." [224]

*Evangelical and Catechetical Functions.* Some of the finest teachers of the early Church, such as Justin Martyr and Tertullian (before he became a Montanist),[225] were laymen. Even catechumens were sometimes taught by laity. The writers of the early Church approved of this practice. Hippolytus writes: "At the close of their prayer, when their instructor lays his hand upon the catechumens, he shall pray and dismiss them; whoever gives the instruction is to do this, whether a cleric or a layman." [226]

Laypeople also engaged in evangelization, as the satirical passage from Celsus indicates. Origen sheds light on this practice:

> Christians do not neglect, as far as in them lies, to take measures to disseminate their doctrine throughout the whole world. Some of them, accordingly, have made it their business to itinerate not only through cities, but even villages and country houses, that they might make converts to God. And no one would maintain that they did this for the sake of gain, when sometimes they would not accept even necessary sustenance; or if at any time they were pressed by a necessity of this sort, were contented with the mere supply of their wants, although many were willing to share with them, and to bestow help upon them far above their need.[227]

Lay Christians also acted as prophets and healers, as this passage from Irenaeus indicates:

> Those who are in truth His disciples, receiving grace from Him, do in His name perform miracles, so as to promote the welfare of other men, according to the gift which each one has received from Him. For some do certainly and truly drive out devils, so that those who have thus been cleansed from evil spirits frequently both believe in Christ, and join themselves to the Church. Others have foreknowledge of things to come: they see visions, and utter prophetic expressions. Others still, heal the sick by laying their hands upon them, and they are made whole.[228]

In the early Church, as today, the vast majority of Christians were members of the laity. Despite the fact that there was a well-defined hierarchy, the laity were not disparaged. On the contrary, they played a vital role in the life of the early Church. Without their active, enthusiastic participation in day-to-day ministries, Christianity could not have survived, thrived, and emerged triumphant in the Roman world.

## CHAPTER 4

# Persecutions and Martyrs in the Early Church

If you ask people what they know about the early Church, the first answer you will get from most people is that early Christians were persecuted, and they hid in the catacombs. The first part of this answer is quite true, but the second part is, as we shall see, doubtful. But even the statement that the Christians were persecuted requires some modification. From 64 to 313, Christianity was, formally and officially, illegal in the empire, and the punishment for being a Christian was death: beheading for citizens, and various forms of cruel and unusual means for noncitizens. There are approximately 1,000 martyrs from this period of whom we know, and countless others that we will never know about.[1] Even though these things are true, the persecutions are best described as intermittent and sporadic, and it might have been possible for a person in some places to have lived his entire life as a Christian without feeling in serious danger of martyrdom.

To understand why this is the case, it will be necessary to take a closer look at the history of the persecutions, but first some general observations. The persecution was intermittent because:

1. Not all the emperors hated the Christians. Some were actually quite sympathetic.

2. Provincial governors and other officials sometimes used their own judgment in enforcing imperial decrees. This happened in all areas of governance, because of the immense size of the empire and the obvious difficulties in communication.

3. The Romans primarily used the tried-and-true method of destroying the leadership of any movement they opposed. The bishops, presbyters, and deacons were usually their primary targets.

Having noted these preliminary observations, let us get into the heart of the subject.

## How the Romans Saw the Christians

The Romans, generally speaking, did not have a strong desire to persecute religious sects. They were like most people in most times: they preferred for things to run as smoothly as possible. They made accommodations with all kinds of religions in all parts of the empire. (The one exception was that they refused to allow the Gauls, the Celts, and the Carthaginians to engage in human sacrifice, as had been the ancient custom of these nations.) Roman accommodationism went so far as to exempt the Jews from the obligation of worshipping the emperors.

It is possible that the Christians could have been granted a similar exemption if things had gone differently. In the early days of Christianity, the Romans seem to have considered it a sect of Judaism. But when Judaism and Christianity came to a definitive split at around A.D. 90, the Christians lost whatever legal protection an association with Judaism might have afforded. But there is no reason to blame the Jews for the persecutions. The Romans had already decided the Christians were dangerous and acted accordingly. In some ways, the persecution of Christians began as a result of a series of historical accidents, but on the other hand, the Romans rightly saw the Christians as the bitterest foes of the established order. Both of these truths require further exploration.

The first "mistake" that led to the persecution of Christians was the Crucifixion of Jesus. This mistake came about because the Romans were always on the lookout for anyone who might have a claim to the throne of a particular territory. In particular, their antennae were up in Judea, which had a long history of unrest. When they heard Jesus referred to as "the son of David", and even "the King of the Jews", they were concerned and took no chances. The Gospel accounts of the trial of Jesus portray the Sanhedrin as the primary mover in the Crucifixion, but the Romans did the deed, and they did it because they wanted no rival claimant to the emperor's throne.[2]

The second historical accident that led to the persecution of the Christians was the Great Fire of Rome, in A.D. 64. No one really knows how this fire started. It is clear, however, that the people of Rome blamed Nero, and Nero decided to deflect blame to a small sect that was always talking about the fiery end of the world. Nero's dishonest and cowardly act established a three-hundred-year precedent that led to the death of countless Christians. In Roman law, once a precedent was established it was extremely difficult to change, and some emperors who had no personal dislike for the Christians felt it necessary to persecute them just to uphold the law.

The third historical accident began with the misunderstanding over the Eucharist. When people heard the Christians talk about eating the "Body and Blood of Christ", they thought the Christians were eating the flesh and drinking the blood of a dead person. Despite their own cruel and barbarous practices, the Romans (and the Greeks) had a genuine horror of cannibalism. Numerous apologists tried to dispel this myth, but the belief that the Christians were engaging in cannibalism lasted well into the third century.[3] The Christians were also accused of engaging in shameful sexual practices during their "love feasts", and the historian Tacitus matter-of-factly described the Christians as "a sect that hates the human race".[4]

These historical accidents are well documented, but they do not tell the whole story. From the Roman point of view, the Christians were indeed a serious threat to the established order. This is not to say that the Romans were justified in persecuting the Christians, but merely to say that the principles of the Christians, if they had been followed by the majority of the people, would have led to the destruction of the existing social order. If there was anything the Romans stood for, it was the existing social order. In this sense, the conflict between the Romans and the Christians was inevitable. The Roman objections to Christianity can be summarized as follows.

The Romans were deeply offended by the Christians' unwillingness to worship the pagan gods. Broadly speaking, people in the Greco-Roman world thought that the growth of crops, the prevention of illness, and military success all depended on the proper worship of the correct gods. The Christians refused to participate in these ceremonies. Worse, from the Roman perspective, they encouraged others to do the same.[5] The Roman attitude toward worshipping the gods was, "Why take a chance?" and they could not understand or tolerate the Christians' refusal to go along. To put the matter as simply as possible, the Christians, from the Roman point of view, by their refusal to worship the gods, were responsible for natural disasters. Tertullian complained: "If the Tiber rises as high as the city walls, if the Nile does not send its waters up over the fields, if the heavens give no rain, if there is an earthquake, if there is famine or pestilence, straightway the cry is, 'Away with the Christians to the lions!'" [6]

The Romans also could not tolerate the Christians' refusal to worship the emperors as gods. For the Romans, this refusal was tantamount to treason. We have numerous documents that show government officials trying to get Christians to "swear by the emperor". Here is one example: "Saturninus the proconsul said: 'We too are religious, and our religion is simple, and we swear by the genius of our lord the Emperor, and pray for his welfare, as you also ought to do.' Speratus said: 'If you will peaceably lend me your ears, I can tell you the mystery of simplicity.' Saturninus said: 'I will not lend my ears to you, when you begin to speak evil things of our sacred rites; but rather you swear by the genius of our lord the Emperor.'" [7]

The Romans also did not care for the fact that Christian leaders discouraged their followers from joining the army. Through parts of the second and third centuries, the empire was in desperate straits, threatened with invasions from the east, the north, and the south. The simple fact is that Christian leaders forbade new converts from joining the army, "lest they despise God". [8] Even more pernicious was the fact that soldiers who became Christians were forbidden to execute anyone or take the soldier's annual oath to Caesar. [9] For these reasons, Christians were seen as a liability to the security of the empire.

To summarize, then, the Romans persecuted the Christians for the following reasons: (1) the Romans were generally suspicious of sects that proclaimed anyone but Caesar as king; (2) Nero set a precedent that could not be broken; (3) the Romans thought the Christians engaged in depraved practices; (4) the Christians were held responsible for natural and military disasters; (5) the Christians' refusal to worship the emperor was interpreted as treason; and (6) the charge of treason was exacerbated by the Christians' attitude toward military service.

*How the Christians Saw the Romans*

With all the Romans did to the Christians, you would expect that the Christians would hate the Roman state and work for its overthrow.[10] One can detect anger at Rome in some Christian writings. The Book of Revelation refers to Rome as Babylon and looks forward to the day when God himself will exact vengeance on her. Angels were depicted as rejoicing over her fall, "Fallen, fallen is Babylon the great, she who made all nations drink the wine of her impure passion."[11] First Peter 5:13 also referred to Rome as Babylon, and the reference was hardly flattering. Babylon was the city that destroyed Jerusalem and took the people of God captive, but in the end, Babylon was destroyed by God. These seem to be the images behind the New Testament comparison.[12]

But there was another stream of New Testament thought regarding Rome. Saint Paul urged Christians to obey those in authority, on the grounds that their authority was allowed by God,[13] and Peter wrote: "Fear God. Honor the emperor."[14] These passages are sufficient to indicate that the attitude of the early Christians toward the Roman state was very complicated. There is a strong strain of anger that runs throughout the writings of this period, coupled with a desire for the Second Coming that would end all suffering. On the other hand, the early Christians were citizens of the empire and understood that their well-being was tied to the well-being of the state. They also understood that they could win more converts by making reasonable accommodations to the surrounding culture.

They even prayed for the emperor. In some versions of Clement's *First Epistle to the Corinthians*, you will find a prayer for rulers: "To our rulers and governors on the earth—to them You, Lord, gave the power of the kingdom by Your glorious and ineffable might, to the end that we may know the glory and honor given to them by Thee and be subject to them, in nothing resisting Your will; to them, Lord, give health, peace, concord, stability, that they may exercise the authority given to them without offence."[15]

As far as we know, Justin Martyr was the first Christian author to quote Jesus' teaching "Render unto Caesar ..."[16] and explain what this passage meant to the Christians of his time:[17]

And everywhere we, more readily than all men, endeavor to pay to those appointed by you the taxes both ordinary and extraordinary, as we have been taught by Him; for at that time some came to Him and asked Him, if one ought to pay tribute to Caesar; and He answered, "Tell Me, whose image does the coin bear?" And they said, "Caesar's." And again He answered them, "Render therefore to Caesar the things that are Caesar's, and to God the things that are God's." Whence to God alone we render worship, but in other things we gladly serve you, acknowledging you as kings and rulers of men, and praying that with your kingly power you be found to possess also sound judgment.[18]

The only thing the Christians begrudged the emperors was the matter of worship. In all other matters, the Christians aspired to be model citizens. Tertullian was convinced that in persecuting the Christians the emperors were alienating their most devoted subjects:

With our hands thus stretched out and up to God, rend us with your iron claws, hang us up on crosses, wrap us in flames, take our heads from us with the sword, let loose the wild beasts on us, the very attitude of a Christian praying is one of preparation for all punishment. Let this, good rulers, be your work: wring from us the soul, beseeching God on the emperor's behalf. Upon the truth of God, and devotion to His name, put the brand of crime.[19]

Tertullian went on to explain a theological reason for praying for the emperor that might strike us as odd today:

There is also another and a greater necessity for our offering prayer in behalf of the emperors, nay, for the complete stability of the empire, and for Roman interests in general. For we know that a mighty shock impending over the whole earth—in fact, the very end of all things threatening dreadful woes—is only retarded by the continued existence of the Roman empire. We have no desire, then, to be overtaken by these dire events; and in praying that their coming may be delayed, we are lending our aid to Rome's duration.[20]

It seems that Tertullian believed that the horrible end of the world was prevented by Rome's continued existence. We do not know how widespread this belief was, but we know that Christian authors throughout the world stated emphatically that all Christians prayed for the emperors.

In looking at the writings of Origen, it becomes clear that over and over again the Christians offered the emperors a very subtle, but powerful, compromise. The outlines of the compromise are as follows: The Christians would (1) pay their taxes promptly and in full, (2) obey all reasonable and just laws to the fullest extent, and (3) pray for the emperor and the good of the empire. In turn, all the Christians asked of the government was (1) freedom to practice their religion without hindrance, (2) freedom from the requirement to worship the emperors, and (3) protection against crime and external enemies.[21]

It is unclear whether Origen foresaw Christians serving in the military if these conditions were met. As we will see, the major obstacles to military service were the religious requirements of the army. At one point Celsus objected that if everyone became a Christian the empire would collapse. Origen responded: "If all the Romans, according to the supposition of Celsus, embrace the Christian faith, they will, when they pray, overcome their enemies; or rather, they will not war at all, being guarded by that divine power which promised to save five entire cities for the sake of fifty just persons."[22]

Origen seems in this passage to have been doubtful about Christian military service, or doubtful about the necessity of military service, if everyone were a Christian. But he had no doubt, with Tertullian, that Christians would make excellent citizens of the empire, if they were given a chance: "Christians are benefactors of their country more than others. For they train up citizens, and inculcate piety to the Supreme Being; and they promote those whose lives in the smallest cities have been good and worthy, to a divine and heavenly city."[23]

The Christians, whatever the Romans thought of them, did not hold an undying hatred for Rome. They recognized government as a necessity and were not even opposed to just warfare, though they preferred not to engage in battle themselves: "While others are engaged in battle, these too [Christians] should engage as the priests and ministers of God, keeping their hands pure, and wrestling in prayers to God on behalf of those who are fighting in a righteous cause, and for the king who reigns righteously, that whatever is opposed to those who act righteously may be destroyed."[24]

The great tragedy of the late Roman Empire, then, is this: it had within it a body of men and women who wanted to be good citizens but were prevented by the injustice of Roman law. The Romans, for their part, felt they could not budge, lest the state fall apart. So the Christians waited, and prayed, and suffered, hoping for a ruler with the wisdom and foresight to use, rather than torture, them. Such an emperor was three hundred years in coming.

### A Brief History of Persecutions and Reprieves

Traditionally, Church historians speak of ten periods of persecution. Since the days of Eusebius, the names of the ten persecutors have been loaded with infamy: Nero, Domitian, Trajan, Marcus Aurelius, Septimius Severus, Maximinus, Decius, Valerian, Aurelian, and Diocletian. The idea of ten persecutors has a certain cachet, but there are two problems with this formulation. First, at least one of the emperors counted among the persecutors (Aurelian) was notably favorable to Christianity, so much so that the Church appealed to him to resolve a matter of internal discipline. Secondly, there were martyrs even during the reigns of reasonably well-disposed emperors.[25]

How could these things be? It would seem that the periods of persecution were not as clear-cut as traditional histories suppose. The truth is that most emperors did not have the absolute control over the empire that some modern dictators enjoy. Edicts would take months to get to the provincial governors. Clarifications might take years. Trials in far-distant provinces could be over long before anyone on the emperor's staff even heard about it. The truth is that most emperors did not necessarily care what happened in the provinces, as long as taxes were collected on time and a rough semblance of order was maintained. Of the emperors that did care what happened in the provinces and maintained as much control as they could, some were shrewd and some were foolish. Some were persecutors, and some were lenient. Sometimes foolish emperors (such as Commodus) were merciful to Christians. Sometimes shrewd emperors (Marcus Aurelius) persecuted Christians. To complicate matters even further, some persecutions had nothing to do with imperial decrees at all, but were initiated by merchants fearful of losing their trade in religious objects, or by the populace, fearful that the crops would not grow if too many people abandoned the old gods.

Fear was the common denominator in the persecutions. Emperors that persecuted were afraid the empire would disintegrate if too many people became Christian. Religious and political leaders who initiated local persecutions were afraid of losing their authority. The poor and uneducated who supported and carried out the persecutions were afraid their meager livelihoods would be endangered if support for the old gods waned. All these elements played a part in the three hundred years of persecution the Church endured.

The deaths of Saint Stephen[26] and James the Righteous were initiated by the religious establishment in Jerusalem. Similar events were taking place in pagan cities as well. In Hierapolis, the Apostle Philip was martyred by the priests of Apollo for preaching against the oracle there.[27] Religious leaders took the lead in persecuting Christians, but before the precedent set by Nero, Roman officials who were interested in defending the law had little idea what to do with the Christians. Events would soon change all that.

In 64, Nero, who had been growing steadily more insane as the years went by, was in serious trouble with the people of Rome. A great fire had broken out in the city. Some citizens were saying that they saw Roman soldiers setting the fire, the implication being that they had done it on Nero's orders. Others remembered that Nero had wanted to destroy Rome and rebuild it in marble. At this point, let the historian Tacitus tell the story:

> To stifle the report, Nero provided others to bear the accusation, in the shape of people who were commonly called "Christians," in detestation of their abominable character. These he visited with every refinement of punishment. First, some were arrested who confessed, then on received information, an immense number were convicted, not so much on the charge of arson but on the charge of ill-will towards mankind in general. Their deaths were turned into a form of amusement. They were wrapped in the skins of wild beasts to be torn in pieces by dogs, or were fastened to crosses to be set on fire, and, when the daylight came to an end, were burned for an illumination at night. Nero threw open his own gardens for the spectacle, and made it the occasion of a circus exhibition, mingling with the populace in the costume of a driver, or standing in his chariot. Sympathy was eventually felt for the sufferers, although the objects of it were guilty people who deserved the most extreme punishment: people felt that they were being destroyed

not for the benefit of the public but to serve the cruel purpose of one man.[28]

Toward the end of Nero's persecution, Peter and Paul were martyred in Rome. Eusebius tells us the story:

> Publicly announcing himself as the first among God's chief enemies, he was led on to the slaughter of the apostles. It is, therefore, recorded that Paul was beheaded in Rome itself, and that Peter likewise was crucified under Nero. This account of Peter and Paul is substantiated by the fact that their names are preserved in the cemeteries of that place even to the present day. It is confirmed likewise by Caius, a member of the Church, who arose under Zephyrinus, bishop of Rome. He, in a published disputation with Proclus, the leader of the Phrygian heresy, speaks as follows concerning the places where the sacred corpses of the aforesaid apostles are laid: "But I can show the trophies of the apostles. For if you will go to the Vatican or to the Ostian way, you will find the trophies of those who laid the foundations of this church." And that they both suffered martyrdom at the same time is stated by Dionysius, bishop of Corinth, in his epistle to the Romans, in the following words: "You have thus by such an admonition bound together the planting of Peter and of Paul at Rome and Corinth. For both of them planted and likewise taught us in our Corinth. And they taught together in like manner in Italy, and suffered martyrdom at the same time." I have quoted these things in order that the truth of the history might be still more confirmed.[29]

Nero's persecution illustrates one strange truth about the persecutions. If the persecutor was an emperor, the persecution could end with great suddenness. In 68, a plot ended Nero's life. The empire was thrown into confusion, and three inferior men, Galba, Otho, and Vitellius, all claimed the purple. When the dust settled, crusty old Vespasian was emperor. He, with his son Titus, who succeeded him in 79, had little interest in persecuting Christians. His second son Domitian, who became emperor in 81, was different. Domitian insisted on being worshipped as a god. He developed an elaborate system to make sure that everyone would make a sacrifice to him at least once a year.[30] Domitian appears to have been the Roman emperor the Book of Revelation refers to in cryptic terms.[31]

Eusebius records that in the fifteenth year of his reign (also the last year of his reign), Domitian initiated a persecution against Christians.[32]

During this persecution, he executed his cousin Flavius Clemens, banished Clemens' niece Flavia Domitilla (who was also Domitian's niece), and executed the consul Acilius Glabrio. There are good reasons for believing that these people, the cream of Roman society, were punished for being Christians.[33] The official charges were treason and atheism.[34] The charge of atheism is mysterious and significant, because it was one of the charges typically brought against Christians. The Romans thought Christians were atheists because they denied the existence of the pagan gods. There is also the curious fact that when archaeologists inspected the catacombs, they found the name Flavia Domitilla carved into one of the walls, with the indication that she was the original owner of the property in which that particular catacomb was located.[35] We will probably never know what really happened within the family of Domitian in A.D. 96, but it is at least possible that some of his family members and close associates were martyred.

Domitian was assassinated later in that year, and, as so often was the case, there was a revulsion against his policies that led to a lightening of the burden of Christians. His immediate successor, Nerva, did not initiate any persecutions. Trajan, who ruled after Nerva, was of no mind to hound the Christians either. We are fortunate to be in the possession of a series of remarkable documents, the letters of Pliny, the governor of Bithynia. In one of those letters, Pliny wrote to Trajan, asking what to do about the Christians. We also have Trajan's reply:

> They [Christians] are not to be sought out; if they are denounced and proved guilty they are to be punished, with this reservation, that whoever denies that he is a Christian and really proves it—that is, by worshipping our gods—even though he was under suspicion in the past, shall obtain pardon through repentance. But anonymously posted accusations ought to have no place in any prosecution. For this is both a dangerous kind of precedent and out of keeping with the spirit of our age.[36]

Trajan's judgment held throughout the second century, until the reign of Septimius Severus, which began in 193. The fact that the government was not seeking out Christians slowed the rate of persecution but did not end it, since many Christians were in fact denounced and had to be tried and punished if they did not recant. Some of the most famous martyrs died under this legal regimen: Ignatius of Antioch, Polycarp, and Justin Martyr are a few whom we have already met. Eusebius summarized the situation the Christians faced during this period:

> On account of this [Trajan's ruling] the persecution which had threatened to be a most terrible one was to a certain degree checked, but there were still left plenty of pretexts for those who wished to do us harm. Sometimes the people, sometimes the rulers in various places, would lay plots against us, so that, although no great persecutions took place, local persecutions were nevertheless going on in particular provinces, and many of the faithful endured martyrdom in various forms.[37]

In the middle of the second century, Marcus Aurelius became emperor. To this day he is well known for his philosophical and spiritual writings. Marcus Aurelius was a Stoic, who disliked what he perceived as the "exhibitionism" of Christianity.[38] At one point, probably due to his nobility of character and high moral standards, the Christians had marked him out as someone with whom they could come to an understanding. Athenagorus of Athens dedicated an apology to him and his son Commodus.

No one knows exactly what set Marcus Aurelius against the Christians, but the fact is that he reissued Trajan's edict against the Christians, and the fiercest persecution of the second century was carried out during his reign. Most of the martyrs of this persecution came from Gaul and Asia. The Gallic martyrs mostly came from Lyons, in one brutal persecution in the spring of 177. Eusebius tells the story.

> The greatness of the tribulation in this region, and the fury of the heathen against the saints, and the sufferings of the blessed witnesses we cannot recount accurately, nor indeed could they possibly be recorded. For with all his might the adversary fell upon us, giving us a foretaste of his unbridled activity at his future coming. He endeavored in every manner to practice and exercise his servants against the servants of God, not only shutting us out from houses and baths and markets, but forbidding any of us to be seen in any place whatever. But the grace of God led the conflict against him, and delivered the weak, and set them as firm pillars, able through patience to endure all the wrath of the Evil One.... First of all, they endured nobly the injuries heaped upon them by the populace; clamors and blows and draggings and robberies and

stonings and imprisonments, and all things which an infuriated mob delight in inflicting on enemies and adversaries. Then, being taken to the forum by the prefect and the authorities of the city, they were examined in the presence of the whole multitude, and having confessed, they were imprisoned until the arrival of the governor. When, afterwards, they were brought before him, and he treated us with the utmost cruelty, Vettius Epagathus, one of the brethren, and a man filled with love for God and his neighbor, interfered. His life was so consistent that, although young, he had attained a reputation equal to that of the elder Zacharias: for he "walked in all the commandments and ordinances of the Lord blameless," and was untiring in every good work for his neighbor, zealous for God and fervent in spirit. Such being his character, he could not endure the unreasonable judgment against us, but was filled with indignation, and asked to be permitted to testify in behalf of his brethren, that there is among us nothing ungodly or impious. But those about the judgment seat cried out against him, for he was a man of distinction; and the governor refused to grant his just request, and merely asked if he also were a Christian. And he, confessing this with a loud voice, was himself taken into the order of the witnesses, being called the Advocate of the Christians, but having the Advocate in himself, the Spirit more abundantly than Zacharias. He showed this by the fulllness of his love, being well pleased even to lay down his life in defense of the brethren. For he was and is a true disciple of Christ, "following the Lamb whithersoever he goeth".

Then the others were divided, and the witnesses were manifestly ready, and finished their confession with all eagerness. But some appeared unprepared and untrained, weak as yet, and unable to endure so great a conflict. About ten of these proved abortions, causing us great grief and sorrow beyond measure, and impairing the zeal of the others who had not yet been seized, but who, though suffering all kinds of affliction, continued constantly with the witnesses and did not forsake them. Then all of us feared greatly on account of uncertainty as to their confession not because we dreaded the sufferings to be endured, but because we looked to the end, and were afraid that some of them might fall away. But those who were worthy were seized day by day, filling up their number, so that all the zealous persons, and those through whom especially our affairs had been established, were collected together out of the two churches. And some of our heathen neighbors also were seized, as the governor had commanded that all of us should be examined publicly. These, being ensnared by Satan, and fearing for themselves the tortures which they beheld the saints endure, and being also urged on by the soldiers, accused us falsely of Thyestean banquets [cannibalism] . . . and of deeds which are not only unlawful for us to speak of or to think, but which we cannot believe were ever done by men. When these accusations were reported, all the people raged like wild beasts against us, so that even if any had before been moderate on account of friendship, they were now exceedingly furious and gnashed their teeth against us. . . . Then finally the holy witnesses endured sufferings beyond description, Satan striving earnestly that some of the slanders might be uttered by them also.

But the whole wrath of the populace, and governor, and soldiers was aroused exceedingly against Sanctus, the deacon from Vienne, and Maturus, a late convert, yet a noble combatant, and against Attalus, a native of Pergamos, where he had always been a pillar and foundation, and Blandina, through whom Christ showed that things which appear mean and obscure and despicable to men are with God of great glory, through love toward him manifested in power, and not boasting in appearance. For while we all trembled, and her earthly mistress, who was herself also one of the witnesses, feared that on account of the weakness of her body, she would be unable to make bold confession, Blandina was filled with such power as to be delivered and raised above those who were torturing her by turns from morning till evening in every manner, so that they acknowledged that they were conquered, and could do nothing more to her. And they were astonished at her endurance, as her entire body was mangled and broken; and they testified that one of these forms of torture was sufficient to destroy life, not to speak of so many and so great sufferings. But the blessed woman, like a noble athlete, renewed her strength in her confession; and her comfort and recreation and relief from the pain of her sufferings was in exclaiming, "I am a Christian, and there is nothing vile done by us."

But Sanctus also endured marvelously and superhumanly all the outrages which he suffered. While the wicked men hoped, by the continuance and severity of his tortures to wring something from him which he ought not to say, he girded himself against them with such firmness that he would not even tell his name, or the nation or city to which he belonged, or whether he was bond or free, but answered in the Roman tongue to all their questions, "I am a Christian. . . ." There arose therefore on the part of the governor and his tormentors a great desire to conquer him but having nothing more that they could do to him, they finally fastened red hot brazen plates to the most tender parts of his body. And these indeed were burned, but he continued unbending and unyielding, firm in his confession, and refreshed and strengthened by the heavenly fountain of the water of life, flowing from the bowels of Christ. And his body was a witness of his sufferings, being one complete wound and bruise, drawn, out of shape, and altogether unlike a human form. Christ, suffering in him, manifested his glory, delivering him from his adversary, and making him an example for the others, showing that nothing is fearful where the love of the Father is, and nothing painful where there is the glory of Christ. For when the wicked men tortured him a second time after some days, supposing that with his body swollen and inflamed to such a degree that he could not bear the touch of a hand, if they should again apply the same instruments, they would overcome him, or at least by his death under his sufferings others would be made afraid, not only did not this occur, but, contrary to all human expectation, his body arose and stood erect in the midst of the subsequent torments, and resumed its original appearance and the use of its limbs so that, through the grace of Christ, these second sufferings became to him, not torture, but healing.

But the devil, thinking that he had already consumed Biblias, who was one of those who had denied Christ, desiring to increase her condemnation through the utterance of blasphemy, brought her again to the torture, to compel her, as already feeble and weak, to report impious things concerning us. But she recovered herself under the suffering, and as if awaking from a deep sleep, and reminded by the present anguish of the eternal punishment in hell, she contradicted the blasphemers. "How," she said, "could those eat children who do not think it lawful to taste the blood even of irrational animals?" And thenceforward she confessed herself a Christian, and was given a place in the order of the witnesses.

But as the tyrannical tortures were made by Christ of none effect through the patience of the blessed, the devil invented other contrivances—confinement in the dark and most loathsome parts of the prison, stretching of the feet to the fifth hole in the stocks, and the other outrages which his servants are accustomed to inflict upon the prisoners when furious and filled with the devil. A great many were suffocated in prison, being chosen by the Lord for this manner of death, that he might manifest in them his glory. For some, though they had been tortured so cruelly that it seemed impossible that they could live, even with the most careful nursing, yet, destitute of human attention, remained in the prison, being strengthened by the Lord, and invigorated both in body and soul; and they exhorted and encouraged the rest. But such as were young, and arrested recently, so that their bodies had not become accustomed to torture, were unable to endure the severity of their confinement, and died in prison.

The blessed Pothinus, who had been entrusted with the bishopric of Lyons, was dragged to the judgment seat. He was more than ninety years of age, and very infirm, scarcely indeed able to breathe because of physical weakness; but he was strengthened by spiritual zeal through his earnest desire for martyrdom. Though his body was worn out by old age and disease, his life was preserved that Christ might triumph in it. When he was brought by the soldiers to the tribunal, accompanied by the civil magistrates and a multitude who shouted against him in every manner as if he were Christ himself he bore noble witness. Being asked by the governor, who was the God of the Christians, he replied, "If you are worthy, you shall know." Then he was dragged away harshly, and received blows of every kind. Those near him struck him with their hands and feet, regardless of his age; and those at a distance hurled at him whatever they could seize; all of them thinking that they would be guilty of great wickedness and impiety if any possible abuse were omitted. For thus they thought to avenge their own deities. Scarcely able to breathe, he was cast into prison and died after two days.

Maturus, and Sanctus and Blandina and Attalus were led to the amphitheater to be exposed to the wild beasts, and to give to the heathen public a spectacle of cruelty, a day for fighting with wild beasts being specially appointed on account of our people. Both Maturus and Sanctus passed again through every torment in the amphitheater, as if they had suffered nothing before, or rather, as if, having already conquered their antagonist in many contests, they were now striving for the crown itself. They endured again the customary running of the gauntlet and the violence of the wild beasts, and everything which the furious people called for or desired, and at last, the iron chair in which their bodies being roasted, tormented them with the fumes. And not with this did the persecutors cease, but were yet madder against them, determined to overcome their patience. But even thus they did not hear a word from Sanctus except the confession which he had uttered from the beginning. These, then, after their life had continued for a long time through the great conflict, were at last sacrificed, having been made throughout that day a spectacle to the world, in place of the usual variety of combats.

But Blandina was suspended on a stake, and exposed to be devoured by the wild beasts who should attack her. And because she appeared as if hanging on a cross, and because of her earnest prayers, she inspired the combatants with great zeal. For they looked on her in her conflict, and beheld with their outward eyes, in the form of their sister, him who was crucified for them, that he might persuade those who believe on him, that every one who suffers for the glory of Christ has fellow-ship always with the living God. As none of the wild beasts at that time touched her, she was taken down from the stake, and cast again into prison. She was preserved thus for another contest, that, being victo-rious in more conflicts, she might make the punishment of the crooked serpent irrevocable; and, though small and weak and despised, yet clothed with Christ the mighty and conquering Athlete, she might arouse the zeal of the brethren, and, having overcome the adversary many times might receive, through her conflict, the crown incorruptible.

But Attalus was called for loudly by the people, because he was a person of distinction. He entered the contest readily on account of a good conscience and his genuine practice in Christian discipline, and as he had always been a witness for the truth among us. He was led around the amphitheater, a tablet being carried before him on which was written in the Roman language "This is Attalus the Christian," and the people were filled with indignation against him. But when the governor learned that he was a Roman, he commanded him to be taken back with the rest of those who were in prison concerning whom he had written to Caesar, and whose answer he was awaiting.

But the intervening time was not wasted, nor fruitless to them; for by their patience the measureless compassion of Christ was manifested. For through their continued life the dead were made alive, and the witnesses showed favor to those who had failed to witness. And the virgin mother had much joy in receiving alive those whom she had brought forth as dead. For through their influence many who had denied were restored, and rebegotten, and rekindled with life, and learned to confess. And being made alive and strengthened, they went to the judg-ment seat to be again interrogated by the governor.... Caesar com-manded that they should be put to death, but that any who might deny should be set free. Therefore, at the beginning of the public festival which took place there, and which was attended by crowds of men from all nations, the governor brought the blessed ones to the judg-ment seat, to make of them a show and spectacle for the multitude. Wherefore also he examined them again, and beheaded those who appeared to possess Roman citizenship, but he sent the others to the wild beasts. And Christ was glorified greatly in those who had for-merly denied him.

To please the people, the governor had ordered Attalus again to the wild beasts. But when Attalus was placed in the iron seat, and the fumes arose from his burning body, he said to the people in the Roman lan-guage: "Lo! this which ye do is devouring men; but we do not devour men; nor do any other wicked thing." And being asked, what name God has, he replied, "God has not a name as man has."

After all these, on the last day of the contests, Blandina was again brought in, with Ponticus, a boy about fifteen years old. They had been brought every day to witness the sufferings of the others, and had been pressed to swear by the idols. But because they remained steadfast and despised them, the multitude became furious, so that they had no compassion for the youth of the boy nor respect for the sex of the woman. Therefore they exposed them to all the terrible sufferings and took them through the entire round of torture, repeatedly urging them to swear, but being unable to effect this; for Ponticus, encouraged by his sister so that even the heathen could see that she was confirming and strengthening him, having nobly endured every torture, gave up the ghost. But the blessed Blandina, last of all, having, as a noble mother, encouraged her children and sent them before her victorious to the King, endured herself all their conflicts and hastened after them, glad and rejoicing in her departure as if called to a marriage supper, rather than cast to wild beasts. And, after the scourging, after the wild beasts, after the roasting seat, she was finally enclosed in a net, and thrown before a bull. And having been tossed about by the animal, but feeling none of the things which were happening to her, on account of her hope and firm hold upon what had been entrusted to her, and her communion with Christ, she also was sacrificed. And the heathen themselves confessed that never among them had a woman endured so many and such terrible tortures.[39]

Other Christians were spared the horrors of the persecution of the martyrs of Lyons by the death of Marcus Aurelius in 180. His son Commodus, who was in his own way a cruel and corrupt ruler, did not continue the persecution of the Christians. They were spared for a brief time, until 193, when a man named Septimius Severus came to the throne. During the early years of his reign, Severus, like Commodus, actually showed some sympathy for the Christians. In 202, however, something turned him against the Christians, and he issued a new edict forbidding conversion to Christianity or Judaism. The Severan persecution focused on new converts, so the regions where the Church was growing, such as Carthage and Alexandria, suffered the most. Perpetua and Felicity were martyred in Carthage. Origen's father suffered martyrdom, and seventeen-year-old Origen barely escaped with his life. Clement of Alexandria fled to escape the persecution, and Origen was appointed to head the catechetical school in his place.

Severus' son Caracalla continued the persecution, but in 217, when Caracalla died, the Church enjoyed more than thirty years of peace. Two emperors, Elagabalus and Alexander Severus, actually showed the Church favor, for different reasons. Elagabalus was a devotee of solar monotheism, and thought Christianity similar. Alexander Severus was fond of Christianity because his mother had once studied Christianity under Origen.[40] Thus, the Church enjoyed thirty-seven years of relative peace, in which to grow and prosper, with only a brief flurry of persecution under Maximinus. This persecution seems to have resulted more in banishment than martyrdom. During Maximinus' reign, Pope Pontianus and Hippolytus were sent to the mines of Sardinia.

After Maximinus, the peace continued until 249. In 242, Philip of Arabia became emperor. Philip was said to be the "first Christian emperor" by Jerome,[41] but the brutality of the means he used to take the throne caused many Christians to look askance upon him. Eusebius records that once he attempted to attend the Paschal Vigil in Antioch, but the bishop refused him, requiring him to do penance instead.[42] Despite the fact that the Church was uneasy about Philip, he showered her with favors, allowing those exiled under Maximinus to return home. His wife, Otacilia Severus, was an open Christian and corresponded with Origen.[43]

The favors Philip showed to the Christians made many pagans envious, and Philip's successors Decius and Valerian resolved to make the Christians pay. Decius came to the throne in 249 with a huge problem on his hands. Germanic tribes were threatening the northern frontier again, and he was concerned about loyalty in the legions. There were at this time a large number of Christians in the legions, but they would not take the soldier's oath or sacrifice to the emperor's genius. Decius interpreted this as personal disloyalty and decided it was necessary to wipe Christianity off the face of the earth. He went about his business systematically. He revived Domitian's idea of giving everyone a *libellus*, or receipt, for worshipping at his temples. Anyone who could not produce the receipt was to be banished and have his property confiscated or be executed, depending on the circumstances. Decius' goal was not to kill all the Christians (he probably could not have succeeded if that had been his goal), but to force them to give up the Christian faith.

Decius' methods produced good results, from his point of view. The Christians had grown soft and lazy from forty years of peace and were ill-prepared for persecution. Decius had the support of the provincial governors, so everyone was enforcing his decrees. A large number of Christians—it is impossible to tell how many—became *lapsi*, those who denied their Christian faith, and *traditores*, those who handed over the sacred books, vessels, and vestments of the Church. It was during this persecution that Cyprian of Carthage and Dionysius, Bishop of Alexandria, went into exile. Fabian, the beloved Bishop of Rome, was also martyred during this time, and Cornelius became his successor.

Despite his successes, in 251 Decius lessened his persecution. He did not rescind his edicts, but events on the Germanic frontier forced his attention elsewhere. He left Rome in the spring of 251 to fight the Goths and perished shortly afterward. At about this time, a plague swept through the empire, and, predictably, the common people blamed it on the Christians. Thus the persecution was revived with hardly any pause at all. In 257, Valerian came to the throne. He was alarmed by the wealth and power of the Christian bishops[44] and revived Decius' persecution, with the following variations: Christians could worship Christ, as long as they also sacrificed to the gods of Rome and the emperor. Valerian also removed any legal basis for Christian assemblies by confiscating their cemeteries. The primary targets of Valerian's edict were the bishops, presbyters, and deacons of the Church. Thus, ordinary Christians would not run into trouble unless they frequented the cemeteries. Visiting the cemeteries was punishable by death.

In 258, Valerian toughened his edict by ruling that bishops, priests, and deacons should be put to death immediately. Men and women of senatorial and equestrian rank, as well as anyone in the imperial household, would have their goods confiscated if they were found to be Christians, and if they persisted, they would be beheaded. Sixtus, Bishop of Rome, was martyred while saying Mass at a cemetery with four of his deacons. Cyprian of Carthage was beheaded after refusing to repudiate his faith. Also in Carthage, a large number of believers were surprised at worship and were decapitated or buried alive.[45]

During this persecution, the Christians behaved with greater steadfastness than they did under Decius. They were better prepared for martyrdom, and some of the lapsed were ashamed of their former behavior and resolved not to deny Christ again.[46] Some Christians voluntarily presented themselves to the authorities and were summarily fed to wild animals.[47]

In 258, a military disaster resulted in Valerian's capture by the Persians. He spent the rest of his life in prison, and his son Gallienus became emperor. He promptly rescinded all his father's edicts against the Christians and the Church, and even directed the bishops to resume their former duties.[48] Gallienus went so far as to make Christianity a *religio licita*, permitting the Church to reclaim cemeteries and church buildings.[49] Gallienus may have been motivated by his wife's Christianity, but evidence is scanty.[50]

Gallienus' peace lasted for thirty years, with the exception of some minor local persecutions during the reign of Aurelian, which may have been carried out without his knowledge, so great was the confusion of that time.[51] The Christians were very close to achieving their goal of permanent acceptance in Roman law, but they had one more storm to endure, and it was quite severe.

In 284, when Diocletian became emperor, he was not badly disposed toward Christians. Indeed, his own wife and daughter appear to have been Christians.[52] From 286 to 292 Diocletian ruled with Maximian, who was a bitter opponent of Christianity. During this period the persecution was fierce, but nowhere near the white heat it would soon reach. In 293, Diocletian and Maximian further divided the empire, with Galerius and Constantius Chlorus appointed as Caesars. Galerius also hated Christianity. Constantius was not a Christian but was inclined to be tolerant.

During this Tetrarchy (293–305), the rulers seem to have concentrated on purging Christians from the military. Eusebius elaborates on this point:

> He [Diocletian] did not wage war against all of us at once, but made trial at first only of those in the army. For he supposed that the others could be taken easily if he should first attack and subdue these. Thereupon many of the soldiers were seen most cheerfully embracing private life, so that they might not deny their piety toward the Creator of the universe. For when the commander began to persecute the soldiers, separating into tribes and purging those who were enrolled in the army, giving them the choice either by obeying to receive the honor which belonged to them, or on the other hand to be deprived of it if they disobeyed the command, a great many soldiers of Christ's kingdom, without hesitation, instantly preferred the confession of him to the seeming glory and prosperity which they were enjoying. And one and another

of them occasionally received in exchange, for their pious constancy, not only the loss of position, but death. But as yet the instigator of this plot proceeded with moderation, and ventured so far as blood only in some instances; for the multitude of believers, as it is likely, made him afraid, and deterred him from waging war at once against all. But when he made the attack more boldly, it is impossible to relate how many and what sort of martyrs of God could be seen, among the inhabitants of all the cities and countries.[53]

After purging the army, Diocletian and his co-rulers moved on to the general population. The change occurred in 299, and it was triggered by an odd incident. Lactantius tells us that one day when the sacrificial victims had been slain and the priests were attempting to inspect the livers, some Christians present made the sign of the cross. The priests informed Diocletian that someone had profaned the rites, and the persecution was on.[54]

In February 303, Diocletian issued the first of his edicts against the Christians, ordering churches leveled, Scriptures burned, and Christians who held high office demoted. This relatively mild edict did not please Galerius, but Diocletian overruled him for the time.[55] In the end, Galerius tricked Diocletian into persecuting the Christians by setting fire to the palace and blaming the Christians.[56] After this incident, Diocletian issued another edict requiring Christians to sacrifice. Still another edict called for the arrest of all Church leaders. The bloodbath was coming, but it took one more event to bring it on. Late in 305, an ill Diocletian abdicated his imperial office (along with Maximian), elevating Constantius and Galerius to the position of Augusti. With Constantius Chlorus occupied in Gaul, Galerius had a free hand to do what he wanted with the Christians of Asia.

Let us allow Eusebius to describe some of the martyrdoms that ensued:

As for the rulers of the Church that suffered martyrdom in the principal cities, the first martyr of the kingdom of Christ whom we shall mention among the monuments of the pious is Anthimus, bishop of the city of Nicomedia, who was beheaded. Among the martyrs at Antioch was Lucian, a presbyter of that parish, whose entire life was most excellent. At Nicomedia, in the presence of the emperor, he proclaimed the heavenly kingdom of Christ, first in an oral defense, and afterwards by deeds as well. Of the martyrs in Phoenicia the most distinguished were those devoted pastors of the spiritual flocks of Christ:

Tyrannion, bishop of the church of Tyre; Zenobius, a presbyter of the church at Sidon; and Silvanus, bishop of the churches about Emesa. The last of these, with others, was made food for wild beasts at Emesa, and was thus received into the ranks of martyrs. The other two glorified the word of God at Antioch through patience unto death. The bishop was thrown into the depths of the sea. But Zenobius, who was a very skillful physician, died through severe tortures, which were applied to his sides. Of the martyrs in Palestine, Silvanus, bishop of the churches about Gaza, was beheaded with thirty-nine others at the copper mines of Phaeno. There also the Egyptian bishops, Peleus and Nilus, with others, suffered death by fire. Among these we must mention Pamphilus, a presbyter, who was the great glory of the parish of Caesarea, and among the men of our time most admirable. The virtue of his manly deeds we have recorded in the proper place. Of those who suffered death illustriously at Alexandria and throughout Egypt and Thebais, Peter, bishop of Alexandria, one of the most excellent teachers of the religion of Christ, should first be mentioned; and of the presbyters with him Faustus, Dius and Arnmonius, perfect martyrs of Christ; also Phileas, Hesychius, Pachymius and Theodorus, bishops of Egyptian churches, and besides them many other distinguished persons who are commemorated by the parishes of their country and region.[57]

The methods used by the persecutor must have been what the framers of the U.S. Constitution had in mind when they banned cruel and unusual punishments:

Why need we mention the rest by name, or number the multitude of the men, or picture the various sufferings of the admirable martyrs of Christ? Some of them were slain with the axe, as in Arabia. The limbs of some were broken, as in Cappadocia. Some, raised on high by the feet, with their heads down, while a gentle fire burned beneath them, were suffocated by the smoke which arose from the burning wood, as was done in Mesopotamia. Others were mutilated by cutting off their noses and ears and hands, and cutting to pieces the other members and parts of their bodies, as in Alexandria. Why need we revive the recollection of those in Antioch who were roasted on grates, not so as to kill them, but so as to subject them to a lingering punishment? Or of others who preferred to thrust their right hand into the fire rather than touch the impious sacrifice? Some, shrinking from the trial, rather than be taken and fall into the hands of their enemies, threw themselves from lofty houses, considering death preferable to the cruelty of the impious.[58]

There was method to Galerius' madness. As in the days of Decius, the goal was to force Christians to renounce their faith. Some did. But many more confessed their faith and died for it. No one knows how long the horror would have continued, with neither side able to give in, until divine providence intervened. First, Constantius Chlorus died, and his son Constantine succeeded him in the Western empire. Then, Galerius developed a mysterious illness, probably cancer of the intestines, that resisted all the healing arts of the ancient world. In desperation, he issued an edict freeing the Christians from persecution, stipulating only that they pray for him.[59]

The storm was almost over. It remained for Constantine to defeat Maximinus Daza, Galerius' successor, at the battle of Milvian Bridge. After that battle, the Edict of Milan granted freedom of worship to all Christians, and the first glimmer of blue sky and sunlight could be seen in the west.[60]

*Conclusion: The Legacy of Martyrs, Confessors, and the Lapsi*

What are we to make of the persecutions of the early Church, the cruelty, the bravery, and, in contrast, the desire to preserve their lives that impelled some, against their will, to deny Christ? Clearly, the Romans felt that their way of life was threatened. Equally clearly, the Christians felt that the principle involved was so compelling that they could not back down. In the course of this study, we have come to understand what made the Romans feel threatened and for what principle the Christians would die.

Let us consider the case of Basilides and Potamiaena, recorded by Eusebius of Caesarea.

> Basilides ... led to martyrdom the celebrated Potamiaena, who is still famous among the people of the country for the many things which she endured for the preservation of her chastity and virginity. For she was blooming in the perfection of her mind and her physical graces. Having suffered much for the faith of Christ, finally after tortures dreadful and terrible to speak of, she with her mother, Marcella, was put to death by fire. They say that the judge, Aquila by name, having inflicted severe tortures upon her entire body, at last threatened to hand her over to the gladiators for bodily abuse. After a little consideration, being

asked for her decision, she made a reply which was regarded as impious. Thereupon she received sentence immediately, and Basilides, one of the officers of the army, led her to death. But as the people attempted to annoy and insult her with abusive words, he drove back her insulters, showing her much pity and kindness. And perceiving the man's sympathy for her, she exhorted him to be of good courage, for she would supplicate her Lord for him after her departure, and he would soon receive a reward for the kindness he had shown her. Having said this, she nobly sustained the issue, burning pitch being poured little by little, over various parts of her body, from the sole of her feet to the crown of her bead. Such was the conflict endured by this famous maiden.

Not long after this Basilides, being asked by his fellow soldiers to swear for a certain reason, declared that it was not lawful for him to swear at all, for he was a Christian, and he confessed this openly. At first they thought that he was jesting, but when he continued to affirm it, he was led to the judge, and, acknowledging his conviction before him, he was imprisoned. But the brethren in God coming to him and inquiring the reason of this sudden and remarkable resolution, he is reported to have said that Potamiaena, for three days after her martyrdom, stood beside him by night and placed a crown on his head and said that she had besought the Lord for him and had obtained what she asked, and that soon she would take him with her. Thereupon the brethren gave him the seal of the Lord; and on the next day, after giving glorious testimony for the Lord, he was beheaded. And many others in Alexandria are recorded to have accepted speedily the word of Christ in those times. For Potamiaena appeared to them in their dreams and exhorted them.[61]

For Potamiaena, her chastity and her relationship with Christ, which in her mind were related, were the things she could not compromise, the things for which she would die. In Eusebius' account, we are presented with two people who are confronted with her convictions, and therein lies the moral drama we are exploring. For the two men, Basilides the soldier and Aquila the judge, responded to Potamiaena in drastically different ways. Her stubbornness and, particularly, her chastity, seem to have inflamed Aquila and inspired him to greater torture. Basilides, on the other hand, responded to her with kindness. What motivated him?

We will never know. We must presume that he was raised as other Romans were, hardened to human suffering by the cruelties of the arena. Why then did he protect her from the abuses of the crowd, whereas other soldiers joined in her torments?

Perhaps there was a moral drama working itself out within his soul. He searched himself and found he could not torment Potamiaena as the others did. The goodness she possessed was a powerful influence. In the end, he found that he too was a follower of Christ.

This moral or spiritual drama was played out numerous times in the Roman world. Some, like Aquila, joined in the torment. Others simply turned away and went about their business. But others, like Basilides, saw the purity and love for which the Christians longed, a purity and love that can be expressed only in sacrifice, and joined them.

What separated Potamiaena and the other martyrs from the *lapsi*? They all were given access to the same graces, the same sacraments, the same prayer life, the same fellowship. In the end, it might have been nothing more than simple desire. The martyrs desired nothing more than unity with Christ, and that unity, once achieved, could not be surrendered for any lesser good.

There were also social consequences of the martyrs' choice, particularly in the ongoing life of the Church. The first direct consequence of the age of martyrs is the development of the cult of martyrs, which evolved into a more general cult of the saints. The development of this cult was probably inevitable, given both the cultural context of early Christianity and the logic of the Christian message, but the large number of martyrs in the first three centuries was a powerful catalyst.

Roman, Jewish, and Greek cultures all gave a special status to the revered ancestors of their communities. In this sense, the cult of the martyrs was natural and inevitable. But Christian theology gave the cult its unique shape. In particular, two aspects of Christian teaching aided the development of the cult: first, the New Testament doctrine of the Body of Christ, which teaches that all believers in Christ are intimately connected with one another with Christ as head, and second, the Christian belief that those who die in Christ will rise to a newness of life just as Christ did. These two powerful ideas made it natural and inevitable for the early Christians to believe that the martyrs would be interested in their concerns and could intercede on their behalf before the throne of God.

The second consequence of the age of martyrs for Christianity was that the presence of the *lapsi* meant that the Church had to deal with the all-too-human phenomenon of failure. The *lapsi* were not strangers to the Christian community. They were brothers, sisters, sons, daughters. They were the people that worshipped next to the faithful on the Lord's Day. And when confronted with the implements of torture, they faltered and denied Christ, and afterward they were ashamed.

Those who bravely underwent torture, then were for some reason released, were a constant living reproach to the *lapsi*. Their twisted limbs, distorted facial expressions, and scars were a living reminder that it was not impossible to endure torture for the sake of Christ. The rest of the Church lionized them:

> We look with glad countenances upon confessors illustrious with the heraldry of a good name, and glorious with the praises of virtue and of faith; clinging to them with holy kisses, we embrace them long desired with insatiable eagerness. The white robed cohort of Christ's soldiers is here, who in the fierce conflict have broken the ferocious turbulence of an urgent persecution, having been prepared for the suffering of the dungeon, armed for the endurance of death. Bravely you have resisted the world: you have afforded a glorious spectacle in the sight of God; you have been an example to your brethren that shall follow you.[62]

But the *lapsi* produced a different reaction in the Church. The Church genuinely grieved for the *lapsi*, as a mother for lost children. Cyprian compared the loss of the *lapsi* with losing a part of one's own body:

> But now, what wounds can those who are overcome show? what gashes of gaping entrails, what tortures of the limbs, in cases where it was not faith that fell in the encounter, but faithlessness that anticipated the struggle? Nor does the necessity of the crime excuse the person compelled, where the crime is committed of free will. Nor do I say this in such a way as that I would burden the cases of the brethren, but that I may rather instigate the brethren to a prayer of atonement.[63]

The case of the lapsed produced anger in the hearts of some and grief in the hearts of others. The lapsed themselves were tormented by guilt and a desire to somehow be restored to fellowship. Out of a lengthy process, some of which has been detailed earlier in this work, the Church as a whole came up with a prescription for restoring the lapsed to communion. The process was agonizing, and some Christians could

not agree with the restoration of the lapsed. Novatian and his followers were particularly outraged by the decision to restore them to
communion.

The problem of the *lapsi* brought schism, heresy, and heartache in
its wake, but the Church made the right decision. Just as Peter, after
his fall, was a better disciple of Christ, many of the *lapsi* who were
restored to fellowship later endured persecution bravely and today wear
the martyr's crown.

CHAPTER 5

# The Early Christians and Slavery

There were many slaves in the Roman Empire at the time of Christ. As we have seen (see Part 1, Chapter 3), in the cities, where Christianity was most prevalent, slaves made up about a third of the total population. We know that there were Christian slaves. Numerous passages of the New Testament deal with slaves and slavery. One of Paul's letters (the Letter to Philemon) was entirely devoted to the problems of one slave. We know of at least one ex-slave who became the Bishop of Rome.[1] We do not know exactly how many slaves were Christian, but if all layers of Roman society were represented in the early Church, perhaps a third of all Christians were slaves.

And yet the New Testament and the early Church documents do not contain a direct condemnation of slavery. No early Christian writer, in the New Testament or elsewhere, stated that slavery itself was immoral or that the Church should work for the emancipation of all slaves. Even more problematic, there are certain passages in the New Testament that have historically been misused to justify slavery.

We now know that slavery is a great moral wrong that was rightly stamped out in Western Civilization. We might wonder what prevented the early Christians from understanding the same thing. But perhaps we are being unfair. Why should we expect the early Christians, who lived in a world where slavery was accepted as normal and even necessary, to decide that slavery should be abolished? That they did not try to abolish slavery may seem to us to be a moral failing on their part. But the gospel works slowly like yeast in dough, and the kingdom of Heaven is like a mustard seed. Such growth takes time.

*Slavery and Early Christianity*

Despite their lack of concern about slavery as an institution, the early Christians were deeply concerned about slaves as individuals. Since slaves had more difficulties in their lives than most people, the early Church lavished more care on solving the problems of slaves than on most other groups, except possibly widows, orphans, and the mentally ill. They took their attitude from Jesus himself, who well understood the problems of slaves. Jesus may have been identifying with slaves when he wanted to explain his mission to his disciples and said: "The Son of Man came not to be served but to serve, and to give his life as a ransom for many." [2]

Not only did Jesus closely identify with servanthood, he sought to instill an ethic of servanthood in his disciples. Just before saying he came to serve, Jesus had told his disciples, "Whoever would be great among you must be your servant, and whoever would be first among you must be slave of all." [3] The early Christians took Jesus' message to heart and institutionalized it in the ecclesiastical office of deacon. The message of this office would have been clear to anyone in the Greco-Roman world: the Christians were here to serve, in the most humble and practical ways possible. When a deacon visited the poor, he was proclaiming to the world, "We are different. We are willing to humble ourselves to serve mankind." This humble service must have been an extremely powerful witness.

Some scholars think they have detected a contradiction in Paul's writings. In Galatians 3:28, he wrote, "There is neither Jew nor Greek, there is neither slave nor free, there is neither male nor female; for you are all one in Christ Jesus." [4] This passage is intended to indicate that all who are in Christ are equal, "for in Christ Jesus you are all sons of God through faith". [5] However, in three places in his letters, Paul wrote that slaves should obey their masters. [6] Nor was Paul the only Christian leader who thought this way. The *Didache* repeats Paul's teaching: "Bondmen shall be subject to your masters as to a representative of God, in modesty and fear." [7]

Why did the early Christians not work for the abolition of slavery? There are, I think, several points that will help us understand their position:

1. They did know slavery was wrong. Every passage telling slaves to be obedient to their masters is followed by a passage telling

masters they will be held accountable for how they treat their slaves.

2. The early Christians were committed to nonviolent resistance in an empire that did not hesitate to use force. Resistance on the behalf of slaves could have resulted in the deaths of a large number of people.

3. The early Christians clearly did not think that spiritual equality in the eyes of God meant equality of position in this world.[8]

4. It was perhaps difficult to imagine a world without slavery, since it was part of their social structure.

5. Many Christian leaders hoped to gain acceptance in the mainstream of Roman society.

There were many things the Christians did to mitigate the fate of slaves. Here are some of them:

1. Christians in positions of authority pushed for the freedom of unjustly enslaved persons. We learn from Hippolytus, for instance, that Commodus' mistress convinced him to free the Christian prisoners in the mines of Sardinia.[9]

2. As we have seen, ordinary Christians made it their business to aid any person in need, including slaves who were being mistreated.

3. The Christians had systems in place for the corporate manumission of slaves.

4. The early Church made allowances for the problems of slaves in the "Church order manuals". For instance, in the *Apostolic Tradition*, slave concubines were not denied baptism (since they were not free to deny their masters), unless they had more than one lover, but men who owned concubines had to marry their concubines, a process which first entailed freeing the woman, before they could be baptized.[10]

5. The early Christians made it a regular practice to retrieve exposed infants and raise them as their own children, thus reducing the total number of potential slaves, since slave

traders also haunted the places where infants were exposed. (See p. 48.)

The early Church welcomed slaves among their number. In the introduction to *The Pastor of Hermas*, the author reveals that he was once a slave: "He who had brought me up, sold me to one Rhode in Rome."[11] We find slaves becoming Christians in the New Testament as well.[12] But being a slave presented some problems to potential Christians:

1. Slaves might find it difficult to get away from their duties to attend the liturgy or meetings.

2. Slaves were sometimes forced by their masters to engage in sexual relations.

3. Slaves had no money of their own and could not contribute to the Church.

4. Slaves lacked the free time to do charitable works or hold office in the Church.

5. Slaves were sometimes incapacitated by beatings. Some slaves were crippled by rage at the injustice of their lives.

We may conclude that slavery presented a difficult problem for the early Church. It was dangerous to encourage slaves to disobey or run away. On the other hand, Jesus had told his followers to take care of those in need, and there was no one group of people in more need than the slaves of the empire. How did the Church respond to this problem?

### The Early Christians and the Manumission of Slaves

There seems to have been a systematic effort in the early Church to manumit as many needy slaves as possible. Saint Paul, who told slaves to be obedient to their masters, seems to have been the originator of this initiative. In 1 Corinthians 7:21, he wrote: "Were you a slave when called? Never mind. But if you can gain your freedom, avail yourself of the opportunity."[13]

Paul did not, in this passage, call upon the Church to aid slaves in attaining their freedom. But in his Letter to Philemon, Paul devoted the entire letter to the situation of one particular slave and ended up asking the slave's Christian master, Philemon, to give him his freedom. The Letter to Philemon requires careful exegesis to understand, and there are numerous theories about what was going on in that Letter,[14] but the basic outline of the situation is as follows: Onesimus was the slave of a Colossian Christian named Philemon. Onesimus ran away from Philemon and joined Paul while Paul was in prison, probably in Ephesus. While with Paul, Onesimus became a Christian. Paul sent Onesimus back to his master, asking Philemon not only not to punish Onesimus, but to treat him like a brother, "no longer as a slave but as a beloved brother."[15]

What Paul was asking of both men is breathtaking. Slave owners were expected to punish runaways. The whole system of slavery depended on giving slaves no hope, except if they obeyed their masters. If Philemon did not punish Onesimus severely, he was risking a general slave revolt. To reward a runaway with his freedom was extremely dangerous. For Onesimus' part, he was being asked to do something even more dangerous. Paul asked Onesimus to trust himself to the mercy of a master from whom he had run away. Philemon could have had Onesimus crucified if he had been inclined to do so. Furthermore, there is no indication that Paul sent an escort with Onesimus. The temptation for the young man not to go to his master must have been intense. Yet, he must have returned to Philemon. Otherwise, how would we have this letter today?[16]

We have every indication that the story ended well, that is, that Philemon gave Onesimus his freedom. First, it seems unlikely that the letter would have been saved if Philemon had not acceded to Paul's wishes. Furthermore, the *Constitutions of the Holy Apostles* records that later Saint Paul ordained as bishop "of Borea in Macedonia, Onesimus, once the servant of Philemon".[17]

In the years after Paul's death, the Christians must have made it a regular practice to free as many slaves as they could. We can infer this negatively from Ignatius of Antioch's letter to Polycarp. In this letter, Ignatius wrote, "Do not despise either male or female slaves, yet neither let them be puffed up with conceit, but rather let them submit themselves the more, for the glory of God, that they may obtain from God a better liberty. Let them not long to be set free from slavery at the public expense, that they be not found slaves to their own desires."[18] To be "set free at the public expense" can mean only that some Christian slaves were being manumitted at the Church's expense. The fact that Ignatius warned Polycarp against the practice indicates that it happened with some regularity.

But why was Ignatius against the practice? Certainly, he had nothing against slaves. He had just finished admonishing Polycarp not to behave arrogantly toward slaves. Even a cursory reading of his letters reveals that Ignatius was very concerned about the poor and oppressed of the world. He was not a hardened man, full of his office, unconcerned about the less fortunate. But he cautioned Polycarp against freeing slaves out of common Church funds. Why? Here are some possible scenarios:

1. He may have been afraid that slaves were faking conversions to gain their freedom.

2. In the secular world, men freed their slaves to gain status and wealth. (See Part 1, Chapter 3.)

3. Ignatius had just finished telling Polycarp not to neglect the widows and orphans. Perhaps he thought limited Church funds should be saved for the widows and orphans.

4. When a secular master freed a slave, he normally set that slave up in a small business. If the Church followed this practice, she would end up running a bank, instead of spreading Christianity. On the other hand, if the Church did not set her freedmen up in business, the freedmen might not be able to make a living.

These may be reasons Ignatius thought it was a bad idea to use Church funds to free slaves. Yet we know that some Christians did work to free slaves. Two famous Christians—Hermas, whose brother was Pope Pius I, and Callistus, who became Pope in the third century— were freedmen. In Callistus' case, it was his owner, Carcophorus, a devout Christian, who gave him his freedom. But Pope Victor, who did not like Callistus for various reasons, sent him to Antium with a monthly stipend for food.[19] Although the Church as a corporate entity did not free Callistus, the Pope made sure his basic needs were met out of the common fund.

We have no direct evidence that at this point in the early Church, Church funds were used to manumit slaves except the negative evidence in Ignatius' letter to Polycarp. Yet it seems likely that churches did manumit slaves. We do know that bishops sometimes ransomed prisoners or appealed to wealthy patrons when the Church lacked the necessary funds, as we can see from this passage from the *Acts* of Archelaus:[20]

> On a certain occasion, when a large body of captives were offered to the Bishop Archelaus by the soldiers who held the camp in that place, their numbers being some seven thousand seven hundred, he was harassed with the keenest anxiety on account of the large sum of money which was demanded by the soldiers as the price of the prisoners' deliverance. And as he could not conceal his solicitude, all aflame for the religion and the fear of God, he at length hastened to Marcellus, and explained to him the importance and difficulty of the case. And when that pattern of piety, Marcellus, heard his narration, without the least delay he went into his house, and provided the price demanded for the prisoners.[21]

The story is clear: the soldiers had a large number of prisoners and assumed that Bishop Archelaus would ransom them if he could. For his part, the bishop assumed it was a part of his duty to ransom prisoners. In the ancient world, there was very little to distinguish prisoners of war from slaves; most prisoners would end up as slaves, if they did not first make their way to the arena. So it seems likely that bishops did consider it a part of their duties to use community funds to manumit slaves when the need arose. We do know for certain that in the age of Constantine, when Roman law was changing to reflect the legal status of Christians, a new form of manumission was recognized, *manumission in ecclesia*.[22]

If we take it as established that the early Church used public funds to free slaves, despite Ignatius' qualms, what are the circumstances under which the Church would do it? We lack hard evidence, but, extrapolating from other cases, I propose that a bishop might use the Church's resources under the following circumstances:

1. If a slave was suffering under a particularly harsh master.

2. If a female slave, especially one vowed to virginity, was in danger of being sexually abused by her master.

3. If a slave showed exceptional promise or spiritual gifts that might suit him for ministry.

Three points must be made in relation to this question. First, any corporate manumission of slaves would be dependent on the wealth of the community. Ignatius made it clear that he thought widows and orphans should receive a higher priority. The Roman community in the middle of the third century was caring for "over fifteen hundred widows and persons in distress, all of whom the grace and kindness of the Master nourish".[23] This community must have been wealthy enough to manumit as many slaves as they saw fit, and even support them after manumission, as they did in the case of Callistus.

The second point that needs to be made is one that would not likely occur to many of us today, the effect of slavery on the slave owner. Clement of Alexandria, for example, considered that owning too many slaves would encourage laziness, gluttony, and sensuality—qualities that Christians have never considered conducive to a sound spiritual life:

> But really I . . . find fault with having large numbers of domestics. For, avoiding working with their own hands and serving themselves, men have recourse to servants, purchasing a great crowd of fine cooks, and of people to lay out the table, and of others to divide the meat skillfully into pieces. And the staff of servants is separated into many divisions; some labor for their gluttony, carvers and seasoners, and the compounders and makers of sweetmeats, and honey-cakes, and custards; others are occupied with their too numerous clothes; others guard the gold, like griffins; others keep the silver, and wipe the cups, and make ready what is needed to furnish the festive table; others rub down the horses; and a crowd of cup-bearers exert themselves in their service, and herds of beautiful boys, like cattle, from whom they milk away their beauty. And male and female assistants at the toilet are employed about the ladies—some for the mirrors, some for the head-dresses, others for the combs.[24]

Clement and other Church leaders encouraged the freeing of slaves on the grounds that a Christian would be better off spiritually without them.

Third, even when Christians did not free their slaves, they generally treated them much better than the average slave could expect to be treated, even to the point of calling them "brother". Aristides wrote: "Further, if one or other of them have bondmen and bondwomen or children, through love toward them they persuade them to become Christians, and when they have done so, they call them brethren without distinction."[25] It is true that Aristides makes it clear that the Christian slave owner only called Christian slaves brothers, but the motivation for any attempt at conversion is love, and we know of very few pagan masters who professed to love their slaves.

Christians who wished to live an ascetic life would find it necessary to free whatever slaves they owned, not only for the sake of the slaves, but in order that they themselves not be too ensnared by the things of this world.

### Christianity and the Ultimate Abolition of Slavery

Not all Christian slaves were freed. We have evidence of Christian slaves and masters through the first three centuries.[26] As we have noted, there was no unified effort to emancipate all slaves or abolish slavery altogether. There was only the acknowledgment that it was a part of Christian charity to free whatever slaves one could. We have examples of Christians as private individuals freeing slaves (in the case of Callistus) and examples of community funds being used to free prisoners (the negative example provided in Ignatius' letter to Polycarp and the positive example in the *Acts* of Archelaus). We also noted, briefly, that the Christian practice of rescuing abandoned infants had the net result of lowering the pool of potential slaves.

When one considers the extent of slavery in the Roman Empire, the actions of the Christians hardly seem effective. Indeed, we find that even in the fourth and fifth century, when Christians had more leverage in shaping public policy, slavery did not die out quickly, and we have evidence that some Christians were still slave owners. Archaeologists have found a metal collar, inscribed with a cross and the words, "I am the slave of the Archdeacon Felix; hold me that I do not flee."[27] This collar came from Rome itself sometime in the fourth or fifth century. We know no more of Felix or his slave than this inscription, but it is hard to imagine Saint Paul, who urged Philemon to forgive and free his erring slave, approving of Felix' conduct.

Other Christians of this period saw it as their Christian duty to manumit their slaves. We have the following fourth-century papyrus: "Aurelius Valerius son of Sarapion ... to my own Hilaria, greetings. I acknowledge that because of my exceptional Christianity, under Zeus, Earth and Sun, together also with your *peculium*, and your loyalty toward me, in order that from here onwards you shall have your freedom."[28]

One could write a whole book on this one papyrus, starting with the arrogance of the writer and moving on to a reflection on fourth-century syncretism! There are two essential points here, however. First, it was considered a Christian duty to free slaves, but the fact that the author boasts of his exceptional Christianity indicates perhaps that not all Christians freed their slaves, only exceptional ones. Secondly, even this "exceptional" Christian kept the *peculium*, the money his slave had saved on her own, as the price of her manumission.

Fortunately, there were other Christians who did more and talked about it less. Slavery was ended in the late Roman world by the deliberate actions of Christians. One thinks of Pope Saint Gregory the Great, who redeemed English slaves in the markets of Rome, or the devout monks who converted the Frankish kingdom, redeeming slaves as part of their Christian duty.[29]

But these events occurred much later. It is considered a scandal, not so much for the early Christians, who were after all powerless, but for the Constantinian Church, that it was not until the sixth and seventh centuries that slavery was finally ended in Christian Europe. But perhaps the failure was not so much a failure of morality as a failure of imagination. For Christianity began in an empire in which a third of the people were enslaved, yet it brought into being a world in which almost everyone knows slavery is wrong. Of course, certain battles have to be fought over and over again, and slavery popped up again and again in the Christian world. It was indeed Christians from Portugal, soon followed by Dutch, French, and English Christians, who joined in the African slave trade in the fifteenth century. But it was also Christians in Europe and the United States who determined to put a stop to that barbarous trade.

The enduring legacy of the early Christians in the matter of slavery is that, relatively powerless as they were, they did what they could. They did not flinch from the issue, or leave later generations with easy excuses. Let us close this chapter with a quote from Hermas.

Hear the similitude which I am about to narrate to you relative to fasting. A certain man had a field and many slaves, and he planted a certain part of the field with a vineyard, and selecting a faithful and beloved and much valued slave, he called him to him, and said, "Take this vineyard which I have planted, and stake it until I come, and do nothing else to the vineyard; and attend to this order of mine, and you shall receive your freedom from me." And the master of the slave departed to a foreign country. And when he was gone, the slave took and staked the vineyard; and when he had finished the staking of the vines, he saw that the vineyard was full of weeds. He then reflected, saying, "I have kept this order of my master: I will dig up the rest of this vineyard, and it will be more beautiful when dug up; and being free of weeds, it will yield more fruit, not being choked by them." He took, therefore, and dug up the vineyard, and rooted out all the weeds that were in it. And that vineyard became very beautiful and fruitful, having no weeds to choke it. And after a certain time the master of the slave and of the field returned, and entered into the vineyard. And seeing that the vines were suitably supported on stakes, and the ground, moreover, dug up, and all the weeds rooted out, and the vines fruitful, he was greatly pleased with the work of his slave. And calling his beloved son who was his heir, and his friends who were his councilors, he told them what orders he had given his slave, and what he had found performed. And they rejoiced along with the slave at the testimony, which his master bore to him. And he said to them, "I promised this slave freedom if he obeyed the command which I gave him; and he has kept my command, and done besides a good work to the vineyard, and has pleased me exceedingly. In return, therefore, for the work which be has done, I wish to make him co-heir with my son, because, having good thoughts, he did not neglect them, but carried them out." With this resolution of the master his son and friends were well pleased, that the slave should be co-heir with the son. After a few days the master made a feast, and sent to his slave many dishes from his table. And the slave receiving the dishes that were sent him from his master, took of them what was sufficient for himself, and distributed the rest among his fellow-slaves. And his fellow-slaves rejoiced to receive the dishes, and began to pray for him, that he might find still greater favor with his master for having so treated them. His master heard all these things that were done, and was again greatly pleased with his conduct. And the master again calling together his friends and his son, reported to them the slave's proceeding with regard to the dishes, which he had sent him. And they were still more satisfied that the slave should become co-heir with his son.[30]

This similitude presents the great gift of Christ to the world: the idea that a slave could become co-heir with the master's son. The early Christians were faithful to Christ's teaching. They passed the vision on, under extremely trying circumstances, and they are not responsible for how that vision was treated by later generations.

CHAPTER 6

# The Rich, the Poor, and
# Charity in Early Christianity

Beginning in A.D. 251, a plague swept across the Roman Empire. At its height, 5,000 people a day died in Rome alone. In Alexandria, possibly as many as two-thirds of the people might have died.[1] Archaeologist Arthur Boak has estimated that Karanis, in Egypt, lost a full third of its population, based on his own excavations of that city.[2]

The plague terrified the people of the empire. Lacking any knowledge of the existence of germs, or any means of curing or preventing the disease, despair reigned. The rich fled to their country estates, hoping isolation would protect them. Doctors, realizing the futility of their treatments, abandoned their charges.[3] Here is what Dionysius, Bishop of Alexandria, had to say about the common response to the plague: "They deserted those who began to be sick, and fled from their dearest friends. And they cast them out into the streets when they were half dead, and left the dead like refuse, unburied. They shunned any participation or fellowship with death; which yet, with all their precautions, it was not easy for them to escape."[4]

In the face of such death and terror, only one group of people would aid the sufferers. They were Christians, and Dionysius, Bishop of Alexandria, was rightly proud of them:

Most of our brethren were unsparing in their exceeding love and brotherly kindness. They held fast to each other and visited the sick fearlessly, and ministered to them continually, serving them in Christ. And they died with them most joyfully, taking the affliction of others, and drawing the sickness from their neighbors to themselves and willingly receiving their pains. And many who cared for the sick and gave strength to others died themselves having transferred to themselves their death.

And the popular saying which always seems a mere expression of courtesy, they then made real in action, taking their departure as the others "off-scouring." Truly the best of our brethren departed from life in this manner, including some presbyters and deacons and those of the people who had the highest reputation so that this form of death, through the great piety and strong faith it exhibited, seemed to lack nothing of martyrdom.[5]

Nor did the Christians help only other Christians. Another city hard hit by this plague was Carthage. Pontius the Deacon records that the intrepid bishop of that city, Cyprian, insisted that Christians should aid pagans as well as believers:

There broke out a dreadful plague, and excessive destruction of a hateful disease invaded every house in succession of the trembling populace, carrying off day by day with abrupt attack numberless people, every one from his own house. All were shuddering, fleeing, shunning the contagion, impiously exposing their own friends, as if with the exclusion of the person who was sure to die of the plague, one could exclude death itself also. There lay about the meanwhile, over the whole city, no longer bodies, but the carcasses of many, and, by the contemplation of a lot which in their turn would be theirs, demanded the pity of the passersby for themselves. No one regarded anything besides his cruel gains. No one trembled at the remembrance of a similar event. No one did to another what he himself wished to experience. In these circumstances, it would be a wrong to pass over what the pontiff of Christ did, who excelled the pontiffs of the world as much in kindly affection as he did in truth of religion. On the people assembled together in one place he first of all urged the benefits of mercy, teaching by examples from divine lessons, how greatly the duties of benevolence avail to deserve well of God. Then afterwards he subjoined, that there was nothing wonderful in our cherishing our own people only with the needed attentions of love, but that he might become perfect who would do something more than the publican or the heathen, who, overcoming evil with good, and practising a clemency which was like the divine clemency, loved even his enemies.[6]

That Cyprian successfully urged the Christians to show mercy to their pagan neighbors is all the more remarkable because only a year earlier the Christians of Carthage had been subjected to the persecution of Decius, which led to the death of many Christians. But there can be no doubt that the Christians really did aid and succor the sick to a much higher degree than the non-Christian population. As we have already mentioned, the satirist Lucian of Antioch made fun of the Christians for what he saw as their naïve philanthropy. A hundred years later, when Emperor Julian "the Apostate" attempted to restore paganism as the official religion of the empire, he encouraged pagan priests to aid the poor as the Christians did: "The impious Galileans support not only their poor, but ours as well, everyone can see that our people lack aid from us."[7]

With both Christian and pagan testimony, there can be little doubt that the Christians cared for the poor, the sick, and the disabled to a degree that their pagan neighbors did not. In this chapter, we will explore the ways in which this behavior changed the world, with particular attention to three questions:

1. How did the Christians go about their charitable work?

2. What were their motivations for doing so?

3. What effect did their work have on the world they inhabited?

As we shall see, in this area, the early Christians initiated a revolution in human thought and behavior that continues in the world to this day.

*The Early Christians and the Social Services of the Ancient World*

The world of the early Christians was quite different than the one in which we live. We are used to the idea that the government will help those in need, but this was not always the case. Before governments got into the business of helping the needy, Christian churches attended to this vital task (as indeed, many do to this day). But before the coming of Christianity, help for the poor was spotty, sometimes even nonexistent. The only people who had a consistent ethic that required aiding the poor as well as an organized approach to it were the Jews.[8] Jewish charity was freely given and likely to be bestowed on those who most needed it, the poorest of the poor. It is unclear, however, whether non-Jews were regularly aided by Jewish philanthropy.[9] But if you were a poor person, alone and in trouble, you would be much more likely to receive aid from a Jew than from a typical Greek or Roman.

Roman indifference to those less fortunate was so widespread that the satirist Juvenal found it necessary to take his fellow citizens to task for it: "Who but the wealthy get sleep in Rome?"[10] Lucian of Antioch (also referred to as Lucian of Samosata), whom we have encountered on several occasions, wrote a satire in which he included the following letter from the god Cronus:

> Cronus to the Rich—Greetings:
> The poor have recently written me complaining that you do not let them share what you have, and, to be brief, they asked me to make the good things common to all and let everyone have his bit. It was right, they said, for there to be equality and not for one man to have too much of what is pleasing while another goes without altogether. . . . Now these requests seem reasonable to me. "How," they say, "can we, shivering in this extreme cold and in the grip of famine, keep festival as well?" So if I wanted them to share in the festival, they bade me counsel you to give them as share of any clothing you might have . . . these things are not at all difficult for you to grant out of all that you are rightly blessed with.[11]

Cronus goes on and on in this manner, making it clear that Lucian thought the rich of his age dealt with the poor heartlessly. Plautus reinforces this notion with the following comment: "He does the beggar a bad service who gives him meat and drink, for what he gives is lost, and the life of the poor is prolonged to their own misery."[12]

There were public and private means by which the poor could receive aid. Following the example of Rome itself, most cities in the empire provided free or cheap grain for the poor. They did this more out of a desire to keep riots to a minimum than out of compassion for the poor, but nevertheless it was a genuine benefit to the poor. Some enlightened cities, like Ephesus, had lower tax rates for the poor. In the private realm, clubs and guilds would keep a fund that could be used for members in distress, but these funds were not available to the general public.[13]

Two cultural values, renunciation and liberality, motivated some prominent pagans to show philanthropy to the poor. Renunciation refers to the philosophical notion, prominent among Cynics, Stoics, and some

Neoplatonists, that wealth and excess were to be avoided. The philosopher Musonius Rufus gave 1,000 sesterces to a beggar who was pretending to be a philosopher. When Rufus' friends protested that the man was a scoundrel who deserved no good, Rufus replied, "Well, then, he deserves money." [14]

The concept of liberality is somewhat more complicated and less altruistic. The idea was that rich men could increase their honor by generosity to people of lower class. But this liberality was carefully metered. The idea was that you should give only to deserving people: talented, hardworking people who had just had a run of bad luck. Men of bad character—the foolish, the criminals, the lazy—should not be helped.[15] The truth is that most wealthy men would help only those who might have something to offer in return, even if it was only public praise.

The early Christians entered into this somewhat heartless world with a new vision of humanity. Christ had taught them: "As you did it to one of the least of these my brethren, you did it to me",[16] and they sincerely believed that their eternal destination depended in part on how they treated the less fortunate.[17] We have already seen how the early Church organized herself so her charities could be done systematically. There is no need to do more than briefly review this system, but it is important to realize that the institutional method was only one of four ways charity could work in the early Church.

1. The institutional method was the most common and probably helped the most people. In this method, people would give their money or food at the liturgy. The bishop would take these items and distribute them to his deacons, deaconesses, or widows.[18] These worthies would then see that those most in true need would receive what they needed.

2. Individual Christians, when confronted with need, would make a spontaneous gift to the person in need. One thinks of Saint Martin of Tours, dividing his cloak with a beggar after his conversion.[19] Ordinary Christians were taught and encouraged by their leaders to look for opportunities to give on their own: "Instead of lands, therefore, buy afflicted souls, according as each one is able, and visit widows and orphans, and do not overlook them; and spend your wealth and all

your preparations, which ye received from the Lord, upon such lands and houses."[20]

3. Sometimes, when confronted with a situation beyond the means of ordinary Church funds, bishops would ask wealthy private individuals to make a sacrificial gift to cover the need. An example of this was provided in the last chapter, when Bishop Archelaus asked the wealthy Christian Marcellus to provide the funds to ransom 7,700 prisoners.

4. When there was a crisis, such as a famine, earthquake, or flood, in one community, the Christian communities that were not affected would take a special collection. There is a clear example of this in sacred Scripture. There was a famine in Jerusalem sometime in the early 50s, and Saint Paul spent a considerable amount of time and energy in collecting relief from the other Christian communities.[21] These things happened all the time. Cyprian of Carthage, for instance, raised 100,000 sesterces to free Numidian Christians who had been held captive by barbarian raiders.[22]

We do not know how much the early Christians gave. The literature does not specify a percentage that people should give.[23] The rich were expected to give more than the poor, but even the poor gave, and if they had no money, they could give cheeses, oils, or some other produce.[24]

### Christian Teaching on Wealth, Poverty, and Almsgiving

The easiest aspect of studying the early Christians is learning what they were taught about a particular subject. You merely have to read the fairly numerous writings of bishops, theologians, and teachers. In the case of the poor, it is even easier than normal to find out what the early Church taught. The New Testament is full of teachings on the subjects of wealth, poverty, charity, and the responsibility of believers. It is perhaps unnecessary to review these numerous passages. Most of them state in a clear and unequivocal way that the poor and sick are to be cared for and that the care given to the poor is a measure of devotion to Christ.

Post–New Testament writers did not deviate from this theme. Clement of Rome, Clement of Alexandria, Tertullian, Origen, Irenaeus, Cyprian, Ignatius of Antioch—all these writers emphasized the duty of the whole community toward the less fortunate. It is not necessary to give a catalogue of what was written by whom, but there are unexpected aspects of the early Church's teaching on wealth and poverty that do need to be explored further. These are the following:

1. In 1 Peter 4:8, Peter wrote, "Above all hold unfailing your love for one another, since love covers a multitude of sins." Furthermore, in Colossians 1:24, Paul wrote, "Now I rejoice in my sufferings for your sake, and in my flesh I complete what is lacking in Christ's afflictions for the sake of his body, that is, the Church." These passages, and others like them, were used in a way that some modern Christians object to, in putting together what some modern scholars refer to as the "doctrine of redemptive almsgiving".

2. Acts 2:44–45 reads: "And all who believed were together and had all things in common; and they sold their possessions and goods and distributed them to all, as any had need." Some modern authors have supposed, on the basis of this passage alone, that the early Christians practiced a primitive form of socialism. But there is really no other evidence, either in the New Testament or in late writings, that this was the case. How did the early Christians feel about wealth and poverty, and was total renunciation required in order to be baptized?

First, let us consider a concept that was actually quite important to the early Christians, to judge by the number of times it appears in the writings of the early Church. The concept in question has been referred to by modern scholars as "redemptive almsgiving".[25] In its crassest form, the concept is described as the idea that forgiveness of sins could be achieved or facilitated by charitable giving. In truth, the early Christians believed that sinners could demonstrate their sincere sorrow for their sins and receive the grace of forgiveness through the performance of charitable acts.

The idea of redemptive almsgiving is repugnant to some modern Christians. We have been conditioned by horror stories of medieval buying and selling of indulgences, and some are influenced by the Lutheran doctrine of *sola fide*. This book is not a work of theology, so I will not delve too deeply into the theological debate, the ins and outs of which would fill up a book much larger than this one.[26] For the present purposes, it is enough to demonstrate that the early Christians emphatically rejected any kind of doctrine that separated faith from works. The doctrine of salvation by faith alone is a product of the nominalism of the late fifteenth and early sixteenth centuries and was not even conceived of by any early Church writer.

I am not insensible to the problems of spiritual corruption and fraud that are associated with a connection between money and salvation. But three considerations minimized the corrupting influence of money in the life of the early Church:

1. The early Church was neither wealthy nor powerful. It was hard to be a Christian, and the only real rewards for being one were spiritual. In such circumstances, it was far less likely that the early Christians would be fooled by spiritual charlatans.

2. The persecutions and hardships of the early Church produced integrity in the leadership of the Church that precluded fraud on their part. Men like Cyprian of Carthage, who gave up their own immense fortunes for the privilege of dying for Christ, were unlikely to attempt to defraud or deceive their followers.

3. If examples of corruption in the Middle Ages are fair game, it is also fair to point out that in modern times, even denominations that subscribe to the doctrine of *sola fide* have been susceptible to corruption. The problems of modern Christianity go far beyond any of the potential problems associated with the teaching of redemptive almsgiving.

What did the early Church actually believe about almsgiving? The early Church was much closer to the actual teachings of Jesus, both in time and in cultural understanding. The world of late first-century Judaism, which shaped the understanding of the early Church, was comfortable with the notion that our earthly deeds would be blessed or cursed by God, depending on their merit. Isaiah 58:9, for instance, says that if you feed the hungry, house the homeless, and clothe the naked, "then you shall call, and the Lord will answer, you shall cry, and he will say, Here I am." Proverbs 10:2 says, "Treasures gained by wickedness do not profit, but righteousness delivers from death."

These two passages are mere examples of the concept that God rewards virtue and punishes greed. Did Jesus, or Paul, or any of the New Testament writers reject this notion? Far from it. Consider, first, the story of the rich man who wanted to receive eternal life.[27] Jesus told him, "Sell all that you have and distribute to the poor, and you will have treasure in heaven; and come, follow me."[28] The early Christians were interested in what it meant to "store up treasure in heaven".

There are other passages that also speak to this "heavenly investment".[29] Jesus said, "Give and it will be given to you. A good measure, pressed down, shaken together, running over, will be put into your lap; for the measure you give will be the measure you get back."[30] The parable of the dishonest steward ends with the following admonition: "Make friends for yourselves by means of unrighteous mammon, so that when it fails they may receive you into the eternal habitations."[31] Luke 11:41 also implies that almsgiving can be used as a means of purifying the ugliness within us. Both Cyprian and Origen interpreted the passage in this way.[32]

In his Letters, Paul placed the focus of almsgiving on love freely given, but he also implied a blessing for giving: "The point is this: he who sows sparingly will also reap sparingly, and he who sows bountifully will also reap bountifully."[33] We have already discussed Peter's statement, "Love one another, for love covers a multitude of sins."[34] The verses immediately following this one make it plain that by love Peter is referring to practical acts of charity.

I have dwelt at great length on the scriptural background for the postapostolic Church's teaching on almsgiving because these teachings have been subject to a great deal of criticism from modern writers, who have implied that the early Church leaders taught that you could buy salvation. They taught no such thing. What they did say was that you could achieve peace of soul, after a life of sin, through the generous giving of ill-gotten gains.

To illustrate this point, let us first look at the *Didache*. This document, remember, was most likely written around 90–110. It stands as a good test of what the Christians who were taught by the apostles were thinking. Here is a sample: "If you have anything, through your hands you shall give ransom for your sins. You shall not hesitate to give, nor murmur when you give; for you shall know who will repay your good deeds." [35] This passage of the *Didache* acknowledges that all good things come from God, for the express purpose of sharing with others, and that God will find a sufficient reward for the giver.

The next document we will look at is one we have not discussed yet, the *Second Epistle to the Corinthians*, also known as *II Clement*. This letter may or may not have been written by the same man who wrote the *First Epistle to the Corinthians*. There is no independent or internal evidence to support or contradict the idea that the same man wrote both letters. The reason it is called *II Clement* is that it was found in a fifth-century collection with *I Clement*, and the notations from that collection indicate that the author was Pope Clement and that *II Clement* was written shortly after *I Clement*. Modern scholars doubt this information, for various reasons. They date *II Clement* to around A.D. 130. They do not think there is any way to know where the letter was written or to whom it was addressed. For these reasons, we cannot attribute *II Clement* to the fourth Bishop of Rome, as I did *I Clement*. Nevertheless, it is a worthwhile document to look at, representing the thought of the fourth or fifth generation of Christians.

Regarding almsgiving, *II Clement* has this to say: "Almsgiving therefore is a good thing, as repentance from sin; fasting is better than prayer, but almsgiving than both; 'but love covers a multitude of sins.' But prayer out of a good conscience delivers from death. Blessed is every one that is found full of these; for almsgiving lightens the burden of sin." [36] Almsgiving, fasting, and prayer are all recommended for the conscience weighed down by sin. Prayer is good, fasting better than prayer, and almsgiving is the best of all: it "lightens the burden of sin." Why?

We must remember the background of many of the early Christians. To understand this, Saint Paul can be consulted: "Do you not know that the unrighteous will not inherit the Kingdom of God? Do not be deceived; neither the immoral, nor idolaters, nor adulterers, nor homosexuals, nor thieves, nor the greedy, nor drunkards, nor revilers, nor robbers will inherit the Kingdom of God. *And such were some of you*" (emphasis added). [37] My point here is that many of the early Christians came from sinful backgrounds, and even after conversion their consciences were uneasy. Some had money gained from prostitution, thievery, murder, or shady business practices. So the author of *II Clement* recommended almsgiving as a means of lightening the burden of sin.

Clement of Alexandria devoted a whole treatise to the question of how the rich could be saved, entitled *Who Is the Rich Man That Will Be Saved?* In this treatise, he used the teaching of Jesus, "store up treasures in Heaven ...", as a starting point for explaining that the rich were given the gifts they had so they could share with others. In this way, both the rich and the poor would benefit. He used an interesting rhetorical device to explain what he meant, a rhetorical device that is easily misunderstood in our current context. He wrote:

> Then to appoint such a reward for liberality an everlasting habitation! Oh excellent trading! Oh divine merchandise! One purchases immortality for money; and, by giving the perishing things of the world, receives in exchange for these an eternal mansion in the heavens! Sail to this mart, if you are wise, Oh rich man! If need be, sail round the whole world. Spare not perils and toils, that you may purchase here the heavenly kingdom. Why do transparent stones and emeralds delight thee so much, and a house that is fuel for fire, or a plaything of time, or the sport of the earthquake, or an occasion for a tyrant's outrage? Aspire to dwell in the heavens, and to reign with God.... He will make thee a dweller with Him. Ask that you may receive; haste; strive; fear lest He disgrace thee.... The Lord did not say, Give, or bring, or do good, or help, but make a friend. But a friend proves himself such not by one gift, but by long intimacy. For it is neither the faith, nor the love, nor the hope, nor the endurance of one day, but "he that endures to the end shall be saved."[38]

This passage begins as though salvation is a crass commercial transaction, but there is a hidden subtlety in Clement's writing. First of all, ordinary people could understand the commercial image he was using. But a closer reading would reveal that Clement was not talking about a cheap commercial transaction at all, but the beauty of a relationship brought to maturity: "The Lord did not say, Give, or bring, or do good, or help, but make a friend. But a friend proves himself such not by one gift, but by long intimacy." All men, whether rich, or poor, or middle class, can build relationships only by giving of the gifts they have. The rich have an obvious gift that they can share with the poor, but all are called to share: "No one is idle, no one is useless. One can obtain your pardon from God, another comfort you when sick, another weep and groan in sympathy for you to the Lord of all, another teach some of the things useful for salvation, another admonish with confidence, another counsel with kindness. And all can love truly, without guile, without fear, without hypocrisy, without flattery, without pretence." [39]

Seen in this light, the admonition that the rich should share their wealth with the poor is a part of the teaching of the Church as the Body of Christ. But in the body, all members must be useful, all members must perform a function. The function of one might be to share their wealth, for another it might be to teach, or pray, or provide succor to the sick, or simply listen sympathetically. And all have a right to share in the good things God brings, as members of the community of salvation. Thus, Clement avoids implying that the rich can buy salvation, while at the same time stating unambiguously that the sharing of the good things God has given are essential in receiving that salvation.

> For this also He came down. For this He clothed Himself with man. For this He voluntarily subjected Himself to the experiences of men, that by bringing Himself to the measure of our weakness whom He loved, He might correspondingly bring us to the measure of His own strength. And about to be offered up and giving Himself a ransom, He left for us a New Covenant: My love I give unto you. And what and how great is it? For each of us He gave His life—the equivalent for all. This He demands from us in return for one another. And if we owe our lives to the brethren, and have made such a mutual compact with the Savior, why should we any more hoard and shut up worldly goods, which are beggarly, foreign to us and transitory? [40]

Clearly, with this context, the early Christians cannot be accused of teaching that salvation can be bought with alms by the rich.

What about the question of socialism in the early Church? In Acts 2:44-45 we read: "And all who believed were together and had all things in common; and they sold their possessions and goods and distributed them to all, as any had need." Also, Jesus asked the rich young man to give up all his possessions. But in other parts of the New Testament, we read of rich persons who were not asked to give up all their possessions. In 1 Timothy 6:17-19, we read, "As for the rich in this world, charge them not be haughty, nor to set their hopes on uncertain riches but on God who richly furnishes us with everything to enjoy. They are to do good, to be rich in good deeds, liberal and generous, thus laying up for themselves a good foundation for the future, so that they may take hold of the life which is life indeed."

Here we see no call to renounce wealth, but merely to use it for good. Here is a potential dilemma. Did the early Church require converts to give up their wealth, or did she merely ask them to use it for the common good? Or did Saint Paul misunderstand and modify the teachings of Jesus? The answer, as usual, is a little bit complicated and does not lend itself to a straight yes or no. Church order manuals, such as the *Didache*, the *Apostolic Tradition*, and the *Didascalia*, certainly did not call for the abandonment of wealth upon baptism. But Clement of Alexandria, whom we just encountered writing so eloquently about the need of the rich to give to the poor, also wrote, "By nature all property which a man possesses in his own power is not his own. And from this unrighteousness it is permitted to work a righteous and saving thing, to refresh someone of those who have an everlasting habitation with the Father."[41]

It seems that most of the early Church authors would have preferred it if all Christians had shared their property equally, but they were insistent that such sharing be voluntary. There was no coercion. As Tertullian wrote, regarding the Sunday collection: "If he likes, each puts in a small donation; but only if it be his pleasure, and only if he be able: for there is no compulsion; all is voluntary."[42]

We know of a few early Christians who did voluntarily give up all their wealth. Cyprian of Carthage did, upon his baptism.[43] Gregory Thaumaturgus, the wonderworker of Pontus, gave up a lucrative career in law to become a missionary in Pontus.[44] Eusebius claimed that it was a common custom in the postapostolic period for itinerant missionaries to give up their wealth, but be gives us no names, dates, or places.[45]

What about communities that held property in common? We read about it in Acts 2, then the practice seems to die out until the fourth century, when the monastic movement begins to gain momentum. In the intervening years, were there no groups of Christians who banded together to share their funds equally? We can only speculate, but it seems likely that some did. We read about groups of virgins, male or female, who lived near each other and prayed together in their respective communities.[46] It seems likely to me that they lived much as religious communities of men and women live to this day, sharing their possessions in common. But we simply do not have the information to say for sure.

For most Christians, the question of selling all and giving the proceeds to the poor or to the Church did not come up, just as few Christians consider it today. The reason is obvious: if the world is going to continue, some people must make money to raise their own families and support the poor. So most Christians continued in the occupations they had before their conversion. Some were rich, some were poor, and some were middle class. Each one was called to do what he could. Some truly were called to abandon their possessions for the sake of the Kingdom. Others simply gave what they could.

## CHAPTER 7

# The Early Christians and Military Service

In A.D. 173, *Legio XII Fulminata*, the "Thundering Legion", was engaged in battle with the Germans along the Danube. The Roman army was in trouble, when a strange thing occurred. The following is Eusebius' description of the events:

It is reported that Marcus Aurelius Caesar, brother of Antoninus, being about to engage in battle with the Germans and Sarmatians, was in great trouble on account of his army's suffering from thirst. But the soldiers of the so-called Melitene legion, through the faith which has given strength from that time to the present, when they were drawn up before the enemy, kneeled on the ground, as is our custom, and engaged in supplications to God. This was indeed a strange sight to the enemy, but it is reported that a stranger thing immediately followed. The lightning drove the enemy to flight and destruction, but a shower refreshed the army of those who had called on God, all of whom had been on the point of perishing with thirst. This story is related by non-Christian writers who have been pleased to treat the times referred to, and it has also been recorded by our own people. By those historians who were strangers to the faith, the marvel is mentioned, but it is not acknowledged as an answer to our prayers. But by our own people, as friends of the truth, the occurrence is related in a simple and artless manner. Among these is Apolinarius, who says that from that time the legion through whose prayers the wonder took place received from the emperor a title appropriate to the event, being called in the language of the Romans the Thundering Legion. Tertullian is a trustworthy witness of these things. In the *Apology for the Faith*, which he addressed to the Roman Senate, and which work we have already mentioned, he confirms the history with greater and stronger proofs. He writes that there are still extant letters of the most intelligent Emperor Marcus in which he testifies that his army, being on the point of perishing with thirst in Germany, was saved by the prayers of the Christians. And he says also that this emperor threatened death to those who brought accusation against us.[1]

This story is odd and somewhat unclear. Why was the Roman army in danger of thirst in well-watered Germany, with the Danube close by? If the Christians saved the army, and Marcus Aurelius knew it, why did he order the savage persecution of Lyons four years later?[2] The most significant question of all is the broadest: What were Christians doing in the Roman legion when it was illegal to be a Christian and the army was a foremost persecutor of Christians? Where, after all, are the letters of Marcus Aurelius, acknowledging that Christians saved his army? The only extant statement from this emperor regarding Christian service to the empire is negative: "They failed the Empire in its time of need."[3]

The casual observer might be forgiven for concluding that the odds are against this story being true. We will return to this fascinating account later and find that most likely there is at least a kernel of truth in the story Eusebius has recorded. We will also find that by the middle of the third century, against all odds, there were a large number of Christians in the legions. And this is the greatest mystery of all. With the teachings of Christ against violence, with some Church leaders fulminating against military service, and with the constant danger of discovery and summary execution, Christians still served in the Roman army.

### Early Christian Teaching on Military Service

Jesus' teachings against violence are some of the most memorable in all the New Testament. The Beatitudes include the statement, "Blessed are the peacemakers, for they will be called the sons of God."[4] Later in the Sermon on the Mount, Jesus spoke even more plainly: "You have heard it said, 'An eye for an eye and a tooth for a tooth.' But I say to you, Do not resist one who is evil. But if any one strikes you on the right cheek, turn to him the other also.'"[5] Jesus also said, "Love your enemies, do good to those who hate you."[6] When Peter assaulted the high priest's servant, Jesus told him, "Put your sword back into its place; for all who take the sword will perish by the sword."[7]

When Pilate asked him if he was a king, Jesus replied, "My kingship is not of this world; if my kingship were of this world, my servants would fight, that I might not be handed over." [8] With these teachings of Jesus, how could anyone doubt that Jesus was a pacifist, and that in his movement, there could be no soldiers? The early Christians, closer to his teachings than we are today, must have known that they could not possibly serve in the army. So how could there be Christians in the Roman legion?

The problem is, of course, that there are other passages in the New Testament that speak favorably of individual soldiers, or use the soldier's life as an analogy for the Christian life. There is even one passage in which John the Baptist teaches soldiers: "Rob no one by violence or by false accusation, and be content with your wages." [9] John did not tell them they had to refuse to fight or leave the service. He simply gave them some basic ethical teachings that were within their reach. One might argue that John the Baptist's teachings were not as strong as Jesus', but John was the one who was given the task of preparing the way for the coming of the Messiah. His job was to teach repentance. If he thought the soldiers were doing grave wrong simply by being soldiers, he would have said so, just as he told Herod he was wrong in marrying his brother's wife.

Individual soldiers are often spoken well of in the New Testament. Here are the most prominent cases:

| Matthew 8:5–13 and Luke 7:1–10 | A centurion asks Jesus to heal his servant. Jesus commends him for his faith |
| --- | --- |
| Mark 15, Luke 23, Matthew 27 | A centurion declares that Jesus truly was the Messiah |
| Acts 10 | The conversion of Cornelius, an upright Roman soldier |
| Acts 27 | The centurion charged with taking Paul to Rome for trial saves Paul in a storm |

These stories reveal some interesting details. Neither Jesus nor John the Baptist, neither Peter nor Paul asked any soldier to give up his office. They merely asked the soldier to perform his duties with more integrity.

Paul in particular was fond of using military imagery to describe the Christian life. For instance, in 1 Thessalonians 5:8, Paul wrote, "Since we belong to the day, let us be sober, and put on the breastplate of faith and love, and for a helmet the hope of salvation." Other passages in which Paul writes in this vein are 2 Corinthians 6:7, 10:3–6, Romans 13:12, Ephesians 6:10–18, 1 Timothy 1:18, and 2 Timothy 2:34.

It is quite clear in these passages that Paul is writing allegorically. The military life is an analogy for the spiritual warfare of the Christian life. But, as Adolf Harnack observed, "Yet war is one of the basic forms of all life, and there are inalienable virtues which find their highest expression at least symbolically in the warrior's calling: obedience and courage, loyalty unto death, self-abnegation and strength. No higher religion can do without the images which are taken from war, and on this account it cannot dispense with 'warriors.' "[10] Harnack reminds us that the virtues one associates with the best soldiers are also virtues for Christians.

If this is true, then there is a deep internal conflict within Christianity that can be reconciled only with great difficulty. On the one hand, Christians are called to be peacemakers and turn the other cheek. On the other hand, the devotion and self-sacrifice of soldiers are to be encouraged in all people. This conflict is usually resolved in real-world situations with some form of just war theory. The early Church had not yet developed just war theory, though some scholars have detected the early stages of it in the writings of Origen.[11]

But other highly significant factors caused most early Christian writers to oppose the enlistment of Christians. In reading through the literature on this subject, it is possible to detect eight distinct objections to Christian service in the Roman army: (1) some Christians on principle rejected war and the shedding of blood; (2) soldiers had to carry out death sentences; (3) the soldier's oath, which had to be taken upon enlistment, was incompatible with Christianity; (4) soldiers were expected to participate in rites of emperor worship; (5) officers had to offer sacrifice to various pagan gods; (6) reverence to the military standards amounted to idolatry; (7) the conduct of soldiers in peacetime conflicted with the Christian ethic; and (8) the rough games, the *mimi*, of the soldiers were morally offensive.[12]

This is a hugely impressive list of reasons for Christians not to enlist in the army. One should note, however, that of these eight reasons, only two have to do with the shedding of blood, both in battle and in the enforcement of the death penalty. Four of the reasons have to do with the paganism of the army, and two relate to the general immorality of a soldier's lifestyle. True pacifists among the early Christians are actually hard to detect. Among them, one would place Justin Martyr, Tertullian, and Origen. Others, such as Hippolytus of Rome and Clement of Alexandria, allowed men who were already in the army upon conversion to stay, with certain restrictions upon their behavior. A third group, among whom I would place Clement of Rome and Cyprian of Carthage, seemed to have few problems with the soldier's life, other than the paganism. Even among those who were adamantly opposed to military service for Christians, one wonders how strongly they would have objected were it not for all the pagan religiosity that surrounded life in the army.

Clement of Rome is the earliest source on Christian attitudes toward military life (the *Didache* had nothing to say on the subject). Clement neither encouraged nor forbade enlistment, nor did he actually mention any Christians who were in the army. However, he was an enthusiastic user of military metaphors to explain the Christian life. His use of these metaphors indicates that he knew a lot about military life, and that he was not at all scandalized by what he knew. This fits our general picture of Clement as a man who must have come from the upper third of Roman society. He compared apostates to deserters: "We should not leave the post which His will has assigned us",[13] and "what world will receive any of those who desert Him?"[14]

Clement also used Paul's favorite metaphor, the Christian as a soldier on hard duty: "Let us then, men and brethren, with all energy act the part of soldiers, in accordance with His holy commandments. Let us consider those who serve under our generals, with what order, obedience, and submissiveness they perform the things which are commanded them. All are not prefects, nor commanders of a thousand, nor of a hundred, nor of fifty, nor the like, but each one in his own rank performs the things commanded by the king and the generals."[15]

Ignatius of Antioch, who had no reason to love the Roman army, used a similar metaphor: "Please Him under whom you fight, and from whom you receive your wages. Let none of you be found a deserter. Let your baptism endure as your arms; your faith as your helmet; your love as your spear; your patience as a complete panoply."[16]

Justin Martyr also used the military metaphor, but in a very clever way, making it clear that Christians were soldiers for peace:

> And when the Spirit of prophecy speaks as predicting things that are to come to pass, He speaks in this way: "For out of Zion shall go forth the law, and the word of the Lord from Jerusalem. And He shall judge among the nations, and shall rebuke many people; and they shall beat their swords into ploughshares, and their spears into pruning-hooks: nation shall not lift up sword against nation, neither shall they learn war any more." And that it did so come to pass, we can convince you. For from Jerusalem there went out into the world, men, twelve in number, and these illiterate, of no ability in speaking: but by the power of God they proclaimed to every race of men that they were sent by Christ to teach to all the word of God; and we who formerly used to murder one another do not only now refrain from making war upon our enemies, but also, that we may not lie nor deceive our examiners, willingly die confessing Christ. For that saying, "The tongue has sworn but the mind is unsworn," might be imitated by us in this matter. But if the soldiers enrolled by you, and who have taken the military oath, prefer their allegiance to their own life, and parents, and country, and all kindred, though you can offer them nothing incorruptible, it were verily ridiculous if we, who earnestly long for incorruption, should not endure all things, in order to obtain what we desire from Him who is able to grant it.[17]

So far no author has directly addressed the question of whether or not Christians should serve in the military. Perhaps the question had not yet arisen. Outside of Cornelius and possibly the centurion who begged Jesus to heal his servant, we have no evidence of Christians in the military until 173. However, after 173, we find an increasingly large number of Christians in the army. For this reason alone, after this time we find more judgments on the validity of Christian military service.

In the *Apostolic Tradition* we read the following: "A soldier of the civil authority must be taught not to kill men [i.e., participate in executions] and to refuse to do so if he is commanded, and to refuse to take an oath; if he is unwilling to comply, he must be rejected. A military commander or civic magistrate that wears the purple must resign or be rejected. If a catechumen or a believer seeks to become a soldier, they must be rejected, for they have despised God."[18] We notice the following. Soldiers already in service are not asked to leave, unless they are governors. Soldiers who choose to stay in the service must refuse to carry out orders regarding capital punishment and refuse to take the military oath. Catechumens and those already baptized are forbidden to join.

In general, all the later Christian teachers adhered to the rule laid out by Hippolytus, though some clearly wished that there were no Christians in the military. Tertullian acknowledged that there were large numbers of Christians in the legions around Carthage in his time: "We are but of yesterday, and we have filled every place among you— cities, islands, fortresses, towns, market-places, the very camp, tribes, companies, palace, senate, forum",[19] and "we sail with you, and fight with you, and till the ground with you."[20]

In writings directed to the general public, Tertullian emphasized the participation of Christians in the military. But when he wrote to other Christians, he did everything he could to convince them that Christians could not honorably serve in the legions. His argument was simple: if men could not join the army after baptism, by what logic could they be allowed to stay in just because they were in the army before conversion? His argument follows:

> In that last section, decision may seem to have been given likewise concerning military service, which is between dignity and power. But now inquiry is made about this point, whether a believer may turn himself unto military service, and whether the military may be admitted unto the faith, even the rank and file, or each inferior grade, to whom there is no necessity for taking part in sacrifices or capital punishments. There is no agreement between the divine and the human sacrament, the standard of Christ and the standard of the devil, the camp of light and the camp of darkness. One soul cannot be due to two masters—God and Caesar. And yet Moses carried a rod, and Aaron wore a buckle, and John is girt with leather and Joshua the son of Nun leads a line of march; and the People warred: if it pleases you to sport with the subject. But how will a Christian man war, nay, how will he serve even in peace, without a sword, which the Lord has taken away? For albeit soldiers had come unto John, and had received the formula of their rule; albeit, likewise, a centurion had believed; still the Lord afterward, in disarming Peter, unbelted every soldier.[21]

As Harnack has pointed out, "Obviously Tertullian does not represent here the general point of view of his Christian brothers."[22] Harnack believes that in his own argument Tertullian reveals himself to be in the minority. He even reveals the arguments of his opponents, that leaders in the Old Testament engaged in wars and that John the Baptist did not forbid military service ("soldiers had come unto John, and had received the formula of their rule"). Thus, it is hard to escape the conclusion that Tertullian knew himself to be in the minority, and an indication that he knew he was in the minority was that he acknowledged that the legions had Christians in them.

Later in his life, Tertullian devoted a whole treatise to Christians in the military. The treatise *The Chaplet* (also known as *On the Crown*) was occasioned by the fact that a Christian soldier had been executed for refusing to wear a crown of laurels signifying victory in combat.[23]

> Lately it happened thus: while the bounty of our most excellent emperors was dispensed in the camp, the soldiers, laurel crowned, were approaching. One of them, more a soldier of God, more steadfast than the rest of his brethren, who had imagined that they could serve two masters, his head alone uncovered, the useless crown in his hand already even by that peculiarity known to every one as a Christian—was nobly conspicuous. Accordingly, all began to mark him out, jeering him at a distance, gnashing on him near at hand. The murmur is wafted to the tribune, when the person had just left the ranks. The tribune at once puts the question to him, Why are you so different in your attire? He declared that he had no liberty to wear the crown with the rest. Being urgently asked for his reasons, he answered, "I am a Christian."[24]

Tertullian commended the soldier for refusing to wear the crown, and exchanging it for the martyr's crown. He made an argument that it is indeed wrong to wear a military crown under any circumstances, but his real argument was against military service in general: "To begin with the real ground of the military crown, I think we must first inquire whether warfare is proper at all for Christians. What sense is there in discussing the merely accidental, when that on which it rests is to be condemned?"[25]

For all his opposition to military service, Tertullian made one concession, but even in the concession is the firm insistence that Christians cannot stay in the military:

> Of course, if faith comes later, and finds any preoccupied with military service, their case is different, as in the instance of those whom John used to receive for baptism, and of those most faithful centurions, I

mean the centurion whom Christ approves, and the centurion whom Peter instructs; yet, at the same time, when a man has become a believer, and faith has been sealed, there must be either an immediate abandonment of it, which has been the course with many; or all sorts of quibbling will have to be resorted to in order to avoid offending God, and that is not allowed even outside of military service.[26]

Tertullian's point is that no one could stay in the army for long without doing something Christians forbid. Sooner or later, a soldier would be expected to sacrifice to an idol, or worship the emperor, or wear a crown, or execute a prisoner. Under those circumstances, the Christian must refuse the command, be exposed as a Christian, and endure martyrdom. Tertullian went on to argue that exceptions could not be made for soldiers, or one would have to be made for everyone: "In fact, an excuse of this sort overturns the entire essence of our sacrament."[27]

Clement of Alexandria did not take the same stance Tertullian took. He expressed what became the orthodox position on military service, albeit with great subtlety and skill: "Practice husbandry, we say, if you are a husbandman; but while you till your fields, know God. Sail the sea, you who are devoted to navigation, yet call all the while on the heavenly Pilot. Has knowledge taken hold of you while engaged in military service? Listen to the commander who orders what is right."[28] The "commander who orders what is right" would be taken to be God himself. The gist of Clement's teaching seems to be that a soldier can stay in the military, but could obey only those commands of which God would approve.

Of all the early Christians, Origen had the most detailed and complex teaching regarding the use of military force. He was clearly opposed to Christian participation in military service. He allegorized the "holy wars" narrated in the Old Testament.[29] He recast the wars of ancient Israel as allegories of individual spiritual warfare. He stated flatly, "Unless those physical wars bore the figure of spiritual wars, I do not think the books of Jewish history would have been handed down by the apostles to the disciples of Christ, who came to teach peace, so that they could be read in the churches."[30] He made sure his readers knew that Paul's teachings on spiritual warfare were metaphorical. The soldiers of Christ, for Origen, were the ascetics, who did not entangle themselves in civilian pursuits.[31]

Origen made a start toward considering the possibility of a just war. In a passage in *Against Celsus*, he wrote about a hypothetical case Celsus had raised involving war among bees:

> Perhaps also the so-called wars among the bees convey instruction as to the manner in which wars, if ever there arise a necessity for them, should be waged in a just and orderly way among men.... But, as I formerly said, we ought on the one hand in these things to admire the divine nature, and on the other to express our admiration of man, who is capable of considering and admiring all things (as co-operating with Providence), and who executes not merely the works which are determined by the providence of God, but also those which are the consequences of his own foresight.[32]

But Origen did not for a minute think that even if there could be just wars Christians could fight in them. A little later in *Against Celsus*, he wrote: "We are come, agreeably to the counsels of Jesus, to 'cut down our hostile and insolent swords into ploughshares, and to convert into pruning hooks the spears formerly employed in war.' For we no longer take up 'sword against nation,' nor do we 'learn war any more,' having become children of peace."[33] Further on, he says, "Christians could not slay their enemies, or condemn to be burned or stoned, as Moses commands, those who had broken the law."[34]

Origen never was able to conceive of a circumstance in which Christians would be anything but a small minority of people. He thought Christians could fulfill their duty to society simply by praying for the good of the emperor, by praying for victory in just wars, and by paying taxes. But in a society where Christians were in the majority, Origen's formula would not work. For if, as Origen granted, some wars are just, then there must be soldiers to fight in them, and if the majority of the population holds itself exempt from warfare, then even just wars cannot be won. So it is that Origen's position cannot be maintained in the real world, unless there are few Christians, who could operate as the spirit in the body, leaving to the unspiritual pagans the bloody work of warfare.

Cyprian of Carthage had fewer contradictions in his thought than Origen. Raised as he was in the upper class of Carthaginian society, with high civic offices under his belt, he was used to soldiers and the soldierly mentality. No early Christian writer uses military imagery as freely and as often as Cyprian.[35] It is perhaps a good thing that Cyprian had an understanding and sympathy for the military. There were evidently many soldiers in his Church, some of them second- or third-generation soldiers and Christians, as the following passage implies:

> Nor is that kind of title to glories in the case of Celerinus, our beloved, an unfamiliar and novel thing. He is advancing in the footsteps of his kindred; he rivals his parents and relations in equal honors of divine condescension. His grandmother, Celerina, was some time since crowned with martyrdom. Moreover, his paternal and maternal uncles, Laurentius and Egnatius, who themselves also were once warring in the camps of the world, but were true and spiritual soldiers of God, casting down the devil by the confession of Christ, merited palms and crowns from the Lord by their illustrious passion. We always offer sacrifices for them, as you remember, as often as we celebrate the passions and days of the martyrs in the annual commemoration.[36]

This short passage tells us so much. Celerinus' grandmother was a Christian. Two of his uncles were Christian soldiers, who were caught up in the persecution of Decius. Cyprian is saying that Celerinus' spiritual ancestry is more worthy of praise than his physical ancestry, to be sure, but it is clear that the fact that Celerinus' uncles served in the army is not held against them. To the contrary, "we always offer sacrifices for them". In other words, Celerinus' uncles were honored highly as martyrs, and their military service was not held against them. Moreover, Cyprian implies that Celerinus himself was a soldier. He writes that his uncles "also were once warring". The person they are being compared to must be Celerinus, since no one else is mentioned in this passage but his grandmother, and women did not serve in the Roman legion.

But it would be a mistake to compare Cyprian to militant bishops of later times. Cyprian had a proper Christian dislike for warfare and other forms of bloodshed: "Consider the roads blocked up by robbers, the seas beset with pirates, wars scattered all over the earth with the bloody horror of camps. The whole world is wet with mutual blood; and murder, which in the case of an individual is admitted to be a crime, is called a virtue when it is committed wholesale. Impunity is claimed for the wicked deeds, not on the plea that they are guiltless, but because the cruelty is perpetrated on a grand scale."[37]

The teaching of the early Church on the subject of military service was not entirely uniform. On the one hand, one could not join the army after conversion. On the other hand, if you were already in the army at the time of conversion, it was acceptable to stay, as long as you did not participate in an execution or engage in pagan sacrifice. Some teachers thought even this concession was too great, and that the Christian life was entirely incompatible with life in the Roman army. But every one of the authors I have listed here knew that the fall of the Roman Empire would be a great humanitarian disaster, and they also knew that the legions helped keep this disaster at bay.

### Christians in the Roman Army

There are excellent reasons for believing that there were Christians, perhaps many Christians, in the army from about A.D. 200 onward. Just how many there were, we shall perhaps never know. But a safe assumption would be that the closer to 300, the more Christians you would be likely to find. The references grow thicker, the number of Christian soldiers cited more numerous, the closer you get to that date.[38]

We know of two Christian soldiers in the New Testament, perhaps three. There is the centurion who asked Jesus to heal his servant, the soldier who proclaimed Jesus as the Son of God after his side was pierced on Golgotha, and the centurion Cornelius, whom Peter converted. But in the post–New Testament period, until the time of the Thundering Legion, there is no sure evidence for Christians in the military. In the twentieth century, a French historian compiled a list of 176 inscriptions, mostly epitaphs, which spoke of Christian soldiers. Of these inscriptions, only six can be dated to the time period with which we are concerned, two of which are from the second century, with four from the third.[39]

But it beggars the imagination to think that there would be soldier converts in the New Testament, no soldiers for 120 years, and then shortly after the first soldiers appeared, relatively large numbers of soldiers. So there must have been some Christian soldiers in the period between 50 and 170. Lack of evidence is not evidence of a lack. If there were Christian soldiers, though, why do we have no evidence?

1. Whatever Christian soldiers there were would have, for obvious reasons, kept quiet. No one would have been walking around with a cross on his shield, like the knights of the Middle Ages.

2. In general, soldiers tend to accumulate fewer personal goods than other people do. The majority of the legions were spread out in strongholds around the perimeter of the empire. Some of these permanent camps have been dug up by archaeologists, but few personal effects of the soldiers have been recovered. The truth is that even after Constantine, when we know from literary sources that there were many Christians in the army, archaeologists have found little evidence of them in the camps.[40]

Evidence for Christian soldiers begins in 173 and grows more prevalent up to 300. The first piece of evidence of Christians in the military is the story of the Thundering Legion, which we discussed at the beginning of this chapter. Eusebius recorded this story (which must have happened in 173, if at all) in 325. His sources were (1) a Christian named Apollinarius, who claimed to be an eyewitness to the events; (2) Tertullian, who devoted a section of his *Apology* to this event; and (3) unspecified pagan writers whose works on this subject appear to be lost to us, or perhaps did not say what Eusebius thought they said.

Did this event occur as Eusebius said it did? Or did something like it happen? What is the actual evidence for or against Eusebius' version of events? The evidence against Eusebius is actually quite strong:

1. Four years after the event, the emperor Marcus Aurelius ordered a savage persecution of the Christians of Lyons (see Part 2, Chapter 4).

2. As already noted, Marcus Aurelius wrote in his *Meditations* that the Christians had failed the empire in its time of need.

3. Nowhere to be found are letters to the Senate, or pagan writings bearing out this version of events.

4. *Legio XII Fulminata* was not named the "Thundering Legion" as the result of this battle. It was given the epithet "*Fulminata*" during the days of Augustus.

Against this relatively strong negative evidence there are also some powerful arguments in favor of Eusebius' story:

1. Tertullian wrote about the event some twenty years later: "So far from that, we, on the contrary, bring before you one who was their protector, as you will see by examining the letters of Marcus Aurelius, that most grave of emperors, in which he bears his testimony that that Germanic drought was removed by the rains obtained through the prayers of the Christians who chanced to be fighting under him." [41]

2. Apollinarius, who wrote an eyewitness account (unfortunately no longer extant) that Eusebius quotes, is known to have lived in the area at the time of the battle. [42]

3. There were Christians in the *municipium* near the camp of the Thundering Legion at the time of the campaign in question. [43]

4. The Thundering Legion was recruited from the region of Melitene in Asia Minor, where we know there were many Christians.

5. The pagan historian Dio Cassius told the same story, though he attributed the miracle to an Egyptian sage who traveled in Marcus Aurelius' entourage. But we at least know the event itself probably happened. [44]

6. In 176, Marcus Aurelius had a column erected in Rome depicting scenes from his reign. Three of the scenes depict the sudden rainstorm that saved his army. [45]

The preponderance of evidence is on the side of Eusebius. There must have been an event in 173 in which *Legio XII Fulminata* was somehow cut off from water during a drought. Perhaps the legion was surrounded and could not get to water. Everyone in the legion must have done what he thought would help. The Christians would have appealed to Christ, the pagans would have prayed to their favorite deity, and Egyptian magicians would have resorted to their best magic. When the storm came, everyone must have had the impression that his form of intervention had been the one that saved the army. But there is no evidence that Marcus Aurelius thought the miracle had occurred through Christian intervention. In fact, the only evidence we have indicates that he was quite certain that Christians had nothing to do with any of it.

But I think we can take it as given that there were at least some Christians in the Thundering Legion. From 173 on, in the midst of persecution, we know there were Christians in the Roman army. As we have already noted, it seems clear from reading Tertullian, Clement of Alexandria, Origen, and Cyprian that there were many Christian soldiers in the third century. The idea fascinates and stirs the imagination. What were their lives like? How did they worship? Did they have "chaplains", presbyters who served their spiritual needs while on campaign? Most importantly, how did they avoid detection? Did they routinely compromise the faith, during the almost incessant pagan rituals of the army? Or did they receive some sort of an informal "pass" from their centurion? We have no firm answers to most of these questions. But we can take some things we do know and make some reasonable guesses.

First, Roman soldiers spent most of their time, not on campaigns, but in more-or-less permanent camps around the fringes of the empire. These camps became the focus of civilian economic activity, and towns and even small cities grew up around them. Christians were among the population of these cities. One such edge of the empire garrison town was Dura-Europos. Dura served as a major fortress guarding the eastern frontier against the Persians, so there were always a lot of soldiers around. Dura had a Christian church, the oldest authenticated church archaeologists have found to this date.[46] One might surmise that Christian soldiers would worship with the local Christian community when they could get off duty.

When on campaign, the prayer life of the soldiers would be highly irregular. The soldiers would probably have to content themselves with private prayer or Scripture reading, with little or no fellowship. Liturgical services would be most likely out of the question, because even when in a temporary camp there would be guard duty, foraging, cooking and cleaning, latrines to dig, and many other tasks to perform.

But closer to 300, with more Christians in the army, it seems likely that some units might have had someone approximating a chaplain. As usual, Eusebius is informative on this point. He records that after Constantine had his famous vision of the cross, accompanied with the anouncement that "in this sign you will conquer", he consulted some Christians in his camp: "Being struck with amazement at the extraordinary vision, and resolving to worship no other God save Him who had appeared to him, he sent for those who were acquainted with the mysteries of His doctrines, and enquired who that God was, and what was intended by the sign of the vision he had seen." [47]

To understand the significance of this passage, it is necessary to know that Constantine and his army were at the crucial phase of a military campaign. Everyone knew that tomorrow the army would fight. Usually at this stage of a campaign all nonessential personnel are left behind. Yet even at this time, Constantine could call upon, and find on short notice, "those who were acquainted with the mysteries of His doctrines".

One might be tempted to think that these men were simply soldiers who happened to know a little bit more about their faith than their comrades, but this is not the impression Eusebius gives. The men who were called forth taught him at a very high level indeed: "They affirmed that He was God, the only begotten Son of the one and only God: that the sign which had appeared was the symbol of immortality, and the trophy of that victory over death which He had gained in time past when sojourning on earth. They taught him also the causes of His advent, and explained to him the true account of His Incarnation." [48] A little further on we read, "he made the priests of God his counselors",[49] in a context which makes it seem as if "the priests" referred to are the same men who informed him about Christianity after his vision.

This is one interpretation that could be put on this passage. Eusebius was writing perhaps twenty years after the events in question. So it might be that there were Christian priests accompanying Constantine's army before the battle of Milvian Bridge, or maybe some other interpretation is in order. It seems quite possible that there were Christian priests with the army. Pagan priests frequently accompanied ancient armies without great difficulty, so why not Christian, especially if there were many Christians in the army, and the commander was not hostile to Christianity?

Before Constantine legalized Christianity, how did Christian soldiers avoid detection? Were they routinely discovered and martyred because of their refusal to go along with pagan sacrifices? Or did they participate in the blasphemous sacrifices in spite of their convictions?

Or did their officers protect them by sending them off on special duties when the sacrifices were scheduled? We have evidence that all three of these scenarios played out at different times. We have seen that Tertullian was convinced that no soldier could be a real Christian for very long without being martyred. In *The Chaplet*, when he was writing about the soldier who was martyred for refusing to wear a crown, he observed that this man was "more steadfast than the rest of his brethren, who had imagined that they could serve two masters".[50] Tertullian thought that most of the soldiers were two-faced in their Christianity, attending liturgies and prayer services when they could but not refusing to participate in the pagan rites of the legion.

It is not hard to imagine what a conflict was faced by the believing soldiers. The guilt, and the continuing sense of unworthiness, must have been intense. Yet the love of Christ and the desire for communion and community must have been equally strong. Finally, the day would come when the soldier could no longer compromise his integrity. He would refuse to participate in some rite, and that refusal would lead to an interrogation that would eventually uncover the truth: the soldier was a Christian. And at that point, execution was the most likely outcome.

We have in our possession, in the *Acts of the Martyrs*, many stories like the story of the soldier about whom Tertullian wrote. One example will suffice, the case of Marcellus, who was martyred in 298. At a festival dedicated to the birthdays of the emperors Diocletian and Maximian, Marcellus broke his vine switch, the symbol of a centurion's authority, and threw down his sword belt. Then, as now, soldiers were expected to appear on ceremonial occasions in complete uniform, so to be lacking his vine switch and his sword belt was a serious infraction in and of itself. But what Marcellus declared was even worse: "I cannot serve under any oath but the one taken to Christ." He was taken to the governor Fortunatus, who told him, "I cannot conceal your rash act, and hence I shall report this to the sacred ears of Diocletian and Maximian."[51]

We do not know how long Marcellus had served before he decided to throw down his vine switch and his sword belt. Perhaps one day he realized how much his integrity was suffering from the double life he was leading, Christian one day, centurion the next, not only participating in pagan sacrifices but making sure his men did as well.

In any case, one day he had enough and decided he could no longer serve two masters. In the end, Marcellus was beheaded on October 30, 298.

Governor Fortunatus, who first tried Marcellus, made one revealing comment. He told Marcellus his behavior could not be concealed. Marcellus' deeds could not be hidden because they were too public, too many people saw them. But Fortunatus' statement leads one to believe that if he could have concealed it he would have.

Did officers and soldiers cover up for the Christians in their midst? There is evidence that this was the case. Take the story of the martyrdom of Marinus:

> At this time, when the peace of the churches had been everywhere restored, Marinus in Caesarea in Palestine, who was honored for his military deeds, and illustrious by virtue of family and wealth, was beheaded for his testimony to Christ, on the following account. The vine branch is a certain mark of honor among the Romans, and those who obtain it become, they say, centurions. A place being vacated, the order of succession called Marinus to this position. But when he was about to receive the honor, another person came before the tribunal and claimed that it was not legal, according to the ancient laws, for him to receive the Roman dignity, as he was a Christian and did not sacrifice to the emperors; but that the office belonged rather to him.[52]

The story is revealing. Marinus was a practicing, devout Christian. His mates knew it and must have known it for a long time. One of them finally gave Marinus up when Marinus received a promotion he wanted for himself.

Two factors would have made it easier for soldiers to cover up for one another. First of all, until the time of Diocletian, common soldiers did not have to sacrifice. Only those of the rank of centurion or higher performed the sacrifice. The others had to be present, in the proper uniform, but they could simply watch the actual sacrifice. Second, as we have seen, not all emperors were interested in tracking down Christians. Many emperors made a political calculation. They needed soldiers, and the Christians were generally good ones. Everyone knew the law forbade Christianity and required at least a twice-annual renewal of the *sacramentum*, or oath of allegiance to the emperor, but because there were so many Christians in the army, a blind eye was turned.

This was particularly the case in the latter half of the third century, until the time of Diocletian and Galerius. A system was worked out by which Christian soldiers would make the sign of the cross while the sacrifice was going on. Presumably, everyone could be satisfied by this arrangement, and the officers would just pretend they did not know what the strange sign meant.[53] No one knows what the Christians thought. Perhaps they thought the power of the sign of the cross would triumph over the rituals they were forced to watch. Or perhaps they just thought that it was enough to register their disapproval of the pagan sacrifice.

Diocletian was initially not ill-disposed toward Christians, but this particular custom angered him and caused a change in his attitude toward Christians, as Lactantius tells us:

Diocletian, as being of a timorous disposition, was a searcher into futurity, and during his abode in the East he began to slay victims, that from their livers he might obtain a prognostic of events; and while he sacrificed, some attendants of his, who were Christians, stood by, and they put the immortal sign on their foreheads. At this the demons were chased away, and the holy rites interrupted. The soothsayers trembled, unable to investigate the wonted marks on the entrails of the victims. They frequently repeated the sacrifices, as if the former had been unpropitious; but the victims, slain from time to time, afforded no tokens for divination. At length Tages, the chief of the soothsayers, either from guess or from his own observation, said, "There are profane persons here, who obstruct the rites." Then Diocletian, in furious passion, ordered not only all who were assisting at the holy ceremonies, but also all who resided within the palace, to sacrifice, and, in case of their refusal, to be scourged. And further, by letters to the commanding officers, he enjoined that all soldiers should be forced to the like impiety, under pain of being dismissed from the service.[54]

It is impossible to know exactly how many Christian soldiers there were in the army when Diocletian first came to power, but the number must have been large. Here is how Eusebius describes the situation in the period of time between the reigns of Valerian and Diocletian:

It is beyond our ability to describe in a suitable manner the extent and nature of the glory and freedom with which the word of piety toward the God of the universe, proclaimed to the world through Christ, was honored among all men, both Greeks and barbarians, before the persecution in our day. The favor shown our people by the rulers might be adduced as evidence; as they committed to them the government of provinces, and on account of the great friendship which they entertained toward their doctrine, released them from anxiety in regard to sacrificing. Why need I speak of those in the royal palaces, and of the rulers over all, who allowed the members of their households, wives and children and servants, to speak openly before them for the Divine word and life, and suffered them almost to boast of the freedom of their faith? Indeed they esteemed them highly, and preferred them to their fellow servants.[55]

The picture Eusebius paints is one with a large number of Christians in positions of responsibility throughout the empire. Eusebius does not specifically mention military service in this passage, but if governors were relieved of the necessity to sacrifice, would not soldiers be as well? Obviously, if Church leaders were forbidding Christians to serve, the laymen were not obeying. But there is no evidence that anyone in authority was forbidding them. Tertullian and Origen, who disapproved of military service, started their careers as orthodox laymen, and both ended their lives out of communion with the universal Church. The only bishop we know of who wrote on the subject, Cyprian, clearly hated bloodshed, but did not forbid Christians to serve in the military. Eusebius, who in addition to being a historian and a prolific writer was Bishop of Caesarea, showed no indication of disapproving of the large number of military Christians about which he wrote. So somewhere between 150 and 250, the Church lost her disapproval of Christian service. Let me be more precise: the Church never forbade people who were already soldiers at time of baptism from continuing to serve. What seems to have changed is that in the late third century, people who were already baptized were enlisting, without any negative consequences from Church leaders.

What was happening? It seems likely that as Christians became more numerous it became increasingly difficult for Christians to sit on the sidelines. The empire was in great difficulty during this period, sometimes fighting against two or three enemies at a time. Barbarian raids across the border were frequent. Christians might not have loved the empire, but they knew that things would be much worse if the empire collapsed. So responsible, civic-minded young Christians joined the army, particularly during the period when it was easy to avoid sacrificing, between the reigns of Valerian and Diocletian.

But soldiers continued to convert after their enlistment, also. What might have induced them to do so? What special attractions might there be for soldiers? In my analysis, the following factors coincided to make Christianity attractive to the Roman soldier:

1. The difficulties of the soldier's lifestyle and the fear of death that is a part of that life made a religion that promised eternal life especially attractive.

2. The personal integrity and courage of Christian soldiers in their unit would have made a strong impression on them.

3. Soldiers were the ones who had to carry out executions in the Roman world, so during periods of persecution they would have encountered martyrs. The story of Potamiaena and Basilides illustrates this point (see above pp. 245–47).

Scholars who claim that Constantine changed Christianity from a persecuted, pacifistic minority sect into a militant religious monster would do well to reexamine the evidence. Long before Constantine, between the periods of persecution, Christians were serving in the military, serving in "Caesar's household",[56] and governing provinces. Those who lived out these difficult and sometimes dangerous vocations did so because they thought the Lord had put them in those circumstances for a reason. The truth is, we find little difference in the behavior and attitudes of Christians from 250 to the time of Constantine, and those of the fourth century. They loved Christ, they loved their families, and they loved the only nation they had ever known, despite all its imperfections. They longed for Rome to be better, more just, and more peaceful, but they defended her.

## CHAPTER 8

# The Early Christians and Family Life

Sometime between the years 170 and 240, a Christian named Minucius Felix wrote a literary apology in which he introduced a friend of his named Octavius. Minucius and Octavius were both lawyers, and dear friends.[1] In his apology, Minucius describes the depth of their friendship, in the process revealing some important things about Octavius' family life: "For the sake of business and of visiting me, Octavius had hastened to Rome, having left his home, his wife, his children, and that which is most attractive in children, while yet their innocent years are attempting only half uttered words, a language all the sweeter for the very imperfection of the faltering tongue."[2]

The picture Minucius Felix draws of Octavius' family is charming: a beloved wife, and young children just learning to speak. We have spent a great deal of time discussing celibate Christians in the early Church, yet it must have been the case that then, as now, the vast majority of Christians were married, and had children. Family, friends, and faith were clearly the three pillars of Octavius' life. He went to Rome to visit Minucius Felix, but clearly it was understood that this was only on account of his great love for Minucius, and if his family had really needed him he would have quickly returned to them.

It is important to bear this charming picture in mind in discussing the family life of the early Christians. We sometimes think them so otherworldly that they would scarcely deign to conceive and raise children, but they were human beings like the rest of us, designed to love and be loved, to procreate and nurture children. And so they did.

And we know the early Christians successfully raised Christian children. In the account of the martyrdom of Justin, we read the following regarding Justin Martyr's friends:

Rusticus the prefect said to Hierax, "And you, are you a Christian?" Hierax said, "Yes, I am a Christian, for I revere and worship the same God." Rusticus the prefect said, "Did Justin make you Christians?" Hierax said, "I was a Christian, and will be a Christian." And Paeon stood up and said, "I too am a Christian." Rusticus the prefect said, "Who taught you?" Paeon said, "From our parents we received this good confession." Euelpistus said, "I willingly heard the words of Justin. But from my parents also I learned to be a Christian." [3]

This passage clearly reveals that Paeon and Euelpistus were raised in the faith by Christian parents.

There are many things we wish we could know about Christian families of the first three centuries. The daily routines of Christian families must have been similar to that of their pagan neighbors, though of course their prayers would have been quite different. (See Part 1, Chapter 3, for Roman family life. See Part 1, Chapter 2, for Roman family religious ceremonies.)

We are hampered in our knowledge of specifically Christian family practices by a lack of both documentary and archaeological evidence. Christian families simply did not leave archaeological trails during the first three centuries for the same reasons Christian soldiers did not. The two main (and fairly obvious) reasons are that Christians would hardly want to advertise themselves in times of persecution, and that in large cities, the chances of archaeologists stumbling onto the private residence of Christians would be slight.

So there are quite a few gaps in our knowledge of Christian families. But there are other things we know quite well. Christian attitudes toward marriage, children, and the role of the family were quite different from those of pagans. We will explore those differences in attitude first, then move into specific areas of family life.


## The Christian Family

As we have seen in Part 1, the father dominated pagan families in the ancient world. The *paterfamilias* of a Roman household was, traditionally, an absolute dictator over his household, with the power to put erring members to death if he felt the situation warranted it. In the first century A.D. the *paterfamilias* lost the right to execute members of his household without a public trial, but the principle of patriarchal rule still held.[4] Children were expected to obey, and discipline was typically harsh. The Romans had advice manuals on child rearing, as they had on almost every subject imaginable, and the manuals recommended "blows and threats" as the best means to obtain desired behavior.[5]

The early Christians, who tended to be influenced more by Jewish practices than by Roman, also subscribed to the theory that the father should be the head of the household. The "household codes" of Ephesians 5:22—6:9 and Colossians 3:18—4:1 make this point clear. Children are admonished to obey their parents, and wives their husbands. The seeming sternness of these passages has led many commentators to suppose that these passages come from a later period, when the Church was more "conservative" and more inclined to make accommodations to Roman culture.

This theory sounds reasonable only if you compare the "household codes" of Paul to modern American family practices. If you compare Paul's teachings on family life to the Roman child-rearing manuals, it becomes clear that the author of Ephesians and Colossians was a social innovator of great daring. Consider certain aspects of Paul's rules that modify and mitigate the harshness of the Roman system.

1. Paul makes sure he constantly explains the reasons for his rules: "Be subject to one another out of reverence for Christ",[6] and "let the peace of Christ rule in your hearts."[7] The "household codes" of Paul were designed to provide for the orderly, harmonious living of the Christian life in families. Love requires sacrifice, and Paul was calling each and every member of the ancient household to make personal sacrifices.

2. Paul asked things of the *paterfamilias* that no Roman manual asked. He asked husbands to love their wives as Christ loves the Church, he asked fathers not to be too harsh with their children, and he asked masters to treat their slaves well. The father, in Paul's understanding, was not to be an absolute master, but was to be guided in all things by the dictates of love.

3. The authority of the father was further mitigated by the understanding that the authority of God is the ultimate guide for

all behavior. Hence, in Ephesians 6:1 we read, "Children, obey your parents in the Lord, for this is right." The key phrase here would be "in the Lord". What would happen if the father's commands were contrary to the teachings of Christ? Christians always knew this problem could come up, but they also knew the teaching of Jesus on this subject: "Whoever does the will of God is my brother and sister and mother." [8]

These three points are sufficient for us to understand that in Paul's mind, families were places where the gospel was to be lived out. But on certain occasions, it would become necessary for a person to renounce family ties for the sake of the gospel.[9] Under such circumstances, Christians could establish a new family, for the Church herself was the "household of God".[10] The Church could and did become the primary kinship group of the early Christians, albeit a "fictive" one.[11]

The net result of the Christian family revolution brought about by the early Church was that families were encouraged to be places of love and mutual respect. People were able to escape from truly bad families and create new, more wholesome ties with people that had the same values and beliefs. Widows were able to escape a life of grinding poverty, because the Church undertook to take care of them. Young girls were able to avoid painful marriages to much older men because the Church valued their virginity. Young men were given a new understanding of their role in society based on Christ's teachings on the greatness of servanthood.

The goal of the Church was not to facilitate people's escape from unpleasant social institutions, but to transform those institutions through the power of the gospel. Just how this transformation took place is a fascinating story.

### Marriage and Divorce

"Moses allowed you to divorce", Jesus told his disciples, "because of the hardness of your hearts. But from the beginning it was not so." [12] In this statement, Jesus acknowledged that the Mosaic law allowed divorce, gave a reason for the allowance, and overrode that teaching, all in one pithy statement. In the world Jesus found, men were allowed to divorce their wives in all societies. There is an unexpected twist to the legal arrangements, though: in Jewish law a man could divorce his wife for virtually any reason. Women could not divorce their husbands. There is no clear data on how frequently Jewish men took advantage of this situation, but it happened often enough that Jesus felt the need to criticize them for their "hardness of heart".

A woman who was cast off by her husband was in a truly pitiable state. Prevented by Jewish custom from earning a living on her own without becoming an outcast, a divorced woman's options were to return to her father's household, if he was still alive and was willing to take her in, rely on grown sons to take care of her, or rely on charity. So divorce was an ugly aspect of first-century Jewish life, although it is unclear how often it happened.

Roman law, by way of contrast, made it easy for both men and women to initiate divorce proceedings. Since Roman women could earn a living on their own, there was no reason—social, legal, or moral— not to divorce. Hence, divorce was common. Frequent divorce and remarriage meant that family life tended to be chaotic: "Members of the Roman upper class married and divorced frequently with their shifting alliances and in their quest for legitimate male offspring. Many also adopted males of allied households, usually young adults, in order to gain suitable heirs. A household might include stepmothers, stepbrothers and stepsisters, and other half-kin."[13]

Christianity encountered this cultural mélange of divorce practices head-on. Jesus forbade divorce categorically in Mark 10:11–12. Matthew 5:32 and 19:9 soften this teaching by allowing an exception for *porneia*, a Greek word best understood as covering all forms of "illicit sexual intercourse in general".[14] The question of whether Matthew or Mark captured Jesus' teaching more accurately is, of course, outside the scope of this study.

The early Christians universally interpreted Jesus' and Paul's teachings on divorce as an absolute prohibition. They went even further: there was a general disapproval of remarriage even when one's spouse died. Justin Martyr wrote, "All who, by human law, are twice married, are in the eye of our Master sinners."[15] Tertullian devoted a whole treatise to convincing his wife not to remarry after his death.[16] But one should not think Tertullian was in the majority. Here is the advice of gentle Hermas regarding the case of remarriage: "And again

I asked him, saying, 'Sir, since you have been so patient in listening to me, will you show me this also?' 'Speak,' said he. And I said, 'If a wife or husband die, and the widower or widow marry, does he or she commit sin?' 'There is no sin in marrying again,' said he; 'but if they remain unmarried, they gain greater honor and glory with the Lord; but if they marry, they do not sin." [17] Hermas and Tertullian had basically the same position, but Tertullian, as was his wont, wrote more forcefully. The basic position was that if your spouse died, you could remarry if you wanted, but it would be better if you remained unmarried at that point.

Two sticky cases troubled the early Church's absolute prohibition on divorce: cases of adultery and cases where a convert was married to an obdurate pagan who would not accept Christianity. In both cases, the prohibition on divorce remained. On the first case, Hermas recorded the following dialogue with the angel that visited him:

> I said to him, "Sir, if any one has a wife who trusts in the Lord, and if he detect her in adultery, does the man sin if he continue to live with her?" And he said, "The husband should put her away, and remain by himself. But if he puts his wife away and marry another, he also commits adultery." And I said to him, "What if the woman put away should repent, and wish to return to her husband: shall she not be taken back by her husband?" And he said to me, "Assuredly. If the husband does not take her back, he sins, and brings a great sin upon himself, for he ought to take back the sinner who has repented." [18]

The second case, the case where the husband or wife was an obstinate pagan, was even more difficult, since husbands could bring legal proceedings against their wives and have them put to death if they wished. Wives could also cause considerable trouble for their husbands if they wished. The general rule was laid down by Saint Paul: "If any brother has a wife who is an unbeliever, and she consents to live with him, he should not divorce her. If any woman has a husband who is an unbeliever, and he consents to live with her, she should not divorce him. For the unbelieving husband is consecrated through his wife, and the unbelieving wife is consecrated through her husband. Otherwise, your children would be unclean, but as it is, they are holy." [19]

Contrary to popular belief, the early Christians did not have a negative view of human sexuality. They lived in a culture where sexual excesses were the norm, where young girls were married at puberty so they would not lose their virginity before marriage. Prostitution, promiscuous orgies, homosexuality, abortion, and child abandonment were all quite common. Some Christians engaged in these acts themselves before their conversion. After discussing Christians who had lived chastely all their lives, Justin Martyr added, "What shall I say, too, of the countless multitude of those who have reformed intemperate habits, and learned these things?"[20]

No one can live an intemperate lifestyle for very long and avoid emotional, physical, and spiritual injury. The Christian lifestyle of chastity and temperance was a cure for those suffering from these wounds and preventative medicine for those who had not yet fallen into worldly ways. Seen in this light, certain passages from the Fathers can be understood in a more positive light. They did not hate sexuality and marriage (indeed, some of them were married), but they understood that every act of sexual intercourse has serious and lasting consequences on those who engage in them. The goal of the Fathers was to maximize the good of human sexuality and minimize sinful relations, which have negative consequences. Many modern commentators have misunderstood the writers of the early Church because of erroneous modern attitudes on the subject of sexual morality.

In order to illustrate these modern misconceptions about the early Church on this subject, let me quote at length from the modern author Willy Rordorf, who includes within his analysis a quote from Clement of Alexandria intended to illustrate his point. In fact, properly understood, the quote does not aid Rordorf's argument but contradicts it, as we shall see:

> From this one phrase alone one can deduce a good part of the marriage ethics of Clement of Alexandria. *All who seek pleasure in marriage are condemned* [emphasis added]. "Marriage for others may find its meaning in voluptuous joy," says he, "but for those who practice philosophy, marriage finds its meaning in accordance with the Logos, because it teaches husbands not to treat their wives as lovers by dishonouring their bodies, but to preserve marriage as an aid for the whole of life and for the excellence of virtue and temperance. Much more precious, it would seem to me, than the sowing of wheat and barley thrown upon the earth at the seasonable time is the fruit of that human sowing. In this regard, that farmer is best who scatters his seed with sobriety."[21]

Notice that Professor Rordorf is convinced that for Clement, "All who seek pleasure in marriage are condemned." But nowhere in the writing he quotes does Clement *say* any such thing. What does Clement really say? First, he says that for the true Christian, marriage does not consist of "voluptuous joy". This phrase seems to refer to more than merely enjoying intercourse with your wife. Clement is really opposed to two things: (1) the dishonor that wives experience when they are used solely as a means of sexual gratification and (2) the separation of intercourse from procreation, which was widespread in the Roman world and was, in the mind of one modern scholar, partly responsible for the decline of the Roman Empire.[22] But Clement clearly loved the institution of marriage in itself and was concerned that it be preserved as "an aid for the whole of life" and for inculcating "the excellence of virtue and temperance".

It would be inaccurate to say that the early Church was opposed to marriage. To the contrary, it was always understood that the majority of Christians would marry. Ignatius of Antioch had the following teachings regarding marriage in his letter to Polycarp:

> Speak to my sisters, that they love the Lord, and be satisfied with their husbands both in the flesh and spirit. In like manner also, exhort my brethren, in the name of Jesus Christ, that they love their wives, even as the Lord the Church. If any one can continue in a state of purity, to the honor of Him who is Lord of the flesh, let him so remain without boasting. If he begins to boast, he is undone; and if he reckons himself greater than the bishop, he is ruined. But it becomes both men and women who marry, to form their union with the approval of the bishop, that their marriage may be according to God, and not after their own lust.[23]

It should be borne in mind that this letter, written around A.D. 107, was addressed to a fellow bishop. Ignatius assumes that physical satisfaction is a part of marriage, which is why he urges husbands and wives to be satisfied with one another. Celibacy is considered an option only for those capable of maintaining that state without succumbing to spiritual pride.

Ignatius also was concerned that those considering marriage first gain the approval of their bishop. I see no reason not to accept Ignatius' stated reason for this rule. Marriage is such an important step in a Christian's life that it is important not to marry for the wrong reason.

At that time, the Church was much smaller, and the bishops functioned on the same scale as a parish priest does today. The bishop would have been the spiritual advisor of his flock, with a personal knowledge of most of them, so he would have been in a good position to give advice on marriage.

Mixed marriages in particular were problematic and required sound spiritual judgment. On the one hand, mixed marriages were a good source of converts. In 1 Peter 3:1, the apostle assumes that many marriages will be mixed: "Likewise you wives, be submissive to your husbands, so that some, though they do not obey the word, may be won over without a word by the behavior of their wives." [24]

On the other hand, marriages with unbelievers carried two related dangers: (1) the pagan spouse might weaken the faith of the Christian spouse, or (2) in certain extreme cases, the pagan spouse might object to Christianity so strongly that he would turn his own spouse in to the authorities. These two considerations account for almost all of the opposition to mixed marriages found in the writings of the early Church. Tertullian, for instance, harshly criticized mixed marriages, in terms that might incline one to conclude that only whores would marry pagans, but his real concern, couched in harsh rhetoric, was for the spiritual well-being of those who were tempted to marry pagans: "What am I to fasten on as the cause of this madness [the desire of a Christian woman to marry a pagan man], except the weakness of faith, ever prone to the concupiscence of worldly joys?" [25]

There is one final question we can address from the early Church literature on marriage. Did the early Christians have Church weddings? The answer to this question would appear to be yes and no. No, in the sense that the Church's wedding liturgy did not develop until the fourth and fifth centuries. [26]

But the Church was indeed interested in marriage in the first three centuries, as the numerous references we have already provided attest. Christians went through the secular process necessary to make sure spouses and children would be protected by the law, but there were also Christian ceremonies associated with marriage.

Marriage is mentioned in the New Testament. In John 2, the apostle records that Jesus attended a wedding feast and changed water into wine. Catholic theologians have traditionally interpreted this passage as Jesus instituting the sacrament of marriage. Some modern scholars disagree, but the Greek word John used to describe the whole event is *semeia*,[27] which indicates "a sign that points to a deeper reality".[28] (The definition of *semeia* is, in fact, quite similar to a modern definition of a sacrament.)[29] At Cana Jesus performed a symbolic act that pointed to a deeper reality behind the act, and it is highly significant that Jesus did this at a wedding.

Similarly, in Ephesians 5:32, Saint Paul writes, "This [marriage] is a great mystery, and I mean in reference to Christ and the Church." Paul is saying here that the love of a man and woman in marriage is a sign of Christ's love for the Church. The Greek word he uses to describe the sign is *mysterion*, which is translated by the RSV as "mystery". However, *mysterion* is best translated into English as "a secret religious teaching or rite".[30] When Jerome translated *mysterion* from Greek into Latin, he chose the word *sacramentum*, which originally referred to a soldier's oath, but in Christian usage was associated with the seven sacraments.[31] With Jerome's translation in mind, let us reread Ephesians 5:32. We might read it, "This [marriage] is a great sacrament, and I am applying it to Christ and the Church."

Paul's usual practice was to write about marriage in practical terms, so we have great difficulty in discovering what rituals might have been associated with it in his mind. We do know, however, that in first-century Judaism there were seven marriage blessings found in various Jewish prayer books: (1) a vine blessing, (2) a blessing for creation, (3) a blessing for the creation of human beings, (4) a supplication for Zion, (5) a supplication for the couple, (6) blessings for the joy of the married couple, and (7) a long blessing for married life.[32] We do not possess a similar list of wedding blessings in the literature of the early Church, but the wedding blessing found in the Gregorian Sacramentary (late sixth century) is remarkably similar to the Jewish blessings discussed above.[33]

What happened in between the first and the sixth centuries? Are we to suppose that Jesus personally attended weddings, and in the sixth century the Church blessed marriages, but in between the Church had no presence in the marriage of Christians? The idea is not credible. In fact, there are four distinct pieces of evidence regarding the wedding practices of the early Church.

1. As already mentioned, in his letter to Polycarp, Ignatius of Antioch wrote that Christians should not marry without

permission from their bishop. This passage indicates that the Church had an interest in marriage from the start.

2. In *To His Wife*, Tertullian spoke of the wedding practices of the Church in the following terms: "Whence are we to find words enough fully to tell the happiness of that marriage which the Church cements, and the oblation confirms, and the benediction signs and seals; which angels carry back the news of to heaven, which the Father holds ratified? For even on earth children do not rightly and lawfully wed without their father's consent." [34] In North Africa, at least at the beginning of the third century, there was an oblation (the Eucharist?) and a blessing associated with weddings.

3. In the apocryphal *Acts of Thomas*, we read that the Apostle Thomas attended a pagan wedding, anointing the groom and giving a blessing for the groom. [35] Elements mentioned in the *Acts of Thomas* that provide clues for the wedding practices of this period are the oil with which Thomas anointed the groom, the crown on the bride's head, seven bridesmaids and seven groomsmen, and the wedding feast. [36]

4. In the art in the catacombs, there are a handful of artistic renditions of Christian weddings. Here is what one standard work on the catacombs has to say: "In a fragment of a sarcophagus of the Villa Albani, Christ is seen behind the bride and groom, who have joined their hands together. Over the head of each of them, our Lord holds a crown." [37]

From these fragments of evidence, we can see that there must have been specifically Christian ceremonies to go with the legal obsequies. We do not have enough information to reconstruct fully the wedding liturgy of the first three centuries, but we can make some general statements. In the third century, nuptial blessings took place within the Church. The minister placed crowns on the heads of the couple, then laid hands on the couple and blessed them both. The blessing was followed by a eucharistic celebration. [38] The passage from Tertullian, the admittedly odd passage in the *Acts of Thomas*, and the funerary artwork described above all point to the same set of practices in the third century. Beyond this, we have no window into the early Church's practices regarding weddings. I can only suggest as a general rule of thumb that the closer one gets to the first century, the more Christian weddings must have looked like Jewish weddings of the same period.

## Children

The early Christians were adamant that sexual activity must be open to the possibility of conception. From this fact, we can deduce that children must have been greatly valued. There is clear and ample evidence in the New Testament that Jesus loved children and wanted his disciples to love them also. Mark 10:13–16, for instance, tells us: "And they were bringing children to him, that he might touch them; and the disciples rebuked them. But when Jesus saw it he was indignant, and said to them, 'Let the children come to me, do not hinder them; for to such belongs the kingdom of God. Truly, I say to you, whoever does not receive the kingdom of God like a child shall not enter it.' And he took them in his arms and blessed them, laying his hands upon them." The story is revelatory on many levels. First of all, it was the parents who brought their children to Jesus. The disciples, meaning well, tried to keep them away. Jesus insisted the children should be allowed to come to him, and then he blessed them. But there is a further point to consider. When children are introduced to Jesus in the Gospels, Jesus shows them great attention and favor, but inevitably he talks to the adults present about their responsibility to children.[39]

Apart from Mark 5:41, where Jesus speaks briefly to Jairus' daughter, there is no record in the New Testament of Jesus speaking directly to children. Instead, he seems to have concentrated on teaching adults what their responsibilities to children were. One thinks, for instance, of Luke 17:1–2: "And he said to his disciples, 'Temptations to sin are sure to come; but woe to him by whom they come! It would be better for him if a millstone were hung round his neck and he were cast into the sea, than that he should cause one of these little ones to sin.' "

Normally, in Jesus' dealing with children, the parents would speak for their children, and in some cases the parent's proclamation of faith was decisive in the healing of the child. Consider, for instance, Mark 9:14–29. The whole scene hinges on verse 24, where the child's father cries out, "I believe; help my unbelief!" After this declaration, Jesus casts out the evil spirit that inhabited the boy. Consider also Luke 7:1–10, where the centurion intervenes on behalf of his servant. It is the centurion's faith, not the slave's, which is decisive in bringing about the cure.[40]

What are we to make of these passages? I think we can infer that for Jesus the role of parents in the faith formation of their children was crucial and should be allowed to work itself out, even in times of crisis. Parents are to mediate the relationship between children and God, particularly in times of distress, and parents are the primary teachers of faith to their children.

We will return to this point later, but before exploring the religious education of children, two other facets of Jesus' attitude toward children need at least a brief mention: (1) Jesus frequently told his disciples to become more like children: "Truly, I say to you, unless you turn and become like children, you will never enter the kingdom of heaven. Whoever humbles himself like this child, he is the greatest in the kingdom of heaven." [41] Jesus wanted his followers to take on the attitude of children, humble, dependent, and willing to learn. (2) Jesus realized that sometimes it would be necessary for people to renounce their biological families for the sake of the Kingdom.[42] But, as one commentator has pointed out, these passages are few and isolated: "In the light of the gospels' whole presentation, we must recognize that Jesus was not attempting to destroy the family." [43]

Given that Jesus was a champion of the family as the place where faith was introduced and allowed to grow, how did the early Church carry out this high calling? Did the leadership support families? Did the Church provide religious education classes for children or have something similar to the parochial school system, where children could learn secular as well as religious subjects?

We have already discussed the baptism of children and concluded the early Church did baptize children in certain circumstances. What about the other sacraments? Did children receive the Eucharist or confess their sins?

We must start by pointing out that children were present in the Church from the start, as the following references will attest:

1. In Acts 21:5, we read that when Paul and his companions left Tyre to progress to Jerusalem, "all of them [the local Christians], with wives and children, escorted us outside the city."

2. In 1 Corinthians 7:14, a passage we discussed earlier in this chapter, Paul tells his followers, "For the unbelieving husband is consecrated through his wife, and the unbelieving wife is consecrated through her husband. Otherwise, your children would be unclean, but as it is they are holy."

3. In Acts 20:7–12, a boy named Eutychus falls asleep during Paul's homily and falls out the window.[44]

4. When Pliny wrote to Emperor Trajan about the presence of Christians in his province (in 112), he wrote that "a great many individuals of every age and class, both men and women", were infected with the contagion.[45]

How did Christians pass on the faith to their children? In the very first communities, it is evident that children worshipped with the general congregation and received instruction with everyone else. We know this because children are included in the "household codes" mentioned earlier. Colossians 3:18—4:1 is an example of one of the earliest teachings to families. Verse 3:20 contains an admonition to children to obey their parents. The very next verse tells fathers not to provoke their children, "lest they lose hope". Paul's Letter to the Colossians was clearly meant to be read during public assemblies; Colossians 4:16 reads: "When this letter has been read among you, have it read also in the church of the Laodiceans." The "household codes", along with the rest of the teachings in this letter, were meant to be taught to everyone in the community, including the children.

In the *Didache*, we find an admonition not to spare the rod, and to teach sons and daughters "the fear of the Lord".[46] Polycarp wrote that husbands should teach their wives "to train up their children in the knowledge and fear of God".[47]

Just how Christian parents trained their children is an open question. Discipline appears to have been neither harsher nor milder than that of pagans, taking all things into consideration.[48] Christians do not appear to have had special schools. Instead, Christian students appear to have studied in pagan schools along with non-Christians. Tertullian, that fierce separatist, quoted approvingly the following argument: "How do we repudiate secular studies, without which divine studies cannot be pursued?"[49]

From Eusebius we gain the following valuable information regarding Origen's education:

> This may be recorded as the first evidence of Origen's youthful wisdom and of his genuine love for piety. For even then he had stored up no small resources in the words of the faith, having been trained in the Divine Scriptures from childhood. And he had not studied them with indifference, for his father, besides giving him the usual liberal education, had made them a matter of no secondary importance. First of all, before inducting him into the Greek sciences, he drilled him in sacred studies, requiring him to learn and recite every day. Nor was this irksome to the boy, but he was eager and diligent in these studies. And he was not satisfied with learning what was simple and obvious in the sacred words, but sought for something more, and even at that age busied himself with deeper speculations.[50]

The important point here is that Origen's father taught him Scripture in the morning, then sent him off to study "Greek sciences", probably a reference to the classics of Greek literature, geometry, mathematics, and basic philosophical systems. Origen does not appear to have suffered from these studies, and even approved the same course of studies for his own students: "When he perceived that any persons had superior intelligence he instructed them also in philosophic branches—in geometry, arithmetic, and other preparatory studies—and then advanced to the systems of the philosophers and explained their writings."[51]

Of course, Origen was highly intelligent, and his educational background may not have been typical. But the basic principle held true. Both Tertullian and Origen testify that Christian students learned the same secular subjects as their pagan neighbors and had Christian studies in the home, either before or after their secular studies.

We have seen that children were sometimes baptized in the early Church, and that practice was believed to have gone back to the time of the apostles. What about other sacraments, specifically the Eucharist? We have no direct evidence until the time of Cyprian of Carthage. But, as one author pointed out, there would be no reason to withhold Communion from children if they were baptized. Paul referred to Jesus as "our Passover lamb" in 1 Corinthians 5:7. Children participated in the Jewish Passover meal, so there would be no reason for Paul to keep children from the Eucharist.

The problem is that the early Christians felt no need to write one way or another on this subject, so we have no data, until we have accidental data from Cyprian of Carthage. In *On the Lapsed*, in a section in which Cyprian is attempting to paint a picture of the spiritual agony of the lapsed, we read the following:

Some parents who by chance were escaping, being little careful on account of their terror, left a little daughter under the care of a wet-nurse. The nurse gave up the forsaken child to the magistrates. They gave it, in the presence of an idol whither the people flocked (because it was not yet able to eat flesh on account of its years), bread mingled with wine, which however itself was the remainder of what had been used in the immolation of those that had perished. Subsequently the mother recovered her child. But the girl was no more able to speak, or to indicate the crime that had been committed, than she had before been able to understand or to prevent it. Therefore it happened unawares in their ignorance, that when we were sacrificing, the mother brought it in with her. Moreover, the girl mingled with the saints, became impatient of our prayer and supplications, and was at one moment shaken with weeping, and at another tossed about like a wave of the sea by the violent excitement of her mind; as if by the compulsion of a torturer the soul of that still tender child confessed a consciousness of the fact with such signs as it could. When, however, the solemnities were finished, and the deacon began to offer the cup to those present, and when, as the rest received it, its turn approached, the little child, by the instinct of the divine majesty, turned away its face, compressed its mouth with resisting lips, and refused the cup. Still the deacon persisted, and, although against her efforts, forced on her some of the sacrament of the cup. Then there followed a sobbing and vomiting.[52]

This story is simple: a child was forced to take bread and wine at a pagan sacrifice, then returned to her Christian parents. The parents took the child to a eucharistic celebration, where the deacon attempted to give the child some of the consecrated Wine, but the child, upset by her previous experience, vomited it up. The story is somewhat horrifying to us today, but it is illustrative of some practices of the early Church. The deacon obviously was accustomed routinely to give children the Eucharist and was not conscious that there was any reason he should not do so in this case.

The *Constitutions of the Holy Apostles*, a fourth-century document, actually has stipulations for the order in which Communion is to be received: "Let the bishop partake, then the presbyters, and deacons, and sub-deacons, and the readers, and the singers, and the ascetics; and then of the women, the deaconesses, and the virgins, and the widows; then the children; and then all the people in order, with reverence and godly fear, without tumult." [53] Children were definitely allowed to receive Communion, in a group before their parents.

We have little information about other aspects of children's lives. We know that the martyr Perpetua nursed her baby while in prison: "I suckled my child, which was now enfeebled with hunger." [54] This might seem like a small point, but pagan women of her class rarely nursed their own children. They used wet-nurses, usually slaves, to nurse their children for them.

Perhaps we can infer from this incident that Christians had a different standard of child rearing than their pagan neighbors. However, we cannot infer that Christians loved their children more than the pagans. The love of children is intrinsic to human nature. But it is equally true that some people take better care of their children than others. It would seem that the Christians were encouraged to take more personal care of their children than their well-off pagan neighbors, who were inclined to hand off such duties to slaves.

### Abortion

Christians' care for their children extended into two areas of vulnerable human life: the life of the unborn and the lives of children unwanted by their parents. In the ancient world, both abortion and infanticide before the eighth day of life were extremely common. In the case of abortions, both abortifacient drugs and surgical implements were used for abortions, though some authorities opposed the use of sharp instruments because it was too dangerous. [55]

The early Church was strong and united in her opposition to abortion. One cannot find a single Christian author willing to defend the practice, but you can find plenty who found the act morally repugnant. Some modern scholars appear confused as to exactly why the early Christians were so opposed to abortion, since, they claim, the

New Testament is silent on the subject. But, as we shall see, the New Testament might not have been as silent as these persons suppose.

Certainly, the Old Testament was not ambiguous on the subject. Numerous passages attest to the belief that God himself was responsible for the life in the womb; he formed the child in the womb and had a plan for that child's life.[56] The one passage in the Old Testament that is sometimes used as a justification for abortion is Exodus 21:22, which reads, "When men strive together, and hurt a woman with child, so that there is a miscarriage, and yet no harm follows, the one who hurt her shall be fined, according as the woman's husband shall lay upon him; and he shall pay as the judges determine." The idea here is that causing a miscarriage is not as great a crime as murder, so the rule "a life for a life" does not apply.

There are two reasons why this passage had no influence on Jewish opposition to abortion: (1) The passage as it stands is ambiguous. The lack of premeditation might be the mitigating factor in this case, not a lower valuation on the life of the unborn child. (2) In the Septuagint, a Greek translation of the Old Testament, verse 23 reads that life is given for life if the embryo is formed. Since the early Christians primarily read the Septuagint, not the original Hebrew, their inclination to honor life in the womb was strengthened, not weakened, by this passage.

In the New Testament, there are more than a few passages that indicate that God has a strong interest in the life in the womb. In Luke 1:40, the infant in Elizabeth's womb leaps when Mary approaches. In Luke 1:42, Elizabeth exclaims, "Blessed is the fruit of your womb." In Matthew 1:19, when Joseph learns of Mary's unexpected pregnancy, he decides to divorce Mary quietly rather than have her stoned for adultery or force her to have an abortion.

These passages speak to a general respect for unborn life, but there might be some more specific references to abortion in the New Testament that we have not properly understood. In Galatians 5:19–21, Paul condemns what he calls "the works of the flesh" (v. 19). Among these works of the flesh is something the RSV translates as "sorcery" (v. 20). But the word translated as "sorcery" is *pharmakeia*, a word that primarily refers to the use and administration of drugs, poisoning, and, only thirdly, sorcery.[57]

If Paul were referring to the administration of drugs, what could he mean here? Remember that there were two main methods of procuring abortions in the ancient world: through the administration of drugs that would force the expulsion of the fetus, and the use of sharp surgical instruments. The second method was not favored because it frequently led to the perforation of the uterus and the subsequent death of the mother. So the primary means of procuring an abortion in the first century was the administration of drugs, *pharmakeia*, which is exactly what Paul was condemning, right after he condemned "fornication, impurity, licentiousness, idolatry".[58]

One finds the same terminology used in Revelation 9:21, which reads, "They did not repent of their murders or their sorceries [*pharmanon*] or their thefts", and 22:15, "outside are the dogs and sorcerers [*pharmanol*] and fornicators and murderers and idolaters, and everyone who loves and practices falsehood."

Since there are three definitions of *pharmakeia*, and the renowned scholars who have created the modern translations of the New Testament are virtually unanimous in translating it as "sorcerer" in the passages mentioned above, one might be forgiven for wondering why I even bring this point up. Why do I think *pharmakeia* should be understood as the giving of a drug to procure an abortion? The answer is that this is exactly the way the word is used in early Christian literature outside the New Testament. *Pharmakeia* is linked with abortion quite unambiguously in the following passages:

1. The *Didache* reads: "You shall not kill. You shall not commit adultery. You shall not corrupt boys. You shall not fornicate. You shall not steal. You shall not make magic. You shall not practice *pharmakeia*. You shall not slay the child by abortions [*phthora*] You shall not kill what is generated. You shall not desire your neighbor's wife." [59] What was wrong with dispensing drugs? Did the early Christians have a problem with the practice of medicine? The answer must be no. Very early, we find the story that Saint Luke was a doctor, and we find that no opprobrium was attached to that fact. It is revealing that *pharmakeia* is mentioned right before *phthora*, which was the technical term for abortion in Greek. It is also revealing that *pharmakeia* is mentioned in the same context as adultery, fornication, lust, and the like.

   One might object that in this passage the ban on *pharmakeia* comes right after the ban on magic. But "magic" and "sorcery" are virtually synonymous, and it makes little sense to suppose that the same act would be forbidden twice. *Pharmakeia* and *phthora*, on the other hand, are two different acts. *Pharmakeia* refers to the act of the abortionist. And *phthora* refers to the decision of the woman.

2. The *Epistle of Barnabas*, which is basically a commentary on the *Didache*, reads, "You shall love your neighbor more than your own life. You shall not slay the child with abortions. You shall not kill what is generated." [60]

3. The clearest link between *pharmakeia* (the administering of drugs) and *phthora* (abortion) is found in the words of Clement of Alexandria, who declared that Christians do not "take away human nature, which is generated from the providence of God, by hastening abortions and applying abortifacient drugs [*phthoriois pharmakois*]". [61]

4. Minucius Felix, a lover of children, records the following: "There are some women who, by drinking medical preparations, extinguish the source of the future man in their very bowels, and thus commit a parricide before they bring forth." [62]

These passages are, I think, sufficient to demonstrate my point. In the minds of the early Christians, *pharmakeia* was linked to a specific type of abortion, which involved the taking of drugs. It seems reasonable to think that the passages in Galatians and Revelation are referring to this type of abortion, since nowhere in the writings of the early Church do we have a condemnation of the practice of medicine for the accomplishment of good.

Despite the frequent condemnations, there were some Christian women who evidently resorted to abortions. Hippolytus, who was probably mistaken in his interpretation of the role of Pope Callistus I, thought that his teachings were responsible for abortions among Christian women:

For even also he [Callistus] permitted females, if they were unwedded, and burned with passion at an age at all events unbecoming, or if they were not disposed to overturn their own dignity through a legal marriage, that they might have whomsoever they would choose as a bedfellow, whether a slave or free, and that a woman, though not legally married, might consider such a companion as a husband. Whence women, reputed believers, began to resort to drugs for producing sterility, and to gird themselves round, so to expel what was being conceived on account of their not wishing to have a child either by a slave or by any paltry fellow, for the sake of their family and excessive wealth. Behold, into how great impiety that lawless one has proceeded, by inculcating adultery and murder at the same time![63]

Behind Hippolytus' ugly interpretation of events, one can discern the truth of the matter. Pope Callistus I, in an act of pastoral charity, allowed the Christian women of Rome to marry men of a lower class. In Roman law, these marriages were illegal, but in the eyes of the Church, they were legal. Hippolytus is charging that the women, in an attempt to hide their illegal marriages, resorted to birth control and even abortion. We know that Hippolytus hated Callistus and lost no opportunity to misrepresent events, but, human nature being what it is, there might have been a few cases where something like this happened.

If these cases happened, they must have been few. Some of the apologists defended Christians against the charge of infanticide by observing that it was well known that Christians would not even condone abortions, much less the slaying of a born child. Athenagorus of Athens wrote, "When we say that those women who use drugs to bring on abortion commit murder, and will have to give an account to God for the abortion, on what principle should we commit murder?"[64] Athenagorus did not argue that Christians opposed abortion; rather, he asserted it, with the expectation that his audience of convinced pagans would accept his assertion on face value. Everyone knew the Christians opposed abortion.

### Conclusion

There are many other aspects of Christian family life we would like to know about, but have no information. We know that many Christians married, but we can only partially reconstruct the ceremony. Most aspects of daily married life remain hidden from us. Regarding children, we know they were loved and wanted, and that some wealthy

Christian women nursed their own children. We know that Christian children went to secular schools to learn what they needed to know to live, while receiving religious education at home. We are amazed that it did not occur to the early Christians to establish their own schools.

The early Christians were strongly opposed to abortion and contraception, on the grounds that the life in the womb was a gift from God. Some authors criticized Christian women for engaging in these practices, so we know some Christian women sinned in these ways. But they would have been in the minority, since everyone knew of the Christian opposition to abortion.

All in all, the picture is edifying. Christian homes must have been warm and loving, though discipline could sometimes be stern. Let us close by taking a look at a passage from Justin's *First Apology*, a passage we considered before, but from a different angle: "Many, both men and women, who have been Christ's disciples from childhood, remain pure at the age of sixty or seventy years; and I boast that I could produce such from every race of men." [65] Justin is writing here about celibacy, but the principle holds true for all Christians. Young men and women were being raised in the faith, and they were remaining true to their calling for their entire life. Christian families in the first three centuries were successful in raising children who were capable of living their faith in the harsh and unforgiving Roman world.

# CONCLUSION

In A.D. 313, the storms of persecution that periodically engulfed the Church for almost three hundred years finally began to recede. By 320, the Church was free throughout the Roman Empire. The thunder and lightning of persecution disappeared, for a time, over the horizon. The winds of scorn and the waves of opprobrium slowly began to die down. And everywhere, Christians began to emerge from their basements, blinking in the sunlight, and they went to work, building new churches, displaying Christian art publicly for the first time, and holding councils of bishops openly. The fourth century, which began with despair and tumult, became a time of hope and growth for the Church.

You can still see signs of the growth of the Church in some of the archaeological sites of the Mediterranean. In the spring of 2004, I walked the ruins of ancient Aphrodisias. Right next to the temple of Aphrodite, you can see the outline of the fourth-century Christian basilica. Aphrodisias eventually became such a strongly Christian city that its name was changed to Stavropol, the "city of the Cross". You can see signs of Christianity emerging everywhere, all at once, in the fourth century. In Sardis, shopkeepers along the main street had crosses carved into the hearthstones of their shops, proud to proclaim their faith to everyone. In Ephesus, formerly the city of Artemis the Great, a cross was carved over the doorway into the council house. The city fathers were happy to tell the whole world that Christ would inspire their deliberations.

You can still see these things today if you take a tour of the archaeological ruins of Turkey. As you sit among the ruins, it is perhaps easy to forget that there were once people living out their lives in thriving cities that took hundreds of years to build. They were not so different than us. They needed food, water, and shelter. They enjoyed entertainment and the company of friends and hoped for a good, happy life. However, deep within their souls, they longed for the love of God.

Unless you understand this about the ancients, you will not understand how Christianity came to triumph in the Roman world. The people of the empire had succeeded in keeping their enemies out for over four hundred years. They had achieved a level of material comfort that was not reached again until the sixteenth century. But these material advances were gained on the backs of slaves, through the blood and tears of others.

For all its greatness, the empire was flawed. Its flaws were moral in nature, and the people must have sensed that one day someone would have to pay for their crimes. They may have been in dread of that day. So when they learned of a religion that told people they could repent of their sins, be washed clean, and live a better life from then on, people responded.

On an individual level, people changed, and that change was reflected, however imperfectly, in society. In the course of the fourth and fifth centuries, the gladiatorial combat and the bloody animal hunts ended, and the chariot races became the primary form of entertainment. Slavery gradually died out, though too slowly for our comfort today.[1]

The first three centuries of the Church's existence can be seen as a massive confrontation between two cultures, or more precisely, a confrontation between an entrenched culture and a vision of a new culture. The confrontation occurred intermittently, on many different fronts. For example, there was the intellectual front, on which apologists sought, mostly in vain, to convince the pagan elites at least to let the Christians exist in peace.

Historians frequently discuss the reasons why Christianity triumphed in the Roman Empire. The ones usually cited are (1) the weaknesses of the pagan religious system, (2) the widespread misery and poverty of the empire, (3) the bankruptcy of the Roman political and legal system, (4) social and economic pressures, (5) the willing self-immolation of the martyrs, and (6) the promise of the resurrection, which brought hope to the darkness of life in the empire.

With some variations, this list has been around for a long time. I would suggest some modifications. First, while I agree that paganism was a false religion, I do not think it could be classified as "weak", if by weak one means lacking in sincere believers or the ability to provide what people want from a religion. Paganism's great weakness was that it provided a false vision of reality, but most people did not know that and found it perfectly acceptable.

I also doubt that misery and poverty were any greater then than they are now. The difference is that poverty and misery were more evenly diffused. In the ancient world, you had rich and poor living together in the same city. Those inclined to do so could see and help the poor. In the modern world, the poor are sometimes invisible to most people in wealthy nations. When one travels through the Mediterranean world, one is struck by the ease with which food is grown in most places. The Romans had food, water, and their own technology. We may look at conditions in the ancient world and imagine they would be unbearable, but the ancients put up with them, simply because they were used to those conditions.

Items three, four, and five get no argument from me. The Roman political system was frequently in chaos, with the army creating half of the emperors, many of whom reigned for no more than a few years. Under these conditions, continuity of policy was impossible. The Roman legal system was rife with corruption and injustice. The martyrs' opposition to that injustice was powerful, and indeed played a major role in the conversion of the peoples of the empire.

With item six, we face some ambiguity. The Greco-Roman world was full of cults to gods and goddesses who died, but were somehow restored to life. Many of these cults promised some kind of personal immortality and, in that sense, offered hope to those who needed it. So if Christianity can be said to offer something the pagan religions did not, one must say that the Christian faith had to be perceived as *true* on a level that the pagan myths were not.

Imagine what must have happened the first time a Christian missionary moved into a pagan community that had not heard of Christ before. The missionary would have explained that Jesus lived in Galilee, "suffered under Pontius Pilate, was crucified, died, and . . . rose again from the dead."[2] His pagan audience would not have been surprised by the story in general, but the specifics would have intrigued them. These events occurred in recent history—when Augustus was emperor and Pontius Pilate was procurator of Judea. Who could say when Isis died and came back to life, or when Mithras slayed the bull? But the Christians claimed there were eyewitnesses who saw Jesus dead, then saw him alive again, eating fish just like anyone else.

So it would appear that the sixth point must be modified. Apostolic succession, in the sense of the orderly handing on of the "chain of evidence", was more important than many think. The chain of witnesses began with those who had personally seen the risen Christ. We see the beginning of this passing on of the tradition in 1 Corinthians 15:3–8. In this passage, Paul was careful to indicate the names of as many eyewitnesses as possible.

The one thing paganism could not claim was eyewitnesses. No one could name anyone who was present when Athena was born. In this sense, there was a certain amount of willful playacting involved in pagan religiosity. But Christianity always had its feet firmly planted on the ground. The claims of the eyewitnesses insured that the Christians mingled this worldly reality with their theological speculations.

It was this need for a connection with the eyewitnesses that insured the rise of the idea of apostolic succession, not some putative will-to-power on the part of some renegade bishops. (The idea is laughable. Second- and third-century bishops plotting and scheming for the privilege of . . . being thrown to the lions?) The ancient world was full of mythmakers, half-poet and half-philosopher, who could make up charming, moving stories that would become the foundation of new religions. The apostles and their successors were not of that ilk. They refused to make up new stories about Christ. When the Gnostics, the Valentinians, and others tried to do so, it was the apostolic authority of the bishops that prevented Christianity from degenerating into another Greco-Roman cult.

If I were making a list of reasons for the success of the early Church against her pagan adversaries, the fact that the Church had bishops would be high on that list. But there is another little-known factor that weighed heavily in the survival and eventual victory of the early Church. Cultural wars are won on the level of ordinary people, and the ordinary Christians of the first three centuries were quite extraordinary. They lived out the vocations God gave them with quiet strength, fulfilling their duties to Church, family, and neighbor. Pagans mocked them for their "naïve" charity, but at the end of the age, when the emperor Julian wanted to bring about a pagan revival, he tried (unsuccessfully) to get the pagans to take care of the poor and sick the way the Christians did.

The hundreds of ordinary Christians became thousands, then millions as the Church spread. Christianity has experienced times when it seemed on the verge of disaster, but it is constantly bursting into new life in unexpected places. Perhaps the love of Christ will diminish in some places where church bells long have rung. Perhaps these places will be reevangelized by new Christians from young cultures. The only thing we know for sure is that Christ, who conquered death, has assured us that even the gates of hell will not prevail against his Church. And in our times we can learn much from the early Church, which survived and grew despite being in a hostile culture.

# APPENDIX A

## The Roman Religious Calendar

| January 1 | New Year |
|---|---|
| February 13–24 | *Parentalia* |
| February 15 | *Lupercalia* |
| February 17 | *Quirinalia* |
| February 24 | *Regifugium* |
| February 27 | *Equirria* |

**Month of War and Agriculture**

| March 6 | Anniversary of Vejovis |
|---|---|
| March 17 | *Liberalia* |
| March 19–23 | *Quinquatrus* |
| March 23 | *Tubilustrium* |

**Month of Female Preeminence**

| April 1 | *Aprilis* |
|---|---|
| April 5 | *Fortuna* |
| April 12–19 | *Cerialia* |
| April 23 | *Vinalia priora* |
| April 25 | *Robigalia* |
| April 28–May 3 | *Floralia* |

**Month of the Ancients**

| May 1 | *Bona Dea* |
|---|---|
| May 9, 11, 13 | Propitiation of the *Lemuria* |

**The Month of Young People**

| June 1 | *Armati Juvenes* |
|---|---|
| June 3 | *Bellona* |
| June 9 | *Vestalia* |
| June 11 | *Matralia* |
| June 15 | *Jupiter Invictus* |
| June 24 | *Fors Fortuna* |

| June 27 | Jupiter Stator |
|---|---|
| July 5 | Poplifugia |
| July 6 | Fortuna Muliebris |
| July 13 | Apollinarian Games |
| July 15 | Transvectio Equitum |
| July 19, 21 | Lucaria |
| July 21 | Neptunalia |
| July 23, 25 | Furrinalia |
| August 9 | Indiges |
| August 13 | Vertumnalia |
| August 17 | Portunalia |
| August 19 | Vinalia Rustica |
| August 21 | Consualia |
| August 23 | Volcanalia |
| August 24 | Mundus Patet |
| August 25 | Opisconsivia |
| August 27 | Volturnalia |
| September 1 | Jupiter Libertas |
| September 4–9 | Ludi Romani |
| September 13 | Banquet to the Capitoline Triad |
| September 20–23 | Anniversary of Several Temples |

**The End of the Campaigning Season**

| October 1 | Tigillum Sororium |
|---|---|
| October 4 | Feast of Ceres |
| October 11 | Meditrinalia |
| October 13 | Fontinalia |
| October 15 | Feast of the October Horse |
| October 19 | Armilustrium |
| Oct. 6–Nov. 1, 4–17 | Circus and Theater Entertainments |
| November 4–17 | Plebeian Games |
| November 13 | Feast of Jupiter (Epulum Jovis) |
| December 3 | Bona Dea |
| December 5 | Faunalia |
| December 11 | Agonalia |
| December 13 | Ceres and Teflus |
| December 15 | Consualia |
| December 17–23 | Saturnalia |
| December 25 | Sol Invictus or Natalis Solis |

# APPENDIX B

## Important Figures in Early Christianity

*Arius* (ca. 250–336). Best known for his heretical position that Christ was subordinate to the Father: "There was a time when the Son was not." He was born and taught in Alexandria, but in 320 he was excommunicated by a synod in Alexandria. In 325 his teachings were rejected by the Council of Nicea, but continued to have influence well into the fifth century.

*Athenagorus* (second century). Wrote one of the earliest apologies for Christianity, dedicated to the emperor Marcus Aurelius.

*Basilides* (second century). A Gnostic teacher in Alexandria. His ideas were opposed by Irenaeus and Hippolytus.

*Cecilia* (second century). Virgin martyr in Sicily in the late second century.

*Clement of Alexandria* (ca. 150–215). Saint and theologian. Born in Athens, he moved to Alexandria, where he headed the famous theological school of that city. His most helpful works are the *Stromateis*, the *Protreptikos*, and the *Paedagogos*. He also wrote commentaries on Scripture and constantly taught against Gnosticism.

*Clement of Rome* (late first century). Saint and fourth Bishop of Rome. He is most famous for two epistles to the Corinthians, the second of which may be incorrectly attributed to him. He also wrote two treatises on virginity.

*Constantine* (ca. 274–337). Emperor. He is most well known for the Edict of Milan, which granted tolerance to Christians. In 325, he convened the Council of Nicea to decide important doctrinal issues. In 330, he moved the capital of the Roman Empire to Constantinople.

*Cyprian of Carthage* (ca. 200–258). Martyr and bishop. He was born in Carthage, became a Christian in 246, and was consecrated bishop of Carthage in 248. He is best known for his controversial position on the rebaptism of heretics. He was martyred in 258 during the Valerian persecution.

327

*Demetrius* (d. ca. 231). Saint and Bishop of Alexandria. He appointed Origen as head of the catechetical school of Alexandria, but later reprimanded him for preaching as a layman.

*Denis* (Dionysius; third century). One of the seven bishops sent from Rome to convert Gaul. He was martyred in Paris, at what later became known as Montmartre.

*Dionysius of Alexandria* (d. ca. 264). A pupil of Origen, he later became head of the catechetical school in Alexandria. In 247, he was consecrated Bishop of Alexandria. During the Decian persecution, he fled into the desert at the urging of his followers. He was opposed to the doctrine of Sabellius. Some have maintained that his teachings influenced the heretic Arius, but Athanasius maintained he was orthodox.

*Eusebius of Caesarea* (ca. 260–ca. 340). Bishop of Caesarea. He is best known as a historian of the early Church. He was a pupil of Pamphilus, who kept a theological school in Caesarea. In his adult life, he was a friend and counselor of Constantine.

*Gregory the Enlightener* (ca. 240–332). Saint, missionary, and bishop. He was a native of Armenia, but spent time in Cappadocia, where he became a Christian. He returned to Armenia, where he converted King Tiridates. He later returned to Cappadocia, where he was consecrated bishop.

*Gregory Thaumaturgus* (Wonderworker; ca. 213–270). Saint, bishop, theologian, and missionary. He was a pupil of Origen. In 238, he was consecrated Bishop of Neocaesarea in Pontus. His ministry was immensely successful, because of his numerous miracles. He turned traditional pagan festivals into Christian feasts and converted large numbers in Pontus. He was the author of a treatise on the Trinity and another work on the teachings of Origen. He combated the heresy of Paul of Samosata.

*Hermas* (early second century). Apostolic Father. Hermas was the author of *The Pastor of Hermas*, a treatise on the Christian life. According to the Muratorian Canon, the author was the brother of Pope Pius I, who died in 154. *The Pastor* was used in the instruction of catechumens well into the fourth century. It stressed the importance of penance and the forgiveness of sins.

*Hippolytus of Rome* (ca. 170–ca. 236). Saint and theologian. Origen heard him preach when he was in Rome for a visit. He was a priest and later a bishop. His major writings were *The Refutation of All Heresies* and *The Apostolic Tradition*. He was estranged from Pope Callistus and even went so far as to set himself up as antipope, but later he was reconciled with

Callistus' successor, Pontian. He was a brilliant man who led a tempes-
tuous life, but in the end he wore a martyr's crown. Legend has it that
he was sentenced to the mines for being a Christian, and there he was
reconciled with Pontian before he died.

*Ignatius of Antioch* (ca. 35–ca. 107). Bishop, theologian, saint, and martyr. Ignatius was Bishop of Antioch. Origen says he was Peter's successor after Peter
moved on to Rome. (Eusebius says Evodius succeeded Peter, and Ignatius
succeeded Evodius.) Ignatius was taken to Rome and martyred in 107. Before
leaving Antioch, he wrote letters to the Churches in Ephesus, Magnesia,
Tralles, Rome, Philadelphia, and Smyrna. He also wrote a letter to his friend
Polycarp. These letters emphasize the threefold ministry of bishop, priest,
and deacon, and the Real Presence of Christ in the Eucharist.

*Irenaeus of Lyons* (ca. 130–ca. 200). Bishop, theologian, and saint. Irenaeus
grew up in Smyrna and heard Polycarp preach as a boy. He moved to
Lyons, where he became a priest. In 177, following a persecution, he
became Bishop of Lyons. His most important writing was *Against Heresies*, a refutation of Gnosticism.

*Justin Martyr* (ca. 100–ca. 165). Saint, martyr, and theologian. He converted to
Christianity in 132, after studying and rejecting pagan philosophies. He taught
in Ephesus and in Rome, where he was martyred. His most important works
were his two apologies and his *Dialogue with Trypho*. His descriptions of baptism and the Eucharist are of great use to liturgists today. He is widely recognized as the most outstanding of the early apologists.

*Lactantius* (ca. 240–ca. 320). Theologian and historian. He was born in North
Africa and received a good pagan education. He was appointed by the
emperor Diocletian to teach Latin oratory in Nicomedia, but he resigned
upon becoming a Christian. After Constantine came to power, he was
appointed tutor to the emperor's son Crispus. He wrote two major works,
the *Divine Institutes*, in which he argued that Christianity was morally
and intellectually superior to paganism, and *Of the Manner in Which the
Persecutors Died*, in which he recounted the grim deaths of emperors who
persecuted Christians.

*Lucian of Antioch* (ca. 240–312). Educator, saint, and martyr. A native of Samosata, he became a priest in Antioch and was appointed head of the theological school in that city. One of his students was Arius. Scholars have
detected the origins of Arius' heresy in Lucian's teachings, but he died a
martyr's death.

*Marcion* (second century). Heretic and sect founder. A native of Pontus, he settled in Rome around 140. He was excommunicated while in Rome, despite attempting to make a huge donation to the Church. He taught that the God of the New Testament was not the same God as the one depicted in the Old Testament. He recognized only the Epistles of Paul and the Gospel of Luke as Scripture.

*Melitius* (late third/early fourth century). Bishop of Lycopolis, Egypt. He thought that Christians who had lapsed during the persecution of Diocletian had been allowed to return to the Church too easily. Melitius is said to have ordained Arius.

*Montanus* (second century). A heretical preacher from Phrygia who taught that the age of the Spirit, in which the New Jerusalem would descend from the heavens, would appear soon. His most prominent follower was Tertullian. He was opposed by Apollinarius and Hippolytus of Rome.

*Novatian* (d. 257). Antipope, sect founder, and martyr. A Roman priest, Novatian thought those who had fallen away during the persecution of Decius were let back into the Church too easily. He was elected Bishop of Rome by his followers, against the existing Pope, Cornelius. He founded a sect called Novatianism. The sect was orthodox in theology and believed in strong discipline. It survived to the fifth century.

*Origen* (ca. 165–ca. 254). Theologian. Born in Alexandria, he was a student of Clement of Alexandria. His father was martyred in 202. He was head of the catechetical school in Alexandria for 28 years, and his teachings influenced thousands of Christians. In 230 he visited Caesarea, where he was ordained. The Bishop of Alexandria objected to his ordination. Origen moved to Caesarea, where he opened an equally successful school. He was martyred during the persecution of Decius. Origen was a prolific writer, and many of his works are still in use to this day. He was an excellent biblical scholar, but there were problems in his speculative theology, particularly in his trinitarian theology, where he may have fallen into the error of subordinationism (the belief that the Son is subordinate to the Father), and in soteriology, where he seems to have believed that in the end everyone, even the devil, will be saved. His most important insight was in the area of prayer, where he taught that prayer was not a matter of asking for things, but of participation in the life of God. His most famous student was Gregory Thaumaturgus.

*Papias* (ca. 60–ca. 130). Bishop of Hierapolis in Asia Minor. According to Irenaeus, he was a disciple of the Apostle John and a friend of Polycarp. His best-known writing was the *Exposition of the Words of the Lord*. In this document is the information that Mark wrote his Gospel based on information given to him by Peter and that this Gospel was accurate but not in the right order. Papias also wrote that Matthew's Gospel had originally been written in Hebrew.

*Paul of Samosata* (third century). Bishop and heretic. He was consecrated Bishop of Antioch in 260, but deposed in 268 because of his heresy. He taught that the divine Word of God was distinct from the human Jesus, and that at some point the Divine Word descended on the human Jesus.

*Perpetua and Felicitas* (late second/early third century). Women of Carthage, in North Africa, who were martyred during the persecution of Septimius Severus. Their martyrdom was recorded in the *Martyrdom of Perpetua and Felicitas*. The most likely author of this work is Tertullian.

*Pius I* (d. ca. 154). Bishop of Rome from 140 to 154. He was the brother of the author of *The Pastor of Hermas*.

*Polycarp* (ca. 69–ca. 155). Bishop of Smyrna. According to Irenaeus, he knew the Apostle John and others who had seen Jesus in the flesh. We have a letter from Irenaeus to him, and a letter he wrote to the Philippians. He was martyred in Smyrna during a pagan festival. His martyrdom is described in the *Martyrium Polycarpi*.

*Sabellius* (third century). Founder of the heretical movement known as Sabellianism, which held that the three persons of the Trinity were simply three different modes of the same being. This heresy is also known as Patripassionism or Modalism. He was opposed by Tertullian and Hippolytus.

*Sebastian* (later third century). Martyr. He was martyred during the persecution of Diocletian by being shot with arrows.

*Sixtus II* (ca. 258). Pope. Martyred during the persecution of Valerian while presiding over a eucharistic celebration. He also is remembered for resuming relations with the Churches of Africa and Asia, which had been broken off during the papacy of Stephen I.

*Tatian* (ca. 100–ca. 172). Pupil of Justin Martyr. He later moved to Syria, where he became an apologist. His most famous work is the *Diatessaron*, an edition of the four Gospels in one continuous narrative.

*Tertullian* (ca. 160–ca. 225). Theologian, polemicist, and apologist. He was born in Carthage to a well-to-do family and educated as a lawyer. When he became a Christian he used his education to argue on behalf of Christianity. In his later life he became involved in the Montanist sect.

# APPENDIX C

# A Guide to the Church Order Manuals
# of the Early Church

The "Church order manuals" are so called because they consist primarily of liturgical rules, prescriptions for baptismal preparation, and rules for Church organization and discipline. The Church order manuals typically claim some sort of connection with the teachings of the apostles, but none of them were written by an apostle, or even while any of the apostles were still alive. It is likely that some of the teachings found in these manuals (particularly those found in the *Didache*) are preserved from the apostolic period, but these documents are "apostolic" primarily in the sense that they reflect the slow accumulation of precedent under the bishops, the successors of the apostles. I refer not to "authors" but to "compilers" of these documents because in my opinion they are not literary creations out of whole cloth, but simply collections of the known rules of Church order at the time they were put together. For this reason, it is understandable that the shortest document, the *Didache*, is the earliest, and that the longest, the *Constitutions of the Holy Apostles*, is also the latest. In this sense, the Church order manuals are useful as snapshots of the developing Church at A.D. 100, 180, 250, and 375.

*The Didache* or *The Teaching of the Twelve Apostles.* The first Church order manual, probably compiled sometime between A.D. 90 and 110, in Syria. It contains the "two ways" catechesis (a contrast between the way of life and the way of death), the earliest description of baptismal practices, some general teachings on prayer, and an early Eucharistic Prayer. The *Didache* was incorporated into later Church order manuals and was praised by Saint Athanasius for the quality of its instruction to neophytes. The *Didache* was most likely intended as an aid to newer Christian communities.

*The Apostolic Tradition.* Most likely compiled by Hippolytus of Rome sometime between 215 and 230. Hippolytus was motivated by the fear that the changes instituted by Popes Zephyrinus and Callistus were damaging the Church and watering down authentic apostolic teaching. *The Apostolic Tradition* probably reflects the practices of the Roman Church when Hippolytus was a young man, around A.D. 180. It was translated into Coptic and survived into our time as the *Egyptian Church Order*.

*The Didascalia Apostolorum.* This document was compiled in Syria at approximately 250. It was originally written in Greek, but there were also Syrian and Latin versions. It deals almost exclusively with the questions of Church organization, finance, and discipline. Many of the passages of the *Didascalia* were copied directly into the *Constitutions of the Holy Apostles*.

*Constitutions of the Holy Apostles.* The last, and largest, of the Church order manuals, it was compiled at around 375, probably in either Syria or Constantinople. It consists primarily of expanded versions of the *Didascalia Apostolorum*, the *Didache*, the *Apostolic Tradition*, certain Jewish prayers, and a lost work of Hippolytus' entitled *Concerning Gifts*. The *Apostolic Tradition* of Hippolytus was expanded into a section that scholars today refer to as the "Clementine Liturgy".

# NOTES

## Introduction

1. This position is admirably summarized in the *Catechism of the Catholic Church*, nos. 355–61.

2. See Philip Jenkins, *Hidden Gospels: How the Search for Jesus Lost Its Way* (New York: Oxford University Press, 2001), for a summary of the reasons the Gnostic writings should be dated to this later period.

3. Moreover, this is the period in which Christianity was transformed from a sparse, regional religion into a significant presence in the Roman world.

## Part I: Life in the Roman World

## Chapter 1: The World They Knew

1. Some of the greatest of modern historians have commented on those similarities, while others counter that every historical period has its own unique circumstances that render comparison impossible. The great historian Michael Grant acknowledged both similarities and differences, then concluded that we could learn many lessons from Roman history, in the introduction of his magisterial work, *A History of Rome* (New York: Scribner, 1978).

2. Thomas Bokenkotter, *A Concise History of the Catholic Church* (New York: Doubleday, 1977), pp. 22–23.

3. Ibid., p. 22.

4. Tim Cornell, *Atlas of the Roman World* (New York: Oxford University Press, 1982), p. 17.

5. These cultural influences were especially strong in the area of religion. More will be forthcoming below, in Chapter 2.

6. Michael Grant, *The Ancient Mediterranean* (New York: History Book Club, 2002), p. 249.

7. Martin Albl, "Alexander", in *Eerdmans Dictionary of the Bible*, ed. David Noel Freedman (Grand Rapids, Mich.: Eerdmans Publishing Co., 2000), p. 40.

8. I use the term "Judah" to describe the Jewish kingdom prior to Roman occupation, and "Judea" to describe the same region under Roman rule.

9. By the time the New Testament was written, *Koine*, or "common" Greek, was the common language of the entire Mediterranean. This explains why almost all of the New Testament was written in this form of Greek.

10. As recorded in Grant, *Ancient Mediterranean*, p. 271.

11. Cornell, *Atlas*, p. 50.

12. Ibid., p. 51.

13. Michael Crawford, "Early Rome and Italy", in *The Oxford History of the Roman World*, ed. John Boardman (New York: Oxford University Press, 1986), p. 43.

14. Elizabeth Rawson, "The Expansion of Rome", in *The Oxford History of the Roman World*, ed. John Boardman (New York: Oxford University Press, 1986), p. 55.

15. See Amy-Jill Levine, "Visions of Kingdoms: From Pompey to the First Jewish Revolt", in *The Oxford History of the Biblical World*, ed. Michael D. Coogan (New York: Oxford University Press, 1998), p. 468. Inside the Holy of Holies one would expect to find the ark of the Covenant, the tablets of the law given to Moses on Mount Sinai, and Aaron's staff. No one knows where these items were hidden, and Pompey never found them. (He was looking primarily for gold. That, also, was evidently spirited away.)

16. See below, Part 2, Chapter 5.

17. The trial of Jesus, recorded in Mk 15, Mt 26–27, Lk 22–23, and Jn 18–19, is a perfect example of how local officials and Roman authorities might cooperate.

18. See Acts 24–26 for a fascinating series of encounters between Paul and the governor Felix, then Festus, then King Agrippa.

19. See Rom 16:23. Erastus, a Christian convert in Corinth, is listed as *oikonomos*, treasurer, of the city. Archaeologists have also found an inscription in Corinth that reads, "In his aedileship, Erastus laid this pavement at his own expense." See Paul Maier, *In the Fullness of Time* (San Francisco: Harper, 1991), p. 289.

20. See Michael Grant, *The World of Rome* (New York: Meridian, 1987), p 39.

21. Cornell, *Atlas*, p. 26.

22. The Senate was encouraged to debate freely, but woe to the senators if they came to a conclusion different than that preferred by the emperor. See Grant, *World of Rome*, pp. 43–45, for a more in-depth discussion.

23. Tacitus, *Annals*, trans. Alfred John Church and William Jackson (Chicago: Encyclopedia Britannica, 1952), 1.2.

24. Herod the Great was actually not a Jew at all, but an Idumean. For a more detailed account of how Herod came to rule, see *Oxford History of the Biblical World*, pp. 467–74.

25. See Josephus, *The Jewish War*, trans. and ed. Paul Maier (Grand Rapids, Mich.: Zondervan, 1982), pp. 280–332.

26. See, for example, Mk 2:13–17.

27. Suetonius, *Lives of the Caesars*, trans. Catharine Edwards (New York: Oxford University Press, 2000), p. 262. Nero fancied himself a virtuoso on the *citar* (the forerunner of the modern guitar) and frequently put on concerts. All present were expected to praise him, and woe to those who failed to be sufficiently impressed!

## Chapter 2: Religion in the Roman World

1. Tacitus, *Annals*, trans. Alfred John Church and William Jackson (Chicago: Encyclopedia Brittanica, 1952), 15.44.

2. R. M. Ogilvie, *The Romans and Their Gods* (New York: W. W. Norton and Co., 1933), p. 10.

3. Ibid., p. 101.

4. Robert Turcan, *The Gods of Ancient Rome: Religion in Everyday Life from Archaic to Imperial Times*, trans. Antonia Nevill (New York: Routledge, 2000), p. 16.

5. Ogilvie, *Roman Gods*, p. 100.

6. See Plautus, *Aulularia*, 3:25, as quoted by Turcan, *Gods of Rome*, pp. 15–16. The poem depicts those who show respect to the *lares* as being successful, while those who fail to show respect die poor.

7. H. J. Rose, *Ancient Roman Religion* (London: Hutchinson's University Library, 1948), p. 25.

8. Ogilvie, *Roman Gods*, p. 103.

9. See Turcan, *Gods of Rome*, pp. 18–19, for a fuller treatment of this subject.

10. Ovid, *Metamorphoses*, trans. Frank Justus Miller (Cambridge, Mass.: Harvard University Press, 1984), pp. 316–45.

11. Tertullian, *A Treatise on the Soul*, trans. Peter Holmes, 37.1, in *The Early Church Fathers* (Gervais, Ore.: Harmony Media, 2000), CD-ROM, hereinafter referred to as *ECF*.

12. Turcan, *Gods of Rome*, p. 2.

13. Rose, *Ancient Roman Religion*, p. 84.

14. Ibid., p. 94.

15. Ibid., p. 124.

16. Ogilvie, *Roman Gods*, p. 110.

17. Rose, *Ancient Roman Religion*, p. 83.

18. Ibid., p. 80. These figures were made out of straw. One might speculate that this practice arose as a substitute for human sacrifice, but there is no evidence that this is the case.

19. Turcan, *Gods of Rome*, p. 53.

20. Ibid., p. 56.

21. Ibid., pp. 53–54.

22. Ibid., p. 7.

23. Ibid., pp. 8–10.

24. Ibid., p. 9.

25. Mt 6:7. All scriptural verses are quoted from the Revised Standard Version, Catholic Edition, unless otherwise noted.

26. Rose, *Ancient Roman Religion*, p. 27.

27. See Acts 19:23–41 for a description of an encounter between Paul and the devotees of Artemis of Ephesus.

28. Turcan, *Gods of Rome*, pp. 109ff.

29. Rose, *Ancient Roman Religion*, pp. 12–16.

30. Ibid., pp. 131ff.

31. Indeed, Attis and Osiris were often spoken of as if they were the same god. In some of the Phrygian myths, Attis was said to have been raised from the dead.

32. See Turcan, *Gods of Rome*, p. 123.

33. Rose, *Ancient Roman Religion*, p. 139.

34. Justin Martyr, *The First Apology of Justin*, 66.4, in *ECF*.

35. Rose, *Ancient Roman Religion*, pp. 136–37.

36. See Jn 12:24. Some scholars think that in this passage Jesus was using images that a Greek audience familiar with the rites of Eleusis would have understood. See Raymond Brown, *The Gospel of John*, vol. 1 (New York: Doubleday and Co., 1966), pp. 471–73.

37. S. Angus, *The Mystery-Religions* (New York: Dover Publications, 1975), p. 76.

38. See Roland H. Worth, *The Seven Cities of the Apocalypse and Roman Culture* (Mahwah, N.J.: Paulist Press, 1999), p. 112.

39. Daniel Showalter, *The Emperor and the Gods: Images from the Time of Trajan* (Minneapolis: Fortress Press, 1992), p. 72. The emperor Trajan, more politically astute than many emperors, maintained a practice of allowing himself to be worshipped as a god in Asia but refused such honors in Rome itself. The natural inference from this would be that in Rome there was strong sentiment against such worship.

40. Worth, *Seven Cities*, p. 116. The people of Asia *made a formal request* to worship the emperor Tiberius.

41. Ogilvie, *Roman Gods*, p. 119.

42. Ibid., p. 125.

43. Worth, *Seven Cites*, p. 114.

44. Turcan, *Gods of Rome*, p. 137.

45. Worth, *Seven Cities*, pp. 118–19.

46. See J. N. Craybill, *Imperial Cult and Commerce in John's Apocalypse* (Sheffield, England: Academic Press, 1996), for an exposition of this theory.

47. Worth, *Seven Cities*, p. 117. Domitian insisted that he be called *dominus et deus* (lord and god) in public.

48. Turcan, *Gods of Rome*, p. 142.

49. The debate over whether or not Constantine was a genuine Christian rages on, with no prospect of resolution. For a fair-minded look at the evidence, see Michael Grant, *Constantine the Great: The Man and His Times* (New York: History Book Club, 1993), pp. 125–55. A Christian appropriation of solar imagery would not necessarily be an unwarranted concession to pagan culture, especially when one considers Malachi 4:2, which predicts that "the sun of righteousness will arise." The early Christians believed that this prophecy referred to Christ. Furthermore, the sun, which rises again each morning, was considered a symbol of Christ. So the equation of *Sol Invictus* with Christ was not necessarily unwarranted.

50. Ogilvie, *Roman Gods*, p. 54.

51. Rose, *Ancient Roman Religion*, pp. 116–17.

52. Ibid., p. 118.

53. Ibid., p. 119.

54. Ibid., p. 109.

55. Josephus, *The Jewish War*, trans. and ed. Paul Maier (Grand Rapids, Mich.: Zondervan, 1982), 2:117ff.

56. Some Scripture scholars believe that this fact is responsible for the difference in the Holy Week chronology between the synoptic Gospels on the one hand and the Gospel of John on the other. In John, Jesus is crucified on the Passover, while in the synoptics, the Last Supper is held on Passover, and Jesus is crucified the next day. But if John was following the Essene calendar, and Matthew, Mark, and Luke were following the conventional calendar, the problem is resolved.

57. See Josephus, *Jewish War*, 2:1–270, for a detailed summary of the events leading up to the Jewish Revolt.

58. Worth, *Seven Cities*, p. 72. Estimates of the Jewish population in the first century vary from two million to nine million. Six million seems a fairly reasonable estimate, but it might be off by quite a bit. Historians arrive at these figures by figuring the population of an area that left quite a few records and extrapolating to the larger population. It might produce accurate figures, but it might not. In any event, we can state with some confidence that the Jewish population in the empire was large enough to make the Jews a political force to be reckoned with.

59. Worth, *Seven Cities*, p. 72. Everything I said in note 58 applies here.

60. Amy-Jill Levine, "Visions of Kingdoms: From Pompey to the First Jewish Revolt", in *The Oxford History of the Biblical World*, ed. Michael D. Coogan (New York: Oxford University Press, 1998), p. 505. This fact, supported by Josephus in *The Jewish War*, explains why the Romans did not carry out a systematic persecution of Jews throughout the empire. The majority of Jews remained loyal to Rome even while the fighting was going on.

## Chapter 3: Social Life in the Roman World

1. Roland H. Worth, *The Seven Cities of the Apocalypse and Roman Culture* (Mahwah, N.J.: Paulist Press, 1999), p. 9.

2. Jerome Carcopino, *Daily Life in Ancient Rome* (New Haven: Yale University Press, 1940), p. 53.

3. Colin Wells, *The Roman Empire* (Cambridge, Mass.: Harvard University Press, 1984), p. 132.

4. Carcopino, *Daily Life*, p. 53.

5. Joseph A. Fitzmeyer, *Anchor Bible Commentary: The Letter to Philemon* (New York: Doubleday, 2001), p. 25.

6. See W. A. Strange, *Children in the Early Church* (Carlisle, England: Paternoster Press, 1996), p. 20. In fact, as we shall see, some exposed infants were rescued and raised to be slaves.

7. John T. Noonan, "Abortion and the Catholic Church: A Summary History", in *Christian Life: Ethics, Morality, and Discipline in the Early Church*, ed. Everett Ferguson (New York: Garland Publishing Co., 1993), p. 180.

8. Ibid.

9. Hippolytus of Rome, *The Refutation of All Heresies*, trans. J. H. Mac-Mahon, 9.12.25, in *The Early Church Fathers* (Gervais, Ore.: Harmony Media, 2000), CD-ROM. Hippolytus actually accused Christian women of engaging in this practice to avoid public knowledge of their illegal marriages to slaves.

10. Strange, *Children*, p. 21.

11. F. R. Cowell, *Life in Ancient Rome* (New York: Penguin, 1961), pp. 61–62.

12. Galen, quoted in Strange, *Children*, p. 23.

13. Strange, *Children*, p. 36.

14. See, for example, Philo, *Special Laws*, in *The Works of Philo*, trans. C. D. Yonge (Peabody, Mass.: Hendrickson Publishers, 1993), 3.110–19.

15. See Prov 13:24, 22:15, and 23:13.

16. Brian W. Grant, *The Social Structure of Christian Families: A Historical Perspective* (Saint Louis, Mo.: Chalice Press, 2000), p. 22.

17. See Mt 19:8. "For your hardness of heart Moses allowed you to divorce your wives, but from the beginning it was not so."

18. From a funerary inscription preserved at the Archaeological Museum of Aphrodisias, in modern-day Turkey.

19. Vincent P. Branick, *The House Church in the Writings of Paul* (Wilmington, Del.: Michael Glazier Books, 1989), pp. 49–50.

20. Bonnie Bowman Thurston, *The Widows: A Women's Ministry in the Early Church* (Minneapolis: Fortress Press, 1987), p. 13.

21. See Deut 25:5–10.

22. Gen 38:14, 19.

23. Ex 22:23–24.

24. Thurston, *Widows*, pp. 11–12.

25. Ibid., p. 15.

26. Ibid., p. 16. This law was a part of Augustus' attempt to increase the population of upper-class Romans.

27. Acts 16:14–15. Purple dye was extremely expensive in the Roman world, which is why it was reserved for the upper class of society.

28. See Worth, *Seven Cities*, pp. 36ff., for a good discussion of this question.

29. See J. Albert Harrill, *The Manumission of Slaves in Early Christianity* (Tubingen: JCB Mohr, 1995), p. 44.

30. Michael Grant, *The Ancient Mediterranean* (New York: History Book Club, 2002), p. 273.

31. Raymond E. Brown, *An Introduction to the New Testament* (New York: Doubleday, 1997), p. 503.

32. Ibid., p. 504.

33. Pliny the Younger, *Letters*, trans. Betty Radice (Cambridge, Mass.: Harvard University Press, 1969), 9.24.

34. Dio Cassius, *Roman History*, trans. J. W. Rich (Warminster, England: Aris and Phillips, 2000), 54.23.2–5.

35. Fitzmeyer, *Philemon*, pp. 27–28.

36. Quoted in ibid., p. 28.

37. See the *Papyrus Oxyrinchus*, 12.1422, quoted in ibid.

38. Fitzmeyer, *Philemon*, p. 28.

39. Ibid.

40. See Jennifer A. Glancy, *Slavery in Early Christianity* (New York: Oxford University Press, 2002), pp. 21ff.

41. For a good discussion of the number of freedmen and freedwomen in the Roman Empire, see Harrill, *Manumission*, pp. 4–5.

42. Ibid., p. 163. Harrill thinks this procedure degrading; the freedman would have to depend on whatever food the master would provide, then hang around until dismissed. I suspect, though, that the degradation of the process depended on the master. A kindly master would take this as an opportunity to make sure

the freedman was getting enough to eat. A cruel master would see it as another opportunity to humiliate a social inferior.

43. Worth, *Seven Cities*, p. 40.

44. Harrill, *Manumission*, p. 54.

45. Worth, *Seven Cities*, p. 38.

46. William V. Harris, "Towards a Study of the Roman Slave Trade", in *The Seaborne Commerce of Ancient Rome* (Rome: American Academy of Rome, 1980), pp. 117–40.

47. Aristotle, *Politics*, 1.2.12.

48. See Euripides, *The Trojan Women*, trans. Shirley A. Barlow (Warminster, England: Aris and Phillips, 1986). This play was written as Euripides' way of protesting the Athenian decision to slaughter all the inhabitants of the island of Melos, which revolted against Athenian rule in 415 B.C. Euripides was much more concerned about the indiscriminate slaughter of noncombatants in the Peloponnesian War than he was about slavery.

49. See Ex 1:10–14 and 5:6–14.

50. This passage was frequently quoted by apologists for slavery in the antebellum South. Paul's Epistle to Philemon was also frequently used by defenders of slavery.

51. See the Pontifical Biblical Commission's document *The Interpretation of the Bible in the Church* (Washington, D.C.: United States Catholic Conference, 1996), p. 33. The authors of this document note, "The writings of the Old Testament contain many imperfect and provisional elements which divine pedagogy could not eliminate right away." Obvious examples are the condoning of slavery in the Old Testament and the seeming endorsement of genocide in the Book of Joshua. The authors suggest that in dealing with contemporary moral problems, "the witness of the Bible, taken within the forceful dynamic that governs it as a whole, will certainly indicate a fruitful direction to go." In other words, to take slavery as an example, the Old Testament begins the movement in the direction that points to the proper end result. Just as the Old Testament limits the rights of slave owners, the end result of the direction Scripture takes us will be the ultimate end of slavery, under the guidance of "divine pedagogy".

52. Lev 25:39–41.

53. Fitzmeyer, *Philemon*, p. 30. However, if Paul considered the Christian community to be the New Israel, he may have applied this law to Christian slaves and Christian masters.

54. For the Essene practice regarding slavery, see Josephus, *Antiquities*, 18.1.5.21. For the Therapeutae, see Philo, *The Contemplative Life*, 9.70–71.

55. Tim Cornell, *Atlas of the Roman World* (New York: Oxford University Press, 1982), p. 108.

56. This possibility is not as farfetched as it might seem. Julius Caesar, for instance, granted citizenship to the people of numerous cities, particularly those who were helpful in the civil wars. See Cornell, *Atlas*, pp. 72–73.

57. Worth, *Seven Cities*, p. 19.

58. Carcopino, *Daily Life*, pp. 52–53.

59. Ibid., p. 52.

60. Wells, *Roman Empire*, p. 129.

61. This did not necessarily mean that they would appear before the emperor in person, though, if one were sufficiently important, one might be granted an imperial audience. For most citizens, it simply meant that one would appear before a Roman magistrate rather than a local court.

62. Carcopino, *Daily Life*, pp. 52–53.

63. Ibid., p. 52.

## Chapter 4: Life in the Roman Army

1. Colin Wells, *The Roman Empire* (Cambridge, Mass.: Harvard University Press, 1984), p. 126. Note: By the fourth century, when the pressure on the frontier was greater, the army had to be much larger (500,000 men), and conscription was again used heavily. But that period is outside the scope of this work.

2. G. R. Watson, *The Roman Soldier* (Ithaca, N.Y.: Cornell University Press, 1995), p. 44. The linguistic derivation is fairly obvious: *via*, meaning "way" + *tecum*, meaning "with you" = "with you on the way".

3. Wells, *Roman Empire*, pp. 143–44.

4. See Nic Fields, *Hadrian's Wall: AD 122–410* (Oxford: Osprey Publishing, 2003), p. 21. The watchtowers along Hadrian's wall in northern England were built into the wall and had primitive living quarters to accommodate eight soldiers. As an additional feature, Hadrian's wall also featured larger structures called mile castles, spaced one Roman mile apart from one another. These small forts had better accommodations and could house sixteen men.

5. Ibid., p. 20.

6. Appian, *Iberica*, trans. J. S. Richardson (Warminster, England: Aris and Phillips, 2000), p. 85, provides a description of how the soldiers would prepare their meals.

7. Fields, *Wall*, p. 50.

8. Simon MacDowall, *Late Roman Infantryman: 236–565 AD* (Oxford: Osprey Publishing, 1994), p. 19.

9. Watson, *Roman Soldier*, pp. 117ff.

10. Ibid., pp. 119–21.

11. Toward the end of his reign, Caligula ordered the Fourteenth Legion to be decimated over a riot that had occurred thirty years earlier, when Caligula was a child. The order was never carried out, and shortly thereafter Caligula was murdered by his Praetorian Guard.

12. For a fascinating list of the religious calendar of a particular legion, unearthed in Dura Europos in the third century, see Brian Campbell, *The Roman Army: 31 BC–AD 337* (London: Routledge, 1994), pp. 127–30.

13. Watson, *Roman Soldier*, p. 130.

14. Ibid., p. 104.

15. Ibid., pp. 58–59.

16. It was a common problem until the Greeks invented helmets with ear and nose flaps.

17. Tacitus, *Annals*, trans. Alfred John Church and William Jackson (Chicago: Encyclopedia Brittanica, 1952), 4:5. In this passage, Tacitus speaks of twenty-five legions in A.D. 23, but we know that there were three legions lost in A.D. 9 in the Teutoberger Forest in Germany. These legions were not replaced, since they had lost their eagles.

18. Wells, *Roman Empire*, p. 124.

19. In an empire of sixty million people, this means that only a quarter of 1 percent of the total population actually served to protect the empire.

20. Tacitus, *Annals*, 4:5.

21. Wells, *Roman Empire*, p. 130.

22. Ibid., p. 127. This particular man actually died before he ever got to enjoy his new rank.

23. Matthew Bunson, "Legions", in *A Dictionary of the Roman Empire* (New York: Oxford University Press, 1991), p. 230.

24. This method is in fact responsible for the establishment of many a city along the Rhine and Danube. The best example is the modern city of Cologne (*Colonia*), which was originally a Roman military camp. A fair-sized city sprang up around the camp as soldiers retired, married local women, and raised families. This process was going on all along the frontier.

25. Eph 6:10–17.


## Chapter 5: The Basics of Life

1. F. R. Cowell, *Life in Ancient Rome* (New York: Penguin, 1961), p. 76.

2. Ibid., p. 86.

3. Karl Christ, *The Romans: An Introduction to Their History and Civilization*, trans. Christopher Holme (Berkeley: University of California Press, 1984), p. 108.

4. Lionel Casson, *Travel in the Ancient World* (Baltimore: Johns Hopkins University Press, 1994), p. 213.

5. Cowell, *Life in Ancient Rome*, pp. 70–71. There were always those among the Romans who worried that the ancient manly virtues were being lost.

6. The famous purple dye was derived from a shellfish called the murex that was common in the Mediterranean. Purple was reserved for the upper class because it was harder to obtain and therefore more expensive and more prestigious to wear.

7. Cowell, *Life in Ancient Rome*, pp. 70–71.

8. The poet Martial considered it bliss to rest clad only in a tunic. See Cowell, *Life in Ancient Rome*, p. 73.

9. D. S. Robertson, *Greek and Roman Architecture* (London: Cambridge University Press, 1969), p. 297.

10. Ian Jenkins, *Greek and Roman Life* (Cambridge, Mass.: Harvard University Press, 1986), p. 11.

11. See Jerome Carcopino, *Daily Life in Ancient Rome* (New Haven, Conn.: Yale University Press, 1940), pp. 36–38, for a detailed discussion of the question of heating in the *insulae*.

12. Ibid., p. 25.

13. Ibid., p. 26.

14. Juvenal, *Satires*, trans. Niall Rudd and Edward Courtney (Bristol: Bristol Classical Press, 1977), pp. 198–202.

15. Carcopino, *Daily Life*, p. 101.

16. Ibid., p. 104.

17. Christ, *Romans*, pp. 103–4. No estimate has been made of the literacy rate of the empire, but the ability to read and write was certainly not universal.

18. Carcopino, *Daily Life*, p. 109.

19. See Irenaeus of Lyons, *Against Heresies*, preface, book 1.3, in *The Early Church Fathers* (Gervais, Ore.: Harmony Media, 2000), CD-ROM. "You will not expect from me, who am resident among the Keltae, and am accustomed for the most part to use a barbarous dialect, any display of rhetoric, which I have never learned, or any excellence of composition, which I have never practiced, or any beauty and persuasiveness of style, to which I make no pretensions."

20. Christ, *Romans*, p. 103.

21. Carcopino, *Daily Life*, p. 152.

22. There are, of course, obvious exceptions. Some people had to start work long before dawn, most notably bakers, who had to have the daily bread baked before the start of everyone else's workday, and carters could move their carts through the streets of Rome only after dark.

23. There were always places where another language was the first language of the people (in North Africa, for example, Punic was always the primary language of the common people), but anywhere you went, some of the people would know either Greek or Latin. See Casson, *Travel*, pp. 115–27, for a summary of the factors that made this universal travel possible.

24. Ibid., p. 150.

25. Ibid., p. 163.

26. An example would be Pausanius, *Description of Greece*, trans. Peter Levi (New York: Penguin, 1971), written between 160 and 180.

27. This might seem unlikely, but the practice was well attested to. The couriers were called *grammatophoroi* (letter carriers) in Greek and *tabellaril* (tablet men) in Latin. See Casson, *Travel*, pp. 219–20.

28. Ibid., pp. 200ff.

29. Ibid., p. 205.

30. See Aelius Aristides, *The Complete Works*, vol. 2, *Orations XVII–LII*, trans. Charles A. Behr (Leiden: E.J. Brill, 1981), pp. 278–355, for Aristides' own account of his stay at the *Asclepion*.

31. Galen, quoted in Fatih Cimok, *Pergamum* (Istanbul: A Turizm Yayinlari, 2001), p. 82.

32. Pliny the Elder, *Natural History*, trans. Philemon Holland (Carbondale, Ill.: Southern Illinois University Press, 1962), 29.12–13.

33. Cimok, *Pergamum*, p. 76. I am indebted to my guide, Ćenk Eronat, for almost all of the insights I gained during my tour of this site.

34. Aristides, *Works*, pp. 278–355.

35. Cowell, *Life in Ancient Rome*, p. 131.

36. Ibid., p. 132.

37. Carcopino, *Daily Life*, p. 40.

38. The author has seen the public latrines of Ephesus, and they were just that, public, without a single concession to personal modesty. Anyone who wished to use them had to be willing to sit inches from the nearest occupant, without a privacy screen of any sort.

39. Cowell, *Life in Ancient Rome*, p. 132.

40. Ibid., p. 132.

41. Saint John the Evangelist, for instance, must have been in his nineties when he died of natural causes.

42. Helen King, *Greek and Roman Medicine* (London: Bristol Classical Press, 2001), p. 51.

43. See Carcopino, *Daily Life*, pp. 39–40. Carcopino had a great admiration for the *construction* of the *Cloaca Maxima* of Rome, but believed that they were inefficient and unclean in actual operation.

## Chapter 6: Entertainment

1. We will discuss the case of Nero in greater detail later in this work. Another well-documented case would be the emperor Commodus (ruled A.D. 180–192), who loved the games so much he sometimes entered the Colosseum and personally participated in the gladiatorial combat.

2. Augustine, *Confessions*, trans. J. G. Pilkington, 6.7, in *The Early Church Fathers* (Gervais, Ore.: Harmony Media, 2000), CD-ROM.

3. See Thomas Wiedemann, *Emperors and Gladiators* (New York: Routledge, 1992), p. 5.

4. Ibid., p. 1.

5. Michael Grant, *Gladiators* (New York: Delacorte Press, 1968), p. 12. Capua was always a center for gladiatorial training, to the very end of the practice.

6. See Alison Futrell, *Blood in the Arena* (Austin: University of Texas Press, 1997), for a good treatment of this whole subject.

7. Wiedemann, *Emperors and Gladiators*, pp. 5–6.

8. Ibid., p. 6.

9. Grant, *Gladiators*, p. 13.

10. See Wiedemann, *Emperors and Gladiators*, p. 47. The author is not unaware of the irony that the two bloodiest festivals of the pagan Romans roughly corresponded with the two holiest feasts of Christianity.

11. Ibid., p. 60.

12. See Robert Payne, *Ancient Rome* (New York: ibooks, 2001), pp. 211–12. Commodus had a habit of engaging unarmed men in the arena and killing them. Commodus was eventually murdered by his wrestling partner, with the approval if not the collaboration of the Senate. Incidentally, this is the young emperor depicted in the movie *Gladiator*.

13. For instance, tigers and lions would be set against one another, or aurochs and bears. Usually, the animals had to be starved before they could be induced to fight one another.

14. Roland Auguet, *Cruelty and Civilization: The Roman Games* (New York: Routledge 1994), p. 93. However, this author provides no actual evidence that the *venatio* originated in North Africa; he simply points out that it might be logical to assume that it originated there.

15. Futrell, *Blood*, pp. 26–27. Evidently these animals were killed in order to teach the soldiers, who were about to embark on a war against Carthage, not to fear elephants.

16. Ibid., p. 28.

17. Wiedemann, *Emperors and Gladiators*, p. 11.

18. The various rooms and chambers under the floor of the Colosseum might lead one to believe that the animals were kept there permanently, but

the truth is that these little cells were used only as temporary holding pens until it was time to release the animals into the arena.

19. Wiedemann, *Emperors and Gladiators*, p. 77.

20. Ibid., pp. 75–76. Later laws, dating to the reign of Marcus Aurelius (161–180), forbade the selling of slaves even under these circumstances. The slave could be forced to fight the animals, but the owner could not profit from the incident.

21. Grant, *Gladiators*, p. 35.

22. It officially opened in A.D. 80, but the work continued for several years after that date.

23. Paul Veyne, *The Roman Empire*, trans. Arthur Goldhammer (Cambridge, Mass.: Harvard University Press, 2002), p. 200. It is still unclear exactly how many people the Colosseum could hold because there were no seats per se, just long stone benches. Payne estimates that the Colosseum could hold 45,000, Auguet says 60,000, and Cornell estimates approximately 70,000. I suspect that for certain special events they could fit even more than 70,000.

24. A caveat is necessary here. As F. R. Cowell, *Life in Ancient Rome* (New York: Penguin, 1961), p. 173, has noted, there exists no ancient Roman source that completely describes what went on in the amphitheater, but from partial descriptions, modern authors have attempted reconstructions of a day at the Colosseum.

25. See Auguet, *Cruelty*, p. 81. Suetonius said that the hunts would proceed "from daybreak". Evidently these events were favored by the lower-class citizens.

26. Ibid., p. 65. Evidently these events did not end in death.

27. Grant, *Gladiators*, pp. 63–64.

28. For a more complete description of the gladiators see ibid., pp. 58–63.

29. Ibid., pp. 74–75.

30. The fresh sand was necessary to ensure a fair fight for later contestants. All the events of the amphitheater were conducted on sand. In fact, the very word "arena" comes from the Latin word for sand, *harena*.

31. Suetonius, *Lives of the Caesars: Nero*, trans. Catharine Edwards (New York: Oxford University Press, 2000), p. 35.

32. Futrell, *Blood*, p. 53.

33. Nîmes was the ancient Roman city of Colonia Nemausus. As its name indicates, it was a Roman colony, populated largely with people of Roman background. You can also view a beautiful amphitheater of the same period in the nearby city of Arles.

34. Wiedemann, *Emperors and Gladiators*, p. 22. By amphitheaters, we mean buildings with a circular seating arrangement that allowed viewing from all angles, built primarily out of stone and masonry.

35. Futrell has made an interesting attempt to estimate the population of Gaul based on the seating capacity of the numerous amphitheaters of the province. Different towns in Gaul had amphitheaters of different sizes, and the size of the amphitheaters seem to correspond roughly to the population of the towns (*Blood*, pp. 66ff.).

36. See ibid., pp. 79–110. The main feast day for this practice was called *lughnasa*, which was held on August 1.

37. This point is borne out by the records of the martyrs. Some, such as Ignatius of Antioch, were transported to Rome for execution. Others, such as Blandina, were executed in the city in which they lived—in Blandina's case, Lugdunum (modern-day Lyons, France).

38. See Wiedemann, *Emperors and Gladiators*, p. 146. Josephus records that Herod Agrippa built an amphitheater in Beirut, and large numbers of gladiators fought there. The Jews found this amphitheater an abomination, but there was nothing they could do about it, since large numbers of Greeks lived in Beirut.

39. Roland H. Worth, *The Seven Cities of the Apocalypse and Roman Culture* (Mahwah, N.J.: Paulist Press, 1999), p. 26.

40. Ibid., p. 27.

41. Auguet, *Cruelty*, p. 120.

42. See Cowell, *Life in Ancient Rome*, p. 171. The Circus Maximus was approximately 600 yards long and 200 yards wide. The first few rows of seats were made of stone, but the back rows were wooden grandstands, built up behind the front rows. Cowell indicates that there were "five or six" circuses throughout Rome.

43. Ibid.

44. The sharp knife blades depicted on the chariot wheels in the movie *Ben Hur* do not appear to have been used.

45. Cowell, *Life in Ancient Rome*, p. 172, records the case of a North African charioteer who won over a million and a half sesterces between the years 115 and 129.

46. Veyne, *Roman Empire*, p. 200.

47. Cowell, *Life in Ancient Rome*, p. 171.

48. Ibid., p. 172.

49. See David Barr, *New Testament Story* (Belmont, Calif.: Wadsworth Publishing Co., 1995), pp. 218ff. Modern biblical scholars are toying with a theory that the authors of the New Testament used some of the production and plotting techniques used by the Greek playwrights. The theory is too young for a thorough evaluation, but in its basic elements it seems plausible, provided one starts with the assumption that in their basic outline the stories in the New Testament are true.

50. Cowell, *Life in Ancient Rome*, p. 145.

51. A *quadrans* was the smallest Roman coin, the equivalent of our penny.

52. See Irenaeus, *Against Heresies*, 3.3, in *ECF*. Irenaeus records an interesting story about the Apostle John using a bathhouse as if it were a common occurrence. Saint John lived out his later years in the city of Ephesus, which had a healthy dose of Greco-Roman culture. One does not know exactly what circumstances allowed Saint John to use this particular bathhouse, but there must have been separate bathing facilities for men and women, or the apostle would not have entered.

53. Cowell, *Life in Ancient Rome*, p. 145.

## Chapter 7: Evaluating the Roman Empire

1. See Alison Futrell, *Blood in the Arena* (Austin: University of Texas Press, 1997), p. 39. The Romans called concrete *opus caementicum*. They spent years fiddling with the formula before they came up with the correct proportions of lime, aggregate (gravel), water, and volcanic ash.

2. There are, of course, smaller communions that have their origins in this period, such as the Chaldean Christians of Iraq and the Coptic Church of Egypt. There is no intent to slight these churches, who can trace their origins to the apostles.

3. Critics of Roman Christianity would have it the other way around, that paganism succeeded in watering down the gospel by introducing pagan elements into Christianity. But you can tell which way things really went merely by reflecting on which religion was still standing at the end of the day.

## Part II: Christians as Salt and Light in the Roman World

## Chapter 1: Baptism by Water, Spirit, Blood, and Fire

1. This might seem an unlikely thing to say. After all, the Christians were prosecuted and executed as public criminals. Nevertheless, at least some people had never even heard of them. The story of Pachomius is instructive. Pachomius was an Egyptian from Thebes. As a young man, at around A.D. 300, he was forcibly conscripted into the army. He was held in prison with the other "conscripts", awaiting transportation to the front. During this time, Christians repeatedly visited him to see to his needs. He expressed astonishment and asked who these people were. Pachomius eventually became a Christian and is known as the father of monasticism. But the immediate point is

that 300 years after Christ, in a city with a good population of Christians, he had no idea what a Christian was until he was thrown in prison.

2. As ridiculous as these charges seem to us today, they were staples of pagan satirists, and the charges appear to have been widely believed. See W. H. C. Frend, *The Rise of Christianity* (Philadephia: Fortress Press, 1984), pp. 181ff.

3. Rodney Stark, *The Rise of Christianity: A Sociologist Reconsiders History* (Princeton, N.J.: Princeton University Press, 1996), pp. 6–8. Professor Stark assumes a total Christian population of 1,000 in A.D. 40, and a total population of 60,000,000 for the entire empire.

4. Mt 28:18–20.

5. See Acts 16 for a perfect example of how Saint Paul would approach a Gentile audience.

6. This was the year of Nero's great persecution in Rome. The precedent he set meant that any Roman authority who became aware of Christians in his district would be obligated to do something about them. To be sure, Christians were persecuted before, but those persecutions were initiated by local authorities.

7. See Justin Martyr's *Dialogue with Trypho*. At the end of their debate, Trypho is unconvinced.

8. Alan Kreider, *The Change of Conversion and the Origin of Christendom* (Harrisburg, Penn.: Trinity Press International, 1999), p. 13.

9. Origen, *Against Celsus*, trans. Frederick Crombie, 3.9, in *The Early Church Fathers* (Gervais, Ore.: Harmony Media, 2000), CD-ROM.

10. Tertullian, *The Soul's Testimony*, trans. S. Thelwall, 1, in *ECF*.

11. Tatian the Syrian, *Address to the Greeks*, trans. J. E. Ryland, 29, in *ECF*.

12. See *The Teaching of the Twelve Apostles (The Didache): The Lord's Teaching through the Twelve Apostles to the Nations*, 1.5, in *ECF* (on CD-ROM Contents page, look under "Apostle"): "Give to every one that asks you, and ask it not back; for the Father wills that to all should be given of our own blessings."

13. Hippolytus of Rome, *The Apostolic Tradition of Hippolytus*, trans. Burton Scott Easton (London: Cambridge University Press, 1934), pp. 5–6.

14. Justin Martyr, *First Apology*, 67, in *ECF*.

15. See E. Glenn Hinson, *The Early Church: Origins to the Dawn of the Middle Ages* (Nashville: Abingdon Press, 1996), p. 64.

16. Basil the Great, *Letter CLXIV: To Ascholius*, trans. Blomfield Jackson, 1, in *ECF*.

17. Justin Martyr, *Second Apology*, 12, in *ECF*. This apology was addressed to the Senate of Rome.

18. Herbert Thurston and Donald Attwater, *Butler's Lives of the Saints*, vol. 3 (New York: P. J. Kenedy and Sons, 1956), pp. 157–58.

19. Hinson, *Early Church*, p. 64.

20. Justin Martyr, *Dialogue with Trypho*, 8, in *ECF*.

21. Justin Martyr, *Second Apology*, 12.

22. See Oskar Skarsaune, "The Conversion of Justin Martyr", in *Conversion, Catechumenate, and Baptism in the Early Church*, ed. Everett Ferguson (New York: Garland Publishing Co., 1993), p. 45.

23. Livy, *The Rise of Rome*, books 1–5, trans. T. J. Luce (New York: Oxford University Press, 1998), p. 4.

24. Cyprian of Carthage, *To Donatus*, Epistle I [1], trans. Ernest Wallis, 3, in *ECF*.

25. We learn this from Pontius the Deacon, *The Life and Passion of Cyprian, Bishop and Martyr*, 6, in *ECF*.

26. Cyprian, *Donatus*, 4.

27. See Tertullian, *On Baptism*, trans. S. Thelwall, 18.4, in *ECF*. In this passage, Tertullian alludes to the dangers sponsors faced.

28. See Acts 2:37–42 for an example.

29. See Kreider, *Change*, p. 4. Justin Martyr, the catechist about whom we have the most personal information, taught in his private rooms above a Roman bath, which also contained his living quarters.

30. Hippolytus, *Apostolic Tradition*, 16.

31. Ibid., 16.

32. See Thomas Finn, *Early Christian Baptism and the Catechumenate: West and East Syria* (Collegeville, Minn.: Liturgical Press, 1992), p. 4.

33. Hippolytus, *Apostolic Tradition*, 15.

34. Lawrence Folkemer, "A Study of the Catechumenate", in *Conversion, Catechumenate, and Baptism in the Early Church*, ed. Everett Ferguson (New York: Garland Publishing Co., 1993), p. 245. "Kneelers" were also sometimes called *competentes*, *illuminati*, or *electi*.

35. Tertullian, *The Prescription against Heretics*, trans. Peter Holmes, 41, in *ECF*.

36. *Didache*, 7.

37. Thomas Finn, *Early Christian Baptism and the Catechumenate: Italy, North Africa and Egypt* (Collegeville, Minn.: Liturgical Press, 1992), pp. 193–94. We have many of Origen's homilies on these subjects, and they reveal a deep and rich baptismal theology.

38. Kreider, *Change*, pp. 27–29.

39. Sometimes this work is titled *Three Testimonies against the Jews*. This title, in my opinion, does not do justice to Cyprian's original intent, which was to present the positive teachings of Christianity. Cyprian's arguments against the Jews were only incidental to his main purpose.

40. Hippolytus, *Apostolic Tradition*, 20.

41. Tertullian, *On Baptism*, 18.

42. See Justin Martyr, *First Apology*, 61.

43. Hippolytus, *Apostolic Tradition*, 20.

44. It is unclear exactly when this occurred. We have an appendix to the works of Hippolytus that makes a clear reference to Lent. If this appendix is authentic, that would mean that in Rome Lent was observed before 215, but the authenticity of this work is in doubt. We find the season of Lent mentioned more frequently in fourth- and fifth-century writings.

45. Tertullian, *On Baptism*, 20.

46. See H.J. Carpenter, "Creeds and Baptismal Rites in the First Four Centuries", in *Conversion, Catechumenate, and Baptism in the Early Church*, ed. Everett Ferguson (New York: Garland Publishing Co., 1993), pp. 367–77. There was no universal creed in the East or the West until the Nicene Creed was agreed upon in 325. There were many local creeds, but they all contained more or less the same points.

47. See Aidan Kavanagh, *The Shape of Baptism: The Rite of Christian Initiation* (New York: Pueblo Publishing Co., 1978), pp. 35–67.

48. Hippolytus, *Apostolic Tradition*, 20–21.

49. *Didascalia Apostolorum: The Syriac Version Translated and Accompanied by the Verona Latin Fragments* (Oxford: Clarendon Press, 1929), p. 16. The New Testament also knew deaconesses (see Rom 16:1 and 1 Tim 3:8–13).

50. See Acts 16:31, 18:8, and 1 Cor 1:16.

51. Tertullian, *On Baptism*, 18:4.

52. Origen, *Homilies on Luke*, trans. Joseph T. Lienhard (Washington, D.C.: Catholic University Press, 1996), 4.5, and Cyprian of Carthage, *To Fidus on the Baptism of Infants*, Epistle LVIII [2], trans. Ernest Wallis, 5, in *ECF*.

53. Origen, *Commentary on Romans, Books 1–5*, trans. Thomas B. Scheck (Washington, D.C.: Catholic University Press, 2001), 5.9.11.

54. These inscriptions were originally catalogued by E. Diehl, *Inscriptions Latinae Christianae Veteres*, 2nd ed. (Berlin, 1961). I am quoting an English translation by Everett Ferguson, "Inscriptions of Infant Baptism", in *Conversion, Catechumenate, and Baptism in the Early Church*, ed. Everett Ferguson (New York: Garland Publishing Co., 1993), pp. 391–400.

55. Heb 10:26–28.

56. See Acts 5:5–50 and 1 Cor 11:30.

57. See 1 Cor 5:2–13. Paul seems to have thought that perhaps this drastic treatment might bring those cast out to repentance.

58. Clement of Rome, *First Epistle to the Corinthians*, Codex Alexandrinus, trans. John Keith, 57, in *ECF*.

59. *Didache*, 4.14.

60. Ibid., 14.1.

61. Barnabas, *The Epistle of Barnabas*, 19.12, in *ECF*.

62. Hermas, *The Pastor of Hermas*, trans. F. Crombie, 2.4.3, in *ECF*.

63. Irenaeus of Lyons, *Against Heresies*, 3.4.3, in *ECF*.

64. 1 Jn 5:16–17.

65. See G.H. Joyce, "Private Penance in the Early Church", in *Christian Life: Ethics, Morality, and Discipline in the Early Church*, ed. Everett Ferguson (New York: Garland Publishing Co., 1993), p. 336. In his later life, when he slipped into heresy, Tertullian evidently did not think the Church could ever forgive these sins. See *On Modesty*, trans. S. Thelwall, 21, in *ECF*.

66. Tertullian, *On Repentance*, trans. S. Thelwall, 9, in *ECF*.

67. H.B. Swete, "Penitential Discipline in the First Three Centuries", in *Christian Life: Ethics, Morality, and Discipline in the Early Church*, ed. Everett Ferguson (New York: Garland Publishing Co., 1993), p. 261, gleaned these points from Origen's *Homilies on Leviticus*, 15.2.

68. Ibid., p. 261.

69. Hippolytus of Rome, *The Refutation of All Heresies*, trans. J.H. MacMahon, 9.7, in *ECF*.

70. Tertullian, *On Modesty*, 1.

## Chapter 2: How the Early Christians Prayed

1. To be sure, there are those who find it of lesser value. See Robert L. Simpson, *The Interpretation of Prayer in the Early Church* (Philadelphia: Westminster Press, 1965), p. 23. Professor Simpson believes that Cyprian owed almost everything that is insightful in his work to Tertullian. Even if this is the case, Cyprian did a great service to the Church by preserving much in Tertullian's thought that might have otherwise been lost.

2. Paul F. Bradshaw, *Daily Prayer in the Early Church: A Study of the Origin and Early Development of the Divine Office* (London: Alcuin Club, 1981), pp. 1–3. Bradshaw thinks the destruction of the Temple in A.D. 70 had a great deal to do with changes in Jewish prayer practices.

3. Ex 29:38.

4. Deut 6:7, 11:19.

5. Bradshaw, *Daily Prayer*, pp. 1–2. In Judaism, a benediction is the type of prayer that begins "Blessed be God ..." and continues with a remembrance of all the things God has done.

6. Dawn was considered the first hour. The third hour would be 9 o'clock, the sixth hour would be noon, and the ninth hour would be 3 o'clock in the afternoon.

7. Tertullian, *On Prayer*, trans. S. Thelwall, 25, in *The Early Church Fathers* (Gervais, Ore.: Harmony Media, 2000), CD-ROM. "Touching the time,

however, the extrinsic observance of certain hours will not be unprofitable—those common hours, I mean, which mark the intervals of the day—the third, the sixth, the ninth".

8. Bradshaw, *Daily Prayer*, pp. 18–20.

9. Acts 2:42. They also continued to attend Temple services, as Acts 2:46 indicates.

10. In Greek, this passage reads: "περι ωραν εκτην", which translates literally: "about the sixth hour".

11. See Phil 4:6, Col 4:2, 1 Thess 5:16–18, and Rom 1:8–9.

12. See Eph 5:18–19 and Col 3:16. Some scholars think Phil 2:6–11 was a part of an early hymn.

13. *The Teaching of the Twelve Apostles (The Didache): The Lord's Teaching through the Twelve Apostles to the Nations*, 8, in *ECF* (on CD-ROM Contents page, look under "Apostle").

14. See Bradshaw, *Daily Prayer*, p. 43. The Book of Psalms is the most quoted Old Testament book in the New Testament.

15. Tertullian, *On Prayer*, 25.

16. Hippolytus of Rome, *The Apostolic Tradition of Hippolytus*, trans. Burton Scott Easton (London: Cambridge University Press, 1934), 41.5.

17. Tertullian seems to have used this point to argue that believers should not marry nonbelievers, since this rising in the middle of the night to pray would be a source of annoyance and jealousy for the nonbeliever. See Bradshaw, *Daily Prayer*, p. 49.

18. Cyprian of Carthage, *On the Lord's Prayer*, trans. Ernest Wallis, 8, in *ECF*.

19. Bradshaw, *Daily Prayer*, p. 59.

20. Tertullian, *On Prayer*, 22.

21. See Felicity Harley, "Invocation and Immolation: The Supplicatory Use of Christ's Name on Crucifixion Amulets in the Early Christian Period", in *Prayer and Spirituality in the Early Church*, ed. Pauline Allen, Wendy Mayer, and Lawrence Cross (Everton Park, Australia: Centre for Early Christian Studies, 1998), pp. 245–57.

22. See Tertullian, *On Prayer*, 19.

23. Tertullian, *Apology*, trans. S. Thelwall, 39, in *ECF*.

24. See Robert L. Simpson, *The Interpretation of Prayer in the Early Church* (Philadelphia: Westminster Press, 1965), pp. 20–28.

25. Cyprian of Carthage, *Lord's Prayer*, 18.

26. Author's translation.

27. See Mt 26:26–29, Mk 14:22–25, Lk 22:15–20, and 1 Cor 11:23–26. Matthew and Mark have the same details in their accounts, and Luke and Paul share similar details in their accounts.

28. See Gregory Dix, *The Shape of the Liturgy* (New York: Seabury Press, 1982), p. 59. Dom Gregory makes the point that, being Jews, the disciples would have eaten this meal many times in their life, but Jesus, by saying, "Do this in remembrance of me", invested the whole meal with an entirely new meaning.

29. It is easy to see how this type of prayer survives in the liturgy to this day. As we shall see, the entire form of the Mass derives from Jewish practices, given a new interpretation by Jesus Christ.

30. See Rev 5:6ff. for an example.

31. See Dix, *Liturgy*, pp. 50ff., for a detailed description of the *chaburah*. Dom Gregory, an English monk of the middle of the twentieth century, was the strongest advocate of the idea of the Last Supper as a *chaburah*.

32. See Mike Aquilina, *The Mass of the Early Christians* (Huntington, Ind.: Our Sunday Visitor Publishing Div., 2001), p. 29.

33. Quoted in Scott Hahn, *The Lamb's Supper* (New York: Doubleday, 1999), p. 33.

34. The Gospel of John might provide the key to understanding how this could happen. In John 19:31, the author states, "Since it was the day of Preparation, in order to prevent the bodies from remaining on the cross on the sabbath (for *that sabbath* was a high day), the Jews asked Pilate that their legs might be broken, and that they might be taken away." (emphasis added). "That Sabbath" was special because Passover Day would fall on the Sabbath. This occurrence, which would happen one year in seven, meant that this Passover was special, and all the solemn observances would be heightened. It is at least conceivable that some people might choose to combine the *chaburah* and the *todah* in this special year. There are other possible explanations, but no one really knows for sure.

35. See Pliny the Younger, *Letters*, trans. Betty Radice (Cambridge, Mass.: Harvard University Press, 1969), p. 294. Pliny was the Roman governor of Bithynia, who took it upon himself to find out about the Christians and wrote a letter to Emperor Trajan to share his findings. He wrote that "on a fixed day", the Christians would gather to "take food of an ordinary, harmless kind". (Pliny emphasized the inoffensive nature of the meal because already rumors were spreading that the Christians were cannibals.) See also *Didache*, 14, which states, "Every Lord's day gather yourselves together and break bread." The early Christians regularly gathered together to do what Jesus had commanded them to do.

36. Ignatius of Antioch, *The Epistle of Ignatius to the Smyrnaeans*, 7, in *ECF*.

37. Hippolytus, *Apostolic Tradition*, 32. Easton considers this section a later addition, but does not indicate when he thinks it was added.

38. A section of the Eucharistic Prayer found in the *Apostolic Tradition*, 4, reads, "Having in memory, therefore, his death and resurrection, we offer thee the bread and cup."

39. Cyprian of Carthage, *Caecilius, On the Sacrament of the Cup of the Lord*, Epistle LXII [7], 14, in *ECF*.

40. In chapters 65 and 66, Justin describes the baptismal liturgy, and in chapter 67, he describes what might be called the basic Sunday liturgy.

41. Justin Martyr, *The First Apology of Justin*, 67, in *ECF*.

42. John Elliott estimates that an unmodified villa could be spacious enough to accommodate thirty to forty worshippers at a time, assuming that there was a Christian in the community that owned such a large house. In any event, the Christians soon found it necessary to knock walls out of houses to make them suitable for worship. See John Elliot, "Philemon and House Churches", *The Bible Today* (May 1984): 147.

43. A. G. Martimort, *The Church at Prayer: An Introduction to the Liturgy*, vol. 2 (Collegeville, Minn.: Liturgical Press, 1987), p. 38.

44. Ibid., p. 37.

45. See Graydon F. Snyder, *Ante Pacem: Archaeological Evidence of Church Life before Constantine* (Macon, Ga.: Mercer University Press, 2003), pp. 144–49. The Basilica of Ss. Giovanni e Paulo was built on top of a part of this site, but enough of the original *insula* was left undisturbed that the archaeologists could see what happened.

46. I first became aware of this find on the internet, at http://news.yahoo.com/s/ap/20051106/ap_on_sc/israel_ancient_church. Further study may require some modification of this information.

47. Dix, *Liturgy*, p. 134. Dom Gregory thinks this custom began in the early years of the second century.

48. *Constitutions of the Holy Apostles*, ed. James Donaldson, 7.57, in *ECF* (on CD-ROM Contents page look under "Apostle").

49. There is little evidence one way or the other for the location of the altar. It might just as well be the case that the altar was against the wall, but that would put the bishop's chair in front of the altar. For what it's worth, Dom Gregory Dix agrees with me (see *Liturgy*, p. 142).

50. *Didascalia Apostolorum: The Syriac Version Translated and Accompanied by the Verona Latin Fragments* (Oxford: Clarendon Press, 1929), p. 124.

51. Ibid, p. 120.

52. Ernest Lussier, *The Eucharist: The Bread of Life* (New York: Alba House, 1977), p. 16.

53. See 1 Cor 11. Dom Gregory Dix thinks this kind of abuse would never have occurred in a Jewish Christian community, since the Jews were used to making entire meals a part of their prayer life, whereas the Greeks

and Romans were more inclined to allow a meal to degenerate into excesses of eating and drinking. See Dix, *Liturgy*, p. 98.

54. 1 Cor 11:34.

55. See Hippolytus, *Apostolic Tradition*, 25–27, and Tertullian, *Apology*, 39.

56. Hippolytus, *Apostolic Tradition*, 26.1.

57. Ibid., 25:2.

58. See Lussier, *Bread of Life*, pp. 209–14, for a detailed discussion of this question.

59. Ibid., pp. 203–8.

60. Cyprian of Carthage, *To Successus on the Tidings Brought from Rome, Telling of the Persecution*, Epistle LXXXI [2], trans. Ernest Wallis, 4, in *ECF*.

61. See Lussier, *Bread of Life*, pp. 205–6. In the *Capella Graeca*, which was in fact a Christian dining room for the *refrigerium*, is the oldest painting of Christ found thus far, representing the raising of Lazarus.

62. *Catechism of the Catholic Church*, no. 1324.

63. Ignatius of Antioch, *The Epistle of Ignatius to the Ephesians*, 20, in *ECF*.

64. See E. C. E. Owen, *Some Authentic Acts of the Early Martyrs* (Oxford: Oxford University Press, 1927), pp. 100–103.

65. See Eusebius Pamphilus of Caesarea, *Church History*, trans. Arthur Cushman McGiffert, 5.1.62–63, in *ECF*, on the Martyrs of Lyons in A.D. 177. "The bodies of the martyrs, having thus in every manner been exhibited and exposed for six days, were afterward burned and reduced to ashes, and swept into the Rhone by the wicked men, so that no trace of them might appear on the earth. And this they did, as if able to conquer God, and prevent their new birth; that as they said, '... now let us see if they will rise again, and if their God is able to help them, and to deliver them out of our hands.'"

66. Ignatius of Antioch, *The Epistle of Ignatius to the Romans*, 4, in *ECF*.

67. This fragment of Caius' writing is preserved in Eusebius' *Church History*, 2.25.7. By "the trophies [*tropaia* in Greek] of the apostles", Caius must have been referring to the graves of Peter at the Vatican, and Paul along the Ostian Way (Paul was beheaded outside the walls of the city, along this road).

68. See Tertullian, *The Chaplet, or (De Corona)*, trans. Peter Holmes, 3, in *ECF*, and Cyprian, *To Successus*, 3.

69. See Orazio Marucchi, *The Evidence of the Catacombs for the Doctrines and Organization of the Primitive Church* (London: Sheed and Ward, 1929), pp. 64–65. Fr. Marucchi notes that the origins of the Jerominian martyrology, which provides the basis for our list of martyrs from the early Church period, can be traced back to the early third century.

70. Paul Allard, *Ten Lectures on the Martyrs*, trans. Luigi Cappadelta (London: Kegan Paul, Trench, Trübner and Co., 1907), p. 323.

71. Ibid., p. 312.

72. Ex 13:19. You can still visit the burial site of Joseph to this day.

73. Marcion at Smyrna, *The Encyclical Epistle of the Church at Smyrna concerning the Martyrdom of the Holy Polycarp*, 17.3, in *ECF*.

74. See Allard, *Ten Lectures*, p. 317.

75. See Ignatius, *Romans*, 1, in *ECF*: "For I am afraid of your love, lest it should do me an injury. For it is easy for you to accomplish what you please; but it is difficult for me to attain to God, if ye do not spare me, under the pretence of carnal affection."

76. Cyprian of Carthage, *On the Mortality (or Plague)*, trans. Ernest Wallis, 9, in *ECF*.

77. Translated and quoted in Marucchi, *Evidence*, p. 56.

78. In Col 1:24, Saint Paul wrote, "Now I rejoice in my sufferings for your sake, and in my flesh I complete what is lacking in Christ's afflictions for the sake of his body, that is, the Church." This passage indicates that Paul thought our sacrifices could somehow be joined to the sacrifice of Christ, for the good of the Church on earth.

79. Marcion at Smyrna, *Martyrdom of Polycarp*, 15.

80. Eusebius, *Church History*, 4.3.

81. H. B. Swete, "Prayer for the Departed in the First Four Centuries", in *Acts of Piety in the Early Church*, ed. Everett Ferguson (New York: Garland Publishing Co., 1993), p. 118.

82. This book is a part of the Old Testament in the Catholic canon of Scripture, but Protestants do not accept it as scriptural, for complicated historical reasons. Therefore, Protestants might not accept this evidence. However, even if Maccabees is not accepted as a part of Scripture, it can be accepted as a reliable guide to Jewish practice at the time of Christ.

83. The Catholic Church does not allow this practice.

84. See Swete, "Prayer", p. 119.

85. *Acts of Paul and Thecla*, 28, in *ECF* (from CD-ROM Contents page, go to "Apostle: Apocryphal Acts of the Apostles: The Story of Perpetua").

86. Tertullian, *On Monogamy*, trans. S. Thelwall, 10, in *ECF*.

87. Some scholars have speculated that Tertullian wrote the first and the third part, and their arguments seem reasonable to me. Tertullian was an active Catholic in Carthage at the time Perpetua was martyred. The style of the work is not inconsistent with Tertullian's other writings.

88. Tertullian, *The Martyrdom of Perpetua and Felicitas*, trans. R. E. Wallis, 2.3–4, in *ECF*.

89. Quoted in Swete, "Prayer", p. 119.

90. Quoted in Marucchi, *Evidence*, p. 52.

91. Ibid., p. 53.

92. Ibid., p. 56.

93. So in the NRSV.

94. Joseph H. Thayer, *Greek-English Lexicon of the New Testament* (Peabody, Mass.: Hendrickson Publishers, 1999), pp. 663–64.

95. Ibid., pp. 665–66.

96. See Mt 1:18 and Lk 1:26.

97. Ignatius, *Smyrnaeans*, 1.1. See also *The Epistle of Ignatius to the Trallians*, 9.1, in *ECF*, and *Ephesians*, 7.2.

98. Justin Martyr, *First Apology*, 33. See also Irenaeus, *Against Heresies*, 3.21, and Origen, *Against Celsus*, 1.34.

99. The dogma states, simply, that "Mary was conceived without stain of Original Sin." See Ludwig Ott, *Fundamentals of Catholic Dogma*, trans. Patrick Lynch (Rockford, Ill.: Tan Books, 1974), p. 199.

100. "Protoevangelium of James", in *The Other Gospels: Non-Canonical Gospel Texts*, ed. Ron Cameron, trans. Oscar Cullmann and A.J.B. Higgins (Philadelphia: Westminster Press, 1982), 4.1.

101. Ibid., 20.

102. See James R. Mueller, "Protoevangelium of James", in *Eerdmans Dictionary of the Bible*, ed. David Noel Freedman (Grand Rapids, Mich.: Eerdmans Publishing Co., 2000), pp. 671–72.

103. Jn 19:26.

104. An excellent short, accessible summary of the history and the evidence for the authenticity of this house is Donald Carroll, *Mary's House* (London: Veritas Books, 2000). Here is Carroll's take on the evidence: "So do I now believe my own reconstruction? Yes, to this extent: I know the facts of the story have been assembled with a scrupulous regard to accuracy, and I know that in no instance has history been reworked to accommodate the demands of the faith. Nonetheless, it has to be admitted that the evidence for Mary's residency on Nightingale Mountain, however detailed and impressive, remains circumstantial, and it will probably always remain so. In that way it is no different from any other unprobable proposition at the heart of religion: it requires a leap of faith. That's what faith is for. But in the case of Mary's house, it is the shortest leap I know" (p. 5). Having personally visited Mary's house, I agree with every word Carroll wrote in this passage.

105. Jo Ann McNamara, *A New Song: Celibate Women in the First Three Christian Centuries* (New York: Harrington Park Press, 1985), p. 80.

106. See *Coptic Apocryphal Gospels*, ed. J. Armitage Robinson (Cambridge, Mass.: Cambridge University Press, 1896). The Egyptian Church of the third and fourth centuries produced a vast array of literature associated with the lives of Jesus, Mary, and the apostles. These tales are contradictory, and many contain details we know to be false. They appear to be what we would call today historical novels, with a religious theme. It is impossible

to know, therefore, how much weight to put on any of the details found in these documents. Modern historical fiction tends to place a great deal of emphasis on accuracy in historical detail, but ancient novels do not appear to have had the same concern.

107. See Eusebius, *Church History*, 3.12.1. Ignatius of Antioch also mentions his predecessor with great reverence in *The Epistle of Ignatius to the Philadelphians*, 4, in *ECF*.

108. *Coptic Gospels*, p. 44.

109. Ludwig Hertling and Engelbert Kirschbaum, *The Roman Catacombs and Their Martyrs*, trans. M. Joseph Costelloe (Milwaukee: Bruce Publishing Co., 1956), p. 72.

110. Marucchi, *Evidence*, p. 74.

## Chapter 3: The Organization of the Early Church

1. See E. Glenn Hinson, *The Early Church: Origins to the Dawn of the Middle Ages* (Nashville: Abingdon Press, 1996), pp. 84–85. The author stresses that the early Christians organized along military lines for the sake of the mission of the Church.

2. I should make my personal opinion clear here. I am assuming that Clement of Rome's *First Epistle to the Corinthians* is authentic, was written in A.D. 96, and was written under the authority of Clement, the fourth Bishop of Rome, as Eusebius and Irenaeus claimed.

3. Alexandre Faivre, *The Emergence of the Laity in the Early Church*, trans. David Smith (New York: Paulist Press, 1990), p. 3.

4. See Mt 4:18–22, Mk 1:16–20, Lk 5:1–111, and Jn 1:35–42. The synoptic Gospels each present a list of the names of the Twelve, in Mt 10:24, Mk 3:16–19, and Lk 6:14–16.

5. Francis A. Sullivan, *From Apostles to Bishops: The Development of the Episcopacy in the Early Church* (New York: Newman Press, 2001), p. 19.

6. William F. Arndt and F. Wilbur Gingrich, *A Greek-English Lexicon of the New Testament and Other Early Christian Literature* (Chicago: University of Chicago Press, 1979), p. 99.

7. See James A. Mohler, *The Origin and Evolution of the Priesthood* (New York: Alba House, 1970), pp. 7–8. The primary duty of the Jewish apostles seems to have been to deliver messages to the communities of the Diaspora and return to Jerusalem with a report of what they observed.

8. See Acts 14:4, 14. Paul and Barnabas are both explicitly referred to as "apostles".

9. See 2 Cor 8:23 and Phil 2:25. In the first case the Greek *apostoloi* is translated "messengers". In the second case the Greek *apostolon* is translated "messenger".

10. I am indebted to Sullivan, *Apostles to Bishops*, p. 28, for this insight.

11. In 1 Pet 1:1, the salutation reads: "Peter, an apostle of Jesus Christ", and in 2 Pet 1:1, "Simon Peter, a servant and apostle of Jesus Christ".

12. Gal 2:9. "When they perceived the grace that was given to me, James and Cephas, and John, who were reputed to be pillars, gave to me and Barnabas the right hand of fellowship, that we should go to the Gentiles and they to the circumcised."

13. See 2 Chron 19:11 and Mal 2:7 for examples of this authority.

14. There is a tradition, with evidence to back it up, that the Apostle Thomas went as far as India, and that several other apostles traveled outside the bounds of the empire to spread the gospel. For a fascinating summary of these traditions, see C. Bernard Ruffin, *The Twelve: The Lives of the Apostles after Calvary* (Huntingdon, Ind.: Our Sunday Visitor Publishing Div., 1997).

15. Sullivan, *Apostles to Bishops*, p. 81.

16. *The Teaching of the Twelve Apostles (The Didache): The Lord's Teaching through the Twelve Apostles to the Nations*, 11, in *The Early Church Fathers* (Gervais, Ore.: Harmony Media, 2000), CD-ROM (on Contents page, look under "Apostle").

17. Ibid., 15.

18. Over and over we will find that throughout the Church, bishops were chosen by the people. We will discuss this process in greater detail shortly, but for now it is enough to know that the process was carefully designed to be orderly and not overly political.

19. The salutation reads, "The Church of God which sojourns at Rome, to the Church of God sojourning at Corinth ..."

20. The occasion for the letter is stated thus: "Owing, dear brethren, to the sudden and successive calamitous events which have happened to ourselves, we feel that we have been somewhat tardy in turning our attention to the points respecting which you consulted us; and especially to that shameful and detestable sedition, utterly abhorrent to the elect of God, which a few rash and self-confident persons have kindled to such a pitch of frenzy, that your venerable and illustrious name, worthy to be universally loved, has suffered grievous injury" (Clement of Rome, *First Epistle to the Corinthians, Codex Alexandrinus*, trans. John Keith, 1, in *ECF*.)

21. See Eusebius Pamphilus of Caesarea, *Church History*, trans. Arthur Cushman McGiffert, 3.38.1, in *ECF*.

22. Sullivan, *Apostles to Bishops*, p. 91.

23. Clement, *I Clement*, 1.

24. Ibid., 21.6.

25. Eusebius, *Church History*, 3.38.1–2.

26. Sullivan, *Apostles to Bishops*, p. 91. The word *hegoumenos* is used to describe the leaders of the Christian community in Hebrews 13:7, 17, and 24.

27. Clement, *I Clement*, 42.2–4.

28. Some scholars date his death as late as 115, but no one dates it any later than that.

29. See Gregory Dix, *Jurisdiction in the Early Church: Episcopal and Papal* (London: Faith House, 1975), pp. 54–56. Dom Gregory points out that canon 6 of the Council of Nicea (A.D. 325) grants to Antioch jurisdiction over the region in accordance with "the ancient customs". Unfortunately, this canon does not define the region Antioch had authority over, nor the date that this jurisdiction began.

30. Eusebius, *Church History*, 3.36.2.

31. Ignatius of Antioch, *The Epistle of Ignatius to the Trallians*, 10.2, in *ECF*.

32. Ignatius of Antioch, *The Epistle of Ignatius to the Smyrnaeans*, 6.2, in *ECF*.

33. Ignatius of Antioch, *The Epistle of Ignatius to the Ephesians*, 4.1, in *ECF*.

34. Ignatius of Antioch, *The Epistle of Ignatius to the Magnesians*, 7.1, in *ECF*.

35. Ignatius, *Ephesians*, 6.1.

36. Ignatius, *Smyrnaeans*, 8.2.

37. See Sullivan, *Apostles to Bishops*, p. 144.

38. Irenaeus of Lyons, *Against Heresies*, 1.1, in *ECF*.

39. Ibid., 3.1.1.

40. Ibid., 3.3.1. In the next two sections, Irenaeus makes good his boast by tracing the bishops of Rome all the way back to Peter and Paul.

41. Ibid., 4.26.2.

42. Sullivan, *Apostles to Bishops*, p. 151.

43. Most bishops about whose election we know something (Cyprian, Ambrose of Milan, Augustine of Hippo) were extremely reluctant to become bishop. In a society where the Church is wealthy and free from persecution, the election of bishops might lead to careerism, base politicking, corruption, and other ills.

44. Hippolytus of Rome, *The Apostolic Tradition of Hippolytus*, trans. Burton Scott Easton (London: Cambridge University Press, 1934), 2.

45. Cyprian of Carthage, *To Antonianus about Cornelius and Novatian*, Epistle LI [4], trans. Ernest Wallis, 8, in *ECF*.

46. Patrick Granfield, "Episcopal Election in Cyprian: Clerical and Lay Participation", in *Church Ministry and Organization in the Early Church Era*, ed. Everett Ferguson (New York: Garland Publishing Co., 1993), p. 48.

47. See Lampridius, *Alexander Severus* (http://penelope.uchicago.edu/ Thayer/E/Roman/Texts/Historia_Augusta/Severus_Alexander/2*.html), 45:64. Alexander Severus, a relatively wise ruler, encouraged the people to reveal any faults that would render candidates unfit for office.

48. *Didascalia Apostolorum: The Syriac Version Translated and Accompanied by the Verona Latin Fragments* (Oxford: Clarendon Press, 1929), 4.1.

49. See Cyprian, *To the Clergy and People Abiding in Spain, concerning Basilides and Martial*, Epistle LXVII [7], in *ECF*, for a case in which the bishop lapsed and the people simply chose another bishop, according to the accepted procedure.

50. *Didascalia Apostolorum*, 7.23.

51. See W. H. C. Frend, *The Rise of Christianity* (Philadelphia: Fortress Press, 1984), pp. 379–80, for a summary of these synods.

52. See Acts 15:1–29. This is the famous Council of Jerusalem, which occurred in A.D. 49 or 50.

53. After all, the Church also went from 1563 (Trent) to 1869 (Vatican I) without an ecumenical council.

54. Cyprian, *Antonianus*, 6.

55. See Cyprian, *Basilides and Martial*.

56. See Eusebius, *Church History*, 7.30. See also Frend, pp. 385–86, for a clear summary of the whole controversy.

57. Alexandrian theology, since before the days of Origen, strongly emphasized the eternal preexistence of Christ.

58. Frend, *Rise of Christianity*, p. 386.

59. Eusebius, *Church History*, 7.30.17.

60. One thinks of Cyprian's letter *To Father Stephanus, concerning Marcianus of Arles, Who Had Joined Himself to Novatian*, Epistle LXVI [4], in *ECF*, where Cyprian asked Pope Stephen to excommunicate Marcianus, Bishop of Arles, because Marcianus was not accepting the authority of the synod that had deposed him. We will explore this letter in greater detail shortly.

61. "In the beginning was the Word ..." The Alexandrians thought this was a clear reference to Christ's preexistence, but the Antiochenes maintained that Jesus and the Word were two distinct entities.

62. The major ecumenical councils of the fourth century were Nicea (325) and Constantinople I (381).

63. Acts 15:2.

64. Acts 15:7–11.

65. Acts 15:7.

66. Eusebius, *Church History*, 3.1.2.

67. See Dix, *Jurisdiction in the Early Church*, pp. 99–100, for a list of some of the leading Protestant scholars who find it impossible to deny the special role of Peter in the New Testament.

68. Eusebius, *Church History*, 2.14. Eusebius says that Peter's initial trip to Rome was occasioned by his dispute with Simon Magus. Jerome and Lactantius both record that Peter first arrived in Rome in A.D. 42.

69. Orazio Marucchi, *The Evidence of the Catacombs for the Doctrines and Organization of the Primitive Church* (London: Sheed and Ward, 1929), p. 77. Fr. Marucchi was not denying that Peter was Bishop of Rome for twenty-five years but was merely observing that from a historical perspective we do not know much about Peter's movements during this period.

70. Catholics observe his feast day on June 29. This date is first mentioned in conjunction with Peter's martyrdom by Tertullian and Origen.

71. This author visited Ephesus in March 2004 and saw the ruins of the Basilica of Saint John, where, according to tradition, his tomb lay. Like Peter, no one knows when John first arrived in Ephesus, but it is fairly certain that he ended his days there.

72. Clement, *I Clement*, 5–6. To be sure, Clement does not directly say that Peter and Paul died in Rome, but he groups them with anonymous martyrs that certainly died in Rome during the persecution of Nero.

73. Ignatius of Antioch, *The Epistle of Ignatius to the Romans*, 4, in *ECF*.

74. Eusebius, *Church History*, 2.25.

75. Clement, *I Clement*, 1.

76. Ibid., 7.

77. 1 Pet 5:3. It is worth noting that many modern scholars think this letter was written after Peter's death, by an anonymous author who wished to claim Peter's authority. Of course, the passage I am quoting here renders this argument irrelevant and even ridiculous. An anonymous author would claim Peter's authority, and then warn against using authority arrogantly? In any case, Raymond Brown, the dean of Catholic New Testament scholars, thinks there is a reasonable chance that Peter really did write this letter.

78. Clement, *I Clement*, 44.

79. Ibid.

80. Ibid., 57.

81. Ignatius, *Romans*, 1.

82. Frend, *Rise of Christianity*, p. 323.

83. Irenaeus of Lyons, *Against Heresies*, 3.3.3, in *ECF*.

84. Ibid., 3.3.2.

85. Tertullian, *The Prescription against Heretics*, trans. Peter Holmes, 36, in *ECF*.

86. Eusebius, *Church History*, 4.14.1.

87. Ibid., 5.24.1–9.

88. Dix, *Jurisdiction*, p. 45. "Rome was the capital of Christendom, and the Popes were the acknowledged 'leaders' of all the Churches without the

shadow of a rival in the first three centuries, in a way that was never quite true again."

89. The story of Marcion can be pieced together primarily from Tertullian's work *Against Marcion*.

90. Dix, *Jurisdiction*, p. 109.

91. Understanding this inscription is difficult, given the highly symbolic language used. I follow Dom Gregory Dix in interpreting it in an anti-Montanist light. (See *Jurisdiction*, p. 110.)

92. Cyprian of Carthage, *To Cornelius, concerning Fortunatus and Felicissimus*, or *Against the Heretics*, Epistle LIV [3], trans. Ernest Wallis, 4, in *ECF*.

93. Cyprian of Carthage, *To Cornelius, concerning Polycarp the Adrumetine*, Epistle XLIV [1], trans. Ernest Wallis, 9, in *ECF*.

94. Cyprian, *Antonianus*, 8.

95. Cyprian of Carthage, *Letter 20*, 3:2, in Sullivan, *Apostles to Bishops*, p. 208.

96. Cyprian, *Father Stephanus*, 1–5.

97. Cyprian of Carthage, *To Stephen, concerning a Council*, Epistle LXXI [3], trans. Ernest Wallis, 3, in *ECF*.

98. Cyprian of Carthage, *To Jubaianus, concerning the Baptism of Heretics*, Epistle LXXII [5], trans. Ernest Wallis, 11, in *ECF*.

99. Ibid., 18.

100. Cyprian of Carthage, *To Pompey, against the Epistle of Stephen about the Baptism of Heretics*, Epistle LXXIII [4], trans. Ernest Wallis, 1, in *ECF*.

101. See Mohler, *Origin and Evolution*, pp. 7–9. The Hebrew word that was translated into the Greek *apostolos* was *selihim*. The *selihim* normally traveled in pairs.

102. A helpful discussion of the early beginnings of Diaspora Judaism can be found in Mary Joan Winn Leith, "Israel among the Nations: The Persian Period", in *The Oxford History of the Biblical World* (New York: Oxford, 1998), pp. 413–15.

103. Ibid., p. 414.

104. Alastair Campbell, *The Elders: Seniority within Earliest Christianity* (Edinburgh: T and T Clark, 1994), p. 239.

105. The synagogue communities did not make up the office of presbyter out of thin air. There were numerous references in the Old Testament to guide them. See, for instance, Num 11:16–17: "Gather for me seventy men of the elders of Israel, whom you know to be the elders of the people and officers over them and bring them to the tent of the meeting, and let them take their stand there with you. And I will come down and talk with you there, and I will take some of the spirit which is upon you, and put it upon them, and they shall bear the burden of the people with you, that you may not bear it yourself alone."

106. Mohler, *Origin and Evolution*, pp. 3–4.

107. See Acts 13:5; 14:43.

108. See Acts 18:7. "Then he [Paul] left there and went to the the house of a man named Titius Justus, a worshiper of God; his house was next door to the synagogue."

109. Acts 18:8.

110. There is not enough time for a detailed exegesis of Revelation in this work, but most of the references to the elders occur between Rev 4:4 and 7:13. Verse 4:4 begins: "Around the throne were twenty-four thrones, and seated on the thrones were twenty-four elders." Dom Gregory Dix thinks this whole section of Revelation reveals a great deal about the first-century liturgy of Ephesus, the community of the Apostle John. See *The Shape of the Liturgy* (New York: Seabury Press, 1982), p. 28.

111. Clement, *I Clement*, 44.

112. Ignatius, *Magnesians*, 6.

113. Ignatius, *Trallians*, 12.

114. Ignatius, *Smyrnaeans*, 13.

115. Ibid., 8.

116. Ibid.

117. Ignatius of Antioch, *The Epistle of Ignatius to the Philadelphians*, 4, in *ECF*.

118. Ignatius, *Magnesians*, 2. "Since, then, I have had the privilege of seeing you, through Damas your most worthy bishop, and through your worthy presbyters Bassus and Apollonius, and through my fellow-servant the deacon Sotio, whose friendship may I ever enjoy".

119. Eusebius, *Church History*, 6.43.11.

120. See Hippolytus, *Apostolic Tradition*, 3, for an example of the imagery the early Church used.

121. See *Catechism of the Catholic Church*, no. 1567.

122. Hippolytus, *Apostolic Tradition*, 7.

123. Polycarp of Smyrna, *Epistle to the Philippians*, 6, in *ECF*.

124. Origen, *Commentary on Matthew*, 16, cited in Mohler, *Origin and Evolution*, p. 65. It should be noted that Origen was undoubtedly bitter toward the entire clergy of Alexandria, from the bishop on down, and his remarks are somewhat biased. Human nature being what it is, though, it seems likely that some of Origen's criticisms had at least some merit.

125. Cyprian of Carthage, *On the Lapsed*, trans. Ernest Wallis, 6, in *ECF*.

126. Cyprian of Carthage, *To the Presbyters and Deacons*, Epistle V [4], trans. Ernest Wallis, 4, in *ECF*.

127. Ibid., 2.

128. Tertullian, *Apology*, trans. S. Thelwall, 39, in *ECF*.

129. Cyprian, *Basilides and Martial*, 4.

130. *Didascalia Apostolorum*, 7, quoted in Mohler, *Origin and Evolution*, p. 58.

131. Hippolytus, *Apostolic Tradition*, 10.

132. For an interesting comment on the ministry of the confessors, see Cyprian of Carthage, *To Rogatianus the Presbyter, and the Other Confessors*, Epistle VI [11], trans. Ernest Wallis, in *ECF*, in which Cyprian warns the confessors against the dangers of spiritual pride.

133. Acts 6:1. The "Hellenists" were probably Greek-speaking Jews who had adapted aspects of Greek culture to Judaism. They may have been looked down upon by "Hebrews", Jews who kept to all the ancestral customs and practices.

134. I have argued elsewhere that this letter was written while Paul was still alive, either at Paul's dictation or by a disciple with Paul's full knowledge of the content. N.B.: This may be a minority opinion among modern scholars. But even if I'm wrong, my argument does not collapse. You simply move the date for these developments back a few years.

135. Phil 1:1.

136. Clement, *I Clement*, 42. The Old Testament reference is Isaiah 60:17, which reads in the RSV: "I will make your overseers peace and your taskmasters righteousness." The Old Testament exegesis of the early Church often differs from that of modern scholars, since the early Christians usually operated from the *Septuagint*, a Greek translation of the Hebrew original, that differs from the earliest Hebrew manuscripts we possess in many passages. The question is, which is closer to the original: the *Septuagint*, or the Masoretic Text, the oldest Hebrew manuscript we possess, which dates to the ninth century A.D., supplemented by fragments found at Qumran? But again, for the purposes of this work, the important question is not what the passage really means, but how the early Christians actually interpreted it, and there is no question that Clement, at least, thought it referred to bishops and deacons.

137. *Didache*, 15.1–2.

138. Edward P. Echlin, *The Deacon in the Church: Past and Future* (New York: Alba House, 1971), p. 17.

139. See Ignatius, *Ephesians*, 2.1, for an example.

140. Ignatius, *Magnesians*, 2.

141. Ignatius, *Trallians*, 2.

142. Ignatius, *Philadelphians*, 11.

143. Ibid., 10.

144. Ignatius, *Magnesians*, 6.

145. Hermas, *The Pastor of Hermas*, trans. F. Crombie, 1.5.1, in *ECF*.

146. Ibid., 3.9.26.

147. Justin Martyr, *The First Apology of Justin*, 65, in *ECF*.

148. Ibid., 67.

149. Tertullian, *On Baptism*, trans. S. Thelwall, 17, in *ECF*.

150. Hippolytus, *Apostolic Tradition*, 8.

151. See Echlin, *Deacon in the Church*, p. 37.

152. Cyprian of Carthage, *To Pomponius, concerning Some Virgins*, Epistle LXI [4], trans. Ernest Wallis, 1–4, in *ECF*.

153. See J. G. Davies, "Deacons, Deaconesses and the Minor Orders in the Patristic Period", in *Church, Ministry, and Organization in the Early Church*, ed. Everett Ferguson (New York: Garland Publishing Co., 1993), pp. 211–12. Though the *Apostolic Tradition* was probably written around 215, it is believed by scholars that it presents the practice of the Church from an earlier period, namely the 170s to 180s.

154. Hippolytus, *Apostolic Tradition*, 14.

155. Ibid., 30.

156. Cyprian of Carthage, *To the Clergy, on the Letters Sent to Rome, and about the Appointment of Saturus as Reader, and Optatus as Sub-deacon*, Epistle XXIII [3], trans. Ernest Wallis, in *ECF*.

157. See Davies, "Deacons, Deaconesses", p. 212, for a discussion of these letters.

158. See Cyprian of Carthage, *To the Clergy, concerning the Care of Poor and Strangers*, Epistle XXXV [5], trans. Ernest Wallis, in *ECF*, and *To Cornelius, about Cyprian's Approval of His Ordination, and concerning Felicissimus*, Epistle XLI [10], trans. Ernest Wallis, in *ECF*. In the former (letter 35), Cyprian went so far as to trust the acolyte Naricus with needed funds.

159. *The Reply of Nemesianus, Dativus, Felix, and Victor, to Cyprian*, Epistle LXXVII [9], trans. Ernest Wallis, 3, in *ECF* (from CD-ROM Contents page, go to "Cyprian of Carthage: The Eighty-Two Epistles of Cyprian").

160. Davies, "Deacons, Deaconesses", p. 216.

161. Justin Martyr, *First Apology*, 67.

162. Hippolytus, *Apostolic Tradition*, 12.

163. Davies, "Deacons, Deaconesses", p. 216.

164. See Mt 8:28–34, Mk 5:1–10, Lk 8:26–39, etc.

165. Cyprian of Carthage, *To Magnus, on Baptizing the Novatians, and Those Who Obtain Grace on a Sick-Bed*, Epistle LXXV [4], trans. Ernest Wallis, 15, in *ECF*.

166. See *The Confessors to Cyprian*, Epistle XVI [1], trans. Ernest Wallis, in *ECF*. (From CD-ROM Contents page, go to "Cyprian of Carthage: The Eighty-Two Epistles of Cyprian".) Lucian was both an exorcist and a lector. See also Eusebius, *Church History*, 7.2.1. Romanus was an exorcist and a deacon.

167. I would not exclude the possibility that at least some of these unfortunate people were authentically demon-possessed, just as I would not deny that demon possession occurs today. But not everyone who appears to be possessed really is, either.

168. *Constitutions of the Holy Apostles*, ed. James Donaldson, 8, 6–7, in *ECF* (on CD-ROM Contents page, look under "Apostle"). The *Constitutions of the Holy Apostles* is a complex document, containing material from the first three centuries and other material from the fourth and even the fifth centuries, so it is hard to tell when to date this section. In any case, here is the prayer: "Ye energumens, afflicted with unclean spirits, pray, and let us all earnestly, pray for them, that God, the lover of mankind, will by Christ rebuke the unclean and wicked spirits, and deliver His supplicants from the dominion of the adversary. May He that rebuked the legion of demons, and the devil, the prince of wickedness, even now rebuke these apostates from piety, and deliver His own workmanship from his power, and cleanse those creatures, which He has made with great wisdom. Let us still pray earnestly for them. Save them, O God, and raise them up by Thy power. Bow down your heads, ye energumens, and receive the blessings."

169. See Davies, "Deacons, Deaconesses", p. 215. These canons were compiled in the fifth century, but Davies thinks they must reflect the practices of an earlier time.

170. John Chrysostom, *Homily LXXI: Matthew XXII:34–36*, in *Homilies on the Gospel according to St. Matthew*, trans. Sir George Prevost, in *ECF*.

171. Jean Danielou, *The Ministry of Women in the Early Church*, trans. Glyn Simon (London: Faith Press, 1961), p. 7.

172. Tertullian, *Prescription against Heretics*, 41.5.

173. Irenaeus, *Against Heresies*, 1.8.3–4.

174. This point is conceded by one of the leading proponents of women in ministry. See Jo Ann McNamara, *A New Song: Celibate Women in the First Three Christian Centuries* (New York: Harrington Park Press, 1985), p. 68. "In our own time, we have surely seen too many contemporary examples of the sexual exploitation of women by self-appointed cult leaders not to agree that Irenaeus had a point." Professor McNamara also points out that Irenaeus could have been mistaken in his belief that Marcus' contact with the women involved sexual intercourse.

175. Dualism involves a radical separation of spirit and matter. Usually the implication is that the spirit is good, and matter is evil. When this conclusion is drawn, sexual intercourse, as a part of the material world, is deemed evil and forbidden. But other dualists hold that only the spirit matters, and therefore what you do with your body is of no importance whatsoever. These

types of dualists are usually charlatans, trying to convince people to engage in hedonistic lifestyles.

176. Pliny the Younger, *Letters*, trans. Betty Radice (Cambridge, Mass.: Harvard University Press, 1969), p. 294.

177. Danielou, *Ministry of Women*, p. 15, takes this approach. It seems to me, however, that the most likely answer is that they were servants (for this is the correct translation of *ancillae*) who were also deaconesses.

178. 1 Cor 14:34–35. Some scholars have argued that this requirement of Paul is a concession to cultural considerations, motivated by a desire to make the churches acceptable to their pagan neighbors. But there is no evidence that women were expected to keep silent in Greco-Roman temples. Actually, Paul seems to have been motivated more by a desire to keep order in the community. In verse 33, he observes, "God is a God not of disorder, but of peace", then begins his ruling on women's silence.

179. In a complicated argument, Danielou, *Ministry of Women*, pp. 10–11, observes that Paul speaks of male and female prophets as equals. The primary role of prophets in the New Testament is to pray. Paul does not forbid this activity to women, but he does forbid women to speak in church. Therefore, women must have been allowed to exercise their prophetic office outside of the liturgy. This argument is plausible, given what we know about the organized prayer life of the early Christians, but the case is not proven.

180. *Didascalia Apostolorum*, pp. 146–48.

181. Ibid., p. 146.

182. Ibid., p. 147.

183. See Aimé Georges Martimort, *Deaconesses: An Historical Study*, trans. K. D. Whitehead (San Francisco: Ignatius Press, 1986), pp. 35–75.

184. See Deut 25:5–10.

185. Bonnie Bowman Thurston, *The Widows: A Women's Ministry in the Early Church* (Minneapolis: Fortress Press, 1989), p. 9.

186. See, for example, Deut 14:28–29.

187. Thurston, *Widows*, p. 14.

188. For example, see Lydia, the wealthy seller of purple cloth in Acts 16:14.

189. Eusebius, *Church History*, 6.43.11.

190. Hippolytus, *Apostolic Tradition*, 11.

191. See Acts 9:36–39. Tabitha (Dorcas) was a widow. When Peter went to her house, the other widows showed him the clothes she had made, evidence of her faithful service.

192. The widow in Lk 18:7, who pestered the magistrate until justice was done, was considered the model of all widows.

193. See Thurston, *Widows*, pp. 74–75. Lucian of Antioch, no friend of the Church, wrote a satire in which one Peregrinus was imprisoned for being a Christian. Lucian has "old hags, 'widows,' they call them" standing outside the prison, praying. One should bear in mind that Lucian was writing a vicious satire and considered what he was writing funny, but satire contains a kernel of truth.

194. See Tit 2:3–5.

195. Polycarp, *Philippians*, 6.

196. See 1 Tim 5:13.

197. The one exception to this statement would be the vestal virgins of Rome, but they did not take a lifetime vow.

198. McNamara, *Celibate Women*, p. 11. Professor McNamara points out, however, that most of the celibates at Qumran were men. It is unclear if women even participated in the practice.

199. Consider the story of St. Agnes, whose pagan suitor had her thrown in a brothel, then had her beheaded. Agnes was only twelve years old when all this occurred, but in Roman culture it was the right age to marry, and neither her suitor nor her parents understood why she didn't want to marry.

200. See Lk 1:27 and Mt 1:23.

201. See Ignatius, *Smyrnaeans*, 1.1, *Trallians*, 9.1, and *Ephesians*, 7.2, 18.2, and 19.1.

202. The apocryphal writings are not useful as historical accounts or sources of doctrine. I am merely using them to provide a window into what the third-century Christians actually believed.

203. Thurston, *Widows*, pp. 79–81.

204. See Acts 21:9.

205. Most scholars assume that Paul thought that Jesus was returning soon, and the whole question would be moot.

206. See 1 Cor 7:7–8. He also added, "It is better to marry than to be aflame with passion."

207. Ignatius, *Philadelphians*, 6.

208. Clement of Rome, *First Epistle of the Blessed Clement, the Disciple of Peter the Apostle*, trans. B. P. Pratten, 5, in *ECF* (look under "Two Epistles concerning Virginity").

209. Justin Martyr, *First Apology*, 15. Justin wrote this apology around A.D. 150. It is possible that some of the 60- or 70-year-old celibates to whom he was referring received their first teaching at the feet of Clement, who wrote his letters in the 90s.

210. See Clement, *First Epistle*, 12.

211. Ibid., 9.

212. Cyprian of Carthage, *On the Dress of Virgins*, trans. Ernest Wallis, 11, in *ECF*.

213. Ibid., 21.

214. Ibid., 4.

215. Celsus, quoted in Origen, *Against Celsus*, trans. Frederick Crombie, 3.55, in *ECF*.

216. See 1 Cor 12.

217. The image of a nation of priests was first expressed in Ex 19:6. Once again, our debt to Judaism is so immense it could never possibly be repaid.

218. See Arndt and Gingrich, *Lexicon*, p. 435.

219. Alexander of Cappadocia, *From an Epistle to Demetrius, Bishop of Alexandria*, trans. S. D. F. Salmond, in *ECF*.

220. Clement, *I Clement*, 41.

221. Justin Martyr, *First Apology*, 67.

222. Hippolytus, *Apostolic Tradition*, 5–6.

223. See Lampridius, *Alexander Severus*, 45.7.

224. Tertullian, *Apology*, 39.

225. St. Jerome wrote that Tertullian was a priest, but he was evidently mistaken, since Tertullian referred to himself as one of the laity in his own writings.

226. Hippolytus, *Apostolic Tradition*, 19.

227. Origen, *Against Celsus*, 3.9.

228. Irenaeus of Lyons, *Against Heresies*, 2.32.4.

## Chapter 4: Persecutions and Martyrs in the Early Church

1. During the persecution of Diocletian, for instance, such vast numbers of Christians were martyred that no one could count them. See Lactantius, *Of the Manner in Which the Persecutors Died*, trans. William Fletcher, 15, in *The Early Church Fathers* (Gervais, Ore.: Harmony Media, 2000), CD-ROM: "Because of their great multitude, they were not burnt one after another, but a herd of them were encircled with the same fire." We will never know the names or anything about the lives of these unfortunate people.

2. The pagan philosopher Celsus made much of the fact that the Christians separated themselves from the rest of society. See Origen, *Against Celsus*, trans. Frederick Crombie, 8.2, in *ECF*: "After having put this question for the purpose of leading us to the worship of demons, he represents us as answering that it is impossible to serve many masters. 'This,' he goes on to say, 'is the language of sedition, and is only used by those who separate themselves and stand aloof from all human society.'"

3. See Tertullian, *Apology*, trans. S. Thelwall, 2, in *ECF*. His pen dripping with scorn, Tertullian responded to this accusation: "The falsehoods disseminated about us ought to have the same sifting, that it might be found how many murdered children each of us had tasted."

4. Tacitus, *Annals*, trans. Alfred John Church and William Jackson (Chicago: Encyclopedia Britannica, 1952), 15:44.

5. See Thomas Bokenkotter, *A Concise History of the Catholic Church* (New York: Doubleday, 1977), p. 24. There is some question as to how sincere pagan beliefs were at the time of Christ. There is the feeling that pagan religion was already dying out in the empire. This may or may not be true, but there are two undeniable facts. First, guilds of craftsmen and temple revenues suffered wherever Christianity took hold. (See Acts 19:21–36.) Second, the Romans certainly believed that their military successes were the result of their assiduous cultivation of divine favor, and they refused to give up pagan worship, for the same reason a man might refuse to walk under a ladder.

6. Tertullian, *Apology*, 40.

7. See *The Passion of the Scillitan Martyrs*, trans. J. A. Robinson, in *ECF*. This particular tale ended with the death of Speratus and his friends.

8. Hippolytus, *The Apostolic Tradition of Hippolytus*, trans. Burton Scott Easton (London: Cambridge University Press, 1934), 16.

9. Ibid.

10. See Oscar Cullmann, *The State in the New Testament* (New York: Scribner, 1956), for a precise expression of this view of the New Testament Church.

11. Rev 14:8. See also 18:2.

12. See Hippolytus, *On Daniel*, trans. S. D. F. Salmond, 33, in *ECF*: "After it, the fourth kingdom of the Romans will succeed, more powerful than those that went before it for which reason also it was likened to iron. For of it is said: 'And the fourth kingdom shall be strong as iron; as iron breaks and subdues all things, so shall it break and subdue all things.' And after all these kingdoms which have been mentioned, the kingdom of God is represented by the stone that breaks the whole image."

13. Rom 13:1.

14. 1 Pet 2:17.

15. Clement of Rome, *First Epistle to the Corinthians* (Bryennios version), *Codex Alexandrinus*, trans. John Keith, 61, in *ECF*. It goes without saying that some scholars think this passage is a much later addition. But there are other passages that speak of Christians praying for secular rulers, even when those rulers were persecuting them. There are, of course, scriptural precedents as well.

16. Mt 22:17.

17. To understand the full force of Justin's argument, one must bear in mind that this apology was addressed to the emperor Antoninus Pius and his son.

18. Justin Martyr, *First Apology of Justin*, 17, in *ECF*.

19. Tertullian, *Apology*, 30.

20. Ibid., 19.

21. The details of this compromise are not explicit in the writings of Origen but are to be found embedded in *Against Celsus*, 8.63–70, where Origen met Celsus' objections to Christianity point by point, and in the process explained what he thought Roman policy to the Christians should be.

22. Ibid., 8.70.

23. Ibid., 8.74.

24. Ibid., 8.73.

25. For example, Antoninus Pius was emperor when Polycarp was martyred in A.D. 155.

26. See Acts 7.

27. See the apocryphal *Acts of Philip* (from *ECF* Contents page, go to "Apostle: Apocryphal Acts of the Apostles") for an account of Philip's martyrdom.

28. Tacitus, *Annals*, 15.44.

29. Eusebius Pamphilus of Caesarea, *Church History*, trans. Arthur Cushman McGiffert, 2.26, in *ECF*.

30. See the section on emperor worship, pp. 30–33 above.

31. See Raymond Brown, *An Introduction to the New Testament* (New York: Doubleday, 1997), pp. 806–9, for a good discussion of this theory.

32. Eusebius, *Church History*, 3.18.

33. Ibid.: "They recorded that in the fifteenth year of Domitian Flavia Domitilla, daughter of a sister of Flavius Clement, who at that time was one of the consuls of Rome, was exiled with many others to the island of Pontia in consequence of testimony borne to Christ."

34. Suetonius, *Lives of the Caesars*, trans. Catharine Edwards (New York: Oxford University Press, 2000), 8.15.

35. Orazio Marucchi, *The Evidence of the Catacombs for the Doctrines and Organization of the Primitive Church* (London: Sheed and Ward, 1929), pp. 89–91.

36. Pliny the Younger, *Letters*, trans. Betty Radice (Cambridge, Mass.: Harvard University Press, 1969), pp. 293–94.

37. Eusebius, *Church History*, 3.23.

38. W. H. C. Frend, *The Rise of Christianity* (Philadelphia: Fortress Press, 1984), p. 171.

39. Eusebius, *Church History*, 5.1.

40. See ibid., 6.2. There is no evidence that Alexander ever actually converted, but he evinced great sympathy for Christians.

41. Jerome, *Lives of Illustrious Men*, trans. Ernest Cushing Richardson, 54, in *ECF*.

42. Eusebius, *Church History*, 6.34.

43. Ibid., 6.36.

44. See E. Glenn Hinson, *The Early Church: Origins to the Dawn of the Middle Ages* (Nashville: Abingdon Press, 1996), p. 125, for a persuasive interpretation of Valerian's motives.

45. Prudentius, *Crowns of Martyrdom*, in *Prudentius*, vol. 2, trans. H.J. Thomson (Cambridge: Harvard University Press, 1961), 3.76–87.

46. Pontius the Deacon, *The Life and Passion of Cyprian, Bishop and Martyr*, 15–18, in *ECF*.

47. See Eusebius, *Church History*, 7.12.

48. Ibid., 7.13.

49. As Hinson points out, this is no more than the Edict of Milan called for some fifty years later (*Early Church*, p. 128).

50. Ibid.

51. Aurelian was interested in promoting solar monotheism. It is unclear whether he saw Christianity as an ally or an enemy in this effort.

52. See Lactantius, *Persecutors Died*, 15. Lactantius states that Diocletian forced them to profane themselves with sacrifices.

53. Eusebius, *Church History*, 8.4.

54. Lactantius, *Persecutors Died*, 10.

55. Ibid., 12. Galerius evidently wanted the Christians to sacrifice or be executed, but Diocletian preferred milder measures.

56. Ibid., 14–15.

57. Eusebius, *Church History*, 8.13.

58. Ibid., 8.12.1–2.

59. Lactantius, *Persecutors Died*, 33–34.

60. I have simplified the confused political situation of this period considerably. It would take diagrams and three hundred pages of text to do justice to this period. My primary purpose here has been to give my readers a feel for the persecutions, not chart the ins and outs of imperial politics.

61. Eusebius, *Church History*, 6.5.

62. Cyprian, *On the Lapsed*, trans. Ernest Wallis, 2, in *ECF*.

63. Ibid., 14.

## Chapter 5: The Early Christians and Slavery

1. Pope Callistus was a slave freed by his Christian master. See Hippolytus of Rome, *The Refutation of All Heresies*, trans. J.H. MacMahon, 9.7, in *The Early Church Fathers* (Gervais, Ore.: Harmony Media, 2000, CD-ROM). Be warned, however. Hippolytus' version of Callistus' life is extremely biased.

2. Mk 10:45. The word translated "to serve" is the verbal form of *diakonos*, which is the Greek word for a household servant.

3. Mk 10:43–44. Again, the word "servant" in verse 43 is *diakonos*, a word with which we are very familiar. But the Greek word in verse 44, which is rightly translated as "slave", is *doulos*, a word that designated the lowest form of slave, who must engage in manual labor, endure constant beatings, and eat bad food.

4. See also Col 3:11.

5. Gal 3:26.

6. See Eph 6:5, Col 3:22, and Titus 2:9. Scholars have their ways of explaining these passages, which they view as highly troubling. Paul became more "conservative" as he got older, they surmise. Or they conclude that Paul did not actually write these Letters. But the second explanation is ruled out by the text. Col 3:22 comes shortly after the passage where Paul wrote, "there is neither slave nor free". If Paul did not write 3:22, he couldn't have written 3:11 either.

7. *The Teaching of the Twelve Apostles (The Didache): The Lord's Teaching through the Twelve Apostles to the Nations*, 4.11, in *ECF* (on CD-ROM Contents page, look under "Apostle").

8. The clearest evidence of this is that some Christians were bishops, presbyters, and deacons, and others were not, despite the fact that the early Church subscribed to the teaching of the priesthood of all the baptized.

9. Hippolytus, *Refutation of All Heresies*, 9.7.

10. Hippolytus of Rome, *The Apostolic Tradition of Hippolytus*, trans. Burton Scott Easton (London: Cambridge University Press, 1934), 16.15–16.

11. Hermas, *The Pastor of Hermas*, trans. F. Crombie, 1.1.1, in *ECF*.

12. In 1 Cor 7:21, Paul asks the rhetorical question, "Were you a slave when called?" knowing that the answer would be yes in some cases.

13. I find the translation used in the Catholic edition of the RSV more accurate than any other. The Greek in this passage lends itself to more than one translation, and some versions of the NT actually have Paul writing that even if a slave had an opportunity to be freed he should remain a slave. But a careful reading of the passage in Greek, with due attention to the context, reveals that the RSV accurately reveals Paul's intention. See J. Albert Harrill, *The Manumission of Slaves in Early Christianity* (Tubingen: JCB Mohr, 1995), pp. 68–126.

14. See Raymond E. Brown, *An Introduction to the New Testament* (New York: Doubleday, 1997), pp. 502–10, for a summary of the problems associated with this Letter, and the most likely solution, which I am summarizing here.

15. Philem 16.

16. The most likely scenario is that Onesimus carried the Letter himself, since Paul does not introduce a letter-carrier, as would have been customary if the letter-carrier was unknown to the recipient. If Onesimus carried the Letter himself, he would have destroyed it if he decided to run away again. Paul sent Onesimus back to Philemon of his own free will, and Onesimus must have gone back to Philemon and been forgiven, otherwise we wouldn't have the Letter.

17. *Constitutions of the Holy Apostles*, ed. James Donaldson, 7.4, in *ECF*. This document is from the fourth century but contains some materials from an earlier period. It seems reasonable to believe that Onesimus was forgiven by his master, given his freedom, and later became a leader in the early Church.

18. Ignatius of Antioch, *The Epistle of Ignatius to Polycarp*, 4, in *ECF*.

19. See Hippolytus, *Refutation of All Heresies*, 9.7. Bear in mind that Hippolytus did not like Callistus and cast all these events in the worst possible light.

20. This document was written in the early fourth century, recounting events that must have occurred around A.D. 270. We do not know who the author was.

21. Archelaus, *The Acts of the Disputation with the Heresiarch Manes*, trans. S. D. F. Salmond, 1, in *ECF*.

22. See Harrill, *Manumission*, p. 189, for a discussion of the circumstances surrounding this type of manumission.

23. Eusebius, *Church History*, 6.43.11.

24. Clement of Alexandria, *The Instructor (Paedagogus)*, trans. William Wilson, 3.4, in *ECF*.

25. Aristides the Philosopher, *The Apology of Aristides the Philosopher*, trans. D. M. Kay, 15.6, in *ECF*.

26. See Jennifer A. Glancy, *Slavery in Early Christianity* (New York: Oxford University Press, 2002), p. 131, for a summary of the evidence.

27. G. H. R. Horsley, ed. *New Documents Illustrating Early Christianity*, vol. 1, *A Review of the Greek Inscriptions and Papyri* (Marrickville, Australia: Ancient History Documentary Research Centre, 1981), pp. 140–41. Some authors have pointed out that the collar, horrible though it seems to us, was actually more humane than the Greco-Roman practice of branding slaves. We progress very slowly, if at all, it seems.

28. Quoted in Glancy, *Slavery*, p. 92.

29. See Richard Fletcher, *The Barbarian Conversion* (New York: Henry Holt and Co., 1997), pp. 146ff.

30. Hermas, *Pastor of Hermas*, 3.5.2.

## Chapter 6: The Rich, the Poor, and Charity in Early Christianity

1. I rely on Rodney Stark, *The Rise of Christianity: A Sociologist Reconsiders History* (Princeton: Princeton University Press, 1996), pp. 76–77, for these statistics. Stark is a sociologist by trade, and his numbers are based on comparable death rates from other plagues, as well as historical sources.

2. Arthur Boak, "The Population of Roman and Byzantine Karanis", *Historia* 4 (1955): 157–62.

3. See Stark, *Sociologist*, pp. 83–86, on this point.

4. Eusebius Pamphilus of Caesarea, *Church History*, trans. Arthur Cushman McGiffert, 7.22.10, in *The Early Church Fathers* (Gervais, Ore.: Harmony Media, 2000), CD-ROM.

5. Ibid., 7.22.8–9.

6. Pontius the Deacon, *The Life and Passion of Cyprian, Bishop and Martyr*, 9, in *ECF*.

7. Julian, *Fragment of a Letter to a Priest*, 290A, quoted in Stark, *Sociologist*, p. 84.

8. See Deut 14:22–28 for an example. The Torah attempted to establish not only an ethic of charity, but a structure by which charity could be efficiently transferred from those who had to those who had not.

9. The story of the Good Samaritan appears to be emblematic of a struggle within Judaism on this point. Jesus, with other rabbis, argued that one should help those in need without regard to their nationality. Eventually, the universalist position won the day, but in the period we are discussing, different schools of thought prevailed in different communities. See Lk 10:25–42.

10. Juvenal, *Satires*, trans. Niall Rudd and Edward Courtney (Bristol, England: Bristol Classical Press, 1977), 3.235.

11. Lucian of Samosata, "Saturnalia", in *Lucian, a Selection*, trans. M. D. MacLeod (Warminster, England: Aris and Phillips, 1991), p. 31.

12. Plautus, *The Pot of Gold and Other Plays*, trans. E. F. Watling (New York: Penguin, 1965), p. 339.

13. Roman Garrison, *Redemptive Almsgiving in Early Christianity* (Sheffield, England: JSOT Press, 1993), pp. 38–45.

14. Cited in ibid., p. 42.

15. See Aristotle, *Nichomachean Ethics*, trans. Martin Ostwald (Indianapolis: Bobs-Merrill, 1962), 4.1.12.

16. Mt 25:40.

17. The early Christians did not subscribe to anything like the Lutheran doctrine of *sola fide*, which cannot be found in Scripture. The early Christians *did* subscribe to the teachings found in the Epistle of James, where the author wrote, "a man is justified by works and not by faith alone." See Jas 2:24.

18. Deaconesses existed in the Eastern parts of the early Church, but the institution died out in the third century. In the West, and in the East after this time, widows handled the special ministries to women.

19. See Sulpitius Severus, *On the Life of Saint Martin*, trans. Alexander Roberts, 1, in *ECF*.

20. Hermas, *The Pastor of Hermas*, trans. F. Crombie, 3.1.8–9, in *ECF*.

21. See 1 Cor 16:1–4, Rom 15:25–27, and 2 Cor 8:1–9:5.

22. Cyprian of Carthage, *To the Numidian Bishops, on the Redemption of Their Brethren from Captivity among the Barbarians*, Epistle LIX [1], trans. Ernest Wallis, in *ECF*. Numidia was a region of Africa for which Cyprian felt the Carthaginian diocese was somewhat responsible.

23. Throughout the literature of this period, authors mention the tithing of the Old Testament period, but never apply it to their own time. Possibly, it was assumed that Christians would give a tenth to the Church, but it is never explicitly stated.

24. Hippolytus of Rome, *The Apostolic Tradition of Hippolytus*, trans. Burton Scott Easton (London: Cambridge University Press, 1934), p. 37. Cheese, olives, oils, and milk are mentioned. There is no mention of livestock, such as the peasants of the Middle Ages might give to the Church.

25. See Garrison, *Redemptive Almsgiving*, and L. William Countryman, *The Rich Christian in the Church of the Early Empire: Contradictions and Accomodations* (New York: Edwin Mellen Press, 1980).

26. See Robert A. Sungenis, *Not by Faith Alone: The Biblical Evidence for the Catholic Doctrine of Justification* (Goleta, Calif.: Queenship Publishing, 1997), for the Catholic side of this debate.

27. Mt 19:16–30, Mk 10:17–31, and Lk 18:18–30.

28. Evangelicals say that Jesus gave this "hard saying" only to convince the young man of the impossibility of "salvation by works". But if so, Jesus was a very poor teacher and missed the chance to save the young man by clearly explaining what he meant. As usual, Jesus meant exactly what he said, but he was not referring to a condition for salvation, but discipleship. In every generation, there are those who are called to give up everything to follow Jesus. The rich young man was evidently called, but unable to answer the call at that time. But this does not mean the rich young man could not still be saved, "for all things are possible with God".

29. Garrison, *Redemptive Almsgiving*, p. 63.

30. Lk 6:38.

31. Lk 16:9.

32. See Cyprian of Carthage, *On Works and Alms*, trans. Ernest Wallis, 2, in *ECF*, and Origen, *Homilies on Leviticus*, trans. Gary Wayne Barkley (Washington, D.C.: Catholic University Press, 1990), 2.4.

33. 2 Cor 9:6.

34. 1 Pet 4:8.

35. *The Teaching of the Twelve Apostles (The Didache): The Lord's Teaching through the Twelve Apostles to the Nations*, 4.6–7, in *ECF*.

36. Clement of Rome, *Second Epistle to the Corinthians, Codex Alexandrinus*, trans. John Keith, 16.4, in *ECF*.

37. 1 Cor 6:11.

38. Clement of Alexandria, *Who Is the Rich Man That Will Be Saved?* trans. William Wilson, 32, in *ECF*.

39. Ibid., 35.

40. Ibid., 37.

41. Ibid., 31.

42. Tertullian, *Apology*, trans. S. Thelwall, 39, in *ECF*.

43. Cyprian most likely placed his property in a trust for the Church of Carthage. Since he became Bishop of Carthage shortly after his baptism, he actually became the administrator of the property he gave away. See Countryman, *Rich Christian*, pp. 183–200, on this point.

44. Socrates Scholasticus, *The Ecclesiastical History*, trans. A. C. Zenos, 4.27, in *ECF*.

45. Countryman, *Rich Christian*, p. 117.

46. See Clement of Rome, *The First Epistle of the Blessed Clement, the Disciple of Peter the Apostle*, in *ECF* (look under "Two Epistles concerning Virginity"). In this letter, we learn many things about the practice of consecrated virginity in the early second century. Unfortunately, we do not receive the answer to the questions we are concerned with here. How did they live? What did they do with their property? The author knew the answer to this question, and his original readers knew, so they felt no reason to mention the subject.

## Chapter 7: The Early Christians and Military Service

1. Eusebius Pamphilus of Caesarea, *Church History*, trans. Arthur Cushman McGiffert, 5.5.1–6, in *The Early Church Fathers* (Gervais, Ore.: Harmony Media, 2000), CD-ROM.

2. See Chapter 4 in Part 2.

3. Marcus Aurelius, *Meditations*, trans. C. Scot Hicks and David V. Hicks (New York: Scribner, 2002), 3.16.

4. See Mt 5:9 and Lk 6:17–23.

5. Mt 5:38.

6. Lk 6:27.

7. Mt 26:52.

8. Jn 18:36.

9. Lk 3:14.

10. Adolph Harnack, *Militia Christi: The Christian Religion and the Military in the First Three Centuries*, trans. David McInnes Gracie (Philadelphia: Fortress Press, 1981), pp. 27–28.

11. John Helgeland, Robert J. Daly, and J. Patout Burns, *Christians and the Military: The Early Experience* (Philadelphia: Fortress Press, 1985), p. 43.

12. Harnack, *Militia Christi*, p. 65.

13. Clement of Rome, *First Epistle to the Corinthians, Codex Alexandrinus*, trans. John Keith, 21, in *ECF*.

14. Ibid., 28.

15. Ibid., 37. It should be noted that Clement takes the image a step further than Paul. In his use of military images, Paul was generally writing about individual preparation for the Christian life. Clement is saying that the Church should be organized like an army, with the bishops as generals, presbyters as legates, etc.

16. Ignatius of Antioch, *The Epistle of Ignatius to Polycarp*, 6, in *ECF*.

17. Justin Martyr, *The First Apology of Justin*, 39, in *ECF*.

18. Hippolytus of Rome, *The Apostolic Tradition of Hippolytus*, trans. Burton Scott Easton (London: Cambridge University Press, 1934), p. 16.

19. Tertullian, *Apology*, trans. S. Thelwall, 37, in *ECF*. The "camp" refers to the camps of the legions.

20. Ibid., 42.

21. Tertullian, *On Idolatry*, trans. S. Thelwall, 19, in *ECF*.

22. Harnack, *Militia Christi*, p. 77.

23. The Roman army handed out crowns in the same way the U.S. military today hands out medals and ribbons. For instance, the Grass Crown could be won for actions that saved an entire army. Soldiers were supposed to wear their crowns on ceremonial occasions, and not wearing a crown was tantamount to being out of uniform.

24. Tertullian, *The Chaplet, or (De Corona)*, trans. Peter Holmes, 1, in *ECF*.

25. Ibid., 11.

26. Ibid.

27. Ibid.

28. Clement of Alexandria, *Exhortation to the Heathen*, trans. William Wilson, 10.100, in *ECF*.

29. See his commentaries on Numbers and Joshua for examples.

30. Origen, *Homilies on Joshua*, trans. Barbara J. Bruce, ed. Cynthia White (Washington, D.C.: Catholic University Press, 2002), 15.1.

31. Harnack, *Militia Christi*, p. 49. Harnack goes on to show that Origen's teachings became the foundation of the ascetic and monastic movements of the fourth century.

32. Origen, *Against Celsus*, trans. Frederick Crombie, 4.82, in *ECF*.

33. Ibid., 5.33.

34. Ibid., 7.26.

35. Harnack, *Militia Christi*, pp. 59–61.

36. Cyprian of Carthage, *To the Clergy and People, about the Ordination of Celerinus as Reader*, Epistle XXXIII [4], trans. Ernest Wallis, 3, in *ECF*.

37. Cyprian of Carthage, *To Donatus*, Epistle I [1], trans. Ernest Wallis, 6, in *ECF*.

38. Roland H. Bainton, "The Early Church and War", in *Christian Life: Ethics, Morality, and Discipline in the Early Church*, ed. Everett Ferguson (New York: Garland Publishing Co., 1993), p. 196.

39. See C. John Cadoux, *The Early Christian Attitude to War* (New York: Gordon Press, 1975), pp. 100–101, for a summary of the scholarly work on these inscriptions. In the past, some scholars have claimed to have inscriptional evidence of Christian soldiers from the reign of Hadrian (117–138), but these inscriptions have either been forged or are from a later period. This is not to say, of course, that there were no Christian soldiers during Hadrian's reign, but we have no evidence of them.

40. G. R. Watson, *The Roman Soldier* (Ithaca, N.Y.: Cornell University Press, 1995), p. 133. Professor Watson thinks the lack of evidence means there were still few Christians in the army, but with a Christian emperor, being a Christian was considered a good means of promotion, and many soldiers converted hoping to gain preference. I stick by my point: pagan or Christian, soldiers don't carry around a lot of personal effects.

41. Tertullian, *Apology*, 5.

42. Helgeland et al., *Christians and the Militiary*, p. 33.

43. Ibid., p. 33.

44. Dio Cassius, *Roman History*, trans. J. W. Rich (Warminster, England: Aris and Phillips, 1990), 82.8.1–10.5.

45. Helgeland et al., *Christians and the Military*, p. 33.

46. See Part 2, Chapter 2. The church at Dura-Europos was actually a house that was converted into a church.

47. Eusebius Pamphilus of Caesarea, *The Life of the Blessed Emperor Constantine*, trans. Ernest Cushing Richardson, 1.32, in *ECF*.

48. Ibid.

49. Ibid.

50. Tertullian, *Chaplet*, 1.

51. *The Acts of Marcellus* (Recension N), as quoted in Helgeland et al., *Christians and the Military*, pp. 59–60.

52. Eusebius, *Church History*, 7.15.

53. Edward A. Ryan, "The Rejection of Military Service by the Early Christians", in *Christian Life: Ethics, Morality, and Discipline in the Early Church*, ed. Everett Ferguson (New York: Garland Publishing Co., 1993), p. 242.

54. Lactantius, *Of the Manner in Which the Persecutors Died*, trans. William Fletcher, 10, in *ECF*.

55. Eusebius, *Church History*, 7.1.1–5.

56. See Phil 4:22: "All the saints greet you, especially those in Caesar's household."

## Chapter 8: The Early Christians and Family Life

1. See W. H. C. Frend, *The Rise of Christianity* (Philadelphia: Fortress Press, 1984), pp. 291–92. The purpose of this apology was to defend the faith on an intellectual level, but the author included personal details about his friend as a literary device. Octavius may or may not have been a fictional character, but the way in which Minucius describes him reveals a great deal about the feeling of the early Christians toward the simpler pleasures of life, family, and children.

2. Minucius Felix, *The Octavius of Minucius Felix*, trans. Robert Ernest Wallis, 2, in *The Early Church Fathers* (Gervais, Ore.: Harmony Media, 2000), CD-ROM.

3. *The Martyrdom of the Holy Martyrs Justin, Chariton, Charites, Paeon, and Liberianus, Who Suffered at Rome*, 3, in *ECF*.

4. W. A. Strange, *Children in the Early Church* (Carlisle, England: Paternoster Press, 1996), p. 7.

5. Brian W. Grant, *The Social Structure of Christian Families: A Historical Perspective* (St. Louis, Mo.: Chalice Press, 2000), p. 24.

6. Eph 5:21.

7. Col 3:15.

8. Mk 3:35.

9. See Mk 13:12, Mt 4:21–22, and Lk 20:35.

10. See 1 Tim 3:15 and Gal 6:10.

11. Rosemary Radford Ruether, *Christianity and the Making of the Modern Family* (Boston: Beacon Press, 2000), p. 13. By this term, Professor Ruether does not mean that the feeling of family provided by the early Church was a false one, but simply that some of the families of the early Church were not biological.

12. Mt 19:8. The author's translation.

13. Ruether, *Family*, p. 15.

14. Joseph H. Thayer, *Greek-English Lexicon of the New Testament* (Peabody, Mass.: Hendrickson Publishers, 1999), pp. 531–32.

15. Justin Martyr, *The First Apology of Justin*, 15.5, in *ECF*.

16. Tertullian, *On Monogamy*, trans. S. Thelwall, in *ECF*. He began this treatise, "Heretics do away with marriage, psychics accumulate them." Tertullian rejected both these positions.

17. Hermas, *The Pastor of Hermas*, trans. F. Crombie, 2.4.4, in *ECF*.

18. Ibid., 2.4.1.

19. 1 Cor 7:12–14.

20. Justin Martyr, *First Apology*, 15.

21. Willy Rordorf, "Marriage in the New Testament and in the Early Church", in *Christian Life: Ethics, Morality, and Discipline in the Early Church*, ed. Everett Ferguson (New York: Garland Publishing Co., 1993), pp. 154–55.

22. Rodney Stark, *The Rise of Christianity: A Sociologist Reconsiders History* (Princeton: Princeton University Press, 1996), pp. 117–22.

23. Ignatius of Antioch, *The Epistle of Ignatius to Polycarp*, 5, in *ECF*.

24. See Stark, *Sociologist*, p. 114. When people of different faiths marry, typically the less religious partner converts to the beliefs of the person whose personal faith is stronger.

25. Tertullian, *To His Wife*, trans. S. Thelwall, 2.8, in *ECF*.

26. Rordorf, "Marriage", pp. 156–58.

27. Jn 2:11.

28. Thayer, *Greek-English Lexicon*, p. 573.

29. See *Catechism of the Catholic Church*, no. 774.

30. William F. Arndt and F. Wilbur Gingrich, *A Greek-English Lexicon of the New Testament and Other Early Christian Literature* (Chicago: University of Chicago Press, 1979), p. 530. In his *Letter to the Magnesians*, 9.2, Ignatius of Antioch refers to the death and Resurrection of Jesus as a *mysterion*.

31. See Cyprian of Carthage, *A Treatise against the Heretic Novatian by an Anonymous Bishop*, trans. Ernest Wallis, 3, in *ECF*.

32. Kenneth Stevenson,"The Origins of the Nuptial Blessing", in *Christian Life: Ethics, Morality, and Discipline in the Early Church*, ed. Everett Ferguson (New York: Garland Publishing Co., 1993), p. 160.

33. Ibid.

34. Tertullian, *To His Wife*, 2.8.

35. *Acts of the Holy Apostle Thomas*, 1–3, in *ECF* (from CD-ROM Contents page, go to "Apostle: Apocryphal Acts of the Apostles"). This is a strange document and contains nothing that actually pertains to the life of the actual apostle. It was written sometime in the third century and must contain details that would ring true to some Christians of that period.

36. The wedding feast mentioned in the *Acts of Thomas* looks more like the heavenly messianic banquet, which is compared to a wedding feast throughout the New Testament.

37. Ludwig Hertling and Engelbert Kirschbaum, *The Roman Catacombs and Their Martyrs*, trans. M. Joseph Costelloe (Milwaukee: Bruce Publishing Co., 1956), p. 194.

38. Stevenson, "Origins", pp. 414–15.

39. W. A. Strange, *Children in the Early Church* (Carlisle, England: Paternoster Press, 1996), p. 62.

40. Of course, there is no evidence that the servant (called a *doulos*) in this passage is a child. But remember, children and servants were both under the authority of the *paterfamilias* in the Roman system.

41. Mt 18:3–4.

42. See for example Mk 10:28–30, Mt 19:27–29, and Lk 18:28–30.

43. Strange, *Children*, p. 60.

44. In verse 9, Eutychus is called a *neanias*, which means "a young man", but in verse 12 he is called a *paidia*, a boy. It seems likely that Luke was trying to say that Eutychus was a teenager.

45. Pliny the Younger, *Letters*, trans. Betty Radice (Cambridge, Mass.: Harvard University Press, 1969), p. 294.

46. *The Teaching of the Twelve Apostles (The Didache): The Lord's Teaching through the Twelve Apostles to the Nations*, 4.9, in *ECF*.

47. Polycarp of Smyrna, *Epistle to the Philippians*, 4.2, in *ECF*.

48. Strange, *Children*, pp. 78–79.

49. Tertullian, *On Idolatry*, trans. S. Thelwall, 10, in *ECF*.

50. Eusebius Pamphilus of Caesarea, *Church History*, trans. Arthur Cushman McGiffert, 6.2.7, in *ECF*.

51. Ibid., 6.18.4.

52. Cyprian of Carthage, *On the Lapsed*, trans. Ernest Wallis, 25, in *ECF*.

53. *Constitutions of the Holy Apostles*, ed. James Donaldson, 8.13, in *ECF*. This document is, as noted, from the fourth century, but is somewhat reflective of customs from the earlier age of the Church.

54. Tertullian, *The Martyrdom of Perpetua and Felicitas*, trans. R. E. Wallis, 2.2, in *ECF*.

55. John T. Noonan, "Abortion and the Catholic Church: A Summary History", in *Christian Life: Ethics, Morality, and Discipline in the Early Church*, ed. Everett Ferguson (New York: Garland Publishing Co., 1993), p. 180.

56. See Jer 1:5, Isa 44:2 and 49:5, Job 31:15–48, Ps 71:6, and Ps 139:13 just for starters.

57. Thayer, *Greek-English Lexicon*, p. 649.

58. For a more complete explanation of this passage, see Noonan, "Abortion and the Catholic Church", pp. 89–90.

59. *Didache*, 2.2.

60. Barnabas, *The Epistle of Barnabas*, 19.5, in *ECF*.

61. Clement of Alexandria, *The Pedagogue*, 2.10.96, quoted in Noonan, "Abortion and the Catholic Church", p. 92.

62. Minucius Felix, *Octavius*, 30.

63. Hippolytus of Rome, *The Refutation of All Heresies*, trans. J. H. MacMahon, 9.7, in *ECF*.

64. Athenagorus of Athens, *A Plea for the Christians*, trans. B. P. Pratten, 35, in *ECF*.

65. Justin Martyr, *First Apology*, 15.


## Conclusion

1. The ending of slavery in the fifth and sixth centuries might have had more to do with a lack of ready cash, which brought about the rise of feudalism, where those who might otherwise have been slaves ended up tied to the land. But in the sixth and seventh centuries, there was a widespread movement, motivated by the love of Christ, to ransom slaves. Many of these slaves in turn became the leaders of a renewed Christianity.

2. From the Apostles' Creed.

# BIBLIOGRAPHY OF ANCIENT AUTHORS

Aelius Aristides. *The Complete Works. Vol. 2, Orations XVII–LII.* Trans. Charles A. Behr. Leiden: E.J. Brill, 1981.

Appian. *Iberica.* Trans. J.S. Richardson. Warminster, England: Aris and Phillips, 2000.

Aristotle. *Nicomachean Ethics.* Trans. Martin Ostwald. Indianapolis: Bobs-Merrill, 1962.

Dio Cassius. *Roman History.* Trans. J.W. Rich. Warminster, England: Aris and Phillips, 1990.

Euripides. *The Trojan Women.* Trans. Shirley A. Barlow. Warminster, England: Aris and Phillips, 1986.

Josephus. *The Jewish War.* Trans. and ed. Paul Maier. Grand Rapids, Mich.: Zondervan, 1982.

Juvenal. *Satires.* Trans. Niall Rudd and Edward Courtney. Bristol, England: Bristol Classical Press, 1977.

Lampridius. *Alexander Severus.* http://penelope.uchicago.edu/Thayer/E/Roman/Texts/ Historia_Augusta/Severus_Alexander/2*.html.

Livy. *The Rise of Rome.* Books 1–5. Trans. T.J. Luce. New York: Oxford University Press, 1998.

Lucian of Samosata. "Saturnalia". In *Lucian, a Selection*, trans. M.D. MacLeod. Warminster, England: Aris and Phillips, 1991.

Marcus Aurelius. *Meditations.* Trans. C. Scot Hicks and David V. Hicks. New York: Scribner, 2002.

Ovid. *Metamorphoses.* Trans. Frank Justus Miller. Cambridge, Mass.: Harvard University Press, 1984.

Pausanius. *Description of Greece.* Trans. Peter Levi. New York: Penguin, 1971.

Philo. *The Contemplative Life.* Trans. David Winston. New York: Paulist Press, 1981.

Philo. *Special Laws.* In *The Works of Philo*, trans. C.D. Yonge. Peabody, Mass.: Hendrickson Publishers, 1993.

Plautus. *The Pot of Gold and Other Plays*. Trans. E. F. Watling. New York: Penguin, 1965.

Pliny the Elder. *Natural History*. Trans. Philemon Holland. Carbondale, Ill.: Southern Illinois University Press, 1962.

Pliny the Younger. *Letters*. Trans. Betty Radice. Cambridge, Mass.: Harvard University Press, 1969.

Suetonius. *Lives of the Caesars*. Trans. Catharine Edwards. New York: Oxford University Press, 2000.

Tacitus. *Annals*. Trans. Alfred John Church and William Jackson. Chicago: Encyclopedia Britannica, 1952.

# BIBLIOGRAPHY OF
# ANCIENT CHRISTIAN AUTHORS

*Acts of Paul and Thecla.* In *The Early Church Fathers.* (From CD-ROM Contents page, go to "Apostle: Apocryphal Acts of the Apostles: The Story of Perpetua".)

*The Acts of Philip: Of the Journeyings of Philip the Apostle.* In *The Early Church Fathers.* (From CD-ROM Contents page, go to "Apostle: Apocryphal Acts of the Apostles".)

*Acts of the Holy Apostle Thomas.* In *The Early Church Fathers.* (From CD-ROM Contents page, go to "Apostle: Apocryphal Acts of the Apostles".)

Alexander of Cappadocia. *From an Epistle to Demetrius, Bishop of Alexandria.* Trans. S. D. F. Salmond. In *The Early Church Fathers.*

Archelaus. *The Acts of the Disputation with the Heresiarch Manes.* Trans. S. D. F. Salmond. In *The Early Church Fathers.*

Aristides the Philosopher. *The Apology of Aristides the Philosopher.* Trans. D. M. Kay. In *The Early Church Fathers.*

Athenagorus of Athens. *A Plea for the Christians.* Trans. B. P. Pratten. In *The Early Church Fathers.*

Augustine. *The Confessions.* Trans. J. G. Pilkington. In *The Early Church Fathers.*

Barnabas. *The Epistle of Barnabas.* In *The Early Church Fathers.*

Basil the Great. *Letter CLXIV: To Ascholius.* Trans. Blomfield Jackson. In *The Early Church Fathers.*

Clement of Alexandria. *Exhortation to the Heathen.* Trans. William Wilson. In *The Early Church Fathers.*

————. *The Instructor (Paedagogus).* Trans. William Wilson. In *The Early Church Fathers.*

————. *Who Is the Rich Man That Shall Be Saved?* Trans. William Wilson. In *The Early Church Fathers.*

Clement of Rome. *The First Epistle of the Blessed Clement, the Disciple of Peter the Apostle.* Trans. B. P. Pratten. In *The Early Church Fathers.* (Look under "Two Epistles concerning Virginity".)

————. *First Epistle to the Corinthians (Bryennios Version)*. Trans. John Keith. In *The Early Church Fathers*.

————. *First Epistle to the Corinthians (Codex Alexandrinus Version)*. Trans. John Keith. In *The Early Church Fathers*.

————. *Second Epistle to the Corinthians*. Trans. John Keith. In *The Early Church Fathers*.

*The Confessors to Cyprian*, Epistle XVI [1]. Trans. Ernest Wallis. In *The Early Church Fathers*. (From CD-ROM Contents page, go to "Cyprian of Carthage: The Eighty-Two Epistles of Cyprian".)

*Constitutions of the Holy Apostles*. Ed. James Donaldson. In *The Early Church Fathers*. (On CD-ROM Contents page, look under "Apostle".)

*Coptic Apocryphal Gospels*. Ed. J. Armitage Robinson. Cambridge, Mass.: Cambridge University Press, 1896.

Cyprian of Carthage. *Caecilius, On the Sacrament of the Cup of the Lord*, Epistle LXII [7]. Trans. Ernest Wallis. In *The Early Church Fathers*.

————. *Letter 20*. In Francis Sullivan, *From Apostles to Bishops: The Development of the Episcopacy in the Early Church*, p. 208. New York: Newman Press, 2001.

————. *On the Dress of Virgins*. Trans. Ernest Wallis. In *The Early Church Fathers*.

————. *On the Lapsed*. Trans. Ernest Wallis. In *The Early Church Fathers*.

————. *On the Lord's Prayer*. Trans. Ernest Wallis. In *The Early Church Fathers*.

————. *On the Mortality (or Plague)*. Trans. Ernest Wallis. In *The Early Church Fathers*.

————. *On Works and Alms*. Trans. Ernest Wallis. In *The Early Church Fathers*.

————. *Three Books of Testimonies against the Jews*. Trans. Ernest Wallis. In *The Early Church Fathers*.

————. *To Antonianus about Cornelius and Novatian*, Epistle LI [4]. Trans. Ernest Wallis. In *The Early Church Fathers*.

————. *To Cornelius, about Cyprian's Approval of His Ordination, and concerning Felicissimus*, Epistle XLI [10]. Trans. Ernest Wallis. In *The Early Church Fathers*.

————. *To Cornelius, concerning Fortunatus and Felicissimus*, or *Against the Heretics*, Epistle LIV [3]. Trans. Ernest Wallis. In *The Early Church Fathers*.

———. *To Cornelius, concerning Polycarp the Adrumetine*, Epistle XLIV [1]. Trans. Ernest Wallis. In *The Early Church Fathers.*

———. *To Donatus*, Epistle I [1]. Trans. Ernest Wallis. In *The Early Church Fathers.*

———. *To Father Stephanus, concerning Marcianus of Arles, Who Had Joined Himself to Novatian*, Epistle LXVI [4]. Trans. Ernest Wallis. In *The Early Church Fathers.*

———. *To Fidus, on the Baptism of Infants*, Epistle LVIII [2]. Trans. Ernest Wallis. In *The Early Church Fathers.*

———. *To Jubaianus, concerning the Baptism of Heretics*, Epistle LXXII [5]. Trans. Ernest Wallis. In *The Early Church Fathers.*

———. *To Magnus, on Baptizing the Novatians, and Those Who Obtain Grace on a Sick-Bed*, Epistle LXXV [4]. Trans. Ernest Wallis. In *The Early Church Fathers.*

———. *To Pompey, against the Epistle of Stephen about the Baptism of Heretics*, Epistle LXXIII [4]. Trans. Ernest Wallis. In *The Early Church Fathers.*

———. *To Pomponius, concerning Some Virgins*, Epistle LXI [4]. Trans. Ernest Wallis. In *The Early Church Fathers.*

———. *To Rogatianus the Presbyter, and the Other Confessors*, Epistle VI [11]. Trans. Ernest Wallis. In *The Early Church Fathers.*

———. *To Stephen, concerning a Council*, Epistle LXXI [3]. Trans. Ernest Wallis. In *The Early Church Fathers.*

———. *To Successus on the Tidings Brought from Rome, Telling of the Persecution*, Epistle LXXXI [2]. Trans. Ernest Wallis. In *The Early Church Fathers.*

———. *To the Clergy and People Abiding in Spain, concerning Basilides and Martial*, Epistle LXVII [7]. Trans. Ernest Wallis. In *The Early Church Fathers.*

———. *To the Clergy and People, about the Ordination of Celerinus as Reader*, Epistle XXXIII [4]. Trans. Ernest Wallis. In *The Early Church Fathers.*

———. *To the Clergy, concerning the Care of Poor and Strangers*, Epistle XXXV [5]. Trans. Ernest Wallis. In *The Early Church Fathers.*

———. *To the Clergy, on the Letters Sent to Rome, and about the Appointment of Saturus as Reader, and Optatus as Sub-Deacon*, Epistle XXIII [3]. Trans. Ernest Wallis. In *The Early Church Fathers.*

———. *To the Numidian Bishops, on the Redemption of Their Brethren from Captivity among the Barbarians*, Epistle LIX [1]. Trans. Ernest Wallis. In *The Early Church Fathers.*

————. *To the Presbyters and Deacons*, Epistle V [4]. Trans. Ernest Wallis. In *The Early Church Fathers*.

————. *A Treatise against the Heretic Novatian by an Anonymous Bishop*. Trans. Ernest Wallis. In *The Early Church Fathers*.

*Didascalia Apostolorum: The Syriac Version Translated and Accompanied by the Verona Latin Fragments*. Introduction and notes by R. Hugh Connolly. Oxford: Clarendon Press, 1929.

*The Early Church Fathers*. Gervais, Ore.: Harmony Media, 2000. CD-ROM.

Eusebius Pamphilus of Caesarea. *Church History*. Trans. Arthur Cushman McGiffert. In *The Early Church Fathers*.

————. *The Life of the Blessed Emperor Constantine*. Trans. Ernest Cushing Richardson. In *The Early Church Fathers*.

Hermas. *The Pastor of Hermas*. Trans. F. Crombie. In *The Early Church Fathers*.

Hippolytus of Rome. *The Apostolic Tradition of Hippolytus*. Trans. Burton Scott Easton. London: Cambridge University Press, 1934.

————. *On Daniel*. Trans. S. D. F. Salmond. In *The Early Church Fathers*.

————. *The Refutation of All Heresies*. Trans. J. H. MacMahon. In *The Early Church Fathers*.

Ignatius of Antioch. *The Epistle of Ignatius to the Ephesians*. In *The Early Church Fathers*.

————. *The Epistle of Ignatius to the Magnesians*. In *The Early Church Fathers*.

————. *The Epistle of Ignatius to the Philadelphians*. In *The Early Church Fathers*.

————. *The Epistle of Ignatius to Polycarp*. In *The Early Church Fathers*.

————. *The Epistle of Ignatius to the Romans*. In *The Early Church Fathers*.

————. *The Epistle of Ignatius to the Smyrnaeans*. In *The Early Church Fathers*.

————. *The Epistle of Ignatius to the Trallians*. In *The Early Church Fathers*.

Irenaeus of Lyons. *Against Heresies*. In *The Early Church Fathers*.

Jerome. *Lives of Illustrious Men*. Trans. Ernest Cushing Richardson. In *The Early Church Fathers*.

John Chrysostom. "Homily LXXI: Matt. XXII:34–36". In *Homilies on the Gospel according to St. Matthew*. Trans. Sir George Prevost. In *The Early Church Fathers*.

Justin Martyr. *Dialogue with Trypho*. In *The Early Church Fathers*.

———. *The First Apology of Justin*. In *The Early Church Fathers*.

———. *The Second Apology of Justin for the Christians*. In *The Early Church Fathers*.

Lactantius. *Of the Manner in Which the Persecutors Died*. Trans. William Fletcher. In *The Early Church Fathers*.

Marcion at Smyrna. *The Encyclical Epistle of the Church at Smyrna concerning the Martyrdom of the Holy Polycarp*. In *The Early Church Fathers*.

*The Martyrdom of the Holy Martyrs Justin, Chariton, Charites, Paeon, and Liberianus, Who Suffered at Rome*. Trans. M. Dods. In *The Early Church Fathers*. (On CD-ROM Contents page, look under "Justin Martyr".)

Mathetes. *The Epistle of Mathetes to Diognetus*. In *The Early Church Fathers*. (On CD-ROM, translated anonymously.)

Minucius Felix. *The Octavius of Minucius Felix*. Trans. Robert Ernest Wallis. In *The Early Church Fathers*.

Origen. *Against Celsus*. Trans. Frederick Crombie. In *The Early Church Fathers*.

———. *Commentary on Romans, Books 1–5*. Trans. Thomas B. Scheck. Washington, D.C.: Catholic University Press, 2001.

———. *Commentary on Romans, Books 6–10*. Trans. Thomas B. Scheck. Washington, D.C.: Catholic University Press, 2002.

———. *Homilies on Joshua*. Trans. Barbara J. Bruce. Ed. Cynthia White. Washington, D.C.: Catholic University Press, 2002.

———. *Homilies on Leviticus*. Trans. Gary Wayne Barkley. Washington, D.C.: Catholic University Press, 1990.

———. *Homilies on Luke*. Trans. Joseph T. Lienhard. Washington, D.C.: Catholic University Press, 1996.

*The Passion of the Scillitan Martyrs*. Trans. J. A. Robinson. In *The Early Church Fathers*.

Polycarp of Smyrna. *Epistle to the Philippians*. In *The Early Church Fathers*.

Pontius the Deacon. *The Life and Passion of Cyprian, Bishop and Martyr*. In *The Early Church Fathers*.

"Protoevangelium of James". In *The Other Gospels: Non-Canonical Gospel Texts*. Ed. Ron Cameron. Trans. Oscar Cullmann and A.J.B. Higgins. Philadelphia: The Westminster Press, 1982.

Prudentius. *Crowns of Martyrdom*. In *Prudentius*. Vol. 2. Trans. H.J. Thomson. Cambridge, Mass.: Harvard University Press, 1961.

*The Reply of Nemesianus, Dativus, Felix, and Victor, to Cyprian*, Epistle LXXVII [9]. Trans. Ernest Wallis. In *The Early Church Fathers*. (From CD-ROM Contents page, go to "Cyprian of Carthage: The Eighty-Two Epistles of Cyprian".)

Socrates Scholasticus. *The Ecclesiastical History*. Trans. A. C. Zenos. In *The Early Church Fathers*.

Sulpitius Severus. *On the Life of St. Martin*. Trans. Alexander Roberts. In *The Early Church Fathers*.

Tatian the Syrian. *Address to the Greeks*. Trans. J. E. Ryland. In *The Early Church Fathers*.

*The Teaching of the Twelve Apostles (The Didache): The Lord's Teaching through the Twelve Apostles to the Nations*. In *The Early Church Fathers*. (On CD-ROM Contents page, look under "Apostle".)

Tertullian. *Apology*. Trans. S. Thelwall. In *The Early Church Fathers*.

———. *The Chaplet, or (De Corona)*. Trans. Peter Holmes. In *The Early Church Fathers*.

———. *The Martyrdom of Perpetua and Felicitas*. Trans. R. E. Wallis. In *The Early Church Fathers*.

———. *On Baptism*. Trans. S. Thelwall. In *The Early Church Fathers*.

———. *On Idolatry*. Trans. S. Thelwall. In *The Early Church Fathers*.

———. *On Modesty*. Trans. S. Thelwall. In *The Early Church Fathers*.

———. *On Monogamy*. Trans. S. Thelwall. In *The Early Church Fathers*.

———. *On Prayer*. Trans. S. Thelwall. In *The Early Church Fathers*.

———. *On Repentance*. Trans. S. Thelwall. In *The Early Church Fathers*.

———. *The Prescription against Heretics*. Trans. Peter Holmes. In *The Early Church Fathers*.

———. *The Soul's Testimony*. Trans. S. Thelwall. In *The Early Church Fathers*.

———. *To His Wife*. Trans. S. Thelwall. In *The Early Church Fathers*.

———. *A Treatise on the Soul*. Trans. Peter Holmes. In *The Early Church Fathers*.

# BIBLIOGRAPHY OF MODERN AUTHORS

Albl, Martin. "Alexander". In *Eerdmans Dictionary of the Bible*. Ed. David Noel Freedman. Grand Rapids, Mich.: Eerdmans Publishing Co., 2002.

Allard, Paul. *Ten Lectures on the Martyrs*. Trans. Luigi Cappadelta. London: Kegan Paul, Trench, Trübner and Co., 1907.

Angus, S. *The Mystery-Religions*. New York: Dover Publications, 1975.

Aquilina, Mike. *The Mass of the Early Christians*. Huntington, Ind.: Our Sunday Visitor Publishing Div., 2001.

Arndt, William F., and F. Wilbur Gingrich. *A Greek-English Lexicon of the New Testament and Other Early Christian Literature*. Chicago: University of Chicago Press, 1979.

Auguet, Roland. *Cruelty and Civilization: The Roman Games*. New York: Routledge, 1994.

Bainton, Roland H. "The Early Church and War". In *Christian Life: Ethics, Morality, and Discipline in the Early Church*. Ed. Everett Ferguson. New York: Garland Publishing Co., 1993.

Barr, David. *New Testament Story*. Belmont, Calif.: Wadsworth Publishing Co., 1995.

Boak, Arthur. "The Population of Roman and Byzantine Karanis". *Historia* 4 (1955): 157–62.

Bokenkotter, Thomas. *A Concise History of the Catholic Church*. New York: Doubleday, 1977.

Bradshaw, Paul F. *Daily Prayer in the Early Church: A Study of the Origin and Early Development of the Divine Office*. London: Alcuin Club, 1981.

Branick, Vincent P. *The House Church in the Writings of Paul*. Wilmington, Del.: Michael Glazier Books, 1989.

Brown, Raymond E. *The Gospel of John*. Vol. 1. New York: Doubleday and Co., 1966.

———. *An Introduction to the New Testament*. New York: Doubleday, 1997.

Bunson, Matthew. "Legions". In *A Dictionary of the Roman Empire*. New York: Oxford University Press, 1991.

Cadoux, C. John. *The Early Christian Attitude to War*. New York: Gordon Press, 1975.

Campbell, R. Alastair. *The Elders: Seniority within Earliest Christianity*. Edinburgh: T and T Clark, 1994.

Campbell, Bryan. *The Roman Army: 31 BC–AD 337*. London: Routledge, 1994.

Carcopino, Jerome. *Daily Life in Ancient Rome*. New Haven, Conn.: Yale University Press, 1940.

Carpenter, H.J. "Creeds and Baptismal Rites in the First Four Centuries". In *Conversion, Catechumenate, and Baptism in the Early Church*. Ed. Everett Ferguson. New York: Garland Publishing Co., 1993.

Carroll, Donald. *Mary's House*. London: Veritas Books, 2000.

Casson, Lionel. *Travel in the Ancient World*. Baltimore: Johns Hopkins University Press, 1994.

Christ, Karl. *The Romans: An Introduction to Their History and Civilization*. Trans. Christopher Holme. Berkeley: University of California Press, 1984.

Cimok, Fatih. *Pergamum*. Istanbul: A Turizm Yayinlari, 2001.

Cornell, Timothy. *Atlas of the Roman World*. New York: Oxford University Press, 1982.

Countryman, L. William. *The Rich Christian in the Church of the Early Empire: Contradictions and Accommodations*. New York: Edwin Mellen Press, 1980.

Cowell, F.R. *Life in Ancient Rome*. New York: Penguin, 1961.

Crawford, Michael. "Early Rome and Italy". In *The Oxford History of the Roman World*. Ed. John Boardman. New York: Oxford University Press, 1986.

Craybill, J.N. *Imperial Cult and Commerce in John's Apocalypse*. Sheffield, England: Academic Press, 1996.

Cullmann, Oscar. *The State in the New Testament*. New York: Scribner, 1956.

Danielou, Jean. *The Ministry of Women in the Early Church*. Trans. Glyn Simon. London: Faith Press, 1961.

Davies, J.G. "Deacons, Deaconesses, and the Minor Orders in the Patristic Period". In *Church, Ministry, and Organization in the Early Church*. Ed. Everett Ferguson. New York: Garland Publishing Co., 1993.

Dix, Gregory. *Jurisdiction in the Early Church: Episcopal and Papal.* London: Faith House, 1975.

————. *The Shape of the Liturgy.* New York: Seabury Press, 1982.

Echlin, Edward P. *The Deacon in the Church: Past and Future.* New York: Alba House, 1971.

Elliot, John. "Philemon and House Churches". *The Bible Today* 22 (May 1984): 145–50.

Faivre, Alexandre. *The Emergence of the Laity in the Early Church.* Trans. David Smith. New York: Paulist Press, 1990.

Ferguson, Everett. "Inscriptions of Infant Baptism". In *Conversion, Catechumenate, and Baptism in the Early Church.* Ed. Everett Ferguson. New York: Garland Publishing Co., 1993.

Fields, Nic. *Hadrian's Wall: AD 122–410.* Oxford: Osprey Publishing, 2003.

Finn, Thomas. *Early Christian Baptism and the Catechumenate: Italy, North Africa, and Egypt.* Collegeville, Minn.: Liturgical Press, 1992.

————. *Early Christian Baptism and the Catechumenate: West and East Syria.* Collegeville, Minn.: Liturgical Press, 1992.

Fitzmyer, Joseph A. *Anchor Bible Commentary: The Letter to Philemon.* New York: Doubleday, 2001.

Fletcher, Richard. *The Barbarian Conversion.* New York: Henry Holt and Co., 1997.

Folkemer, Lawrence. "A Study of the Catechumenate". In *Conversion, Catechumenate, and Baptism in the Early Church.* Ed. Everett Ferguson. New York: Garland Publishing Co., 1993.

Frend, W. H. C. *The Rise of Christianity.* Philadelphia: Fortress Press, 1984.

Futrell, Alison. *Blood in the Arena.* Austin: University of Texas Press, 1997.

Garrison, Roman. *Redemptive Almsgiving in Early Christianity.* Sheffield, England: JSOT Press, 1993.

Glancy, Jennifer A. *Slavery in Early Christianity.* New York: Oxford University Press, 2002.

Granfield, Patrick. "Episcopal Election in Cyprian: Clerical and Lay Participation". In *Church Ministry and Organization in the Early Church Era.* Ed. Everett Ferguson. New York: Garland Publishing Co., 1993.

Grant, Brian W. *The Social Structure of Christian Families: A Historical Perspective.* St. Louis, Mo.: Chalice Press, 2000.

Grant, Michael. *The Ancient Mediterranean.* New York: History Book Club, 2002.

————. *Constantine the Great: The Man and His Times.* New York: History Book Club, 1993.

————. *Gladiators.* New York: Delacorte Press, 1968.

————. *A History of Rome.* New York: Scribner, 1978.

————. *The World of Rome.* New York: Meridian, 1987.

Hahn, Scott. *The Lamb's Supper.* New York: Doubleday, 1999.

Harley, Felicity. "Invocation and Immolation: The Supplicatory Use of Christ's Name on Crucifixion Amulets in the Early Christian Period". In *Prayer and Spirituality in the Early Church.* Ed. Pauline Allen, Wendy Mayer, and Lawrence Cross. Everton Park, Australia: Centre for Early Christian Studies, 1998.

Harnack, Adolph. *Militia Christi: The Christian Religion and the Military in the the First Three Centuries.* Trans. David McInnes Gracie. Philadelphia: Fortress Press, 1981.

Harrill, J. Albert. *The Manumission of Slaves in Early Christianity.* Tubingen: JCB Mohr, 1995.

Harris, William V. "Towards a Study of the Roman Slave Trade". In *The Seaborne Commerce of Ancient Rome.* Rome: American Academy of Rome, 1980.

Helgeland, John, Robert J. Daly, and J. Patout Burns. *Christians and the Military: The Early Experience.* Philadelphia: Fortress Press, 1985.

Hertling, Ludwig, and Engelbert Kirschbaum. *The Roman Catacombs and Their Martyrs.* Trans. M. Joseph Costelloe. Milwaukee: Bruce Publishing Co., 1956.

Hinson, E. Glenn. *The Early Church: Origins to the Dawn of the Middle Ages.* Nashville: Abingdon Press, 1996.

Horsley, G. H. R., ed. *New Documents Illustrating Early Christianity.* Vol. 1, *A Review of the Greek Inscriptions and Papyri.* Marrickville, Australia: Ancient History Documentary Research Centre, 1981.

Jenkins, Ian. *Greek and Roman Life.* Cambridge, Mass.: Harvard University Press, 1986.

Jenkins, Philip. *Hidden Gospels: How the Search for Jesus Lost Its Way.* New York: Oxford University Press, 2001.

Joyce, G. H. "Private Penance in the Early Church". In *Christian Life: Ethics, Morality, and Discipline in the Early Church*. Ed. Everett Ferguson. New York: Garland Publishing Co., 1993.

Kavanagh, Aidan. *The Shape of Baptism: The Rite of Christian Initiation*. New York: Pueblo Publishing Co., 1978.

King, Helen. *Greek and Roman Medicine*. London: Bristol Classical Press, 2001.

Krieder, Alan. *The Change of Conversion and the Origin of Christendom*. Harrisburg, Penn.: Trinity Press International, 1999.

Leith, Mary Joan Winn. "Israel among the Nations: The Persian Period". In *The Oxford History of the Biblical World*. Ed. Michael D. Coogan. New York: Oxford University Press, 1998.

Levine, Amy-Jill. "Visions of Kingdoms: From Pompey to the First Jewish Revolt". In *The Oxford History of the Biblical World*. Ed. Michael D. Coogan. New York: Oxford University Press, 1998.

Lussier, Ernest. *The Eucharist: The Bread of Life*. New York: Alba House, 1977.

MacDowall, Simon. *Late Roman Infantryman: 236–565 AD*. Oxford: Osprey Publishing, 1994.

McNamara, Jo Ann. *A New Song: Celibate Women in the First Three Christian Centuries*. New York: Harrington Park Press, 1985.

Maier, Paul. *In the Fullness of Time*. San Francisco: Harper, 1991.

Martimort, A. G. *The Church at Prayer: An Introduction to the Liturgy*. Vol. 2. Collegeville, Minn.: Liturgical Press, 1987.

———. *Deaconesses: An Historical Study*. Trans. K. D. Whitehead. San Francisco: Ignatius Press, 1986.

Marucchi, Orazio. *The Evidence of the Catacombs for the Doctrines and Organization of the Primitive Church*. London: Sheed and Ward, 1929.

Mohler, James A. *The Origin and Evolution of the Priesthood*. New York: Alba House, 1970.

Mueller, James R. "Protoevangelium of James". In *Eerdmans Dictionary of the Bible*. Ed. David Noel Freedman. Grand Rapids, Mich.: Eerdmans Publishing Co., 2000.

Noonan, John T. "Abortion and the Catholic Church: A Summary History". In *Christian Life: Ethics, Morality, and Discipline in the Early Church*. Ed. Everett Ferguson. New York: Garland Publishing Co., 1993.

Ogilvie, R. M. *The Romans and Their Gods*. New York: W.W. Norton and Co., 1933.

Ott, Ludwig. *Fundamentals of Catholic Dogma*. Trans. Patrick Lynch. Rockford, Ill.: Tan Books, 1974.

Owen, E. C. E. *Some Authentic Acts of the Early Martyrs*. Oxford: Oxford University Press, 1927.

Payne, Robert. *Ancient Rome*. New York: ibooks, 2001.

Pontifical Biblical Commission. *The Interpretation of the Bible in the Church*. Washington: United States Catholic Conference, 1996.

Rawson, Elizabeth. "The Expansion of Rome". In *The Oxford History of the Roman World*. Ed. John Boardman. New York: Oxford University Press, 1986.

Robertson, D. S. *Handbook of Greek and Roman Architecture*. London: Cambridge University Press, 1969.

Rordorf, Willy. "Marriage in the New Testament and in the Early Church". In *Christian Life: Ethics, Morality, and Discipline in the Early Church*. Ed. Everett Ferguson. New York: Garland Publishing Co., 1993.

Rose, H. J. *Ancient Roman Religion*. London: Hutchinson's University Library, 1948.

Ruffin, C. Bernard. *The Twelve: The Lives of the Apostles after Calvary*. Huntingdon, Ind.: Our Sunday Visitor Publishing Div., 1997.

Ryan, Edward A. "The Rejection of Military Service by the Early Christians". In *Christian Life: Ethics, Morality, and Discipline in the Early Church*. Ed. Everett Ferguson. New York: Garland Publishing Co., 1993.

Showalter, Daniel. *The Emperor and the Gods: Images from the Time of Trajan*. Minneapolis: Fortress Press, 1992.

Simpson, Robert L. *The Interpretation of Prayer in the Early Church*. Philadelphia: Westminster Press, 1965.

Skarsaune, Oskar. "The Conversion of Justin Martyr". In *Conversion, Catechumenate, and Baptism in the Early Church*. Ed. Everett Ferguson. New York: Garland Publishing Co., 1993.

Snyder, Graydon F. *Ante Pacem: Archaeological Evidence of Church Life before Constantine*. Macon, Ga.: Mercer University Press, 2003.

Stark, Rodney. *The Rise of Christianity: A Sociologist Reconsiders History*. Princeton: Princeton University Press, 1996.

Stevenson, Kenneth. "The Origins of the Nuptial Blessing". In *Christian Life: Ethics, Morality, and Discipline in the Early Church.* Ed. Everett Ferguson. New York: Garland Publishing Co., 1993.

Strange, W. A. *Children in the Early Church.* Carlisle, England: Paternoster Press, 1996.

Sullivan, Francis A. *From Apostles to Bishops: The Development of the Episcopacy in the Early Church.* New York: Newman Press, 2001.

Sungenis, Robert A. *Not by Faith Alone: The Biblical Evidence for the Catholic Doctrine of Justification.* Goleta, Calif.: Queenship Publishing, 1997.

Swete, H. B. "Penitential Discipline in the First Three Centuries". In *Christian Life: Ethics, Morality, and Discipline in the Early Church.* Ed. Everett Ferguson. New York: Garland Publishing Co., 1993.

——. "Prayer for the Departed in the First Four Centuries". In *Acts of Piety in the Early Church.* Ed. Everett Ferguson. New York: Garland Publishing Co., 1993.

Thayer, Joseph H. *Greek-English Lexicon of the New Testament.* Peabody, Mass.: Hendrickson Publishers, 1999.

Thurston, Bonnie Bowman. *The Widows: A Women's Ministry in the Early Church.* Minneapolis: Fortress Press, 1989.

Thurston, Herbert, and Donald Attwater. *Butler's Lives of the Saints.* Vol. 3. New York: P. J. Kenedy and Sons, 1956.

Turcan, Robert. *The Gods of Ancient Rome: Religion in Everyday Life from Archaic to Imperial Times.* Trans. Antonia Nevill. New York: Routledge, 2000.

Veyne, Paul. *The Roman Empire.* Trans. Arthur Goldhammer. Cambridge, Mass.: Harvard University Press, 2002.

Watson, G. R. *The Roman Soldier.* Ithaca, N.Y.: Cornell University Press, 1995.

Wells, Colin. *The Roman Empire.* Cambridge, Mass.: Harvard University Press, 1984.

Wiedemann, Thomas. *Emperors and Gladiators.* New York: Routledge, 1992.

Worth, Roland H. *The Seven Cities of the Apocalypse and Roman Culture.* Mahwah, N.J.: Paulist Press, 1999.

# INDEX

Abercius, Bishop, 188
abortion, 41–42, 302, 312–16, 340n9
acolytes, 204
Acts: apostolic succession, 161, 162;
  charity, 267, 272; children's presence,
  308, 309; deacons, 199, 200; Eucharist, 138; Hellenists dispute, 198–99,
  368n133; miracles, 148; Paul's citizenship, 55; Peter's authority, 179–80;
  Philip's daughters, 214; prayer, 131;
  presbyters, 192; soldiers, 277; syna-
  gogues, 367n108; widow care, 211
Acts of Archelaus, 256, 378n20
Acts of Barnabas, xiii
Acts of Bartholomew, 154
Acts of Paul and Tecla, 149
Acts of Saints Perpetua and Felicity,
  150–51
Acts of the Martyrs, 291
Acts of Thomas, 306, 385n35
adultery, 44, 127, 301
aediles, 13
Aeneas, 4
Against Celsus (Origen), 284
Against Heresies (Irenaeus), 169
agape (love feast), 142, 224, 358n53
Agnes, Saint, 372n199
agriculture, 66
Agrippa, 37
Alemona, 19
Alexander, Bishop of Cappadocia, 219
Alexander, in Irenaeus' list, 186
Alexander Severus, 220, 240, 364n47,
  375n40
Alexander (soldier), 112
Alexander the Great, 6–7, 32, 100
Alexandria: bishop functions, 174;
  catechetical school, 116, 118;

divinity dispute, 176–77; lay
  preaching, 219; persecutions of
  Christians, 244; plague statistics, 261;
  prayer practices, 132; synods, 174;
  traveler accommodations, 76–77
almanah, defined, 210
almsgiving: and institutional charity,
  110–11, 265, 266, 380nn23–24; laity
  responsibilities during liturgy, 220;
  teachings about, 267–71, 273. See
  also charity work
altars, 137, 138, 140, 147, 213, 357n49
Ammon, 25
amphitheaters, 92–94, 96, 348n34,
  349n35, 349n38
amulets, 133
Amyntas, 50
Anacletus, in Irenaeus' list, 185
ancestral spirits, Roman world, 18–20,
  31
angels, 20, 125, 226
Anicetus, Pope, 169, 186
animal spectacles: Christian martyrdom,
  94, 230–31, 237–38, 239, 244;
  as Roman entertainment, 86,
  87–89, 92–93, 347nn13–15, n18,
  348n20
Anthimus, Bishop, 243
Anthochus III, 7
Anthony, Mark, 11
Antonianus, 171
apartment buildings, 70–71
Aphrodisias, 44–45, 319
Apocryphal writings, 214, 372n202
Apollinarius, 275, 287, 288
Apollo, 78, 230
Apollonius, 201, 367n118
apologists, 108–9